Straight On Till Morning

Beryl pictured shortly before her transatlantic flight at Estree Airport, England, 1936.

Straight On Till Morning

The Biography of
Beryl Markham

MARY S. LOVELL

ST. MARTIN'S PRESS
NEW YORK

Library of Congress Cataloging-in-Publication Data
Lovell, Mary S.
    Straight on till morning.
    1. Markham, Beryl.   2. Air pilots—Great Britain—
Biography.   I. Title.
TL540.M345L68   1987   629.13′092′4 [B]   87-16329
ISBN 0-312-01096-6

First published in Great Britain by Century Hutchinson Ltd.

First U.S. Edition

10 9 8 7 6 5 4 3 2 1

To Clifford,
who introduced me to Beryl.
Feet on the ground, heart in the sky!

'How do you get to Neverland?' Wendy asked.
'Second star to the right, and straight on till
morning.'

J.M. Barrie, *Peter Pan*

CONTENTS

PREFACE

During the weeks that Mary Lovell has been in Nairobi, she has spent each day but one at my house on the Ngong Racecourse. We have become friends.

She tells me that people are interested in the things I have done in my life which were not written about in my own book *West with the Night*. I cannot think why this should be so, but I accept her assurances, and have made my collection of papers available to her.

Day after day, I have listened while she read these papers to me. I have remembered times long past and people long dead. And when she has asked me I have tried to tell her about them. But some memories I have kept for myself as everyone must. And because she understands this I have tried to help her, as she – in her own way – has helped me.

Beryl Markham
Nairobi, 3 April 1986

PROLOGUE

When I first met the man I was to love more than any other human being, I was aware immediately of some sixth sense – a warning frisson. Some people might call it love at first sight.

So, when I first heard the name Beryl Markham mentioned at a dinner party in 1985 and experienced a similar spine-tingling sensation I was surprised for as far as I could remember I had never heard the name before. My inquiries elicited the information that she had led a somewhat sensational life but was now in her eighties, retired and living in Kenya. As a pioneer aviatrix she had been the first woman to fly the Atlantic from east to west, she had written a book called *West with the Night* in the year I was born, and had been a leading racehorse trainer. She had also been a friend of Karen Blixen and Denys Finch Hatton whose story had recently been filmed in *Out of Africa*.

My former husband had supplied his Gipsy Moth aeroplane and flown in some of the flying scenes in the film, which is based loosely on Karen Blixen's book of the same name. Over dinner, shortly after his return from Kenya, he told me of the people he had met during his three-month stint in Kenya. One of the names was Beryl Markham.

I couldn't think why I'd experienced this odd feeling – almost of *déjà vu*, until he said, 'Someone ought to write a book about her life. It would make the most wonderful story . . .'

I read Beryl's lovely book three days later, the earliest I could get hold of a copy. Before that I had already ransacked the reference division of my local library to find only the bare details of Beryl's epic flight across the Atlantic. I tried the aviation section in the lending division and went through the indexes at the back of books which provided me with a little more information.

For years I have collected antiquarian books on horses and foxhunting. Among this collection is the personal hunting diary of a lady from Leicestershire. Flicking idly through this diary one evening I was astonished to see the name of Beryl's father, Charles B. Clutterbuck. I had seen it only two evenings earlier in Beryl's autobiography. Surely a coincidence? No, probably not, for hadn't Beryl said he had been a successful steeplechaser?

I was well into work on another book when this happened, and so my agent was surprised when I called and told him I was abandoning it to write a biography of Beryl Markham. 'Who is Beryl Markham?' he asked. I replied defensively, not yet ready to share Beryl with anyone else. 'I don't know yet. But I just know I've got to write about her.'

Within weeks I had gathered enough material to draft what I thought was an outline for the book. Luckily I had a week's holiday and I spent that entire time and every spare minute of the succeeding weeks, driven purely by instinct and almost in a frenzy to learn more. I wrote to Beryl Markham via her English publishers, Virago Press Limited, and went on with the early research. I realize now that never for a moment did I consider that the project might be brought to a halt.

I was saddened to receive a reply from Jack Couldrey, who advised me that he was Beryl's solicitor and that though he had read my letter to Beryl he wasn't sure that she had understood it. '. . . to all intents and purposes she is now virtually senile,' he wrote. If I went to Nairobi, the letter continued, I could certainly see her and would even be able to carry on a conversation but her mind was apt to wander.

This was a blow, but I knew I had to see her. The same day I went into my local travel agents and booked a return trip to Nairobi. Then I started writing to people whose names appeared in the research material I had already gathered. Interviews followed. I was astonished at the sweep of interests of Beryl's life. Disappointing as it was, I felt it might not be essential to question Beryl in order to write her story, but I still desperately wanted to see her. Besides there were many people in Kenya who could help me to piece the story together, if they would.

I arrived in the lovely city of Nairobi in March 1986. I had expected blasting heat and searing shades of yellow, so the warm but sparkling air, the wealth of colour and the beauty of shrubs and flowers was an unexpected enchantment.

It was Sunday and I spent the rest of the day on the telephone setting up appointments and arranging to hire a car. On Monday I collected it and eased myself with trepidation into the indiscipline of Nairobi's traffic streams.

My first call was on Jack Couldrey. He seemed concerned that I might have wasted my time and money. With great kindness he told me how he first became involved with Beryl and a little of his involvement. 'Beryl can be difficult at times,' he warned me. 'And she doesn't particularly like women. She has very few friends now and is sad, and rather lonely. She has cut herself off. She swears terribly at her two servants, I don't know why they stay with her. She has good times and bad . . . last night when I called in on her she was brighter than I've seen her for a long time . . . If you want anything photocopied please bring it here and we'll copy it for you. I think a lot of things have been taken away over the years, but you wouldn't do that, would you? No, of course not.'

I thanked him and left, stopping off to buy a large bouquet of flowers, although I had already been told by many people that I'd do better to take a bottle of vodka.

I found the cottage on the racecourse without any difficulty. The door was wide open and I could hear the murmur of voices speaking in Swahili. I knocked at the door which opened directly into a sitting room. 'Oh hello, do come in,' said a cultured voice. 'How lovely to see you.' I went in and she saw the flowers. 'How lovely, thank you *so* much!' she said graciously. She was instantly recognizable from the photographs I had already collected in my researches. Just an older version of the once stunningly beautiful woman whose features I already knew so well. On that day there was little of the celebrated glamour but her classical bone structure identified her. Her hair was pure white, combed close to the head, and had clearly not seen a hairdresser for some time. She wore blue jeans and a loose shirt.

She was holding her arm and clearly there was some domestic crisis for the servants were hovering around anxiously. Her left hand covered the upper part of her right arm. She removed it and showed me an ugly wound. Somehow she had torn away a large triangular flap of skin, and it was folded back almost surgically, exposing nerves and muscle. She admitted that it 'hurt rather' but she was very stoic about it, merely expressing annoyance. I inquired about dressings, for there were a number of flies in the room and it was very warm. Adiambo, the woman servant, went off to the recesses of the house and came back with a bottle of cream shampoo saying that was all she could find. Beryl looked at me questioningly.

I knew the Jockey Club could not be far away, and telling Beryl to keep her hand over the wound, I drove off to find it. There I was treated with great courtesy and offered the contents of the first-aid box. I returned to the cottage and dressed the wound. She did not flinch. 'Oh that's better. How kind,' she said when I was finished. 'What time is it – would you like a drink?' It was noon and the sun technically over the yardarm, so I agreed.

There was only vodka and orange. I watched with alarm as Adiambo poured for me what seemed to be half a tumbler of alcohol topped up with orange squash. When I sipped it I found it very weak and realized that the vodka was well watered down. Later I found that each bottle was magically turned into two bottles; Beryl was not, apparently, aware of the deception. As the afternoon wore on I saw that she sipped delicately at the drink from time to time, and it was still unfinished when I left at six o'clock.

I told her I was there to write a book about her but she knew this already from Jack Couldrey. I pressed on. 'Do you mind?' 'No sweetie, of course not. When can I see it?' During the course of conversation she told me to open the black tin trunk lying under the window. 'Everything is in there . . . bring me some of it and I'll show you,' she said. I had already ascertained that she could not walk and had not done so since the previous October when she had suffered a thrombosis. 'I probably could walk if I only had the right people around me,' she told me briskly.

I took out a few of the things from the trunk. The first batch was mainly letters and cables which Beryl had received at the time of her flight across the Atlantic. I read them to her and she laughed delightedly. 'Oh I say . . . how funny.' There was no evidence of the senility I had been warned to expect, nor of her mind wandering. I had clearly been lucky enough to pick a good day. 'May I come back tomorrow?' 'Oh please do, I'd love that . . .'

Every day for the next weeks I drove out to Beryl's cottage about ten o'clock each morning. We sat in her modestly furnished sitting room whose walls were lined with framed photographs. They were mainly of her aeroplane and her arrival in New York, but there were a few of her horses and over her chair hung a portrait of the aviator Tom Campbell Black. She was interested to learn that I had interviewed Florence Desmond (Tom's wife until his death in 1936) before flying out to Kenya.

The first few days I spent going through Beryl's trunk, handing the items to her one by one and reading the contents or, in the case of maps, talking about them. She seemed never to tire of this and we spent several days poring over each flight in her log book. She wanted to hear about everything I'd discovered. 'How did you find out about that?' At first she gave little away. When I asked a direct question she'd hedge. 'Such and such a person said you did this . . .' I'd tell her. 'Is it true?' 'What do you think?' she'd ask, turning her china-blue eyes on me questioningly. 'I think it's true,' I'd say. 'Well then . . .'

Our conversation was not always about the biography. Within two days I realized that Beryl was unhappy about her appearance. Given the fact that she was obviously confined to her chair, I tentatively suggested that I could shampoo and set her hair for her. We arranged that I should borrow a hairdryer from the beauty salon at my hotel and that we'd have a hairdressing session over the weekend. We talked about horses, and about vintage aeroplanes – interests we had in common. I told her about my own horse, Flashman, and of hunting in the New Forest. She remembered then that she had hunted in England as a young woman. It was the first time she had volunteered information for which I had not asked.

Meanwhile my interviews with other people were also being conducted. Sometimes I had to leave Beryl for a short time to have lunch with someone, or I might arrive a little late because I'd met an informant for breakfast beside the pool at my hotel;

my absences annoyed her. Generally I tried to see interviewees
in the evenings and I was the recipient of an unequalled degree
of hospitality from everyone with whom I came into contact. I
noted everything down, and was initially sidetracked by the
huge amount of rumour, gossip and innuendo.

'She drinks like a fish, you know.' 'She had an affair with the
Prince of Wales.' 'Prince Henry fathered her son.' 'She was paid
by the royal family never to return to England.' 'She was paid
an astronomical amount by the Palace and spent the lot.' 'Her
family won't have anything to do with her.' 'She could never
have written that book, she's totally illiterate!' The names of
Beryl's supposed lovers were given with surprising candour. It
took me some days to realize that gossip is the main social
amusement in Kenya. People who provided me with
information which I knew from earlier researches could not
possibly be true were not being malicious or mischievous. They
were simply repeating part of the legend which has built up
about Beryl since the early part of the century.

Within days of my first visit to the cottage at the racecourse I
noticed that Beryl had started to wear make-up, and my regular
ten a.m. arrival found her carefully dressed and sitting facing
the door. I told her I'd like to learn Swahili, hated it when
people were talking around me and I couldn't understand
them. After that, each day she taught me five new words, and
was amused at my halting efforts to converse with Odero and
Adiambo. So were they. Adiambo smirked openly but Odero
was kind enough to pretend I was word perfect and obediently
brought water, let the dogs out, or brought a shawl for Beryl.
Jambo; *Hodi*; *Kwaheri*; *Maji*; *Hapana* ... Whenever she spoke to
someone in Swahili I would pick out a word and ask her what it
meant. 'What does *kidogo* mean, Beryl?' 'Small.'

The hairdressing session was not a total success. I thought her
hair looked very attractive, snowy white and surprisingly thick
once it was washed and set. Beryl could not wait to see it, but I
realized where I'd gone wrong the moment I showed her the
result in a hand looking glass. 'But it's still *white*,' she said,
disappointed. It was not until a hairdresser from my hotel had
been persuaded to visit her and apply a delicate silvery-blonde
tint and cut and shape it that Beryl was really satisfied with the

result, and each day I acted as her lady's maid, applying make-up and styling her hair while we talked.

One day I left at lunch time to drive up into the Ngong hills to find Denys Finch Hatton's grave and to see Karen Blixen's house (now a museum). On my return I took Beryl a book of pictures taken during the filming of *Out of Africa*. She was scathing about the pictures of Karen, 'Blix' and Denys. 'Who are these people?' 'That's supposed to be Tania [Karen Blixen was known to friends as Tania] and Blix getting married,' I explained. '*Nothing* like them!' 'Well, these people are just actors...' 'What's he supposed to be doing here?' 'That's Denys washing Tania's hair.' 'What? Oh no, that's quite wrong. He would never have washed her hair. The other way round perhaps – only he didn't have much to wash...'

Occasionally her mind would wander off. I came to know the symptoms, for she would start to repeat herself or trail off in her sentences. Sometimes this lasted for minutes and sometimes for an hour or more. It was pointless to try to make sense of what she said during these periods. Patience was the only answer so I would sit quietly, often reading to her, or if she was talking, to myself. Suddenly she'd demand, 'Why aren't you saying anything?' Mercifully she didn't know of her lapses, but 'growing old and losing her mind' was a fear she spoke of. 'I hate to think that people will be laughing at me,' she confessed sadly. Often she could not summon a word to mind and became upset, but I noticed no such hesitancy in her Swahili speech. It was almost as if, towards the end, she was more at home in it than English.

One day she told me that before my arrival she had walked to the door and back. I was very surprised. 'Really? That's wonderful news.' Beryl's friend Paddy Migdoll arrived shortly afterwards en route to see her horses in training for the races on the following Sunday. She often interrupted her busy routine to call and to sit with Beryl for a while. I told her about Beryl walking. Paddy was equally surprised and questioned Adiambo out of Beryl's hearing. The woman apparently denied that Beryl had walked. 'I'm afraid it's her imagination,' Paddy told me when I walked her to her car. But it wasn't, for after lunch Beryl suddenly announced, 'I'm going for a walk.' Calling

Odero who held her hands, and with me supporting her at the waist, she pulled herself instantly to her feet. Her face was a study in concentration as she walked slowly to the door. 'Outside now,' she said. I supported her as she stepped down on to the veranda and then stood back ready to move in if needed. She was relying on Odero only as a crutch as she walked twice around the veranda and back. I was surprised at her height (having only seen her in her chair previously), and her upright stance.

Seated in her chair again, with a vodka by her elbow, she was triumphantly elated. 'I told you I could walk. Call the girl and have your drink topped up. Come on – let's have some fun, shall we?' I was equally delighted. Having had to learn to walk again after major spinal surgery some years earlier, I knew what it felt like, that first walk. She seemed young and coquettish, and for the remainder of the afternoon she talked happily of what she was going to do once she was walking properly and driving her car again. 'The first thing I'm going to do is go to the bank and get some money out. I've quite a lot, you know, from my book, only I can't get out to go to the bank without a car.' 'Your book is a tremendous success at the moment, isn't it?' 'Yes, I *know*,' she said. 'It's astonishing. I'd forgotten all about it, you know.'

'Why did you never write anything else?' I asked. 'Oh but I did – lots of little things for those other people.' Gently I probed and was rewarded with the names of several magazines which I carefully noted for future research. 'You know that some people say you didn't write the book alone?' I suggested. She was contemptuously dismissive of this rumour, as she had been to others who had asked the same question before me, telling me that of course she wrote it herself. What had Raoul Schumacher done, I wondered, to deserve the dedication and thanks. 'He helped me at the end, he was very good at that sort of thing, very clever but I wrote the book myself while he was away... he wasn't even there.' I wanted to believe she had written it. If the doubt had not been placed in my mind by innumerable informants, it would never have occurred to me to question it. Talking to her, being with her, she unconsciously embodied my expectations.

I found her highly intelligent and cultured. She had at times an air of detachment which could have been taken for vagueness, but I was left with the impression of an immensely strong and complex personality. My subsequent researches resolved all my personal doubts. Beryl wrote her book and the autobiographical short stories that came later. There are still a few rumoured incidents in her life which I have not been able to verify to my personal satisfaction and so they are not included here. Her ability to have written the book was not one of them.

Sometimes I read to her from her collection of books, about which she could talk lucidly. She had not read them for some time because a cataract in one eye had affected her reading sight. But she remembered enough to convince me that she had read them and many were old friends. Once I suggested that perhaps Jack Couldrey could arrange a driver if she wanted to go out, now that she was able to walk a little. 'No, I prefer to drive myself about. I'm a good driver, you know.'

No matter what I asked her, she always answered politely. When she did not wish to answer a question she would reply evasively, 'I'm afraid I can't remember, it's so long ago now.' However, I quickly learned that when she had genuinely forgotten something, she became distressed. 'I really can't remember – I was thinking about it in the night and wanted to tell you, but now I can't remember... I *really* want to tell you... I'm so sorry.' She was very interested in all my work, though I admit to filtering the results of my other interviews which I was afraid she might find offensive. She was amused at the extracts from old copies of the *East African Standard,* which I'd looked up in Nairobi's McMillan Library, and the results of other researches conducted very early in the morning at the Kenya National Archives. She allowed me to take some of her documents away each evening for photocopying the following morning in Nairobi.

On only one day during my time in Kenya did I fail to see Beryl for the major part of the day. I drove up country to visit Miss Pamela Scott at her home Deloraine, near Njoro. She kindly drove me to Beryl's childhood home, the old Clutterbuck farm which now belongs to a wool-spinners' cooperative. One of the men who works there, an African who as a child lost a leg in Clutterbuck's saw mill, still remembers Beryl well and is able to recall her happy relationship with her father, and her love for horses.

It was magical, that day I drove up country to Njoro. I was unprepared for the moment when, having wound tortuously along a road following a line of trucks, the car rounded a curve and the trees lining the side of the road ended, revealing over the edge of the escarpment a view of the Rift Valley stretching into apparent infinity, thousands of feet beneath the road. Like many before me I was overwhelmed. I stopped the car and sat for a long time, trying to imprint it on my mind, the heat shimmering above a landscape so beautiful that I could not tear myself away. Far away in the distance I could see the shining patches of water that I knew must be the lakes Naivasha and Elmenteita, which lay on my route. I stopped the car many times on that journey, and as a result I was late for my appointment. 'There are no signs,' I was told. 'After you leave Nakuru go exactly twenty-eight kilometres and then you cross two rivers, then you come to...' Living on the banks of a fast-flowing Wiltshire river I was misled by this simple instruction and looked in vain for what I called rivers. One turned out to be a narrow stream and the other one I never saw at all because it had obviously dried up.

Miss Scott showed me not only Beryl's home but also the gallops where as a girl she herself had ridden. 'Beryl always kept them beautifully level and perfectly maintained,' she told me. I drank it all in, the views across to distant mountains in one direction and down the length of the Rift Valley in another. 'Of course in Beryl's day all this was forest.' Now the only trees to be seen were dotted about in small clumps and the landscape was divided into small shambas. Still, to me it was inescapably lovely. It was spoiled only to those who had known it as virgin land.

Beryl was pleased to see me next morning, and listened with interest as I told her about my day at Njoro. 'My little house? Oh yes, I remember that so well. It had a proper roof, I loved it though it was quite tiny... it was lovely up there... we used to ride up into the hills. I had the gallops when I was training. No, they weren't my father's, they were mine... I used to land my aeroplane there sometimes.'

One day I asked her, 'Beryl, you wouldn't consider writing an introduction to my book about you, would you?' She agreed instantly. 'Now?' I asked, and we decided that she would dictate and I would type her words on her little portable typewriter which lay among dusty mounds of copies of *Horse and Hound* on her dining table. 'What do you think, is it any good?' she'd ask.

'Mmm, I'm not sure...'

'I don't like it much either.'

It took her two days to hone innumerable drafts. 'No, I don't like that,' she said repeatedly when I read each out, so that I began to doubt that there would ever be a finished one, but eventually the three-paragraph introduction was approved and signed.

On the following day some unexpected visitors arrived – a Danish couple who had never met Beryl brought by a man who'd known her years ago and had come to see her whilst on holiday in Kenya. Beryl was gracious and funny, signing their copy of *West with the Night* with aplomb. I asked her to sign another copy of the introduction. 'What again?' she laughed. I told her I'd found some mistakes in my typing and wanted it to be perfect for the book. She agreed and signed it after I read it to her once again. 'It's very good, isn't it?' she asked. I said I thought it excellent and was very pleased to have it. Actually I had only wanted witnesses that the work was hers.

Not every day was a good day. Sometimes she was tired, and querulous with the servants. Her physical frailty obviously irritated her and she took this out on Adiambo particularly. Her biggest problem though was loneliness and boredom. She had no television, radio, nor even a record player – not since the burglary. She had a large collection of records – Burl Ives in particular, but some classical and popular music, as well as a sound recording of the Derby being won by her famous race-horse Niagara. She had not been able to play them for years. She had fairly regular visitors; perhaps every other day whilst I was there someone popped in to chat. But I could see that these visits took up a short time in what were very long days of inactivity to her. The worst thing of all for her was the lack of mental stimulation, and that, I think, was the reason she looked forward to my daily visits. Each day I took a little gift. Nothing much. A packet of English cigarettes, a plastic lighter, a bottle of cologne, a mirror, a new hairbrush. And each day I brought the *Standard* and *Nation* newspapers from which I read to her.

By now I had become so attached to her that at one time I

even toyed with the idea of remaining in Nairobi permanently, though I knew even as I thought of it that it was a thoroughly impractical idea. I extended my visit however, and took advantage of Jack Couldrey's and Beryl's permission to have all her photographs copied. My collection of papers, notes, photographs and photocopies weighed nearly twenty kilos and as I would not be parted with them on the aeroplane, I had to pay excess baggage and share my narrow seat with the lot.

On the final day of my time in Kenya I was joined in my visit to Beryl's house by George Gutekunst, the enthusiast who arranged for the republication of *West with the Night*. He had arrived two days earlier to pay a flying visit in connection with the film rights to Beryl's book. At Beryl's request I had also asked her neighbour, the vet 'VJ', to join us. I noticed that she never behaved well when more than one person was present – she seemed to lack the concentration needed to cope with a number of people talking. However, it was a pleasant morning and when the conversation turned inevitably to the Derby, to be run later that day, Beryl said, 'I'd like to go to the Derby.' There was a moment's silence as Beryl's guests looked at each other in surprise, but it was soon arranged. I would drive Beryl in my car accompanied by George. A call to the Jockey Club arranged special provisions for an honoured guest.

When she was dressed and ready to leave she stood waiting on the veranda. Her hair, recently tinted ash blonde, had been brushed and patted carefully into shape. Her china-blue eyes sparkled with triumph, and she graciously acknowledged the tribute I paid to her appearance. She was still beautiful and she still had that indefinable something which is instinctive in some women. Glamour.

It is the way I will always recall her. She suffered a fall as we left the races and on our return to her cottage she was obviously shocked. I left her almost immediately to rush back to the race course to find a doctor, for her own doctor could not be reached. I was fortunate to find Sir Charles Markham in the owners' enclosure and he wasted no time, cutting short my breathless explanation, and arranging for the course doctor to go out to Beryl's cottage. I did not see Beryl again after that for I had to leave, but I later telephoned Paddy Migdoll, who'd looked in on Beryl and found her sedated and resting comfortably.

Shortly after returning to England I gave up my job to concentrate on the book. I could not think of, nor concentrate on, anything else, and was totally obsessed with Beryl and her story.

In late July 1986 I was in California, having spent the afternoon at Beryl's old home in Santa Barbara, when I first heard that she'd fallen over Tookie, her little pug dog, and suffered a broken hip. I didn't like the sound of it, but as the days wore on the news was good. 'She's holding her own,' I was told. 'They're very pleased with her progress.' After Santa Barbara I drove up to San Francisco to visit George Gutekunst and I was there on 3 August when the news of Beryl's death was telephoned by Paddy Migdoll. It was a devastating blow.

I think it was the fact that I should never see her again which hurt more than anything; the sense of loss was intolerable. In the weeks that followed I helped with the arrangements for her Thanksgiving service in London and met Beryl's grand-daughters Fleur and Valery. Neither of them is a replica, but in composite one can see Beryl quite clearly. I was proud and sad on the fiftieth anniversary of Beryl's famous flight to see Fleur receive the replica Vega Gull trophy from the hands of the station commander at RAF Abingdon. Beryl would have loved it.

And how she would have loved to know that her republished book *West with the Night* had climbed briskly through the best-seller charts in the United States. By Christmas 1986 it reached number one and stayed there for weeks on end, after interest generated by the television documentary *World without Walls* brought her story into public focus. Now, a full-blown television series is to be made, and perhaps a full-length feature film.

She has become so much a part of my life that I will never stop searching for more information, and long after this book has been published I will still be turning first to the indexes of books rather than introductions. It is hard to believe that I knew her personally for such a short time – only a matter of weeks – and yet she changed my life. Her advice '. . . never look back. You've got to keep looking forward. Something will always happen if you try to make it happen . . .' inspired me to take the step of resigning my well-paid job, which I enjoyed. But I had always wanted to work full time as a writer and had lacked the necessary courage to cast myself adrift from a regular monthly salary. 'If it's what you want to do you must do it ... it will all work out. It won't always be easy ... hardly anything worth doing is easy.'

She is the most remarkable person I have ever met, and perhaps even greater than her own great adventure with life was her ability to inspire others. For myself, I love her still, with a passion which often takes me by surprise.

CHAPTER ONE

[1890-1906]

In the spring of 1898 the long Victorian era was drawing to a close. The gay nineties were still in full swing however, and in high Leicestershire it was possible to hunt the fox in great style on five days a week, provided one had the money, the horses and the inclination. Charles Baldwin Clutterbuck certainly had the inclination. Horses were easy to come by, for people would always lend him a bad horse, and Charles could ride anything on four legs. Money was more of a problem.

Some months earlier he had been asked to resign his army commission, and debt was almost certainly the reason for this request. His career and reputation, at least among his army contemporaries, were in ruins. It was a pity. An intelligent man, with a good, though not wealthy, family background and a classical education, Charles had enjoyed the army, and he had been a good officer.

The younger of two sons of his father's first marriage, after attending school at Repton[1] where he was considered a very bright boy in the classics stream, he entered the Royal Military Academy at Sandhurst as a gentleman cadet. The courses he took whilst at the academy were all military subjects: Military Law and Administration, Tactics, Fortification, Topography and Reconnaissance, Drill and Gymnastics. His conduct, according to his record, was exemplary.[2]

Commissioned shortly before his nineteenth birthday in 1890 into the 1st Battalion, King's Own Scottish Borderers, Charles had taken to regimental life with ease. He served in Burma for a while, catching the last six months of the regiment's service there, and was awarded the Indian General Service Medal with the bar Chin Lushai. The battalion returned to England in early 1891.[3]

The remainder of his service life was spent in England, mainly at Aldershot. In 1893 he was promoted to first lieutenant. He had an undoubted ability to make and ride horses, even very difficult horses. He often rode in regimental races, and he often won.

The peacetime life of an officer in those days could be very pleasant. Duties were not onerous, and the social life was good. In addition to an endless round of mess activities, bachelor officers were in constant demand at dinner parties in the town, and there were steeplechasing and polo. London with its hotels, gentlemen's clubs, Weatherby's and Tattersall's, was within easy reach of Aldershot, and Charles, a slim, good-looking man with a good deal of address, made full use of its amenities.

Above all though, there was the hunting. The army had always encouraged officers to hunt, on the grounds that it encouraged bold horsemanship, an asset in the days of cavalry warfare. Wellington declared of his victorious officers that they had 'picked up their excellence in riding across country when hunting in England'. Charles had enjoyed it all, but increasingly found that he could not afford to maintain the social standards set by his brother officers.

Charles's mother died whilst he was a child, and his father, a Carlisle solicitor, remarried. This second marriage produced a clutch of five children so that when, in 1891, Mr Richard Henry Clutterbuck died suddenly of influenza, within weeks of his wife producing a son, the estate had a great number of calls upon it. All Charles received when his father died was two silver candlesticks, three silver salt cellars, some shares in the County Hotel Company and the residue of the sale of a modest London property after all bank debts and overdrafts of the deceased had been met.[4] It was unlikely that this was more than a few hundred pounds, far short of the expectations of the young officer. The main part of his inheritance was a half share in the substantial family home and contents, but his stepmother and her young children were to enjoy those for her lifetime.[5] No officer could manage indefinitely on army pay alone, and by 1897 Charles could no longer afford to continue his military career.

At the age of twenty-seven Charles was out of the army, and living on a small farm at Knaptoff in Leicestershire. He was not quite dishonoured, though his record in the army lists bears the terse comment 'removed from the army',[6] the usual synonym for slow horses, fast women or debts. No one, ever, could accuse Charles of slow horses, so it was certainly one of the latter.

At that time and in that place the horse was king. A good hunter was almost worshipped, and cosseted beyond belief.[7] Charles had already found that he could buy badly-schooled or poorly-made horses cheaply, and make them into good hunters, selling them on for acceptable profits. He had done this with some success in the army, but not, it seems, enough to keep him out of financial deep water.

It was whilst he was hunting with the Cottesmore Hounds that Charles first saw Clara Alexander. He had an eye for a beautiful girl and at nineteen Clara was undoubtedly a lovely creature. Tall, reed-slim, and strikingly handsome, she sat and handled a horse in a manner which turned heads. In addition she had a particularly sweet clear voice[8] and a pouting, appealing manner. Her classical features and silken brown hair turned Charles's head and he and Clara were married on a hot August day in 1898 in the parish church of Wintringham, York, where Clara had been living with her mother after the family returned from India following the death of her father.[9]

In July 1900, at Scarborough in Yorkshire, Clara gave birth to a son, Richard Alexander Clutterbuck. She must have travelled to the North Riding for her confinement, for the couple had resided since their marriage in Uppingham, Leicestershire. Two years later the Clutterbucks had moved to Ashwell, in the heart of the Cottesmore country. From here they could hunt with the three best packs in the kingdom – The Quorn, The Belvoir and The Cottesmore.[10]

A second child was born on 26 October 1902, at Westfield House, Ashwell in the county of Rutland. It was a girl. The parents evidently could not think of a suitable name, and even by 3 December when the child's birth was registered, no name was mentioned. The birth certificate merely records that the child was 'female' and Charles declared his occupation as 'farmer'. Eventually the baby was christened Beryl at the lovely old Norman church of St Mary in Ashwell on 7 December.[11]

Charles and Clara continued to hunt, mixing easily in the hunting set. For many years after the Clutterbucks left the area, they were reputed to have been the best-looking couple and the hardest riders to hounds in Melton.[12] Charles often rode in hunt races on his two good horses, Hot Chocolate and Snape, and when his regular successes became noticed he also began to train chasers, as an additional source of income to that earned from his farming and horse-coping.[13] But money was always a problem, and the domestic obligations which two babies brought with them could not have helped the situation. The couple began to have serious disagreements and in the summer of 1903 they separated. Charles stayed at Westfield House with the children and Clara went to live in Melton Mowbray where she ran a tea shop in Burton Street.[14]

Beryl was only starting to walk when her father decided to emigrate to South Africa. It was generally believed that there were fortunes to be made in farming there: it was another India, just opening up. Everyone knew how much money had been made in India, but Africa, it seemed, was even better, for there were no feudal princes in Africa, land was to be had cheaply and a well-run farm could make one a millionaire. A man could breathe in the vastness of Africa. In the spring of 1904 Charles and Clara made an attempt at reconciliation, following which Charles sailed for the Cape where his intention was to farm and to train horses. If he were successful Clara would join him there with the two children.

Charles did not stay in South Africa long, for as soon as he arrived he became interested in the East African Protectorate, then known as British East Africa or simply BEA. Almost certainly his imagination was caught by the virtues being widely advertised for the territory in an attempt to encourage white settlement of the newly opened country.

The British government had spent an enormous sum mainly in the building of the famous railway line from Mombasa on the coast to Kisumu on the shores of Lake Victoria.[15] This railway to Uganda, dubbed the Lunatic Express, opened up a vast territory of great potential value – the White Highlands of Kenya.[16] However, maintaining the sparsely populated protectorate would remain a very expensive enterprise. Following recommendations from Sir Charles Eliot, HM

Commissioner in East Africa, that white settlement was the essential route towards making the project self-supporting, it became a matter of prime importance to encourage the 'right sort' of settler. The Commissioner of Customs, Mr A. Marsden, was therefore dispatched to South Africa to advertise the potential of the country.

Probably as a direct result of this action, Charles sailed for East Africa, arriving at the old Mombasa harbour, subsequently named Kilindini, on 29 July 1904. As the steamer slowly edged through the gap in the coral reef, he had his first view of the town with its white beaches fringed with palm and mango trees.[17] Above the shoreline, the lush tropical vegetation, with its climbing carpet of flowering bougainvillea, palms and the peculiar, unique baobab trees, gave every indication of swamping the whitewashed, red-roofed houses.[18] He would have been prepared for the humid heat, but the vibrant colours of the abundant flowers, and the alien sounds of the cosmopolitan town with its population of Arabs, Africans and Europeans, must have burst upon his senses after the monotony of the sea voyage. He stayed for one night at the Grand Hotel before boarding the train for Nairobi.[19] 'Mombasa...', wrote Winston Churchill after his visit in 1907,

> is the starting point of one of the most romantic and most wonderful railways in the world... all day long the train runs upward and westward, through broken and undulating ground clad and encumbered with superabundant vegetation. Beautiful birds and butterflies fly from tree to tree and flower to flower. Deep ragged gorges, filled by streams in flood, open out far below us through glades of palm and creeper covered trees, every few miles are trim little stations with their water tanks, signals, ticket offices, and flower beds backed by impenetrable bush. In the evening a cooler crisper air is blowing... at an altitude of four thousand feet we begin to laugh at the equator... After Makindu station the forest ceases and the traveller enters upon a region of grass... the plains are covered with wild animals.[20]

From the windows of the carriages the passengers gazed upon the great herds of antelope, gazelle and zebra. Giraffe, lion and ostrich were also to be seen in this Garden of Eden. The trains

stopped at Voi which enabled the passengers to take dinner in a
dak bungalow. When the engine driver gave the signal the
passengers returned to their carriages and tried to get what
sleep they could as the train chugged on through the night; but
they were all awake early next morning, anxious to see the
promised glory of Kilimanjaro, its ice-crowned summit tinted
coral in the rays of the rising sun.[21]

The hot and dusty train journey ended for Charles at
Nairobi, then merely a collection of shabby, tin-roofed shacks
around the railway station. Situated on a treeless plain, it had
been chosen as a halt for trains to take on water, before the line
began a dizzying series of contortions over the Kikuyu
escarpment into the Rift Valley. It was an unhealthy place and
only two years earlier had been affected by bubonic plague. A
huge swamp bordered the river along the length of modern-day
Nairobi's city centre, a constant breeding ground for malaria.

> ... the railway station consisted of a wooden platform roofed
> by a few strips of corrugated iron and a godown with a
> kitchen clock suspended over the door. The arrival of the bi-
> weekly train was a great event. Naked natives flocked onto
> the platform to see the miracle... in the dry weather
> passengers arrived coated with a thick layer of red dust. The
> particles clung to everything – clothes, baggage, fingernails,
> hair, food. Faces were fantastically streaked as though they
> had been smeared with chocolate war-paint. The passengers
> had to walk from the station. There were no rickshaws or
> buggies to meet them. There was one small hotel, easily filled.
> The only alternative was to camp... The town consisted of
> one cart-track, recently labelled Government Road, flanked
> by Indian dukas [shops]... one European store and one
> office. Beyond lay the swamp where the frogs lived. Every
> night at dusk they used to bark out their vibrant chorus and
> spread a cloak of deep, incessant sound over the little
> township.[22]

Charles's favourable impression of Nairobi was no doubt
coloured by the fact that he arrived there during Race Week.[23]
This was a far cry from the formal green turf of Ascot, but not
too unlike the hurly-burly of a hunt point-to-point and Charles
would have been instantly at home in such company. Soon after

arriving in Nairobi he met Lord Delamere. The great pioneer of Kenya was quick to spot the ability of the young, well-educated farmer and undoubtedly encouraged him to settle. This included the offer of a job as manager of his farm at Njoro (where Delamere had over fifteen hundred head of cattle including imported pedigree Herefords), and suggestions about several good parcels of land for which Clutterbuck could apply.

Hugh Cholmondeley, third Baron Delamere,[24] had left his ancestral estate, Vale Royal in Cheshire, for a couple of grass huts in BEA. He had, it must be admitted, also acquired 100,000 acres, but this was virgin land, virtually valueless at that time. In subsequent years he brought the Vale Royal estates to bankruptcy for the sake of the land in Kenya, and dedicated the rest of his life to making Kenya one of the most efficient and prosperous colonies in Africa.

Charles travelled up country to look at several sites, two of which were serious possibilities. One was at Thika, which he rejected.[25] The other was a large tract near Njoro in the White Highlands, which marched with, and was originally part of, Delamere's own property which was known as Equator Ranch because the equator ran through one corner of it.[26] Charles eventually purchased 1000 acres of this land at three rupees an acre,[27] but first he got to know the land by working it for Delamere.

The land at Njoro consisted of raw and untamed bush on the slopes of the mighty Mau Escarpment, which forms the western edge of the great Rift Valley. Much of it was covered in dense forests of juniper (known as cedars), acacia and mahogo, but there were also areas of open pasture. The climate was pleasant: the site was situated at some 7000 feet, so the heat never became oppressive even in the strong sunlight of the equator, and mild frost at night was not unusual. During the day the air had an alpine sparkle to it, dry and clean.

The views were breathtaking. No man or woman alive could fail to be stirred by the sweeping vistas of the rift down to the distant Aberdare Mountains on one hand, and the multi-hued blues and greens of the Mau Forest stretching across the Rongai Valley to the slopes of the extinct volcano Menengai on the other. Game abounded in the forests, as did lions and leopards.

In one of his letters home Lord Delamere described the area around Njoro:

> I measured a cedar yesterday on the road through the forest close here – 24 ft and 22 ft, three feet above the ground and round the butt, and there are many larger in the heart of the forest I believe. The more I see of the place the more I like it. This is the hottest time of the year and the thermometer has never been above 70° since I have been up here and is down to 50° in the mornings in my hut. After the rains I expect it to be very much cooler. At the next station on the place, Elburgon, it freezes even at this time of the year, but that is up in the forest.[28]

Charles Miller outlines the difficulties of the new settler who

> made the initial stage of his African journey by rail from Mombasa to Nairobi, and thence to the station nearest his holding on the Kikuyu escarpment, the floor of the rift or the slopes of the Mau. The final lap was covered on ox- or mule-drawn wagons, whose axles screamed out under the weight of disc ploughs, harrows, grindstones, bags of seed, rolls of barbed wire, steamer trunks, chop boxes, bedsteads, tin bath tubs, toilet seats and veritable flea markets of household goods. Practically no roads existed outside a radius of a few hundred yards from any station. The grass rose above a man's head. The ground was strewn with rocks that smashed wagon wheels, pitted with ant-bear holes capable of snapping an ox's foreleg like a dried twig. During the rains, wagons would swamp easily while being wrestled through the mill races of bloated streams. A farm no further than fifteen miles from the nearest railway station might not be reached in a fortnight.[29]

With his few personal belongings, Charles settled on the land and, helped by African labour, started the task of making the farm which he optimistically called Green Hills.

In *West with the Night* Beryl wrote a poetic summary of the years which in reality must have involved a backbreaking, often heartbreaking struggle for her father. Much has been written about the difficulties besetting the pioneer settlers.[30] There was often too much sun and not enough rain. Then, when the rain did come there was often too much of it. The dirt roads became impassable in hip-deep mud; the only movement possible for weeks at a time, was on horseback or on foot and the great ox-drawn wagons, scotch carts used for supplies, and water carts, stood idle.

Clearing the land could take months. A coarse outer beard of tall grass and dense knotted scrub had to be shaved clean with bush knives, or pangas as they were known. There were forests of gum, thorn trees and giant cedar to be felled, and their great stumps extracted like decayed teeth. As Charles Miller wrote:

> Boulders and man-high anthills harder than concrete must be swept away. These chores, in turn, meant on-the-job training for the African farmhands, who were patiently taught how to wield axes, picks and hoes without amputating their legs or fracturing their shoulders. The workers also had to learn the rudiments of handling the ox teams that would drag the tree stumps from the earth with chains attached to their yokes. Even the oxen required education, being local beasts that had never known any sort of halter and that were deaf to the command of the human voice. More than one farmer harnessed his oxen by dropping the yokes on them from a tree, provided that one of the African workers could drive the animal under the branches.
>
> When ploughing finally began, the settler was likely to discover to his exasperation, that it was a rare African indeed who could comprehend the meaning of a straight line. Furrows in the infant years of pioneering on the highlands, often resembled the paths left by gigantic pythons.[31]

At first the Clutterbuck homestead was, like that of all newly-arrived settlers, a hut called a rondavel, made of mud and daub with a grass-thatch roof and sited on a high sunny clearing. Whatever your social standing, these native-type huts were your introduction to living in Kenya. Their dark interiors remained cool in the sun, and at night the thick mud walls were snug against the cold air of the highlands. Lord Delamere continued to live for years in his collection of huts on the Mau Escarpment – although in his case this was from personal choice. Lord Francis Scott recalled some years later: 'For the first nine months I lived in a tent on my estate – then my wife and two young daughters came out and we put up . . . mud and wattle huts, until about nine months later when the house [Deloraine] was ready.'[32] In *The Flame Trees of Thika* Elspeth Huxley wrote of her first African home that it 'was most companionable, for a great many creatures soon joined us in the roof and the walls. The nicest were the lizards, who would stay for hours spread-eagled on a wall quite motionless, clinging to the surface with small scaly hands . . . the thatch was always full of sounds, little rustling, secretive noises from unseen fellow-residents.'

These huts had no proper doors, but usually some sacking provided a little privacy. The windows were merely openings cut into the walls, but they looked out on to some of the best views in the world. Langley Morris, who was taken out to East Africa as a child to live near Njoro, recalled, 'I can remember kneeling on my bed and looking out of the window at the Molo Hills to the north of us, it is my earliest real memory. The hills were deep blue – as blue as your dress [cobalt]. I asked one of the African boys if they were really that blue – he told me it was the mist hanging over the hills that made them appear so.'[33] The cold night air often made fires at night a necessity, and the main hut on the Clutterbuck homestead nearly always had a big cedarwood fire burning after dark.

Furnishings were a strange mixture. Treasured antique pieces shipped from 'home' stood shoulder to shoulder with upturned packing cases which served as makeshift chairs and tables. Beds were often animal skins on wooden stretchers. The legs of tables, chairs and beds stood in tins of water – or, if available, in paraffin – to discourage the ever-present ants.

The main diet was 'tommies', the plentiful Thomson's gazelle, though most of the settlers tried a wide variety of plains game when the need arose. Langley Morris, describing their food, said, 'Once my father killed a python but my mother wouldn't let me have any in case it was poisonous. My father said it was very stringy! I did eat ostrich once and *that* was stringy. Also it looked very unattractive – covered in pits like craters of the moon, where the quills had been pulled out.'[34]

Cooking was done by Africans who coped admirably in preparing European food on primitive cooking ranges. These usually consisted of three flat stones over a fire, but the Morris household had managed to acquire a Somali cook who had his own ideas: '...our cooking range consisted of a sheet of corrugated galvanized iron on which several small fires of charcoal were kept burning.'[35]

The pioneer settlers had little in the way of entertainment and social life, but what there was revolved around horses. Within months Charles had established his interest, and began advertising 'For Sale at Njoro, several high class ponies 14hh–15hh. Prices Reasonable apply C.B. Clutterbuck, Njoro.'[36] His remarkable talent with horses was immediately apparent when the newly organized Turf Club held a race meeting in Nairobi in February and Charles rode in many of the races on behalf of clients. He won on Lord Delamere's Dawn and also managed several places, riding horses owned by the Delameres, R.B. Cole and others.[37] From this date onwards he rode regularly in the owner-ridden Somali or country-bred horse races and was among the first to import horses to improve the blood lines.

According to Charles, or 'Clutt' as he became known in the protectorate, 'Delamere was never really keen on racing, only he saw it as a way of improving horse blood.'[38] Clutt imported two Australian mares; Gladys, which he owned in partnership with Berkeley Cole, and Kathleen, which was owned by Lady Delamere. Both were trained by Clutterbuck and became famous in the early days of Kenyan racing. By 1906 Clutt was well established in racing circles. In a poem which starts 'To the races I went and I had a good time, There was racing and laughter and Scotch Whisky wine', his name features heavily.[39]

Race meetings were only held twice a year in those early days. Handicapping was an invidious task, for the horses ranged from English thoroughbreds to Somali 'rats'. On one occasion the handicapping steward was bitterly upbraided for putting 16 stone on the horse of a prominent settler and making it give 8 stone to a Somali pony. One might suppose that the settler's complaint was justified until one learns that his horse started hot favourite and that he won the race 'pulling up, in a hunting saddle.' Whenever possible Clutt personally rode the horses he trained, and despite the vagaries of the handicapper, won with what must have seemed, to rival stables, maddening consistency.[40]

Clara went out to join her husband in late 1905, taking

Richard and Beryl with her. As was the custom, after a few months living at the unaccustomed altitude of Njoro she went down to the coast for a few days in April 1906 to spend a short time at sea level.[41] She was staying there with friends at Mombasa in April 1906 when she met Richard Meinertzhagen who recorded the meeting in his diary:

> Bowring gave a dinner party this evening at which were present Mr & Mrs Coombe, Mrs Clutterbuck, Stanley of the railways, my old Fort Hall friend Ronald Humphrey and myself. Mrs Clutterbuck told me a good story which she declared to be true. Her husband wounded an old bull elephant near Molo on the Mau Plateau but failed to recover him that day. On the following day they found that he had wandered off to a small stream, and in his efforts to get water had sunk down and died, actually in the bed of the watercourse. The stream was thus dammed but instead of the water rising and flowing over the carcass it found for itself a new course underground and now flows for over a mile in this fashion.[42]

By 1906 the Protectorate of East Africa was beginning to flourish and lose some of its wildness. Nairobi had changed considerably from the tin shanty town which Charles had found two years earlier, and Meinertzhagen recorded his surprise when visiting Nairobi in 1906:

> ... the town has trebled in size. Trees have sprung up everywhere, hotels exist where zebra once roamed. Private bungalows in all their ugliness now mar the landscape where I used to hunt the waterbuck, impala and duiker. The place is full of strange faces and ... where two years ago I knew every soul of the twenty or thirty Europeans ... there are now over 1200 Europeans in the town.[43]

The Clutterbuck farm was already well established by the standards of the day. A friend who visited Green Hill Farm in that year to recuperate from an illness recalled a 'pretty little house, with a garden full of English cottage-garden flowers', and later recalled with amusement that she was fed on 'roast mutton, boiled onions and tea for every meal'.[44]

Clutterbuck was still working for Lord Delamere and ran regular weekly advertisements in the *East African Standard*: 'FOR SALE at Lord Delamere's Njoro Farm: Broken bullocks at 50 Rupees, Unbroken Bullocks 40 Rupees, also young large White Yorkshire, Middle white and Berkshire Pigs, Boars and Gilts at 30 Rupees each... a quantity of the above always for sale. Apply C.B. Clutterbuck Njoro.'

In August 1906 the Ladies' Column in the same newspaper proved that it was not 'all work and no play' even in the pioneering days, when it carried a report of the Turf Club Ball at Nairobi.

> The Ball Room was most tastefully decorated with flags and long trailing garlands of flowers and when everyone was dancing it was a very pretty sight. There were lots of pretty women in lovely frocks. Mrs Clutterbuck wore a perfectly lovely frock of pink chiffon which suited her to perfection, Lady Delamere was in wine-coloured velvet, Mrs Bowker in a dress of fine black lace...[45]

The rival newspaper, *The Times of East Africa*, noted at the end of that week that 'The Delameres and the Clutterbucks have left for Njoro.'[46]

Life up country was not without its excitement, however. There were constant rumours of native unrest – particularly from the Nandi and Sotik tribes a little way to the north of Njoro. Trains were not allowed through the disturbed areas at night and up-country passengers had to sleep at Nakuru and go on next day.[47]

When Lord Delamere returned to England to raise capital to develop his farming interests in Kenya his admirable wife Lady Florence wrote calmly:

> I suppose you have heard of our scare. The Sotik looted two Masai villages on the other side of the line from here. Wiped them out I understand. Then the Government sent word to the el moru [elders] on our land that another party of Sotik were coming. So I borrowed 200 cartridges from Mr Clutterbuck to reinforce Casaro [the head Masai on the Delameres' property]; but as nothing more happened, I

conclude the government were misinformed. Personally I never thought they would come here but I thought it as well to get more cartridges.

Rather amusing, the district officer at Naivasha wired... to say a loot was expected. The said loot had taken place two days before. Beauties aren't they?[48]

Native raids were not the only excitement at Njoro. There were periodic scares from lions and leopards who prowled around bomas (cattle enclosures built of thorn trees) where the oxen were herded for the night. There was always the chance of running into one after dark.[49]

Langley Morris, whose family lived on a farm at Njoro from 1906 to 1914, remembered that his father had once walked three miles home in the dark and had been 'shadowed' by a lion. 'It kept parallel to him the entire time, about fifty yards away. When he stopped the lion did too. He had only a pistol on him so it was pointless his trying to do anything unless the lion attacked. So he just kept on walking... and so did the lion.'[50]

Lions were classed as vermin, and were shot at will, although technically only proven cattle-killers could be shot unless the hunter had the requisite licence. They were not the only 'game' presenting problems to pioneer farmers. Elephants, rhino, buffalo, zebra, giraffes and gazelles grazed on the crops. Lions, leopards and cheetahs threatened livestock.[51]

Almost from the first, Richard, the elder Clutterbuck child, ailed. He had always been a sickly infant, slight and fair, but he now suffered a series of distressing illnesses which his parents attributed to the climate and altitude. Early settlers were by no means convinced that it was possible to rear children in the highlands, despite the views of H.M. Commissioner Sir Charles Eliot who in 1905 wrote that the fearful hazards of altitude, equatorial sun and disease had been exaggerated; fever was certainly not more prevalent than influenza in England: '... it will no longer sound incredible that European children can be reared [in the highlands] without danger or difficulty. The number of fat, rosy infants to be encountered on an afternoon's walk at Nairobi is quite remarkable.'[52] The young Winston Churchill disagreed: 'It is still quite unproved that a European can make the highlands of East Africa his permanent home...

still less that he can breed and rear families [at heights of] from five to eight thousand feet above sea-level.'[53] In September 1906 Richard was sent home in the company of friends.[54]

Settler life, despite the obvious improvements brought about since 1904, had not suited Clara. She enjoyed a busy social existence, loved parties and dancing, and could not accustom herself to the rigours, nor the social isolation, of her new life. Her single regular contact with civilization seems to have been a friendship with Lord Delamere's wife Florence, daughter of the Earl of Enniskillen. Before being taken to India by her parents, Clara too had been gently raised in a succession of 'big houses' belonging to the Alexanders, a great Irish family. The two women undoubtedly shared the trauma of their changed circumstances, and the friendship between them was noted by Lord Cranworth:

> If D[elamere] was a remarkable character, no less remarkable was his wife Florence. I do not think that I have ever met a more delightful companion or a more devoted wife. She loved hunting, dancing, every form of society and every joy of life. Yet she shared an existence of the utmost discomfort without any one of these amenities with the utmost cheeriness. On their personal expenditure... the very closest watch was kept. Two poor mud huts, which would have been condemned instanter by any housing authority in England, served them for years, and there was no garden nor indeed any other amenity whatsoever. D. was away nearly all day and every day on the farm and about his various enterprises and until the coming of the Clutterbucks she had a very lonely life...[55]

But the friendship of Lady Delamere could not compensate Clara for the living standards and society she missed so much, and she was not able to adapt, nor accept the privations, so well as her neighbour. Three months after young Richard had sailed for England, Clara embarked on the SS *Djemnah* bound for Marseilles and home.[56]

In 1986 Beryl stated that her father always told her that Clara 'ran off to England with Harry Kirkpatrick'. Major Harry Fearnley Kirkpatrick (whom Clara married some years later),

was serving at the time in East Africa attached to the 3rd King's
African Rifles,[57] so this must be considered as a possible reason
for the separation. But Clara's decision not to take Beryl back to
England with her may have been because she originally
intended to return to Njoro, and since Beryl was obviously
suited to life in Africa there seemed no justification for
uprooting her for the long and arduous journey to England.
Whatever the reason, it was decided that Beryl would remain
with her father at Njoro.

It will probably never be known whether Clara ever seriously
intended returning to Charles and the farm at Njoro. Beryl
would be a grown woman before she saw her brother or her
mother again. In the little time she knew him as an adult, she
loved her brother. But she never forgave her mother for
abandoning her.

CHAPTER TWO

[1906-1918]

After Clara's departure for England, the African house-servants were given the responsibility of watching over the little girl while Clutterbuck worked to establish the farm. Before 1909 when a series of governesses appeared on the scene, Beryl's regular companions were African contemporaries, the children of the increasing number of migrant workers employed by Clutterbuck, or 'Clutabuki' as he quickly became known to them.[1] From them Beryl learned to speak the languages of Africa, exactly as the other totos (small children) learned. The African workers on the farm were mainly Kikuyus and people from the Kavirondo district; but there were also a number of Kipsigis – a pastoral tribe allied to the warrior Nandis who hailed from the country to the north of the farm – who made particularly good herdsmen. The child's days were filled with sunshine, the soft murmur of African voices, and the cracking whips of the Boers who drove the huge teams of oxen which were used to drag away the felled timber.

The night sounds were those of the occasional roar of a lion in the distance, the snap and crackle of cedarwood fires, and the continuous shriek of hyraxes – attractive, small furry creatures, rodent-like but in fact the nearest living relative of the elephant.

The absence of her mother and brother undoubtedly had an influence on Beryl's character; indeed the strength and independence she was to show later almost certainly had their roots in this deprivation. Her lifelong habit of going barefoot whenever possible stemmed from these years, and her necessary intimacy with the African families who lived in squatter villages on the farm caused her to become almost more African than European in her thinking and attitudes. True, she acquired a veneer of European manners as she grew up, but these early years which did so much to shape her strength of personality also created within her a deep well of insecurity, and an inability to handle personal relationships. She simply 'never knew what was required of her and her instincts were to survive at any price, no matter what the cost to other people', a friend told me.[2] Her own comments about her father are also revealing:

> He is a tall man my father – a lean man, and he husbands his words. It is a kind of frugality, a hatred of waste I think. Through all his garnered store of years, he has regarded wasted emotion as if it were strength lavished on futile things.[3]

Beryl was always full of life and energy, and from contemporary recollections she might today be classified as a hyperactive child. But her charisma even as a young girl was outstanding, and she was regarded as having 'powerful *dawa*' (Swahili for magic or medicine) by the African workers on the farm. Her ideas were treated with respect even by adults.[4]

Although the highlight of her day was to 'do the stables with daddy',[5] her father, with his immense workload, had little time to spare. Lady Delamere kept a watching brief over her welfare. The Delameres' own child Tom, two years older than Beryl, had been left behind in England when the couple went out to Kenya in 1902 and it therefore is hardly surprising that Clara's child on the neighbouring farm provoked a kindly interest from Lady D. Interviewed in the spring of 1986 Beryl still retained a vague childhood memory of riding over to the Delameres' house on her pony,[6] and of 'a white frock' that she had been given by the woman described by Meinertzhagen as 'very lovely, graceful and charming, and quite out of place in this savage country'.[7]

Clutterbuck intended to make a success of his venture in Kenya from the start. He was more resourceful than many of the early settlers and he had the constant support and advice of Delamere; indeed it is difficult to separate Clutterbuck's early projects from Delamere's own concerns and interests. Much of Clutterbuck's initial work was performed on Delamere's behalf and was subsequently taken over by Clutterbuck, probably on very favourable terms.

Delamere pointed out to him the fact that the railway company had a number of redundant engines at various points along the line, and so Clutterbuck purchased two old engines and used them to power a mill to grind the maize and wheat grown by himself and his neighbours.[8] There was no easy living to be had, but Clutt's Mill, as it was known to the settlers, slowly prospered, in spite of numerous farming difficulties affecting the protectorate. Over the years Clutterbuck astutely acquired government contracts to provide posho (ground maize) for the workers on the Uganda Railway.

He was also quick to act on Delamere's early concern that despite the enormous quantities of trees available in the country, timber for building had to be imported because of lack of processing facilities in Kenya. Clutt bought two more engines in the autumn of 1906 and built a saw mill at the side of the railway track where it crossed his land. Delamere had spotted the potential of saw mills some time earlier and had ordered his agent in England to acquire and send out 'two small circular saws, a large rack circular saw and other woodworking equipment'.[9] The equipment took a long time to arrive, but Delamere had postdated the cheque for the equipment by a year.

Timber processed by Clutt was used by a newly arrived carpenter, Mr Francis Morris, to build his own and then Lady Delamere's house in 1907.[10] Lady Delamere, writing to her husband, told him, 'The rain has been awful, and the cold intense. I hope you won't be annoyed but I couldn't stand it any longer and have bought a little house and have hired a carpenter to build it.'[11]

'Intense' cold, on a farm which has the equator running within its boundaries, is an interesting paradox, but Equator Ranch was more reminiscent of the Scottish Highlands than anywhere in Africa. Mr Morris lined the inside of Lady Delamere's house with bamboo. When he subsequently built a house for Berkeley Cole (Lady Delamere's brother), Mr Morris lined the walls with tapestry, a source of wonderment to his young son Langley, who thought it the ultimate in luxury.

Gradually the number of Africans working on the Clutterbuck farm increased until there were over a thousand. When Winston Churchill briefly halted his train journey at the farm in 1907 there were nearly nine hundred employed solely on cutting timber and clearing the forest. Much of the timber was used to fuel the trains – a lucrative contract. Churchill described Clutterbuck as 'A young English gentleman... a model employer of native labour'.[12] This labour force sounds huge by today's standards, but it was not unusual. Karen Blixen, for example, was welcomed to her farm in 1914 by a similar number of African workers.[13]

The amount of effort involved in clearing land from the bush and forest was herculean. At that time there were no machines to pull the unyielding stumps from the ground even after the mass of timber was cleared. Many willing hands were needed, and teams of oxen. The Dutch who had trekked north from the Cape were the experts with oxen, and Clutterbuck took full advantage of their skills.[14] Beryl was later to write of her father's heroic work in

> clearing the trees from our farm – or rather... fighting the Mau Forest, which, in its centuries of unhampered growth had raised a rampart of trees so tall I used to think their branches brushed the sky. The trees were cedar, olive, yew and bamboo, and often the cedars rose to heights of two hundred feet blocking the sun. Men said this forest could not be beaten, and this was true but at least my father made it retreat. Under his command a corps of Dutchmen with hundreds of oxen and an axe to every man assaulted the bulwark day after day, and in time its outer walls began to fall.[15]

For Churchill's visit, Clutterbuck had a path cleared through the forest which linked a loop in the railway line. The path consisted of a leafy tunnel, about a mile and a half long, through the forest which Churchill described as dense and confused.

> The great giants towered up magnificently to a hundred and fifty feet. Then came the ordinary forest trees, much more thickly clustered. Below this was a layer of scrub and bushes and under, around and among the whole flowed a vast sea of convolvulus-looking creeper. Through this four-fold veil the

sunlight struggled down every twenty yards or so in gleaming chequers of green and gold.

Characteristically, Churchill was not only observant of the scenery.

> What a way to cut fuel! A floating population... pecking at the trees with native choppers more like a toy hoe than an axe... Each of the nine-hundred natives employed costs on the whole six pounds a year. The price of a tree-felling plant, with a mile of mono-rail tram complete, is about five-hundred pounds, and [would] effect a sevenfold multiplication of power. It is no good trying to lay hold of Tropical Africa with naked fingers. Civilization must be armed with machinery if she is to subdue these wild regions to her authority.

He talked of this to Clutterbuck as they scrambled through the forest path. But Churchill's conclusion – 'It is of vital importance that these forests should not be laid waste by reckless and improvident hands. It is not less important that the Uganda Railway should have cheap fuel' –[16] is oddly poignant, for in 1986 a visit to the site he describes reveals treeless farmland.

As time went on there was no sign of Clara's return to Kenya with Richard, but the farm thrived, thanks to Clutterbuck's efforts and administrative ability, and Beryl thrived along with it. The horses were her special love. Her father was not slow to notice the special affinity Beryl had with all animals, but particularly with horses. Even as a child she had the ability to make a horse 'quiet', simply by touching it. She was, like both her parents, a natural rider totally without fear, and rode all horses on a long rein, with great sensitivity.[17] Her own special horse, acquired when Beryl was only six years old, was an arab pony stallion called Wee Macgregor.[18] Years later Beryl wrote about her childhood friend:

> Wee Macgregor maintained throughout his life a gentle contempt for men and the works of men, and I am convinced that his willing response to their demands was born wholly of tolerance. He rarely ignored a word or resisted a hand...

Wee Macgregor was an Arab. His coat was chestnut and his
mane and tail were black, and he wore a white star on his
forehead – jauntily and a little to one side, more or less as a
street urchin might wear his cap. He was an urchin too by the
standards of our stables. He was perfectly built but very
small, and though he was a stallion, he was not bought to
breed, certainly not to race, but only to work carrying myself,
or my father – and even if need be to pull a light pony cart.[19]

Before race days Beryl helped her father and the syces
(grooms) to load the horses, including her own Wee Macgregor,
on to the down train bound for Nairobi. She always
accompanied her father to the race meetings, she recalled, and
they slept in tents... 'nearly everybody did'.

One race meeting in 1909 must have been especially exciting
for the little girl, for her father won the Produce Plate riding
Sugaroi, a horse he trained for Berkeley Cole. This race was
being run for the first time in 1909 and soon it was regarded as
one of the feature races in East Africa. No wonder Beryl grew up
hero-worshipping her father when so often she saw him as king
in his own country.

As well as stables full of glossy thoroughbreds, there were
always innumerable pets around Green Hills: 'orphans mostly',
Beryl recalled: lambs, fawns orphaned by hunting 'accidents',
goat kids and dogs. There was a pure-bred bull terrier (her
father's favourite dog, given to him by Lord Delamere), which
was the sire of Beryl's own crossbreed, Buller. Clara had left
behind the large and very beautiful English sheepdog she had
originally taken out to Kenya with her, and there were also two
imported greyhounds called Storm and Sleet, and two great
danes. Beryl recalled sadly that nearly all of them were killed by
disease or 'taken by leopards'.[20]

However, and despite Beryl's assertions to the contrary in her
memoir, there was another woman besides Lady Delamere who
had some influence on her upbringing. It was her Aunt Annie.
Clutterbuck's elder brother Henry[21] together with his wife
Annie and their son Jasper had moved to Kenya from India in
1908 when the climate there proved too much for Henry's
constitution. They settled at Molo, about half a day's ride from
Njoro, and there was naturally some intimacy between the two

families. Jasper was two months younger than Beryl and the two were occasional playmates.

Before her marriage, the tall and elegant Annie had been brought up in a very luxurious manner, one grandfather being Wykeham-Martin of Leeds Castle and the other the Earl of Cornwallis. Her photograph in court dress at the time of her presentation shows a poised and very lovely woman. In India she had been used to running her sizeable household with the aid of efficient, well-trained servants, and the privations of the farm at Molo came as a considerable shock. But she made the best of it and grappled valiantly with the odds. On one occasion during her husband's absence on business her servants told her, 'Some men have threatened to come and break in in the night and kill everyone and steal the stock.' Annie calmly took out a revolver and loaded it before their eyes, slowly and deliberately. Then she lit a storm lantern and sat down in a chair facing the door. 'Tell them,' she said, 'that I shall be patrolling the house all night. If I see *anyone* moving at all I shall kill them immediately.'

Another time when she was alone with her small son they heard something walking on the roof. The servants who were outside called out, 'Don't come out – there is an animal on the roof who will kill you and eat your brains. Shoot at it through the roof.' 'Mother, who did not know how to use a rifle, but did not want the servants to know this, called out that the bwana [master] would be angry if she shot holes in the roof and instead prodded the thatch with a native spear. The animal went away and later the servants told us it had been the nandi bear. This creature was long assumed by Europeans to be a mythical animal, but there has been evidence recently that it was a small species of bear. The Africans were quite correct, it had a tendency to kill its victims and eat the brains.'[22]

On Christmas Eve 1910 Annie gave birth to a second son, Nigel, and Beryl saw both cousins, as well as her aunt and uncle, as frequently as was convenient given the circumstances and the difficulties of travel. Beryl does not mention her aunt or her two cousins in her memoir, but it is inconceivable that during six important formative years of her life she would have been ignored by Annie, nor could she have failed to be affected by Annie's intrepid nature.

Undoubtedly Beryl's ability later in life to merge into London society, her cultured manners and accent, her pleasantly high, slightly nasal speaking voice, were developed by contact with expatriate upper-class Europeans. But these were external attributes. Beryl's character was developing in a complex manner; for instance without regular parental guidance her instinct led her to adopt the belief that 'the end justifies the means' – a basic premise in the art of survival – and this characteristic was to reveal itself noticeably as she grew older when her tendency to 'use' people – and their possessions – blatantly, was even described as amoral. Her extraordinary energy, zest for life and the remarkable freedom she was allowed (or took), led her into many childhood adventures which would normally have been denied to girls, whether of European or African backgrounds. As an old lady she recalled, 'I admire my father for the way he raised me. People go around kissing and fussing over their children. I didn't get anything like that. I had to look after myself, and then I used to go off and read by myself and think by myself. Funnily enough it made me.'[23] Admirable from her point of view it may have been, but it is difficult to rid oneself of the impression of a lonely child deprived of the affection she outwardly eschewed but inwardly craved, for she undoubtedly adored her father and for the remainder of her life never met another man who measured up to him.

If Clutterbuck, a former classics scholar, was worried about the lack of formal education for his daughter, his concern was not readily apparent. Beryl told me: 'Daddy used to teach me things'; but this seems to have been limited to the retelling of stories of ancient Greece, and answering the child's constant stream of questions. As an eight-year-old she went to stay with a neighbour's wife and son, while Clutterbuck and the husband, Mr Lister, went off to the Congo on an ivory-hunting expedition. During this time Mrs Lister taught Beryl to read from Mee's *Encyclopedia,* an invaluable source of reference for colonial mothers.[24] Beryl was an intelligent child and learned quickly, but she was no lover of organized lessons. By the time her father returned she could both read and write, and from then on she became an avid reader, but given half a chance she 'ducked lessons, in favour of horses and games with her African playmates'.[25] Doreen Bathurst-Norman recalled how Beryl told her of 'wrestling matches with the African boys, which she often won. She grew immensely strong and knew how to use her physical strength to its best advantage.'

During her stay with the Listers, Beryl met Langley Morris, then aged about seven years old. According to him, European children were as scarce as hen's teeth – the farms themselves were widely scattered and the children seldom travelled off them. Beryl was the first white girl he had ever seen and he remembers her as looking like '... Alice in Wonderland... I don't mean pretty or missish, it was a sort of style of dressing that all the girls of that period affected. Loose fair hair, worn long and caught up in a ribbon. Rather Victorian than Edwardian, but fashions took a long time to reach East Africa. She was an intelligent girl, tall and slim with a bright vivacity... as I recall she knew the sort of things that I knew; what to do in case of snake-bite, where to shoot a charging elephant, where to hit a lion (in the shoulder to lame him; you couldn't hope to kill him with the first shot), how to skin a buck, the effects of strychnine poisoning'[26] ... 'these were the important things to us as children. The emphasis of the educational process was on survival.'[27]

Soon after his return from the Congo expedition, Clutterbuck hired as Beryl's governess Mrs Orchardson, the wife of a newly arrived English settler. Beryl took an instant dislike to her, and this dislike grew into open antagonism as the years passed. The reason for her hostility was almost certainly rooted in jealousy and still, nearly eighty years later, she referred to her former governess as 'that bloody woman!'

There was a Mr Orchardson,[28] an artist of Royal Academy standard, turned anthropologist, but he was seldom in evidence since his objective in going to Africa was to conduct a serious study of the Kipsigis tribe and he spent the next nineteen years living in Kipsigis villages, returning occasionally to visit Mrs Orchardson and their son Arthur, who was the same age as Beryl.

Around this time the farm acquired a house built strongly of cedar. At night the light from the blazing log fires flickered on the polished floor and reflected in the panelled walls, and their warmth drew out the aromatic fragrance from the wood. In the main living room on the huge stone chimneybreast, Clutter-

buck used to measure Beryl's height in charcoal on the stones.
These marks remained until the farmhouse burned down in
1983 and the fireplace was dismantled.[29] But Beryl, rebellious
and defiant, was unwilling to move into the house under Mrs
Orchardson's constant supervision, and she continued to sleep
in her own mud rondavel some distance away.

Poor Ada Orchardson! She saw it as her duty to bring order
and conventionality into the life of this strong-willed child.
Until that time Beryl's father had treated his daughter like a
boy. She was allowed to plan her own life, to work or play as she
wished, to accompany her father as he worked about the farm,
and occasionally to read a little and learn by listening to
Clutterbuck. Her father was fair but firm and was not above
taking a stick to her if she transgressed.[30] Beryl accepted this –
she loved and respected him. But she loathed Mrs Orchardson.
Whenever she could, she ran off with her African friends to play
in the cool Mau forests, or hid in the stables which by now had
expanded to over twenty horses, in training and being brought
on, by the enterprising Clutterbuck. 'Daddy was very good
about it – he understood how I felt,' Beryl recalled. 'It was a
very hard upbringing,' stated a friend.[31] But it was the
upbringing Beryl wanted. She revelled in it.

If she disliked Mrs Orchardson, she adored her father single-
mindedly. The two became a familiar sight, for as she grew into
adolescence she continued to accompany him when he went to
Nairobi a hundred-odd miles to the south-east, for business
reasons or to the races. They travelled down by the twice-
weekly train, with their horses. By the time she was eleven Beryl
was already riding out on her father's racehorses[32] and had
become an accomplished and competent horsewoman.

On some of these trips south the pair would hunt with the
Masara Hounds. Jim Elkington, a huge Old Etonian with a
genial countenance and sparkling blue eyes, was the Master
and huntsman of this pack of imported foxhounds, and both a
good friend and a rival of Clutterbuck on Nairobi's race course.
The Elkington farm was a regular stop for Clutterbuck and
Beryl when they came in from up country.

The Elkington homestead was 'complete with bleached and
horned animal skulls lining the walls, a veranda ran all round
the ramshackle wooden bungalow, littered with riding crops

and bits of saddlery with dog bowls and . . . a huge population of dogs and cats, waiting to trip you up.' A caged parrot acted as an early-warning system for approaching visitors, and above all there was Paddy.[33]

Paddy, the unusual companion of the Elkingtons' only child Margaret, was a huge black-maned lion. He was the only survivor of a litter of three cubs, the offspring of a lioness shot by accident.[34] Raised by the Elkingtons on a mixture of egg and milk fed to him in a baby's bottle, he was regarded by the family as totally tame and was allowed to roam about the property like a pet dog, 'loose about the house until he got so big that he could pat Mrs Jim [Mrs Elkington] and she fell down'.[35]

Beryl had already been told by her father not to trust this animal, but she ignored the warnings. In 1911 she was attacked by Paddy. How serious the attack was seems to differ in the telling. Beryl's own description is a dramatic and highly readable account.[36] But Margaret Elkington claims it was no more than 'a slight scratch'.[37]

Margaret's version of the story may have been coloured by a natural sense of injustice at Paddy's fate, for the eighteen-month-old lion was thereafter confined to a cage for the rest of his long life. It is quite likely that Paddy had merely attempted to play with Beryl in the way he was used to tumble about with other members of the Elkington family. Beryl, though, claimed that he attacked and would have eaten her, if she had not been rescued by Jim Elkington and some of his servants. It does not need a lot of imagination to picture a fully grown lion in his prime attempting to romp with a nine-year-old girl. From the child's point of view it must have been a terrifying ordeal, whatever the lion's motives.

Beryl soon recovered from her adventure. She even regretted Paddy's incarceration. She often saw him in his cage, for as she grew into womanhood the Elkingtons (including Paddy in his cage), moved from Nairobi up country, and Beryl was a frequent visitor to their home.[38]

In 1914 tragedy struck the Clutterbuck relations at Molo. Henry Clutterbuck had been ill for some time, and after major surgery, performed on the kitchen table, he died, leaving the valiant Annie and her two sons on a farm that was, like most in Kenya, mortgaged to the hilt. Annie's troubles were not

restricted to grief, for in the general hysteria which surrounded
the advent of war, no unprotected women and children were
allowed to remain alone on isolated farmsteads. All their
farming implements were confiscated and Annie had no option
but to pack up and leave. She took the two boys to stay at Green
Hills for a while before returning reluctantly to England.
Hardships there may have been, but few settlers gave up and
went home willingly. At this time Beryl was a lanky twelve-
year-old.

Her cousin's last memory of her was of a typical Beryl prank.
She packed the huge fireplace in the sitting room with tinder-
dry kindling and set it alight. It virtually exploded into life,
setting the chimney on fire and threatening the nearby thatched
huts and dry grassland surrounding the house. For a while there
was utter pandemonium. 'Beryl simply looked on in wide-eyed
amazement at all the fuss as though she had nothing whatsoever
to do with it,' Nigel Clutterbuck told me.

Earlier the same day she had, with the assistance of her cousin
Jasper, killed a black mamba – one of the most poisonous snakes
in Africa – with sticks. The two children then paraded around
the yard with the dead snake held aloft on poles. 'She was
absolutely wild and would try anything, no matter how
dangerous it was,' her cousin Nigel recalled.[39]

As she grew to womanhood, Beryl's close association with the
Africans, of whom she undoubtedly saw a great deal more than
she saw of her father or any other European, continued to shape
the young girl. It was her African friends who provided her with
a companionship she enjoyed, and an education which she
preferred to her dreary textbooks. In many ways it was the
education given to a young boy of the tribe. She was tall, lithe
and strong, fearless to a degree, or if she knew fear she quickly
learned never to show it.

It was the Africans who taught Beryl to handle a spear, to
shoot with a bow and arrow, and to play the complicated
mathematical game of *bao* using stones or tiny round sodom
apples in shallow depressions in the earth. She joined the young
men and listened to the advice given to them by the tribal
elders. The instructions meted out regarding hunting were
given in the knowledge that hunting was a life or death affair to
the young audience. When the African youth hunted lion, no

friendly white hunter stood at his shoulder with a covering rifle should the spear fail in its attempt to kill the quarry. Beryl's version of such a hunt – a young man's test of skill and courage to determine his fitness to hold the title *moran* (warrior) – has about it the realism of a scene actually witnessed by the writer:

> The lion breathed and swung his tail in easy rhythmic arcs and watched the slender figure of a human near him in a cleft of rock. On one knee now [Temas] waited for the signal of the lifted spears. Of his comrades he could see but two or three – a tuft of warrior's feathers, a gleaming arm. He gripped the shaft of his spear until pain stung the muscles of his hand. The lion had crouched and Temas stood suddenly within the radius of his leap. Around the lion the circle of warriors had drawn closer, and there was no sound save the sound of their uneven breathing.
>
> The lion crouched against the reddish earth, head forward. The muscles of his massive quarters were taut, his body was a drawn bow. And, as a swordsman unsheathes his blade, so he unsheathed his fangs and chose his man...
>
> He charged at once, and as he charged the young Temas was, in a breath, transformed from doubting boy to a man. All fear was gone – all fear of fear – and as he took the charge, a light almost of ecstasy burned in his eyes, and the spirit of his people came to him.
>
> Over the rim of his shield he saw fury take form. Light was blotted from his eyes as the dark shape descended down and upon him – for the lion's leap carried him above the shield, the spear and the youth, so that, looking upward from his crouch, Temas, for a sliver of time, was intimate with death.
>
> He did not yield. He did not think or feel or consciously react. All was simple – all now happened as in the dreams, and his mind was an observer of his acts. He saw his own spear rise in a swift arc, his own shield leap on the bended arm, his own eyes seek the vital spot – and miss it. But he struck. He struck hard, not wildly or too soon, but exactly at the ripened moment, and saw his point drive full in the shoulder of the beast. It was not enough. In that moment his spear was torn from his grasp, his shield vanished, claws furrowed the flesh of his chest, ripping deep, and the weight, and the power of the charge overwhelmed him.[40]

In the evenings she sometimes sat around the fires with the

African totos and listened to the endless legends handed down
from generation to generation. These traditional fables concerned moral attitudes or myths about man's origins. 'Long
ago,' runs one,

> in the days when mountains spat fire, elephants were men
> and these men were very rich. They had *ngombi, kondo, mbuzi,*
> *kuku* [cattle, sheep, goats and chickens] in numbers like grass
> on the plains. They were indeed so wealthy that they had no
> need of work. They simply lolled about all day, covering
> themselves with oil and red earth and making love in the
> noonday heat. They had so much milk they did not know
> what to do with it. Then one day one of them washed in milk,
> and when the others saw him they did the same thing, so that
> it became a practice with them, every morning and every
> evening to toss this white water over their polished bodies.
> Well, it came to pass on a certain evening that *Muungu* [God]
> came through the forest to see if all was in order with the
> animals he had created – with the rhinoceroses, with the
> hyenas and with the lions, and with all the others. And all was
> in order. On his way back he suddenly caught the sound of
> man's laughter and turned aside to see if they also were doing
> well. Now it chanced that it was the time of their evening
> washing, and when God saw the good milk splash over their
> bodies he fell into a great passion. 'I created cows to give them
> the white water of life and now they throw it away or do worse
> with it.' And he called the men to him as he stood there in the
> shadow of the forest. And the men, when they heard God's
> voice louder than the roaring of a lion when its belly is full,
> trembled and came creeping to him on hands and knees like
> so many baboons. And God cried out, 'In so much as you
> have proved yourselves unworthy to receive my gifts... you
> shall become *Nyama* [wild animals], a new kind of *Nyama*,
> bearing on your head milk-white teeth so that you will be
> constantly reminded of your guilt.' So God transformed them
> all into elephants and they moved off into the forest, huge
> grey forms with gleaming tusks set in their bowed heads for
> ever and ever...[41]

Beryl never tired of hearing the stories which began 'Long
ago...' or 'There once was a man...'

In her unique upbringing, she had two very special African

friends, the stately *arap* Maina, (assigned as Beryl's personal servant by Clutterbuck), who was to die in the 1914-18 war, and his son Kibii, who was a little younger than Beryl. It was with him that she formed her greatest childhood friendship.[42] Another companion was Arthur Orchardson, but he was too hampered by obedience to his mother to join in Beryl's more adventurous exploits. As a leggy teenager Beryl's other constant companion was her dog Buller, named after General Buller, the reliever of Ladysmith in the Boer War. Buller the dog was the unlikely cross between Clutterbuck's favourite bull terrier and the old English sheepdog left at Green Hills by Clara. The cross had failed insofar as he resembled neither. Though thoroughly unlovely to many eyes he was possessed of undeviating loyalty to Beryl and she could not have had a more suitable companion for her youthful adventures. To her at least he was beautiful, for in 1986 she still recalled him as 'my lovely dog'.[43]

Buller and many other canine companions shared Beryl's mud rondavel, away from the farmhouse. It had a floor of beaten earth and cow dung, trodden down to the consistency of polished tile. An unglazed window looked out on the breathtaking Liakipia Escarpment.[44] Whenever she thought she could get away with it, Beryl escaped from the daily round of chores and lessons, clad in khaki shorts and shirt, and sometimes merely in a lungi (a single piece of material tied lengthwise around the body), always barefoot[45] and carrying her Masai spear, accompanied by her eager accomplice, Buller, before her father and the household were around to put a stop to her plans.[46]

With her African friends Beryl would disappear into the Mau forest to hunt one of the species of buck – reedbuck, waterbuck, bushbuck – or the species of wild pig, the wart hog. The Mau forest is all gone now, but then it was dense with junipers.

> Their trunks were straight and tall, and a sort of lichen hung like drooping grey-green whiskers from their crown of dark foliage... dwarfing the paler olives which shared the mountain with them. All through the forest were natural glades where a traveller walked suddenly into bright sunlight after the cold gloom of the woods. Brilliantly coloured butterflies darted in and out of the shadows and hovered,

orange and turquoise blue, over the tall pale grass. In the
morning you might come upon a party of grey-furred
waterbuck grazing in the open, spangled all over with tiny
shining beads of dew. If you rustled the grass they would
freeze instantly into immobility and listen with heads lifted
and big fur-lined ears erect to trap the faintest tremor of the
air-waves. Then they would turn suddenly, dark and solid in
the sunlight, and vanish noiselessly into the forest as though
they had flown apart into a million particles of light and flecks
of shade.[47]

In the air birds flapped about and shouted raucous calls and
monkeys screamed their sharp cry. On the ground 'the subtle
skinned leopard moved as softly as a current of air'.

There were other dwellers in the forest. These were members
of the shy Wanderobo tribe who hunted with poison-tipped bows
and arrows, and with whom settlers occasionally established
a trading relationship – honey in exchange for the soft colobus
monkey skins, and meat in exchange for duties as trackers and
guides.[48] In those days the charming black and white colobus
monkeys were numerous in the forests of the highlands, and
would swing through the trees above the traveller's head, or sit
looking down with bright intelligent eyes, 'like so many tiny
nuns peering out of the branches', one old settler recalled.

Through these forests Beryl ran as a fair-haired, often half-
naked girl carrying her spear.[49] She had learned well how to
move swiftly and silently, with animal-like stealth, on the balls of
her feet so that she almost skimmed over the forest floor and
disturbed not so much as a dried twig. She knew that the slightest
noise would draw the instant contempt of her companions, as
would any sign of weakness or exhaustion. This unique way of
moving remained with Beryl all her life. 'She walked and moved
as though she had wings on her ankles until she was nearly
eighty,' said a friend.[50]

Beryl's hunting activities, which today appear somewhat
sensationally unusual, are described in vivid detail in *West with
the Night*.[51] Many settler children enjoyed similar close
relationships with the Africans, but as usual, Beryl went further.
Women contemporaries interviewed for this book sometimes
doubted the total accuracy of Beryl's exploits as recorded in
West with the Night. Indeed it seems, on the face of it, surprising

that her father should have allowed the adolescent girl – tomboy though she then was – to roam about the forests, sometimes remaining away from home overnight engaged in hunting sorties. It also seems unlikely that native warriors would allow their hunting expeditions to be trammelled by the presence of a young girl, particularly a European child.

However, close friends of Beryl in later years state that Beryl told them tales of her hunting exploits in the bush which were simply too detailed to have been imagined. 'The Africans were her servants. When she wanted to go hunting she simply ordered them to take her. She was perfectly capable of commanding them to take her along. She was the memsahib kidogo [little memsahib] and very imperious even at that age. But it's not surprising that Clutterbuck let her roam about as he did. I raised two children myself in Kenya,' said an informant who knew Beryl well. 'You always felt that the children were as safe out in the bush with the Africans as they would have been in Hyde Park with a nanny. They were infinitely patient with European children.

'Beryl often told me how she hunted with the Africans, there were some Nandi herdsmen on the farm. She was allowed to roam free . . . completely wild, like a little savage. She told me she wore nothing but a lungi tied around the bottom half of her body, and she went barefoot and carried a spear. I can vouch for the fact that she knew how to handle a spear, and a bow and arrow in exactly the way that the Africans did. It wasn't the sort of thing you knew unless you were taught as a child.'[52]

Doreen Bathurst Norman, one of Beryl's greatest friends in later life, also recalled Beryl telling her of her hunting feats and has no doubts that the stories in Beryl's book are based on fact. Another, perhaps surprising champion of this part of Beryl's life was Ernest Hemingway, who met her during his African safaris and wrote about her book: '. . . the only parts I know about personally, on account of having been there at the time and heard the other people's stories are absolutely true. So you have to take as truth the early stuff about when she was a child which is absolutely superb . . .'[53]

That Beryl's own poetic descriptions of the hunts were written from personal experience is beyond question; whether or not she exaggerated her own part in these activities will probably never be known. It is claimed by several informants that the Africans she would have accompanied on the hunting expeditions were members of the Kipsigis tribe, and not the more colourful warrior Nandis. *Arap* Maina and his son Kibii were Kipsigis – a tribe allied to the Nandi but with a more pastoral culture.[54] However, the aristocratic Nandi are a more colourful and widely known race, and perhaps Beryl was merely indulging in a little poetic licence.

Beryl certainly developed a relationship with the Africans and a knowledge of them which was rare. A close friend told me, 'Beryl really thought more like an African than a European; she had no trace whatsoever of the expatriate view of Africans. She was almost the only person I knew who really understood them.'[55]

Beryl seemed to tread easily between the two cultures, taking from each what she needed. Had she remained in England with her mother and brother, her life would have been vastly different and it is difficult to resist wondering what would have become of the supercharged child if she had been brought up within the confines of Edwardian county society. Had she been born African she would certainly never have been allowed to participate in the hunting pastimes which are purely the preserve of the male warrior.

Beryl's self-reliant nature was apparent at an early age. When she was ten years old and staying at the home of her father's friend Berkeley Cole, who farmed in Naro Moru, she rode accompanied by *arap* Maina from Naro Moru across the Aberdare Mountains on her pony stallion Wee Macgregor in order to attend a party – a three-day journey there and back. 'I can tell you,' said the informant, 'that it was pretty rough country then. She must have been some kid to have done it.'[56]

In 1914 Beryl's friend and possibly the only European woman she cared for, Lady Delamere, died in Nairobi. She was thirty-six years old and had been suffering from heart trouble for some time. Her death must have removed an important influence – certainly the only maternal influence that Beryl could ever remember. Lady Florence was charming and amusing. 'Her courage and gaiety in the face of many troubles had won the admiration of all who knew her, and her death was a very real sorrow to the East Africans.'[57]

Beryl's riding skills led her to increasing contact with the children of European neighbours. Mrs Hilda Furse (née Hilda Hill-Williams) told me, 'Our home Marindas at Molo was not so very far on horseback from the Clutterbuck home at Njoro, where Clutt had started a stud of thoroughbreds. We used to send our mares down to visit his beautiful imported stallions.'[58]

One such stallion was Camsiscan, son of the 1906 English Derby winner Spearmint, and on his dam's side, grandson of Carbine by Musket, 'two of the best racehorses Australia has ever known'.[59] Camsiscan was a magnificent horse, imperious, maintained in the prime condition required of a stud stallion, and difficult to ride. Thirteen-year-old Beryl nevertheless rode him out daily. Once during exercise with the string, Camsiscan threw her, and she suffered serious concussion.[60] For weeks after her recovery Beryl fought a battle of wills with this horse until an understanding was gradually reached between them that neither was master of the other. During this time Beryl slept in his stable at night.[61] She always bore the faint scars on her back of his teeth marks, and at the age of eighty-three she recounted how he had once picked her up in his teeth and shaken her 'like a terrier with a rat . . . what a horse he was; wonderful breeding', she recalled with a smile.[62]

A contemporary remembers a visit to the Clutterbuck farm around 1915 to enable her mother to 'talk horses with Clutt . . . My mother found us sitting in the corner of a huge loose-box, watching in awe and admiration, as Beryl groomed a large, and very beautiful but reputedly savage imported stallion. He was squealing and snapping but never touched her. She had a truly wonderful gift of understanding and handling animals. She adored them and was quite fearless.'[63]

The same friend met Beryl a year later in different circumstances. It had been obvious for a long time that the wilful teenager would not learn anything from Mrs Orchardson. Jealousy was almost certainly the reason for this since her father and Mrs Orchardson were by then living together. But none of the governesses who succeeded her fared any better than Mrs Orchardson. Beryl '. . . got rid of them by putting spiders in their beds'. A particularly stubborn one threw back the covers to look for a suspected spider and found a black mamba.[64] Two male tutors were engaged in succession and Beryl remembered them as being more successful, but these arrangements were curtailed by the war.

Towards the end of 1915 or early 1916 Miss Hilda Hill-Williams and her sister 'Tuppence' were sent to school in Nairobi. The school was run by Miss Secombe who had been a former governess of the Hill-Williams girls. 'Beryl had been there some little while when we arrived,' wrote the elder of the two girls. 'Looking back we must have been a very difficult bunch of independent young things for the poor starched teacher-ladies to try and manage.' The school was housed in a 'ghastly little old wood and iron building on The Hill [the part of Nairobi where Government House was located]. We, boys and girls, had mostly come from farm homes where we ran free and rode our ponies and had wonderful lives. We were suddenly confined in what we felt was a prison. It was not easy for staff or pupils. I remember that Beryl didn't care for authority at all. We were very awe-inspired by her, as she was older and taller and *very* beautiful. She was one of the loveliest girls I have ever seen.'[65]

Another pupil at the school, the late Sonny Bumpus (who would later join Beryl in one of the highlights of her life), described her differently. 'She was a gawky girl, two years older than me . . . She tried to organize cricket, which never interested me, so I avoided playing and didn't see very much of her. She was all arms and legs – no chocolate-box beauty. I think she was a very serious-minded person though, she was grown up from the time she was small.'[66]

Beryl remained at the school for some two and a half years, the only formal education she was to receive. She was a bright pupil but once again she resented the discipline. Cast as Alice in Wonderland in the school play she looked the part, but she was anything but the 'butter-wouldn't-melt-in-her-mouth' child she appears in the photograph of the event. 'Beryl always did things better than anyone else – not popular at school,' a friend noted with amusement.[67] Eventually the teachers tired of her trouble-making and she was expelled – probably to considerable mutual relief. The same friend told me, 'She didn't get the sack just for being naughty, I think she tried to organize a revolt.'[68]

The previous few years had been especially difficult for Beryl.

Lady Delamere had died, and – soon after he had joined the KAR (King's African Rifles) – *arap* Maina had been killed fighting in Tanganyika. Then, later in that same year Beryl learned that her mother, Clara, had divorced her father 'on the grounds of adultery, coupled with desertion'. Clutterbuck having failed to comply with a decree for restitution of conjugal rights dated 30 November 1913,[69] Clara married Harry Fearnley Kirkpatrick in England on the day after the divorce became absolute, following which Charles Clutterbuck and Mrs Orchardson announced their intention to marry as soon as she too could obtain her freedom. After this, but not necessarily as a direct result, Beryl had been sent away to school in Nairobi where she was expected to conform and behave like a conventionally reared Edwardian child.

Any one of these incidents could have been traumatic; coming, as they did, in close succession, it is hardly surprising that the naturally intelligent youngster sought some outlet for her feelings of repression. A latent talent surfaced while Beryl was at school. It was a love of music. She showed great promise at the piano and had she pursued this, could have been a passable player.[70]

In 1916, following her expulsion, Beryl found herself at home in her beloved Njoro again. There was no more nonsense about Mrs Orchardson being her governess,[71] and in time Mrs Orchardson became the second Mrs Clutterbuck, Beryl's stepmother. Beryl continued to dislike her and refused to live in the farmhouse with her. Instead she remained independent in her own little house, a 'gingerbread' structure built for her by Clutterbuck, and made of cedar shingles from their own forest and saw mill.

It was a building to enchant a teenager, a low single-storey cottage with just three rooms. Each room had a pretty gabled roof whose point was topped with a decorative spike. The wooden floors and glass windows were a novelty after her grass hut and it was furnished with two chairs, a table and shelves for her books: 'I used to read all the time – I could never get enough books.'[72] Beryl's little house is still there today, as are the huge barn-like stables. The cluster of buildings stands on a high sunny plateau under hot clear equatorial skies, surrounded by views that defy description.

In these stables the teenage Beryl was soon acting as head lad. It was her special responsibility to foal down the highly strung thoroughbred mares, and for this alone she must have been an invaluable aid to her father. Clutterbuck was more and more involved with farming and financial matters as the rains failed and he struggled to meet contractual obligations for the supply of posho at a fixed rate. True, he had gained a reputation as 'the best trainer in the country', but this was technically a sideline to the farm even though he had over eighty horses in his stables, among them the most successful racehorses in the country. Some belonged to him and the rest to leading figures in the protectorate.[73]

In 1917 Beryl supervised the foaling of a horse that was to mean a great deal to her – Pegasus. He was by an imported thoroughbred stallion out of a native mare. She remembered him still in 1986 as 'a big bay gelding. I could do anything with him.' In her memoir she explains the allegorical references to the name Pegasus that she chose for him on the night he was born, but friends thought she actually got the idea from the name of a brand of petrol widely available in Kenya at that time, which pictured a horse with wings. 'Pegasus – the spirit of mileage and power' ran the slogan.

Beryl became a well-known figure on Pegasus as the pair roamed the countryside together and won events at race days, gymkhanas and shows.[74] One occasion has become a Kenya legend. In the show-jumping ring one of the jumps was a huge double which was causing some distress among the competitors. To the amazement of the crowd, Pegasus successfully cleared it in one enormous leap.[75]

Another horse came into Beryl's life at this time, one of the few that she was to remember into old age. He was a big half-bred dark bay with a white blaze, his thoroughbred quartering obvious only in his courage for he had a large common head, and feathers, where Beryl was used to the clean-legged grace of her father's thoroughbreds.

This horse was brought to Njoro by two men from F.O.B. Wilson's Scouts.[76] They had come to recuperate from the fighting with Von Lettow Vorbeck's forces in German East Africa. When the party arrived they were all sick – the two men and the six horses. Beryl sat up for several nights nursing the horse to health. Afterwards she rode him out and came to know and love him for the generosity of his temperament. 'If Camsiscan was the prince,' she said later, 'The Baron was the general, he was more capable than many men.' He was a gallant campaign horse who had seen dreadful sights and had carried his unconscious rider to safety through some of the fiercest fighting on the front. The rider had half his face shot away and the horse too was badly injured.[77]

His rider, a captain whose name was Dennis, was tall, fair and a good horseman. He played endless games of cricket with Beryl while his face healed to a mass of scar tissue. They went shooting for the pot on horseback. In a short story published in 1944 Beryl wrote:

> They taught me how to use a revolver. Mounted on their best horse called The Baron, I would go off with them. Those days stick in my mind as some of the happiest and most exciting in my life. We would come home tired and happy and in the evenings when my father had finished working, we would all play whisky-poker. I say when my father finished working – at times he would work up till all hours of the morning, as he seldom got back from the forest and the mills etc., before dark. Then he had all his book work and accounts.[78]

Eventually men and horses went back to the war and she never saw them again, but the horse left behind a bright and ever-present memory of a gallant animal, and a hatred of the sheer stupidity of war. First her friend *arap* Maina had been sacrificed to its senseless brutality, and now this horse with whom she had developed a special relationship had returned to almost certain slaughter. Many years later she wrote about the episode, as usual subtly altering the facts to provide a moving climax to her story.[79]

Again and again, people who had known Beryl as a growing teenager paid tribute to her horsemanship and fearlessness. 'There was no horse she could not ride – even as quite a young girl.' 'She used to ride fearsome stallions with the reins held up loosely under her chin. Even as a child of eleven she was riding out alone on her father's racehorses.' It is difficult to deny that for Beryl, animals were her only real friends.

As she left her childhood behind, her extraordinary personality was beginning to emerge. She was fearless, strong and physically able to undertake any task she set herself. She was thoroughly at home in her surroundings and as at one with her adopted country as it is possible to be. She had great ability and was competent and knowledgeable at her work; and she had a unique facility for developing relationships with animals. What she lacked was the ability to handle human relationships. During her formative teenage years, when she perhaps could have achieved the closeness with her father for which she subconsciously yearned, she was driven from his presence more and more by her (self-inflicted and unreciprocated) dislike for her stepmother; and apart from her friendship with Kibii she developed no close relationship with anyone. In consequence she was a complex mixture of physical self-confidence and emotional awkwardness.

About this time, a clairvoyant told her, 'You will always be successful, but you will never be happy.'[80] It was a remarkably succinct summary. Beryl seemed to spend her adult life searching for something. Neither she nor anyone else knew what that something was, but she drove herself on in seemingly relentless determination to attain it. At sixteen Beryl had no way of knowing that it was to be a life full of adventure and incident, and would take her far from her beloved Njoro.

CHAPTER THREE

[1918–1927]

At sixteen Beryl was a tall, long-limbed and wilful beauty. She was afraid of nothing and was able to talk and compete with men on their own level. She knew and spoke her own mind and she had the reputation for upsetting people, especially female contemporaries. 'She wasn't very friendly...' said one.[1] She had virtually been raised as a boy and was hardly ever seen wearing a skirt after she left school.

Despite this she was intensely feminine. She took great pains over her appearance, and there was now no tomboyishness about her patrician beauty, which was enhanced by her sense of fun and an extraordinary energy. She developed the unconscious mannerism of patting her long hair into docility with her long shapely hands. With her clear, fair skin tanned to a golden brown, her light brown hair bleached by the sun because she never wore a hat, and her vivacious energy, she was in great demand as a dancing partner in the celebrations held to mark the end of the Great War. As yet she was unpolished. She did not know how to dress, and she had no one to tell her; socially she was gauche and awkward, with an appealing vulnerability.

Her life was a full one. She worked happily and competently for her father, spending her spare time riding or travelling round to race meetings, and there was a crowd of young people to provide a round of social activities. She was confident in herself and her skill with horses, and as a friend told me, 'She was just not like other girls of that age.'[2] Evanston Muwangi worked for Beryl in the stables at Green Hills, and still works on the farm which is now owned by a weaving cooperative.[3] He remembered that Beryl loved horses more than people. She was very strict with syces: 'If you did good work she had no quarrel, but to those who did not do right she was tough.' Another friend said, 'She was very particular about feeding and grooming. A syce hadn't to behave badly more than once and he was out . . . If he failed to clean out his horse's feet when he should have, or something like that, she would say, "Look for a job somewhere else – I don't want you in my stable."'[4] She was hard but fair, she knew her job and worked hard and expected the same of others.

With around a hundred horses in his stables, both Clutt and Beryl were kept busy. Clutterbuck rarely involved himself in politics or any other non-equine activities. It is difficult to find much trace of him, outside of faded memories, and innumerable reports of racing successes, but a number of letters written by him to the editor of the *East African Standard* reveal something of his character.

The following letter, written in September 1918, was in response to a letter printed the previous week in the *Standard,* from Berkeley Cole – an old friend from the early days of European settlement in Kenya, and one of Clutt's horse owners:

I have just read Mr C.B. Cole's letter in your issue of 21st, in which he apparently condemns the action of the authorities in calling on the Masai[5] to produce 400 men for the KAR [King's African Rifles] and upholds the attitude of the Masai in refusing to do so.

I fail to understand Mr Cole's arguments. Large numbers of every other tribe in the protectorate have been called upon to do their share in the war, many of them both as Askaris [guards or policemen] and Porters; and practically all the Masai have done is to sell cattle and sheep for cash, which I consider they ought to have been compelled to do even before the war for their own good and the country at large.

There have always been a number of 'Masai Maniacs' in the country, some honestly so, and some because they think it is the swagger thing to be followed about by a Masai boy, who is too tired to speak unless he can lean against something to support him while he is doing so, and who would have a fit if requested to carry his master's bag! The Masai boast that they are a fighting people. They were told to supply only 400 fighting men, which they refused to do. In my opinion they should no longer be given the chance, but 2000 of them should now be taken, not as fighting men but as porters.

It appears to me to be a most undesirable thing if... Lord Delamere has been asked to 'clean up the mess'. He has always been the arch Masai Maniac, when not engaged in writing letters on behalf of the Somalis and equally useless and objectionable people. To the uninitiated savage (and there is no greater savage than the Masai), this must appear a confirmation of the weakness of the authorities. Mr Cole seems to be rather frightened about his herd boys. This, to the man in the street, might suggest the possibility of his letter being not altogether uninterested. I have not heard the employer of the Kavirondo, Wakikuyu or Wakamba labour complain, when thousands or hundreds of these tribesmen were taken as porters, nor would the tribes in question have been given the chance of listening to the soft persuasive utterances of the noble Lord, before being punished if they had the temerity to refuse to obey orders.

As far as I can see, the Masai, when competing with other tribes in the protectorate, have not done their bit in any way since the war was declared. If, as Mr Cole states, they are not amenable to discipline, then the sooner they are taught to do so the better, and as they are apparently too proud or too frightened to fight, a little load carrying would act as a very useful tonic for their swollen heads.

A further letter in a lighter tone appeared in August 1919, complaining about a recent article by the *Standard*'s racing correspondent regarding the merits of moving the race course[6] to another site. It gives an insight into his pithy sense of humour.

... It is a pity that if you must publish articles on racing, that you do not get them written by someone who understands a little of the game. The gentleman who wrote the article in your issue of last Tuesday would appear to be more conversant with whippets than horses!

In rapid succession Clutterbuck took every major racing trophy, among them the Jubiland Cup, the Produce Stakes, Kenya Steeplechase Cup, Naval and Military Cup, War Memorial Cup and the *East African Standard* Gold Cup. Camsiscan ran often and with great success in spite of being heavily handicapped. There can be no doubt that Clutterbuck had a genius for bringing out the very best in horses. All the knowledge he had, he passed on to his daughter.

There was another talented youngster around the Clutterbuck farm. Arthur Orchardson, the son of Mrs Orchardson and her ever-absent anthropologist husband, also grew up with a tremendous knowledge of horses and was a good rider.[7] In later years he was to be a great help to Beryl as a trusted aide and jockey.

Meanwhile, the drought which had been creating severe problems for settler farmers caused even greater concern to Clutterbuck. He had contracted to supply large quantities of grain to the authorities at a fixed price. He could not grow sufficient grain to meet the contract, and as the rains failed the price of grain rocketed and grain stores emptied. In order to meet his obligations Clutterbuck had to buy grain for more than his contracted sale price for the milled product. He purchased all he could get from his neighbours, among whom was 'Jock' Purves.

Alexander Laidlaw Purves, known to all and sundry as Jock, had recently returned to his farm having served as a captain in the 3rd King's African Rifles during the First World War. He was then in his early thirties, a powerfully built and athletic man. Born in England in August 1886, the eldest of four brothers, Jock had been educated at Fettes College, Edinburgh. During his years at Fettes the school was turning out scholars and international sportsmen in profusion, many of them combining both learning and athletic skills, and 'the 1st XV must have been very hard to get into'.[8] Nevertheless Jock had won his place in the rugby team playing centre three-quarter beside the brilliant K.G. Macleod, as a consequence of which he was somewhat overshadowed on the playing field. He was halfway up the Modern VIth form when he left (the scholars were in the Classics VIth), and was considered to be bright but 'a late developer who would have made more of a mark academically if he had stayed a year longer'.[9] His father was Dr. William Laidlaw Purves, the founder of the prestigious Royal St George's Golf Club, and Jock's three brothers all carved distinguished army careers for themselves and were renowned all-round sportsmen.

In 1905, at the age of eighteen, Jock joined the London

Scottish regiment. In 1906 he played in his first rugby international, and during the following two years he was capped ten times as a Scottish International. *The Times* described him as 'that type of Rugby footballer who, with half a try in sight made it a whole. He took part in Scotland's memorable victory over the South Africans in Glasgow in 1906, in which season Scotland also beat England, Ireland and Wales.'[10] In 1908 he left the regiment and went to Madras to seek his fortune. At the outset of war he joined the Madras Volunteers and shipped to Kenya, where he later transferred to the King's African Rifles. At the end of the war he managed, with the help of his family, to buy 600 acres of land at Njoro, and in the early days, before his own farm was self-supporting, he worked for Clutterbuck on a part-time basis.

There is a story, which may be no more than rumour, that Jock became one of Clutterbuck's biggest creditors and arrived at some sort of deal regarding the amount of money he was owed. The story goes that Jock agreed to forget the debt if Clutterbuck would allow him to marry Beryl.[11] Beryl smiled serenely at this story and claimed she couldn't remember, but recalled Jock as 'a very nice man, and a kind man, very strong...'

Beryl was only sixteen when she became engaged to Jock in August 1919. There is also a story that Clutterbuck could not remember her exact age and 'aged' her along with the racehorses,[12] so that on 1 August each year Beryl became a year older.[13] Assuming this story is true, even by Clutterbuck's reckoning Beryl would have been seventeen when she married Jock on 15 October, though in fact she was still only sixteen, and roughly half the age of her bridegroom. The marriage certificate gives her age as eighteen and this was witnessed by her father and Lord Delamere, both of whom must have known very well that she was not eighteen. But this was probably done in order to meet the legal age requirement for marriage in the protectorate.[14] Delamere was always prepared to sacrifice strict accuracy where expediency was at stake.

There were the inevitable newspaper reports of the wedding: in *The Leader* the report was headlined 'A Sporting Wedding', whilst the report in the *East African Standard* was accompanied by a typically wooden photograph of the wedding party, in which Beryl appears a very mature sixteen-year-old, and could easily have passed for eighteen. Jock Purves was over six foot tall and powerfully built, but Beryl is very nearly his height and is inches taller than her father.

East African Standard Saturday 18 October 1919

NAIROBI WEDDING

Miss B. Clutterbuck & Captn A.L. Purves

Local Society Event

There was a large influx of up country folk for the wedding at Nairobi on Wednesday afternoon of Captain Alexander Laidlaw Purves KAR, and Miss Beryl Clutterbuck daughter of Mr Charles B. Clutterbuck of Njoro. The friends and relatives made a congregation that filled All Saints Church. The bridegroom's brother officers of the KAR were strongly represented.

Just on 2.30 pm the bride, accompanied by her father who gave her away drove to the church and amid the strains of 'Lead us heavenly father lead us' proceeded up the aisle followed by her train bearer Miss Elizabeth Milne. The bridegroom was attended by Captain Lavender, his best man... The bride looked charming in a dress of ivory satin with an embroidered corsage, veiled *ninon* ornamented with pearl trimmings and a girdle of orange blossom. Her train of ivory satin was embroidered with roses and thistles. Her veil was white silk net with a garland of orange blossom.

After the wedding ceremony a very largely attended reception was held at the Norfolk Hotel when photographs of the wedding group were taken. The KAR band played outside the hotel. The newly wedded pair received the congratulations of a host of friends and left for the honeymoon which is to be spent in India.

Mrs Purves' travelling costume was a tailored suit in white gabardine, pleated shirt and neat coat with a long rolled collar.

The dress with its symbolic motif consisting of roses for England (the bride), and thistles for Scotland (the groom), implies that a considerable amount of planning went into the event. The list of gifts included all the usual paraphernalia: a number of cheques, a cake stand, a gold chain, a silver cigarette case, a silver calendar and vase, silver napkin rings etc. Lord Delamere gave a silver spirit kettle; and the more unusual items included a cutting whip and a box made from a rhino's foot.

While the couple departed for 'India where they stayed with Jock's relatives, and enjoyed a honeymoon which Beryl remembered as 'great fun and very glamorous – we both had people out there and played a lot of polo', the protectorate, shortly to become a colony, experienced the first influx of soldier settlers. The Soldier Settler Scheme was a lottery for which the participants qualified by virtue of war service.

Two ballots were held, one at the Theatre Royal in Nairobi in May 1919, and the other a few weeks later at the Colonial Office in London. Since the prizes consisted of plots of land which were to be offered to the winners at virtually give-away prices, it is hardly surprising that the scheme was a huge success and many thousands of applications were received. Before the year ended some fifteen hundred new settlers had arrived in British East Africa to settle mainly in the highlands.

Clutterbuck was still experiencing financial problems and watching the profits of his good years on the farm drain away as he continued to meet his contractual obligations. Beryl and Jock returned from honeymoon and settled on Jock's farm which adjoined Green Hills. To Beryl's great delight her brother Richard, whom she had last seen in 1906, came out to live with Clutterbuck.

Richard was a good rider and rode in several races, never winning but sometimes placed, and there are several records of him riding in races with his father. He never beat his father, and in the end the climate again beat Richard. The handsome fair young man died aged twenty-one. The cause was either cerebral malaria or tuberculosis – possibly the effects of both.[15]

In the summer of 1920 Clutterbuck was photographed receiving the prestigious *East African Standard* Gold Cup, which he won with his beautiful little mare Ask Papa. At the Nairobi meeting in July his horses won six out of the seven races. But in November 1920 he announced that he was selling up his entire holdings to meet his creditors' demands. Even the good harvest did not save Green Hills. In addition to the problems Clutterbuck experienced over grain he was badly affected by the revaluation of the rupee in February 1920. He would have been in the minority if he had not been heavily in debt to the bank. The revaluation of the rupee, a decision taken in far-away London, brought many farmers to the verge of bankruptcy since overnight their indebtedness increased by 50 per cent. The settler who went to bed owing £5000 woke up owing £7500, as well as suffering the continuing injustice of interest at eight per cent on the £2500 he had never borrowed.[16]

The *East African Standard* records Clutterbuck's decision with regret. '... as a lover of the racehorse, he took risks in bringing to the country English thoroughbreds with a view to breeding. As a horseman Mr Clutterbuck has always proved himself one of the best and today he holds pride of place in the list of winning jockeys for 1920.'

The farm was sold off lock, stock and barrel. Jock bought the flour mill and the stables by private arrangement and took Beryl away whilst the sale of her old home and its contents was effected by auction. Miss Alice Scott (subsequently HRH Princess Alice, Duchess of Gloucester) attended the auction on behalf of her uncle, Lord Francis Scott. Her only purchase, she recalled, was a wheelbarrow.[17] The horses were sold in two auctions. The first was held on 14 December, at which Lord Delamere was quick to snap up Camsiscan, then an eight-year-old. Forty-seven horses, including the best stallions and mares, were sold along with some very promising yearlings and two-year-olds. Lord Francis Scott bought much of Camsiscan's progeny.

The East African Derby was held on New Year's Day 1921 and Clutterbuck entered My Tern, riding her himself under his colours of black and yellow. He must have desperately wanted to win, not only for the prize money but for the added value that would accrue to the horse, but everything was against him. Exceptionally heavy rains had made the going very heavy and My Tern slipped rounding the final bend, unseating her rider. He had entered a great number of runners that day, for the races were a prelude to the second auction of his horses which was to be held at Nairobi Race Course on the following morning. Richard, Arthur Orchardson and Clutterbuck all rode in races that day but without success: 'It is some time since we saw the Njoro stable in such bad form,' said the *East African Standard*'s racing correspondent, 'for it did not saddle a winner during the afternoon. Mr Clutterbuck's horses prefer galloping on the top of the ground and the mud on Thursday did not suit them.'[18]

Prior to the auction it was announced by the Kenya Jockey Club (until this time it had been known as the East African Turf Club) that a special race meeting would be held in February so that buyers at the auction would have an opportunity of running their horses without waiting until the June meeting. Even this inducement did not persuade the crowd to bid generously, although all of the horses bar five (who failed to reach the reserve) were sold under the hammer. Jock bought three horses on behalf of himself and some partners. The best price of the day was paid for Ask Papa, a brilliant mare bred by Clutterbuck out of Gladys (the first thoroughbred he had imported into the colony). It fetched 8000 rupees[19] from Mr Eric Gooch.

Clutterbuck rode in the special February meeting, gaining two second places on the horses that had remained unsold, and it was somehow fitting that he should win the last race of the meeting for he had resigned from the Jockey Club and it was to be his last race meeting before he left the colony. Having placed an insolvency notice in the official gazette[20] he accepted a position as trainer in Peru. He could hardly have chosen a more distant point on the map to escape from the stigma of bankruptcy, and Beryl was devastated. She later told friends that she felt totally abandoned, but to be fair to Clutterbuck he must have thought that Beryl was happily settled in her own household. Before he left he discussed with Beryl the possibilities of her becoming a trainer in her own right and as a parting gift he gave her Reve D'Or, a promising filly that had failed to reach her reserve at auction. He had already sold two of the five unsold horses, and the remaining two he left with Beryl to be trained by her, run under his colours, and sold when a suitable buyer came along.

Beryl obtained a trainer's licence, the first ever granted to a woman trainer in Kenya. She engaged a professional English jockey called Walters to ride for her, and, operating from part of the old Green Hills stable, she began training a handful of horses. On 25 June there was a meeting at Nakuru and it was there at the age of eighteen that Beryl started her career. She ran two horses that were owned by Jock and his partners, obtaining a second place with Goblimey in the first race. But the important race of the day was a trial stakes for two-year-olds and Beryl had entered Cam, a previously untried son of Camsiscan. 'To a good start, Cam took the lead, led all the way and won easily. Winner trained by Mr B. Purvis [sic],' the *East African Standard* reported. On the following day the young trainer led in a further three winners.

A month later in more select company at Nairobi she repeated her success with three winners, including the Dewar Cup race. Shortly afterwards Cam won the Produce Stakes, confirming Beryl's suspicions that he was a Derby candidate. At first owners did not flock to her stables. She had to prove her mettle. But by October her blue and gold colours had been seen in the winner's enclosure enough to convince Mr A. Hogg and Mr A. Anstey to send horses to her for training. Beryl repaid their confidence by promptly securing a winner for each of them and in addition Cam romped home to win the big race of the day.[21]

Her success made Beryl the toast of Kenya society and now other owners, including Major Ben Birkbeck, sent horses to her. The name Mrs Purves began to appear frequently in the lists of winning trainers, as the name C.B. Clutterbuck had done previously, and in December she won four races on the eight-race card. Her own Pegasus came home to an exciting finish: 'A great neck and neck finish was seen all the way down the straight and both Pegasus and Miller's Daughter passed the post together, five lengths ahead of Vixen . . . the dead heat was divided.'[22]

Her first big test came in January 1922 with the East African Derby. Cam started favourite at odds of 10 to 1 on, with the horse's half-brothers Cameo and Camargo (ridden by Richard Clutterbuck) also entered. 'To a good start Camargo settled down in front of the field and led them to the bend for home where Cameo challenged and running on led Cam up the straight. Here the favourite looked beaten and Cameo ran on to win by a length. Two lengths between the second [Cam] and third.'[23] The result was hotly discussed by the losing punters and in a subsequent edition of the *East African Standard* the racing correspondent was moved to comment on the dispute and the ugly rumours circulating in the colony.

> Who would have thought that the Cameo we saw finish last at the September meeing would win this year's Derby? I remember the Sunday morning she was picked up at Mr C.B. Clutterbuck's sale for something like £90. After the [Derby] I listened to all sorts of suggestions as to how the favourite might have won the race. How absurd ... who could have known better than Walters how to ride the favourite. He had lived with it and had ridden it in all its work. I hold no brief for Walters. He is a superior jockey, hence all the more reason that the public should be told when he makes a mistake. But upon this occasion he made no mistake. He rode Cam as any experienced jockey would. Knowing Cam had a superior turn of speed he was content to remain behind Camargo and allow the stable companion to make the running. As it was when the straight was reached Camargo ran wide and Cameo who was going smoothly all the way, seized the opening. Walters realised this and asked his horse to go on but he could not respond and the Derby was lost and won.
>
> Unfortunately it was one of Cam's off days ... all in the glorious uncertainties of racing, and as it happens a favourite has yet to win this event. Now that all suggestions as to how the race should have been won have fallen to the ground the last excuse to fall back on is that Cam was 'got at'. To my mind it is both childish and unfortunate.
>
> Who are the persons supposed to have 'got at' the favourite? Could we not have discovered this by the position of the market? Would the books have laid 10 to 1 on the favourite if anything else had been expected to win? It is too absurd.[24]

To have achieved even a second place in the Derby at her first attempt, and at the age of nineteen, was hardly a disgrace. But the controversy upset Beryl and she promptly put all her horses on the 'ease list'.[25] By March, however, she had recovered her confidence and was racing again. During that year she obtained seven firsts (among them the Jubiland Cup and Lord Delamere's Gold Cup), and numerous places for Jock's

consortium and other owners. But in December Beryl's name
vanished from the trainers' lists; all the horses she had
previously trained were run under the auspices of other stables
and Jock sold his horses to Major Birkbeck.

The reason was that Beryl and Jock had begun to fight,
sometimes physically, and their domestic circumstances were
desperately unhappy. Despite her successes, Clutterbuck's
departure and Richard's death during that year were traumatic
events for Beryl. According to her contemporaries Beryl became
'very wild and unhappy'.[26] Jock and Beryl often had rows after
which Beryl 'went off'. Once she stayed away for three weeks –
Jock had no idea where she was or how to set about finding
her.[27] There is a story – well known among the couple's friends –
that Beryl had a number of lovers during this period, and that
each time she took another lover, Jock knocked a six-inch nail
into the post by their front door '... until eventually there was
quite a long row of nails. We all knew what they represented ...'
said a member of their set.[28]

When Beryl married Jock two years earlier she was little more
than a child. She had had an extraordinary upbringing and
could hardly have known about the duties expected of a wife in
normal circumstances, or even how to behave within a family
unit. Jock was probably not as sensitive to her distress over her
father's departure as he might have been, and he was jealous of
the time she spent with the horses. He could never have
measured up to Clutterbuck in her eyes (few men could) and
Beryl's attitude towards him was often scornful. It was when
Jock began to suspect that she was being unfaithful to him that
the problems escalated into public violence. Almost certainly
she stayed with Jock longer than she would have done if there
had not been the horses to consider, but eventually she ran away
from home, taking only Pegasus and what she could carry. She
had no money and nowhere to go, except to friends.

It was during this period that she first became involved with
Karen Blixen[29] and Denys Finch Hatton. Beryl could not
remember how they had met. She said she had 'always known
them'. They all attended race meetings, and in 1986 Beryl
recalled that as a child she used to walk the Blixens' dogs.
Whenever Beryl was in Nairobi at race meetings or on business,
she used to visit the baroness at her home on the outskirts of the

town.[30] Karen – or Tania as she was known to her friends –
wrote to her mother, Ingeborg Dinesen, every Sunday for many
years and her letters are an elegant chronicle of those years in
Kenya. In April 1923 Tania[31] wrote:

> Beryl Purves is staying with me at the moment... she is only
> 20, really one of the most beautiful girls I have seen, but she
> has had such bad luck. She is married to a man she doesn't
> care for, and he won't agree to a divorce, nor will he give her
> any allowance, so she is pretty stranded – but full of life and
> energy, so I expect she will manage... I have thought of
> painting Beryl as soon as I get them [paints from France]. It
> should make a beautiful picture, she really is unusually lovely
> – something like Mona Lisa or Donatello's Holy Cecilia...
> Beryl's mother, who was divorced from her father, married
> again and widowed – is probably going to rent the Mbagathi
> house for a year. It would be nice to have them as neighbours,
> Beryl and I could always have some fun together. She has her
> horse here and you know how pleasant it always is to have
> someone to go riding with...[32]

Beryl stayed with Tania for some weeks at her farm overlooking the Ngong hills outside Nairobi, and Tania was happy
to have her company; but it was the rainy season and they could
not ride much, or get about. On one occasion they drove into
Nairobi to have dinner with Lord Carbery[33] and his wife Maia
who were leaving for America on the following day. 'We really
had an awful drive in, we slid from one side of the road to the
other like a ship at sea, and several times we stuck fast and
couldn't move despite the fact that we had chains on... The
dinner was most enjoyable, there were a lot of us. We stayed at
Muthaiga last night but drove back here for breakfast...'[34]

In May Beryl's mother, a widow since 1918, arrived from
England bringing her two little Kirkpatrick sons. As arranged
she moved into Tania's empty house at Mbagathi where it was
intended that Beryl should stay with her since she was now,
clearly, estranged from Jock. All did not go smoothly however,
as Tania related to her mother: 'I have been having such
trouble – I had just let the house to a Mrs Kirkpatrick – Beryl
Purves's mother, who is staying with me – but after she had been
there for a few days she said it was raining in everywhere and

today has gone back to Nairobi. I had taken so much care to get the house cleaned up and in order and to repair the roof, but with all the rain we have had recently practically nothing can keep it out... the unfortunate Mrs Kirkpatrick was quite desperate, she has her two small boys with her, and had to keep moving the beds around to find a spot where it didn't rain in on them...'[35] Later she wrote: 'I am really sorry for Beryl, she is so "lost" just now – it is all very fine for the people who are born and brought up out here as long as everything goes well for them, but if things get difficult for them in this country they are not really suited for anywhere else in the world.'[36]

Beryl returned to Jock in the autumn of 1923 but after a row at Christmas, she took Pegasus out of his stable at ten o'clock at night and fled to Soysambu and the protection of Lord Delamere. Lord Delamere had known Beryl since she was three years old, and was a surrogate uncle to her, present at all important family occasions. His son Tom, two years older than Beryl and a lifelong friend to her, was also staying at Soysambu at the time. Beryl recalled that Lord Delamere and Tom bickered and fought, mainly because Tom did not share his father's fanatical ambitions for the colony. One day after a typical scene between the two over the tea table, Tom got up to leave. His parent threw the teapot full of scalding tea after him, shouting, 'How did I ever come to father that?'

Tom claimed later to good friends that he had lost his virginity to Beryl in the stables at Soysambu, and that his great generosity to her in later years was entirely due to his affectionate memory of this event.[37] Whatever the reason, Jock attacked and beat up Lord Delamere, claiming that both Delamere's farm manager and his son had been Beryl's lovers and he wanted 'satisfaction'. Tania Blixen wrote to her mother:

'I met Beryl Purves [in Nairobi], I expect you can remember her, I am so sorry for her, her life is in such an awful mess and she is such a child and cannot cope at all with it, let alone even realize what is happening. A frightful thing has happened over her *shauries* [troubles; affairs] – her husband, who thinks he has been treated badly, partly by Delamere's manager Long and partly by the Delameres' son Tom Cholmondeley, and thinks that they have lured his wife away from him, attacked Delamere outside the Nakuru hotel the other day, knocked him down and injured him quite seriously... He will be in bed at least six months. For the sake of his son and Beryl, Delamere does not want the cause of his injuries made public, but everybody knows about it. Long has gone home in a panic as Purves threatened to shoot him. They say Delamere is very worried and depressed and of course it is very damaging for the whole country, most of the political meetings take place at his house now. I think it would be better if Beryl stayed away from the races now but I don't think she has the slightest idea that in some ways people are blaming her, and how indignant they feel about Purves – after all Delamere has a special position here...'[38]

Lord Delamere's injuries were severe – he suffered several broken bones in his arm and his jaw, and injured his neck in the brawl with Jock who had jumped into Delamere's car outside the hotel and refused to get out.[39] Jock was a very strong, fit and athletic man, clearly distraught over the break-up of his marriage – for that was what it amounted to. There is a distinct impression of a man head over heels in love with his much younger wife, not knowing how to bring her to heel and lashing out savagely in all directions.

After this incident Beryl left Jock permanently, and most people blamed her for the break. 'She behaved very badly.' 'Jock put up with a lot.' 'I think she was very bored with Jock. He was a good chap but not very exciting.' 'He played a bad game of bridge and told rather boring stories.'

Rose Cartwright, who knew the couple, was more forthright: 'We all went round with the same crowd of young people, it was very jolly... Jock was delightful – a lovely man and absolutely devoted to Beryl. She was very naughty and started going off with other men. It was Beryl's infidelities that ended the marriage.'[40] Beryl's rumoured promiscuity became legendary even in a society in which casual morals were perfectly acceptable and gossip was a major social pastime.

Beryl told a different story. Interviewed by a reporter in 1983, she claimed she left Jock 'because he drank'.[41] Friends who knew the couple dispute this. 'Neither of them drank much – just the usual amount that everyone did.'[42] But there was a court case in 1924 when Jock was charged with causing an accident whilst under the influence of alcohol. Witnesses claimed he was 'very drunk and behaved aggressively' after he had driven into another car.[43]

Clearly Beryl had no deep feeling for Jock and possibly resented his casual assumption that his position as her husband gave him an automatic dominant role in her life. She wanted to continue to live her life as she always had, without interference, and this was apparently impossible within the framework of their marriage. None of the extra-marital relationships meant anything to her, except as a gratification of her sexual desires. She seemed not to know, or care, that her behaviour was unacceptable, nor realize how it affected Jock. She had obviously asked for a divorce – Karen Blixen's statement that Jock would not agree to such a course makes this clear – but it was some years before she was legally free.[44]

Jock remained in the colony for a long time after the separation, a lonely figure. He continued to play rugby for the Njoro and Nairobi teams. Eventually, after his marriage to Beryl was dissolved, he remarried, to the great disappointment of at least one fervent admirer, and returned to England where until 1939 he was a rugby football correspondent for *The Times*. At the outbreak of the Second World War he rejoined the London Scottish regiment, with which he had been associated since the age of eighteen. He had joined the regiment originally as a private but was commissioned during the Second World War and achieved the rank of lieutenant colonel – an impressive climb through the ranks. He served in the Ethiopian, North African and Italian campaigns until he was invalided home in 1944. He died in 1945 as a result of the wounds he had received. His obituary in *The Times* described him 'as a man of adventurous nature, placid and gentle in manner, but most formidable to those who dared to trespass upon his good nature'.[45]

In January 1924 Beryl made her first visit to England. A friend believed her mother had loaned her the fare (about £47) and she certainly had very little money when she arrived there. Tania Blixen recorded: 'On Friday I went into Nairobi to say good-bye to Beryl Purves who left for home today. I was so sorry for the poor child, she is so boundlessly naive and confused, and has more or less fallen out with all her friends – particularly after that *shaurie* with her – former – husband, who attacked Lord Delamere so violently. A year ago she was the most feted person out here, now she is travelling home second class and when she gets to England she will have only £20 in her pocket and will have to manage for herself – only Flo Martin and I were at the station to see her off. But she was cheerful enough and has no idea of the difficulties she will have . . . she is very beautiful – but it's not certain whether that will help her or not.'[46]

In London Beryl stayed with a friend, the wife of Lord Delamere's manager, 'Boy' Long. Another friend who had met Beryl in Kenya and was then living in London was Cockie Birkbeck.[47] 'I had been out for the day,' Cockie recalled, 'and when I returned my maid told me that a woman had been waiting all day to see me. I asked her what she was like and she told me she was very beautiful and was wearing a badly hand-knitted suit. I knew immediately it was Beryl. She had no money at all; one of my friends gave her a lovely dress and I took her shopping . . . I remember the thing she wanted more than anything else was a pair of sunglasses with tortoise-shell rims. They were not at all fashionable at the time and I told her so, but she insisted on having them! She opened an account and charged them to it.'[48] Beryl stayed in England for about six months and then went back to Kenya – without paying the account, and probably others like it. All her life she had a total disregard for money, but then she very seldom had any. Her entire career, all her adventures and travels were carried out without money, and she quite blatantly opened accounts with no thought of how she was to pay them. She always assumed that she would get by somehow – and somehow she always did!

During this visit to England she met many people whom she had known previously in Kenya – among them Tania Blixen's brother Thomas, Denys Finch Hatton (who had hurried home to his mother's sickbed – an illness which resulted in her death), and Frank Greswolde-Williams. The latter had a farm in the Kedong Valley about forty miles to the north of Nairobi. He was a very wealthy man but, having been more or less brought up by his parents' grooms, had a rough manner. Despite this apparent coarseness, Tania Blixen found him 'an unusually kind and nice person'. He had been one of Clutt's owners for years and had known Beryl since she was a child – indeed he had been a guest at her wedding. In addition to his farm in Kenya Greswolde-Williams had several properties in England, including the family seat in Worcestershire. He was a keen shot and lost an eye shortly after the First World War in a shooting accident when a rifle exploded in his face, adding to his craggy appearance. He was nearly thirty years older than Beryl but for the remainder of her stay in England Greswolde-Williams became her generous protector and lover. When she returned to Kenya Beryl was beautifully dressed and possessed of a wardrobe with somewhat more chic than the badly hand-knitted suit in which she had arrived in England six months earlier.

In July Tania Blixen wrote to her mother Ingeborg Dinesen: 'Beryl Purves was back again, dressed like Solomon in all his glory with big pearls around her neck, and as she was in the greatest need when I saw her last and nothing in her situation has officially changed, it was quite hard to know how to behave towards her. They say Frank Greswolde-Williams is paying for it, she is living with him anyhow. I'm almost inclined to think it would be better if they got married, though actually it is too ghastly to want anyone to marry Frank. He was as drunk as a lord at the races...'[49]

The affair with Greswolde-Williams was a shooting star – over before most people knew about it – but he continued in his generosity to her for a long time afterwards and helped her to get back into training racehorses by lending her money. Later that year, according to friends, Beryl joined forces with John Drury and Gerald Alexander of Molo in a training venture which enjoyed some early success, for all three were knowledgeable horsemen. A sympathetic friend of Beryl's, Mrs Carsdale-Luck,[50] who had a farm at Molo, loaned Beryl a block of stables and a hut in which to live. Hilda Hill-Williams, Beryl's old school chum, recalled that there were a lot of young people in the district by that time and they all had a lot of fun. 'David Furse, an attractive young farm manager, moved into the district and came into our lives with a bang. He fell heavily for Beryl, and she and I both cared for him. But he later became my husband in 1926 and we all remained friends.'[51]

Initially Beryl had three horses in training at Molo, the best of these being Wrack, a yearling son of Camsiscan, owned by the

Carsdale-Lucks. The other two were The Baron, owned jointly by her friends Tom Campbell Black and Gerald Alexander; and Timepiece, owned by H.D. Stanning. She did all the work herself with one of the Carsdale-Lucks' houseboys as a syce but when her childhood playmate Kibii, (now a fully grown moran called *arap* Ruta), returned to Njoro to find Clutterbuck gone, he sought out Beryl in Molo and worked for her from then on as her right-hand man. Kibii was an African of great character. Although a few years younger than Beryl he was tall, grave and aristocratic in his bearing and he seemed instinctively to know what Beryl wanted of him.

'He took all the rough edges off and dealt with people for Beryl. He was honest and intelligent and altogether a likeable chap,' said Sonny Bumpus, who knew Ruta well and thought that the Scottish expression 'having a good conceit of yourself' particularly applied to him. 'They seemed to be on terms of friendship rather than that of master and servant, although he always referred to Beryl as madam, and memsahib.'[52]

All Europeans were given Swahili names by their servants, and often these were excruciatingly accurate caricatures of some facet of personality – Bwana Samaki (fish) for example, for a man whose face had a solemn expression and protuberant eyes, or Memsahib Maua (the lady of flowers) for a woman who had a particularly sweet and gentle nature and who was often seen gathering flowers for the house.[53] Beryl was no exception. She had one particularly complicated African name which translated to 'she who cannot fall off a horse', and a Somali once said of her, 'To see her, she is like a spear' – an evocative description of the hard, upright and fit young woman. 'She was as strong as a man and far more capable than most men,' said a friend.[54] But the name which stuck all her life was Memsahib wa Farasi (lady of the horses).[55]

Predictably it was only a short time before Beryl's horses appeared 'in the frame'. In July 1925 she took two second places – Wrack on his first time out taking a close second in the feature race, the Produce Stakes. He won on his next outing,[56] and the colt's early performance on the race course must have given Beryl considerable encouragement. She soon had other successes with Melton Pie (also owned by the Carsdale-Lucks) and Timepiece.

She continued to get around the country attending race meetings in her car, and sometimes used a rickety old motorcycle for local transport. On one occasion, driving over to the Blixen house in the dark from Nairobi Race Course, Beryl hit a pot-hole and came off her motorbike, smashing her nose in the process. With her nose streaming with blood she walked the rest of the way. Her nose, previously aquiline, was to mend with an unsightly (to her) small bump which annoyed her for years until she had an operation to correct the damage in London in 1936.[57]

As her success grew, Beryl found the loaned premises at Molo too small, and after a disagreement with the Carsdale-Lucks she moved her training establishment to Nakuru Race Course. Here she was able to use the permanent stable blocks but there was no accommodation for her and she lived in a tent under the stands. A friend who had known her for some years recorded an incident from Beryl's time at Nakuru. One day he met an English friend in a hotel bar in Nakuru and during the conversation they discussed Beryl and the shabby way in which she was living. They decided to drive out to the race course and invite her to have dinner with them as a treat. When they arrived they walked over to the stable block to look for Beryl. As they rounded a corner they saw her.

> She was dressed very smartly in boots and safari shorts, and was standing with her back against a stable wall, leaning with her legs neatly crossed at the ankles. She hadn't seen us and was quietly watching the sun go down. It was a wonderful sight. The surface of the lake was like molten gold in the setting sun, across the lake we could see the dark green forest in the distance, and against the brilliant colours of the sky rose great clouds of pink flamingoes. She stood quietly watching the sun go down and looked very lovely. It was a picture I will never forget, this lovely girl in such a setting. When the sun had gone down we spoke to her. She was delighted to see us and invited us to come and see the horses. The stables were very poor and Beryl herself was living in a tent with very little furniture. She invited us in and she sat down on the bed which served as a seat. My friend took the only chair and I sat on a bale of hay. The humble surroundings had no effect on the atmosphere which was very happy as we talked and drank a

bottle of wine which we had brought with us. Later we had dinner at the hotel which was great fun and I was glad afterwards that we had been able to make a change for her in her loneliness. She was so charming...' [58]

Her humble surroundings did not affect her training ability either, and her horses were soon winning with daunting regularity. By then she had a useful string of horses from a number of owners. At a meeting held in Nakuru in July the winning horse, Ruddygore, was 'trained by Mrs Purves and owned by Mr Frank Couldrey'. Mr Couldrey, one-time editor of the *Kenya Weekly News*, was the father of Mr Jack Couldrey, Beryl's solicitor and friend until her death in 1986. Beryl had two other winners and two good second places at this meeting – she was moving inexorably to take over her father's old position as leading trainer.

It must have been difficult at first for owners to accept that this attractive young girl, still childlike in her manner, could possibly make a successful trainer in such circumstances. Of course she had had a spell of success some years earlier, but then she had the backing of a husband, and operated from established racing stables, and it was easy to assume that she had merely inherited the work and support of an existing team. Now Beryl had to prove her ability all over again by producing winners from unknown horses. She had as her working capital a remarkable talent and capacity for hard work and she was supremely fit. Doreen Bathurst-Norman recalled a story which Beryl had told her of her time at Nakuru. Once, when mounting a particularly temperamental horse, Beryl was flung across the yard and slammed down on her back across the stone water trough. This was enough to break her back but she escaped with minor injuries, and although the muscle webbing had been torn from her ribs, she got back on the horse immediately and rode it. [59]

In April 1926 Tania Blixen wrote to her mother: 'I saw Beryl recently, she seemed very happy, working hard training racehorses, I think she is probably very good at it. It seems to give her only just enough to live on but she finds it a very pleasant change from marriage. She looked fine, had just driven her car down from Nairobi along the most impossible roads where nobody else could get through...'[60]

Wrack, the chestnut colt, was fancied by Beryl as a potential winner of one of the two big classic races – the East African Derby or the St Leger. When she moved to Nakuru, Wrack went with her, sold by the Carsdale-Lucks to Mr E. Ogilvie-Boyle along with Melton Pie. Beryl trained Wrack to the hilt with the St Leger in mind, and was deeply hurt when, after an argument, his owner removed him from her stable three months before the race and placed him with a rival trainer.[61] Ogilvie-Boyle sold his other horse Melton Pie to Major Cavendish-Bentinck and Beryl continued to train this horse until she bought it herself in the following year. And fortunately there was another horse on which to pin her hopes of a classics winner – Wise Child, a filly which belonged to Captain Eric Gooch, a family friend of long standing.

This filly was impeccably bred out of Clutterbuck's good mare Ask Papa by Wise Dove – a stallion imported by Eric Gooch. The Wise Dove progeny were to shine in subsequent years in Kenya racing circles and Wise Child was among the best of them. She was considered to be the best three-year-old in 1925 but developed 'a leg' before the Derby and could not run. Knowing that the horse needed special training, Beryl took her on and got her fit again. Sonny Bumpus, then a very young amateur rider but nevertheless one of the best in the colony, had also suffered a disappointment when the horse he had in training for the race broke down. Beryl asked him to ride Wise Child in the St Leger.

On Saturday 7 August 1926 under the headline 'Wise Child Wins the St Leger' the *East African Standard* stated: 'This day can be written down as one of the most successful in the history of racing from any point of view. It certainly indicates that racing in Kenya is increasing in popularity... Scotch Bitters lost six lengths at the start. Restless made the running for a mile when Wise Child came on to win in a canter.' The result was: first Wise Child; second Restless; third Foolish Pride and fourth Scotch Bitters.

The report does not reveal that Wise Child broke down a few yards from the winning post when a tendon gave out, and she passed the post on three legs. Nor did the report give Beryl credit for training the winner, which was described as 'trained by owner'. But the people who mattered knew that Beryl had been training the horse, and the nail-biting finish gave Beryl her first classic winner. She gave Sonny Bumpus a silver cigarette box to commemorate the occasion, which he treasured until his death in 1985.[62]

Wrack did not run in this St Leger, although he was a declared entry, and in *West with the Night* Beryl uses the race as the scene of a dramatic contest between Wrack and Wise Child. In fact the race that Beryl wrote about so convincingly never took place. It was merely a vignette, the sum of Beryl's experiences, triumphs and disappointments distilled into what has been described as the most exciting and moving description ever written of a horse race.

The two horses did race together on other occasions but never in the manner which Beryl described. In February, whilst Beryl was still training Wrack, the colt had romped home by three lengths clear to Wise Child's poor third place. On another occasion described in the *East African Standard* in October 1926 when Beryl was training Wise Child but not Wrack:

> Camiknickers (owned by Mr & Mrs Birkbeck), lost a length at the start, Wrack was early in the lead followed by Wise Child and Trouble. Five furlongs from home Dovedale improved and joined issue with the leaders, and with Wise Child breaking down a good race was seen for the post... Result 1st Dovedale, 2nd Wrack, 3rd Trouble, 4th Wise Child.

This result also indicates how Beryl embellished the facts in her memoir, for in *West with the Night* the story ends happily ever after, with the owner declaring that the gallant little mare deserves never to have to race again. In reality, despite her weak tendons Wise Child made regular and successful appearances on the race course for some years.[63] When she did eventually retire she proved a gold mine to her owner at the stud.[64]

At twenty-four, Beryl had every right to enjoy her success. She had worked hard, and had earned her place in the male-dominated racing circle. She often rode Pegasus to winning places in local gymkhanas and races,[65] and had a wide circle of admirers. She would have been a saint if she derived no pleasure from a comment in the 15 January 1927 edition of the *East African Standard*: 'Wrack is an unlucky horse, continually running second. He has not won a race since leaving Mrs Purves' stable. Evidently the air at Nakuru agreed with him better than that at Nairobi does!' She was no saint, but the perfectionist within her would have been deeply sorry that the talented colt had not achieved the brilliant career she could have helped him to gain.[66]

Lord Delamere invited her to train from his farm at Soysambu, but here Beryl's personal accommodation consisted of one of the horse-boxes, tastefully furnished with a table, chair and a bed which, with a zebra-skin thrown over it, also served as a sofa for visitors. Yet it was an improvement over Nakuru.

An acquaintance remembered her father, one of Beryl's owners during these years, saying that Beryl always submitted her accounts written meticulously in her own hand and always accurate.[67] Later, there were many people in Kenya who said that Beryl was virtually illiterate, but these claims are at the very least exaggerations. Beryl's learning process was ill-disciplined, not absent.

It took a particular type of intelligence, as well as immense skill, for a young, unprotected woman to succeed in 'a man's game' in Kenya, at a time when women in England were still excluded from the profession of racehorse training. It is therefore tempting to compare Beryl's life at that time, when she was successfully competing with long-established male trainers such as Spencer Tryon (a contemporary of Clutter-buck's who had a clear field until Beryl's entry into the lists), with the advice being ladled out on the women's pages of the *East African Standard*. There, more homely virtues for women were stressed, in notes on 'The Registration of Servants' and 'Comfort for the Convalescent'. No one seemed to think her position in any way odd, and in the same edition of the newspaper appears the comment: 'Mrs Purves holds a very strong hand with both Charlatan and Welsh Guard (ex Camsiscan) in her stable.'

Beryl achieved her pole position in a remarkably short time, chiefly because of her ability, but also because she was free from the feelings of constraint that beset many of her female counterparts.

By the mid 1920s Kenya society had undergone a significant change from the days of the pioneer communities. This has been attributed to the huge influx of Soldier Settlers and other hopefuls, together with a new prosperity and the general frivolity of the bright young things in the Jazz Age after the horrors of the First World War. Many of the new farms which had sprung up in the highlands were large and comfortable, built of stone with panelled rooms, containing sumptuous furnishings. They were surrounded by smooth, well-groomed green lawns and staffed by armies of servants, in the style of English country houses.[68]

In the more opulent of these homes dwelt the lotus eaters of the so-called Happy Valley set; many were the younger sons of wealthy English families, victims of the English law of primogeniture. Unlike the hard-working settlers they had regular incomes and with no need to work they established a lavish and frivolous lifestyle which included a seemingly endless round of picnics and house parties, where champagne flowed and casual love affairs between the guests were the order of the day. Their meeting place in Nairobi was the Muthaiga Country Club, and it was here that Beryl was to meet many of this privileged (and some say much-maligned) coterie.

Beryl's involvement with the people of the Happy Valley was insouciant. She was always attracted by the titled, rich and famous, and although she joined in the high-spirited activities at the fabled Oserian (or the Djinn Palace as it was known), and other up-country retreats, she never became a full-blooded member of the set.[69] But she enjoyed the fun and high spirits of their never-ending parties and for the next decade Lady Idina, the Errolls, the Carberrys, Kiki Preston, Alice de Janze, the Soames, the Broughtons – all the leading members of the now infamous clique, were among her closest circle of friends. However she was never a party to the reported wilder excesses such as drug-taking.[70] 'I always thought she was a very quiet person,' said the late Sonny Bumpus. 'At a party you would often see her quietly sitting in a corner talking seriously to someone. She was not pretty, more inclined to be beautiful with a tall, slim figure and a graceful, sort of slinky walk.'[71]

Her close friend and one-time jockey Buster Parnell disagreed with this quiet image of Beryl, though he himself was not living in Kenya at the time, as Sonny was. Buster recalled that Beryl told him with glee of the time when at a Djinn Palace party, she climbed into the back of a parked Buick with an amorous companion. To her astonishment she found herself sitting on the naked bodies of a lady and gentleman she knew rather well, and who had got there first. The lady, who was to become a neighbour some years afterwards, was not amused and bit Beryl's little finger nearly through to the bone. The incident cooled the ardour of both couples and the two women never spoke to each other for forty years.[72]

The description given by Sonny Bumpus of her 'sitting quietly' seems to describe a peculiar characteristic which several informants mentioned, and which I noticed particularly. There was, at times, a stillness about her which somehow conveyed an immensely powerful personality. It was not done consciously and she was quite capable of throwing off the mood with a bright remark, 'Oh for heaven's sake, let's have another drink!'

On Saturday 19 March 1927 the colony read the following announcement in the *East African Standard* over their breakfast coffee:

> Engagement. Watson–Clutterbuck
> The engagement is announced between the Hon. Robert Fraser Watson, 2nd son of the late Lord Manton and Claire, Lady Manton of Offchurch, Bury, Leamington and Beryl, only daughter of Mr C.B. Clutterbuck late of Njoro and Mrs Kirkpatrick.

Clara Kirkpatrick and her two Kirkpatrick sons were now living at Limuru. When her second husband died he left her the sum of £173, and she was therefore forced to rely upon the generosity of her relatives for her income. Probably her allowance provided a better standard of living in Kenya than in England, otherwise it is difficult to know why she chose to resettle there. If she sought a reunion with her daughter she was disappointed. Beryl enjoyed the company of the two young boys and referred to them as her brothers,[73] but she was always cool towards Clara, though she saw her often and even stayed with her on occasions. Pamela Scott remembers Clara and Beryl as being 'very alike physically. Both were very tall and slim, with brown hair and blue eyes, and both were very striking.'[74]

The engagement was far from a blissful interlude, and spiteful rumours regarding Beryl's behaviour circulated in Muthaiga and throughout the colony.[75] Whilst preparing for her forthcoming marriage to Bob Watson, she continued with her career and at the July race meeting she not only won the two major events but also won three races on each day. She was in great demand socially and despite the ostentatious presence of a large engagement ring was seen out 'on the town' with several well-known gentlemen. One of these was Mr Mansfield Markham. Karen Blixen again: 'Bror, whom I met in town last Monday ... has been taken on by Mansfield Markham, and his brother Sir Charles Markham.'[76]

The colony had hardly digested the news of the Watson–Clutterbuck engagement announcement, and decided whether or not to accept the wedding invitations, when another announcement appeared on 27 August 1927. This time Beryl's surname is given as Purves rather than Clutterbuck, as in the previous notice.

> Engagement. Markham–Purves
> The engagement is announced and the marriage will shortly take place between Mansfield Markham, second son of the late Sir Arthur Markham Baronet, and Mrs James O'Hea of 20 Hyde Park Gardens, London, and Beryl, only daughter of Mr Charles B. Clutterbuck and Mrs Kirkpatrick of Kenya Colony.

This second advertisement not unnaturally provoked a great deal of amused speculation within the colony, whose chief occupation and innocent delight was social gossip. But the amusement was not confined to the colony. The story reached London, and the watchful eye of Rose Cartwright, who was back in London for a while, working for the *Daily Express* on society stories.[77] The next morning UK readers were able to discover:

REAL LIFE SERIAL STORY

Two Engagements in Three Instalments

A serial story with the facts set down, but with all the explanations provocatively left out, has been running since Friday of last week in Newspaper columns. It is a disappointing story in one way, for the last chapter leaves the reader with an unsatisfied middle-chapter curiosity. The first instalment appeared on Friday. Here it is:

The engagement is announced between the Hon. Robert Fraser Watson, second son of the late Lord Manton and Claire, Lady Manton of Offchurch, Bury, Leamington Spa, and Beryl, only daughter of Mr C.B. Clutterbuck late of Njoro and Mrs Kirkpatrick, of Sey, Kenya Colony.

Tuesday's instalment brought a complication, for it was announced that 'the marriage arranged between the Hon. R.F. Watson and Mrs B. Purves will now not take place.'
    The serial concluded yesterday, only three days later [sic] with the announcement:

The engagement is announced from Kenya Colony between Mansfield Markham, second son of the late Sir Arthur Markham Bt, and Beryl, only daughter of the late [sic] Mr Charles B. Clutterbuck and Mrs Kirkpatrick of Kenya Colony.

The English papers got it wrong on two counts; firstly there was a gap of five months between engagements, but the news of the first engagement had only reached London in August, hence the 'story'; secondly the 'late' Mr Clutterbuck was very much alive and was only 'late of Njoro'! I was unable to discover any information about the first engagement except a generally held opinion that 'Watson had a lucky escape!'
    Tania Blixen kept her mother up to date on Beryl's affairs with the report that she was lending her house to Beryl and Mansfield to use for a honeymoon: 'Beryl's wedding takes place on Saturday and I am going into Nairobi for it so I don't know if I will be able to write on Sunday, but I will send a postcard anyway... I do hope they will be happy, and won't express any

more of my well-known doubts about marriage – but this one seems to be more of a lottery than usual!'[78]

The newspaper reports of the wedding followed shortly, as promised, only a week after the engagement announcement.

Saturday September 3rd 1927.
The Markham – Purves Wedding.
————

A quiet but fashionable wedding took place on Saturday morning at St Andrew's Church Nairobi when Mrs B. Purves of Njoro, was married to Mr Mansfield Markham the second son of the late Sir Arthur Markham, Baronet.

The service was choral and the church was beautifully decorated for the occasion with most artistically arranged bougainvillaea and arum lilies. The bride entered the church escorted by Lord Delamere who subsequently gave her away.

She wore a simple bridal frock of cream crepe-de-chine, with plain tight-fitting sleeves. The bodice of the frock was figured in silk and over the skirt was a long silver fringe which emphasized the softness of a very becoming gown. A narrow scarf with deep fringe to match the dress was worn around the neck. The close fitting hat of fine silver plaited straw was trimmed at the side with soft white feathers and cream stockings and silver kid shoes completed the toilet.

The bride received at the door of the church, from a Somali servant, her bouquet of lilies. The bridegroom was attended by Mr A.C. Hoey of Eldoret, and the best man and Mr Pelham-Burn acted as M.C.'s

After the service which was conducted by the Rev. J. Orr, minister of the parish, the bride and groom left the church amid a shower of confetti under crossed racing whips bearing the bride's racing colours and marking her association with the world of racing in Kenya, where her activities have been so prominently and beneficially centred.

A wedding luncheon was held at the Muthaiga Club when Lord Delamere toasted the health of the bride and groom and Mr Markham responded.[79]

Tania's weekly letter home recorded: 'The wedding took place yesterday and went well in every way – the ceremony... and lunch at Muthaiga. Delamere gave away the bride, who looked so lovely – I had provided the bouquet of lilies and white carnations. We were 65 at lunch. Delamere and the bridegroom spoke... the lunch was excellent. I sat on the bridegroom's right, then the "best man" and then the bride's mother, so that was really very nice. They went off joyfully covered with confetti, poor things.'[80] Later, mentioning a blocked tear duct which was causing her problems, Tania wrote that tears had been running down her face at Beryl's wedding 'so unceasingly that everyone must have thought I [was] in despair at not getting Mansfield myself – or plunged in the most sorrowful memories...'[81]

The wedding photograph pictures Beryl with her brown hair worn close-cut in a shingle. Her wedding outfit is the height of 1920s fashion, and she is surrounded by a host of friends including her mother and two small half-brothers, and leading members of Kenya high society, among whom were Lord Delamere and Tania – Baroness von Blixen.

Beryl is seated next to her groom, but on her face there is none of the radiance one might expect in the bride of one of the richest young aristocrats in the colony.

CHAPTER FOUR

[*1927–1930*]

Mansfield Markham was the wealthy son of the late Sir Arthur Markham, Member of Parliament for Mansfield in Nottinghamshire and the first holder of the baronetcy created in 1911. Sir Arthur died in 1916 leaving three sons, the eldest of whom, Charles (father of the present Sir Charles), was only seventeen when he inherited. The two younger sons, Mansfield and Arthur, also inherited a great deal of money at a very early age. Too early, in the opinion of the present Sir Charles, for the two elder brothers had both run through their entire fortunes within two decades.[1] After leaving Radley, Mansfield spent the best part of a year in a Swiss sanatorium undergoing treatment for tuberculosis which involved painful liver injections. At the age of twenty he was appointed honorary attaché to HM Embassy in Paris. He went to Kenya in early 1927 aged twenty-two, intending to go on safari and explore East Africa.[2]

Safaris had become a fashionable pursuit in the early part of the century. A new field of sport had been opened up to the wealthy, and stories filtered back to England and America of a 'paradise on earth' where unlimited game, exciting sport and a marvellous climate combined to provide the best of everything. After the much-publicized Roosevelt safari[3] there was 'a virtual flood of wealthy young sportsmen from the aristocratic and officer classes'.

Bunny Allen, a youthful big-game hunter in the twenties, remembered that: 'Life was pretty wild, very colourful, and it took a long time to get anywhere. Every time you went out in a car you got stuck in the mud, so most of the safaris were done on horses, mules and donkeys, that's why they took so long.' Bunny's first safari car was a Rugby 'with wooden wheels that squeaked and squawked, a radiator which spurted water the whole time, always ready to make a cup of tea, in fact I used to put cornmeal in the radiator to seal it up at times!' The famous hunter Philip Percival would send out his staff and all the supplies days before the hunters were expected to arrive. The journey to camp could take up to a week and often the safaris lasted months 'but it didn't matter in those days because people not only had money to burn, but time to burn too'.[4]

Bror Blixen introduced Mansfield to Beryl in Nairobi after the Markham party had returned from their safari.[5] Mansfield fell for the striking young woman immediately, despite the fact that she was engaged to someone else. Sonny Bumpus said of Mansfield: 'He was a nice enough young man, a bit quiet, but there was nothing extraordinary about him.' Several friends commented 'I don't know why she married him,' which of course could equally be said of Mansfield. Beryl told friends that she 'wasn't in love with Mansfield, but she rather liked him'.[6] Perhaps it was this which occasioned Tania Blixen's remark that Beryl's marriage was 'more of a lottery than usual'. Mansfield was slim, rather slight, not much above medium height, fair-haired, good-looking and a man of considerable, quiet charm and cultured intelligence.

After the wedding the pair spent some time at Tania's farm. She wrote, 'I have had such pleasure lending my house to my newly-weds – but the climate out here makes everything like that easier.'[7] They repaid their hostess by presenting her with an unusual gift. 'This morning a lorry came out with the bed the Markhams have given me – it's as big as a car in itself!' their hostess wrote after they had left her farm.

'They had ordered it to be made 7 ft wide, but I managed to get that altered, but it is 5' 6" and could not be made any less by the time I had a hand in it. In a way it is wonderful to have such a wide bed but my sheets are not wide enough – and I have had to buy two blankets and sew them together as I have no bedspread either, or can't use the beautiful coverlet Aunt Lidda gave me as a wedding present, which is a shame, but I have made one out of a curtain which will do quite well. I didn't think I could refuse it as it really was nice of them to have ordered it for me – and they paid £45 for it you will hardly believe, to extortioners in Nairobi. I have had it put with its

Beryl Markham July 1936. *(B.M.E.)*

The house at Ashwell, Leicestershire, where Beryl was born in 1902.

Charles Clutterbuck in the uniform of the Kings Own Scottish Borderers Regiment *circa* 1895. *(Neil Potts)*

Paddy (the lion who attacked the ten year old Beryl) with his owners: Margaret and 'Mrs Jim' Elkington. *(Elspeth Huxley)*

The house which Clutterbuck built for Beryl in 1915.

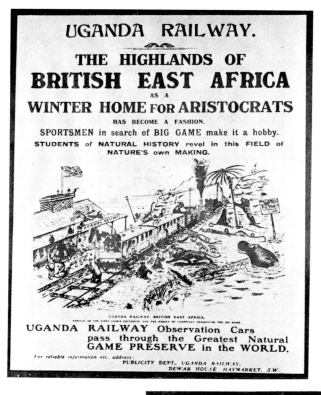

Early travel poster.

Beryl's first marriage to Jock Purves in Nairobi, October 1919. *l. to r.* Jock, Beryl, Charles Clutterbuck, Captain Lavender, Miss Eliza Milne.

Beryl's brother,
Richard
Clutterbuck

(B.M.E.)

Prince Henry with the lion he
killed whilst on *safari* in 1928.
(British Library)

l. to r. Bror Blixen; Edward, Prince of Wales; Denys Finch Hatton.

The home of Karen Blixen on the outskirts of Nairobi; Beryl was a frequent visitor.

Beryl before presentation at Court, London, 1928. *(V. Markham)*

Beryl's 2nd marriage to Mansfield Markham, Nairobi, 1927. *l. to r.* Bottom row: Karen Blixen, Clara (Beryl's mother); Mansfield; Beryl; Lord Delamere; unknown. The two boys seated in the foreground are Beryl's step-brothers. *(British Library)*

Mansfield and Gervase. *(V. Markham)*

Tom Campbell Black, Beryl's one and only flying instructor.

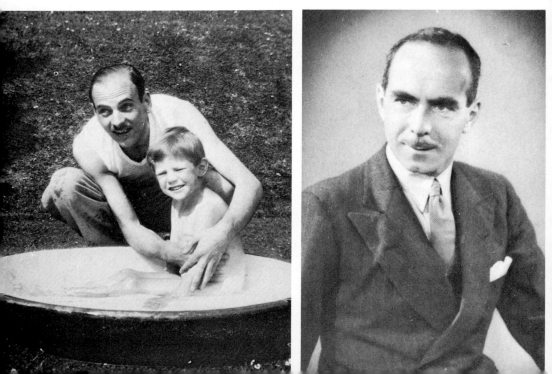

back to the window and you can lie in it and see the Ngong Hills through the door out to your veranda...'[8]

The newlyweds sailed for Europe to continue their honeymoon and en route to London stopped over in Paris where Mansfield introduced Beryl to a lifestyle hitherto unknown to her. The constant round of diplomatic parties and social engagements demanded a wardrobe she did not possess. Mansfield took her to Chanel, and bought her a wonderful trousseau including evening dresses and furs.[9] No expense was spared, and probably Mansfield got as much pleasure out of this as Beryl did, for there was undoubtedly an element of satisfaction to him in engineering the transformation of the handsome country girl into a chic, bejewelled international beauty.

If Beryl had been a success in the small, albeit smart circles in Kenya she was doubly so in Paris and London. With her tall, slender figure, so perfect for the 1920s fashions, draped in beautifully designed and cut clothes, she was seen and admired everywhere. Despite her unconventional upbringing her clear light voice had the cultured accents of the English upper class, and there was a charisma about her, a luminosity which attracted men to her side without fail. Soignée is a word often used to describe the young Mrs Mansfield Markham,[10] but there was also a quiet presence and an appealing combination of radiance and childlike insecurity to which men could not fail to respond.

In England that winter the couple hunted with some of the smarter foxhound packs known years earlier to Beryl's parents – The Belvoir, Cottesmore and Quorn. Beryl had never ridden sidesaddle and after inspecting the stiffly fenced country, sensibly opted to ride astride. This was still unusual enough to cause raised eyebrows at meets in high Leicestershire, but her bold cross-country riding quickly put paid to any disapproval.[11] Furthermore a beautiful woman, well turned out and with a good seat on a horse, is difficult to resist. It was whilst hunting in Leicestershire that Beryl first met Prince Henry, Duke of Gloucester, who was a regular visitor to the Melton country and a keen rider to hounds.[12]

During that season Beryl was presented to the king and queen, presumably sponsored by her mother-in-law as convention dictated. The formal portrait of this event shows a serious, dark-haired young woman, dressed in a richly embroidered satin gown with a train, and the requisite plume of three Prince of Wales feathers atop a twenty-seven-inch white veil adorning a bejewelled contemporary headdress. The normal rules were circumvented to allow Beryl to make her curtsey to their majesties, for in 1928 divorced women were not presented at court.

However the Markhams' marriage ran into difficulties almost from the start. Beryl's remarks that she was not in love with Mansfield imply a less-than-ideal relationship. Mansfield was not a highly-sexed man,[13] while throughout her life Beryl was regarded as having a warm sexual appetite. He may well have been jealous of her popularity with other men.

Mansfield's nephew, the present Sir Charles Markham, also felt that the couple 'were poles apart. Mansfield had come from an entirely different background, had attended public school and though not an intellectual he had been very well educated and had been brought up in a very rich background with a large number of well-trained servants. He was sophisticated and not very keen on living in the middle of the wilds surrounded only by horses. In contrast, Beryl had received a scanty formal education, had virtually no conversation but horses, and was very much an outdoor girl.'[14]

Doreen Bathurst-Norman, a close friend of Beryl's, stated that Mansfield was 'simply not up to weight'. On Mansfield's side, after initial infatuation and pride at having captured the colony's golden girl, he found her lack of sophistication irritating. Moreover her openly casual morals were not at all to his taste, and though he was not himself averse to 'a bit of slap and tickle in the back of a car', it was not the sort of behaviour he expected his wife to adopt.[15] Beryl's code of morals had been forged in a country where relationships outside marriage could hardly be disguised, and where few people bothered to hide participation in illicit love affairs – wasn't it all part of the fun? Mansfield's upbringing in England had taught him that love affairs were necessarily handled with the utmost secrecy and discretion.

In March 1928 the couple returned to Kenya and immediately called upon Tania Blixen, asking her to look after their two dogs (a borzoi or Russian wolfhound, and a red setter) for a fortnight, while they went to look at a farm property near Njoro where Beryl could take up her role as trainer again. 'Lady Markham told me the marriage was a complete fiasco,' Tania wrote to her mother, 'but I thought they seemed very pleased with each other. Beryl looked well and lovely and I had the impression that she is very keen on behaving properly and making a success of it.'[16]

Before leaving England the couple had been to the sales at Newmarket to buy some bloodstock to take back to Kenya. A horse called Messenger Boy, which had the reputation of being totally savage and unmanageable, was put up for sale. It had killed its groom, put the famous English trainer Fred Darling in hospital, and was considered by many to be unrideable. This did not influence Beryl in the slightest, she was after its breeding line and she picked up the horse at a knock-down price. Mansfield was a little doubtful but Beryl was confident that she could handle him. She wrote a story about this horse many years later, as usual in her writing subtly moulding the incident to her dramatic purpose and renaming him Rigel:

Rigel had a pedigree that looked backwards and beyond the pedigrees of many Englishmen – and Rigel had a brilliant record. By all odds he should have brought ten thousand guineas at the sale, but I knew he wouldn't for he had just killed a man.

He had killed a man – not fallen upon him, nor thrown him in a playful moment from the saddle, but killed him dead with his hoofs and with his teeth in a stable. And that was not all, though it was the greatest thing. Rigel had crippled other men, and, so the story went, would cripple or kill still more, so long as he lived. He was savage, people said, and while he could not be hanged for his crimes, like a man he could be shunned as criminals are. He could be offered for sale. And yet, under the implacable rules of racing, he had been warned off the turf for life – so who would buy?

Well I for one . . . I know this horse, he is by Hurry On[17] out of Bounty – the sire unbeaten, the dam a great steeplechaser – and there is no better blood than that. Killer or not, Rigel has won races and won them clean. God and Barclays Bank stay with me, he will return to Africa when I do.

And there at last he stands. In the broad entrance to the
ring, two powerful men appear with the stallion between
them. The men are not grooms of ordinary size; they have
been picked for strength, and in between the clenched fist of
each is the end of a chain. Between the chain and the bit there
is on the near side a short rod of steel, close to the stallion's
mouth – a rod of steel, easy to grasp, easy to use. Clenched
around the great girth of the horse, and fitted with metal
rings, there is a strap of thick leather that brings to mind the
restraining harness of a madman. Together the two men edge
the stallion forward. Tall as they are, they move like midgets
besides his massive shoulders. He is the biggest thoroughbred
I have ever seen. He is the most beautiful. His coat is chestnut,
flecked with white, and his mane and tail are close to gold . . .
he looks upon the men who hold his chains as a captured king
may look upon his captors. He is not tamed. Nothing about
him promises that he will be tamed. Stiffly on reluctant hoofs
he enters the ring and flares his crimson nostrils at the crowd,
and the crowd is still . . . upon this rebel the crowds stare, and
the rebel stares back.

His eyes are lit with anger, or with hate. His head is held
disdainfully and high, his neck an arc of arrogance. He
prances now . . . and the chains jerk tight. The long stallion
reins are tightly held – apprehensively held – and the men
who hold them glance at the auctioneer, an urgent question
in their eyes.[18]

Within weeks of Messenger Boy arriving in Kenya, Beryl was
riding him out every day. The present Sir Charles Markham
said, 'Mansfield told me she had absolutely no fear of anything.
One could only have the greatest respect for her courage.'[19]
Doreen Norman was told the story of Messenger Boy by Beryl. 'I
asked her how she had managed to subdue and ride him. She
told me in an off-handed way that she had just turned the horse
out in the field for a few weeks and then got on and ridden him.
However, much later she admitted to me that he had been a *bit*
of a handful at first.'[20]

The couple must have left England in the latter half of
February in order to be back in Nairobi by mid March when
they called on Tania, for they returned by steamboat and 'one
had to allow a good three weeks for the journey'. They had
brought a gift for Tania '. . . the sweetest, loveliest deerhound

you can imagine – Beryl asked if I would keep her two for
another fortnight so my whole life at present is in the Sign of the
Dogs – I now have six of all sizes and shapes from Beryl's big
borzoi to my or Denys's little Sirius...'[21]

The Markhams were up country looking at farms for two
weeks and then were occupied with settling in, but they called
towards the end of the month for tea and to collect the dogs.
Poor Tania had had a wretched and worrying time for the
borzoi ran away and Tania and Denys had to go out searching
for it on horseback – only to find it 'standing as large as life in
front of the house' on their return.[22]

On 2 June a major social event was reported by the *East
African Standard*. It was the marriage during the preceding week
of Gwladys, the former Lady Markham, to Lord Delamere at St
Andrew's Church, Nairobi. The list of 'principal guests' at the
wedding included Mr and Mrs Mansfield Markham and
Baroness von Blixen. Gwladys had divorced Mansfield's
brother Sir Charles in the previous year, but Mansfield and she
remained friends. Beryl was there in the role of adopted niece of
the groom, as well as being 'family' of the bride.

Beryl and Mansfield settled on a farm called Melela at
Elburgon near Njoro, where Beryl arranged the provision of
gallops. Now she could afford to buy top-class horses, and she
did so. Almost immediately after their arrival Beryl's name
appeared in the racing columns: 'Winner owned and trained by
Mrs Markham.' 'Owner Mr Mansfield Markham, Trainer Mrs
Beryl Markham.' It is hardly surprising to see that some of these
horses had formerly been Clutterbuck's; indeed most were
progeny of horses from his old stud at Njoro six years earlier.
And now, to Beryl's delight and reportedly at Mansfield's
expense, her father returned from Peru and took up residence in
a cottage on the farm. Her relationship with Ada Clutterbuck,
her stepmother, was no better than before – a mutual tolerance
was the best that could be hoped for, but at least she had Daddy
back. Mansfield could have given her nothing in the world
more calculated to please.

There are various reports of Beryl and Mansfield in the social
columns of the period, and they are pictured receiving the Rift
Valley Plate after the horse Clemency (owned by Mansfield and
trained by Beryl) had won the race in great style in late June.

The couple were seen together often during this period and, at least on the surface, seemed happy together. This is important, for some time around May Beryl conceived, and the parentage of this child was to cause rumour and conjecture for decades. It is not possible to say for certain who was the father of her child, but it is possible to say, with conviction, who could not have been.

The present Sir Charles Markham told me that Mansfield was already unhappy about Beryl's behaviour before they left England. 'She liked to go out a lot, and she loved parties. She must have been a very striking woman with her blonde hair and lovely skin, and would have stood out in a crowd. I think Beryl had already met Prince Henry in England before she and my uncle returned to Kenya.' Mansfield was suspicious of Beryl's relationship with the prince from the start.

When in the summer of 1928 Beryl discovered she was pregnant she was furious and immediately talked about an abortion.[23] 'She just didn't have time for a baby and anyway she certainly wasn't the maternal type.'[24] Mansfield was equally furious and they had a row in which Beryl allegedly flung at him the angry words: 'You don't even know that it's yours anyway, so why should you worry?' If this report is true, it was probably this remark which accounted for Mansfield's subsequent behaviour towards his son.[25] Tania Blixen reported in July to her mother that she had lunched with the couple at Muthaiga, and that Beryl 'looks ill and I think they are rather unhappy'.[26]

Throughout August and September whilst Beryl continued her successful training activities,[27] Nairobi became a hive of activity. The forthcoming visit of the Prince of Wales and his brother Prince Henry was the major topic of conversation. Perhaps because Beryl had met both men socially she was asked to help with the hostessing arrangements for the safari.[28]

The life of a safari hostess is really a social and administrative one. Safari life was certainly adventurous and hard at times, but the camps themselves were as comfortable as money was able to make them. The weary hunters could expect to find sundowner cocktails awaiting their return to camp. A relaxing drink was followed by a relaxing hot bath, in a canvas bathtub.[29] The guests, clad in pyjamas and dressing gowns, then sat down to dinner (often game shot by the hunters), which was served on tables in the open, and if the evening became chilly a huge camp fire blazed with entire tree trunks as logs. Usually the administrative details of providing this comfort – stores, furnishings, the provision of constant hot water for baths etc. – was the responsibility of a camp hostess, and Beryl was clearly delighted to be involved in planning these details.[30] When the princes arrived in Nairobi on 1 October she was in the vanguard of those waiting to welcome the royal party. A description of the event is recorded in *Sport and Travel in East Africa*, a book compiled by Patrick Chalmers from the diaries of the Prince of Wales.

> As the train came to the platform it got an ovation which must have surprised it. The station looked like a flower show and circus combined. Around it sat or stood in the street, many thousands of spectators of all races and colours attired in all conceivable schemes of personal decoration. On a red carpeted dais, under banners and flags and a mile of bunting the Governor... made Their Royal Highnesses welcome. They... then got into a waiting car and drove at foot pace, under triumphal arches and the fluttering of a thousand flags to Government House. The route, roses all the way, was... solid with folk and wild with enthusiasm.[31]

For the next few weeks the two princes were feted and entertained in the grand manner with balls at Government House, outdoor supper parties, luncheons, race meetings and private parties at Muthaiga Club and leading night spots. Beryl was constantly present at these social occasions and from the start interested onlookers noted the marked preference that Prince Henry showed for her company.[32]

The Prince of Wales had arranged several safaris and although he claimed to be more interested in shooting with his camera than his gun he particularly wanted to bag an elephant and a lion.[33] Prince Henry was not so keen to hunt, Bunny Allen stated. 'He was riding horses a lot, doing trips up into the mountains and thoroughly enjoying himself, but not actually doing a lot of hunting.' Before leaving civilization both princes spent some time racing at Nairobi. Prince Henry rode well, far better than his brother who was, according to local opinion, 'a brave though somewhat poor horseman'.[34] Significantly the

Prince of Wales was always provided with better horses though
he only managed a second place riding the Markhams' best
horse Cambrian, a few days after his arrival. At a subsequent
meeting the Prince of Wales won a race with his brother a close
second. Surely the informant who hinted that the other riders
had hung back was being less than generous?

Bunny Allen first met Beryl on one of the Prince of Wales's
safaris:

> ... she was in and out of camp as a friend of His Royal
> Highness and his aides. It's history that Prince Henry was
> very fond of Beryl and that she reciprocated... They were
> constantly together and they were a very handsome pair. He
> was tall, slightly arrogant, good looking; a fine figure of a
> man. She was a magnificent creature, with a beautiful
> movement, very feline. It was like watching a beautiful
> golden lioness when she walked across the room, or the green
> lawns of the Muthaiga Club.
>
> She was always so beautifully dressed and she had such
> wonderful legs for a pair of slacks. Slacks were only just
> coming into vogue at that period – all the dear old ladies who
> had hunted in the past (which weren't many) were still
> wearing voluminous skirts. She was the first girl to bring a
> good looking pair of legs into a good looking pair of slacks! If
> one went into the club during the visit of Prince Henry, more
> often than not Beryl and the Prince were there together
> having a splendid time with a crowd of friends.[35]
>
> Beryl was several times in our camps in the Mount Kenya
> and Northern Frontier areas, accompanied by Prince Henry
> on at least one occasion. Whilst camps were being moved
> from one place to another, the 'inmates' hied themselves off to
> Muthaiga Club, which was the Royal 'Waiting Room'. One
> has to remember that in those days safaris moved on slower
> wheels. A move from one camp to another took about a week
> to set up and get the champagne chilled.[36]

Bunny also felt confident that Beryl had accompanied Prince
Henry on at least one safari as a member of his party, where
there was ample time for what he termed 'bushy experiences'.[37]

In the authorized biography *Prince Henry: Duke of Gloucester*
the prince's time in East Africa is reported:

Prince Henry felt that he had met everyone in Kenya. 'There are some very nice people,' he observed, 'and some very much otherwise.' Kenya, with its uniquely beautiful scenery, and its rather relaxed European society ranging from the highest quality as represented by Lord Frances Scott ... to some of less reliable background, did indeed offer a combination of enjoyments and hazards for two of such eligible status as the Prince of Wales and the Duke of Gloucester. From here they were to take their separate safari routes, Prince Henry travelling to Longido, spending some days in the shadow of Mount Kilimanjaro ... he was in search of big game but he resolved not to shoot more than two of each species unless the need for meat dictated a greater ration.

The record of Prince Henry's trip continues with reports of the races in which the princes rode, with particular note of the race where

... the Prince of Wales won and Prince Henry was second 'which was great fun'. Prince Henry was mounted on a horse trained by Captain Clutterbuck, a Kenya notable and the father of Beryl, who won a name for herself on account of her remarkable beauty and also her outstanding feats of airmanship.[38] They then dined with the Governor of Kenya and Lady Grigg. This was followed by a municipal ball and then a supper party which the Princes gave at a club. No wonder the Governor, Sir Edward Grigg, described the Princes as 'indefatigable'. He also noticed 'what a charming and simple person' Prince Henry was and he reckoned he would be 'a great asset when he has gained a little more confidence' ... By 20th October, when [the prince] was writing to the Queen under an extension to his tent with a yellow lining on the M'hata Plains near Kilosa in a lovely breeze, 'the kind of weather you would like', he was able to tell his mother that he was enjoying himself, had 'never felt so well' and that his party was a happy one.[39]

On 9 November Tania wrote to her mother of the small dinner party she had given for the Prince of Wales at which Beryl, shortly to leave for England, had been present: '[Beryl] looked absolutely ravishing that evening...'[40] Karen Blixen's biographer, Judith Thurman, states:

Beryl was a sort of Circe ... Tania could not have been blind to her allure, and it speaks highly for her dedication as a hostess – and her sense of fairplay generally – that she still invited her to dinner, placed her beside Denys and later reported to her mother that she looked ravishing. It was the evening of Kamante's [Tania's cook] greatest triumph, with a meal that began with his famous clear soup and was followed by Mombasa turbot served with hollandaise, ham poached in champagne, partridge with peas, a pasta with cream and truffles, green, pearl onions and tomato salad, wild mush-room croustades, a savarin, strawberries and grenadines from the garden. Denys provided the wines and cigars. Afterward, the guests went out to watch the *ngoma* [tribal dance]. The chiefs had not let her down, and there was a crowd of enthusiastic dancers around the bonfires. The drive was illuminated with several smaller fires, and Tania hung a pair of old ship's lanterns – brought back from Denmark for Berkeley Cole – outside the house.[41]

The next day the Prince of Wales's party left on safari. Beryl was now five months into her pregnancy, though 'no one would have guessed to look at her. She was riding out up to the day she left.' Some time in mid November she left for England to spend Christmas with her mother-in-law and to have her baby. From the day of her departure her father took over the training of all the horses.

Within weeks the two princes were made aware of a potential crisis when the king became gravely ill. The Prince of Wales was hunting with Bror Blixen when he received a cabled summons back to England. It said: 'The King has been attacked with congestion of and pleurisy of the lung due to microbic infection. The condition of the heart makes the immediate future anxious and uncertain. I advise the Prince to get in touch near home. Dawson.'[42]

Not unnaturally, after receiving this message, the prince became pensive. 'At any moment he might have to open a blue and white envelope informing him that he was no longer Prince of Wales.'[43] Before he left, the prince remarked to Cockie (Bror Blixen's second wife), 'To think that in a few days I may be King of England.'

The whole nation held its breath. On 27 November, the Prince of Wales who was at Dodoma received the news. His Assistant Private Secretary Captain Alan Lascelles, immediately telegraphed Lord Stamfordham to say that they would stay there to await further developments. He also telegraphed to Captain Howard Kerr at Buckingham Palace to see if he could contact Prince Henry, whose whereabouts neither he nor the Prince of Wales knew. Then on 1 December at Ndola, Prince Henry got the news. 'Am so distressed to hear of Papa's illness,' he telegraphed to his mother, 'and am proceeding home as soon as possible via Cape Town.'[44]

Owing to the seriousness of the situation, a series of special transport arrangements were laid on for the Prince of Wales's party and by travelling day and night the prince arrived home only ten days after leaving Dar es Salaam. He drove straight to Buckingham Palace and went to the king's room. 'Now,' commanded his father, 'tell me about the elephants.'[45]

But the king was a desperately sick man and his illness reached a crisis on 11 December, the very day that the Prince of Wales reached London. The king was suffering from pleuropneumonia and a severe case of toxaemia caused by an untreated abscess seated behind the diaphragm. By 12 December he was unconscious and his physician, Lord Dawson of Penn, decided that it was a 'do or die' situation. In a daring piece of surgery he located the abscess and drained it. By the end of the month the papers and medical journals were reporting that 'convalescence is now in sight'.[46]

The Times of 27 February 1929 carried the announcement, 'Markham: On February 25th, at 9 Gerald Road, Eaton Square, to Beryl, wife of Mansfield Markham, a son.'

Beryl's son was called Gervase. According to the birth certificate, the birth was not registered for sixteen months, which delay actually rendered the mother liable to prosecution. None the less, an adequate explanation for the delay was given to the registrar general, who personally approved the certificate.[47]

The precise date of the child's birth is of obvious importance, for it completely invalidates the theory that Prince Henry could have been the father of the boy. This theory, which has been given much credence in Kenya and was never denied by Beryl, was even believed by members of the Markham family. However, it was almost a year before Gervase's birth that Beryl had embarked on her voyage to Kenya with her husband. On arrival in Kenya her whereabouts are well documented. Prince Henry's movements too are well documented. He was in England and his diary crammed with formal duties at the time when, even allowing for an unusually long or short pregnancy, Gervase was conceived. Beryl had been in Kenya for some time before she conceived her child, and it is therefore impossible that Prince Henry could have been the father. One wonders why Beryl did not deny the speculation during the years which followed – perhaps she enjoyed the notoriety, though this seems out of character. Much more likely is the theory that she didn't care what people thought.[48] Tania Blixen, writing to her mother of the child's birth, said, 'They are probably not coming out here again for the time being. The Duke of Gloucester, who was out here, is said to be very attentive and attending on [Beryl] day and night, and I think everyone in Kenya was counting on their fingers like Corfitz in *The Lying-in Room*[49] to see if the child could be reckoned to have royal blood, but unfortunately it doesn't work out.'[50]

The name chosen for the baby was an old family name, and in view of his mother's background at least, it was highly appropriate. Gervase Markham, his ancestor and namesake, wrote a book on horses and training as long ago as 1599:

> The secrets and arte of trayning and dietting the horse for a course: which we commonly call running Horses.
>
> Touching the day in which your horse must runne for your wager, thus shall you use him; First, the night before, you shall gui him but a verie little supper, so that he may be passing empty in the morning, when you are to haue him out and ayre him an howre or two before day, taking great care that he empty himself thorowly while he is abroad, then bring him in; and after you have well rubd all his four legges, and annoynted them thorowly either with Neates-foot oyle, Treame oyle, Sheepes-foote oyle, or Linceed-oyle, all which may be the most excellent oyles that may be had for a horse, then give him this food: Take a good bigge penny white loafe

and cut the same into toastes, and toaste them against the fire,
then steep them in Muskadine, and laye them betweene hot
cloathes, and dry them, and so give them to your horse...
This be so comforting and pleasant that your horse's empties
shall little aggreive him. When he hath eaten this, put on his
mussell, give him great store of lytter, unloose his sursingle
that his cloathes may hang loosely upon him, and so let him
stand to take his reste till the howre in which he must be led
forth to runne, not suffering any man to come within your
stable, for fear of disquieting your horse. When the howre has
come for you to lead him out, gyrd on his cloathes
handsomely, bridle him up and then take your mouth ful of
strong vinegar and spirt it into your horse's nosethrils,
whereof it will search and open his pypes, making them apt
for the receite of wind. This done, lead him to the race, and
when you come at the end therfor where you must uncloathe
him, having the vinegar carried after you, doo the like there,
and so bequeath him and yourself to God, and good fortune.[51]

Beryl and Prince Henry took up their friendship surprisingly
soon after Gervase's birth, and this is given by those interviewed
as the reason that the prince 'tried to wriggle out of going to
Japan'. That the prince was not keen to go on this Garter
Mission is a well-recorded fact.

Plans for his Garter Mission to Japan had by now for some
months been the subject of exchanges between the Foreign
Office in London and the British Embassy in Tokyo. The
decision, however, rested with the King, or such as in his
grave illness, could speak for him. On the morning of 8
January 1929 the Prince of Wales summoned into his almost
regal presence at St James's Palace Mr F.G. Gwatkin of the
Foreign Office. He said that although the King was
somewhat better he would be unable to undertake any public
engagements before the summer. The Duke of Gloucester,
the Prince of Wales therefore explained, could not be spared
for the Garter Mission to Japan. Perhaps, the Prince
suggested, some non-royal eminence could be spared to take
his place or perhaps the Japanese could wait until 1930. By
that time, the Prince of Wales thought, Prince Henry would
be serving with his Regiment in India and therefore might the
more easily visit Japan. The British Ambassador, Sir John

Tilley, was to be consulted. And so, in these senses the matter was ventilated in the Foreign Office and with Sir John Tilley in Tokyo until on 21 January Lord Stamfordham put the issue beyond doubt. He then told the Foreign Office that the matter was not for the Prince of Wales but for the Queen 'who alone', he boldly asserted, 'I regard as the mouthpiece of the King. Her Majesty', he continued, 'told me that the previous evening she had explained to the Prince of Wales that what had been arranged by the King could not be changed and that His Royal Highness understood that it must now be settled that the Duke of Gloucester goes as previously arranged with the Garter Mission'.[52]

So, despite the Prince of Wales's assistance it was decided that the Garter Mission would depart at the end of March, and in the meantime Prince Henry officially, according to his biographer, 'kept up his spirits by galloping up and down steep hills at Melton Mowbray and then, when hard frosts made hunting impossible, by coming up to Buckingham Palace and skating on the lake'. Many years later when Prince Henry was told of the attack on Pearl Harbor, he retorted, 'To think they made me travel ten thousand miles to give the Garter to that damned Mikado!'[53] In fact Prince Henry spent much of his time with Beryl. She was a frequent visitor to his apartments at Buckingham Palace where, James Fox says, 'She ran about the palatial corridors, barefoot, like a Nandi warrior.'[54] Beryl confirmed her visits to the palace and told a close friend of an incident when the prince's mother, Queen Mary, paid an unexpected call on her son. Beryl hid in a cupboard until the visit was over.

Until his father's illness Prince Edward had had no state role or responsibilities. Now, for the first time, he was given the feel of the reins of power, serving on the council which temporarily absorbed the power of the monarch. For many years Prince Edward had hunted and steeplechased in defiance of his parents' fears and wishes. But following a visit to the coal fields in the bitterest winter Europe has known this century, he decided to sell his string of horses. On the evening before the sale in late February the stablehands were astonished to receive a visit from the prince, exquisite in evening clothes. Sadly and all alone, he visited each horse in turn, with a pat and a whispered goodbye. In his autobiography the prince recalled this event as a reluctant abandonment of the only pursuit which gave an outlet to his competitive spirit.

Between the birth of Gervase and Prince Henry's departure for Japan, Beryl and Henry had only a few short weeks to enjoy each other's company. On the eve of his departure Beryl gave him a small silver cigarette case. Inside, engraved in her own handwriting, was the message '28th March 1929. From Beryl. A sad day after many happy times.'[55]

When Gervase was only months old, Beryl and Mansfield separated and Beryl left the baby with her mother-in-law, Lady Markham. This incident followed a tremendous row between Beryl and Mansfield, which reportedly erupted after Mansfield found some love letters from Prince Henry addressed to Beryl in her writing table. Beryl was more annoyed that her privacy had been broached than that her royal liaison was discovered. Indeed, if Mansfield had not known about the affair until that time, he must have been the last person in London and Kenya to find out. Gervase was subsequently raised by his grandmother; he saw very little of his mother during his entire childhood.[56] A close friend said, 'It wasn't an entirely selfish action. She knew she would make a hopeless mother and thought the baby would be better off with the wealthy Markham family, who could give him far more than she could provide.'[57] My own belief is that because of her own peculiar childhood, when she was abandoned by her mother and – because of his work – received insufficient attention from her father, she had no understanding of normal family life and any maternal feelings she might have developed were submerged in her love for animals. One must not, either, overlook the fact that a baby would have been a distinct hindrance to the continuance of her liaison with Prince Henry.

When Prince Henry returned to England in July after his mission to Japan, he had several months free with no employment. He was appointed a personal ADC to the king, but since he had no regimental duties he was placed on half pay of eleven shillings and one penny per day.[58] With Beryl now free of all strings and the prince himself at a loose end, the couple were able to be together a great deal and were anything but discreet. According to journalist James Fox, when the prince

took her to the races Beryl tied ribbons in HRH's racing colours
to her dog's collar, and the prince hired a pony cart drawn by a
Shetland pony and sent cartloads of white flowers to the Royal
Aero Club in Piccadilly where Beryl had been staying since she
left Mansfield.[59]

Beryl introduced Prince Henry to her circle of friends at the
London Aeroplane Club[60] and he decided he would like to learn
to fly. This caused ripples of concern in royal circles because
neither Prince Henry nor his brother Prince George (who also
wanted to learn to fly) held commissions in the RAF and it was
felt that there might be some criticism if they were to learn in
RAF machines. Eventually however a private aeroplane was
purchased in which both princes were taught. Prince Henry
subsequently soloed in 1930.[61]

Meanwhile Beryl's royal romance had begun to cause
Mansfield such embarrassment and annoyance that he could no
longer tolerate it. Towards the end of 1929, acting on the advice
of his elder brother, Sir Charles, he approached his solicitors in
London armed with the packet of love letters, and advised them
that he intended to divorce Beryl, citing Prince Henry as co-
respondent. Although the Markham family believe that a
petition was actually lodged, there is no evidence that this is so,
and Cockie Hoogterp, whose brother Ulick was Keeper of the
Privy Purse at the time,[62] says that her brother told her that it
merely reached the stage of a threat. Beryl, questioned in 1986,
remained as discreet as ever, and claimed it was all so long ago
she could not remember. The solicitor who, according to the
present Sir Charles Markham, handled the matter for
Mansfield, died on the very day that I contacted him.[63]

What is known is that Sir Charles Markham (Mansfield's
elder brother and the titular head of the Markham family) was
hastily summoned to the palace to be interviewed by Queen
Mary, who told him very severely that it would not do. 'One
simply could not cite a Prince of the Blood in a divorce
petition.'[64] However, Mansfield was understandably reluctant
to maintain his wife when she was seen everywhere with the
duke, and the pair provoked almost constant gossip in society.
His response therefore was that unless some satisfactory
settlement could be reached, and quickly, he was going ahead
with the divorce proceedings with the implication that the

prince would be charged with enticement and Mansfield would sue for appropriate damages.[65]

The law in England at that period did not cater for amicable divorces. Apart from desertion, adultery was the only acceptable way out of an uncongenial union. Under the rules of play, the gentleman concerned usually provided the evidence in a situation where a woman (usually met only once for this specific purpose, which was known as collusion) would be seen by hotel staff who were prepared to swear that the two had spent the night together. The problem with this arrangement was that unless the wife was proven to be 'the guilty party' the husband had, necessarily, to continue to support her, and this Mansfield was clearly not prepared to do.

It is not difficult to imagine the concern and distress that Mansfield's decision caused the queen. A divorce case involving the prince would have caused an almighty scandal. Further, the implication was that after the divorce, Beryl would be free to marry Prince Henry – indeed in such a situation he would have been almost obliged to consider marriage to her. The prince was third in line of succession to the throne, and such a possibility must have lurked heavily behind all the discussions. Divorce still carried the stigma of social disgrace in England and it was inconceivable that the action should be allowed to continue. And of course it did not.

The conjectures about the actual amount settled on Beryl by the palace, so that she would no longer represent a financial burden to Mansfield, have been many and various. That such a settlement was made has never been in doubt. Various pieces of documentary evidence were produced by interviewees during research for this book, which showed that Beryl received an annuity from 1929 until her death, and this annuity is traceable to a single source.[66]

Informants close to palace circles had actually discussed the matter with members of the royal family, and Cockie Hoogterp confirmed that her brother told her of the matter.[67] In the main, though, informants requested anonymity, and in one case, though the informant did not specifically ask for anonymity, it would be irresponsible to divulge the name.[68] A woman friend who had looked after Beryl's financial affairs during her illness some years ago told me of her 'surprise that the monthly amount was so small, given the speculation I had heard over the years... everyone thinks she got a fortune out of it.'[69] Cockie Hoogterp's brother Ulick, who as Keeper of the Privy Purse must have been involved in the transaction itself, told her that Queen Mary had insisted that a sum of £15,000 be set aside for the matter. The Markham family were sure that £10,000 was the sum involved. Many other informants stated that they knew the full story – the amounts varying in each case from £10,000 upwards, and one well-placed informant suggested it was nearer £30,000.

It is clear that gossip and speculation over the years are responsible for the fog of misinformation that surrounds Beryl's story. Many thought that Beryl was on the Civil List[70] but this is not so. Others thought she had been bought off with a substantial capital sum and annual payment, on condition that she never returned to live in England. Again, incorrect. After Beryl's death in 1986, through the kindness of Beryl's executor, I was privileged to have sight of the contract.

Cockie Hoogterp's recollection of events was in fact very nearly accurate. The capital sum involved was £15,000 – a generous sum in those days – but it was Prince Henry himself, not his mother, who provided the money. The trust was administered by a firm of solicitors but although the prince is not named in the contract (which is signed by Beryl and a solicitor), a handwritten note dated 1939 on the back of the document makes it clear that it was Prince Henry who had provided the necessary funds.

The capital sum was used to create a trust based on bonds with a fixed-rate return, providing an annuity which was paid into Beryl's account each year from December 1929 until her death in 1986. The annual figure that Beryl actually received appears modest by today's standards, though it would have been quite sufficient to maintain a certain style in 1929, particularly in Kenya, where doubtless those most nearly concerned with the prince's reputation heartily wished she would return with utmost speed. In 1982, during a period of severe financial hardship, the annual amount was increased temporarily. The informant who thought the initial capital sum was £30,000, an old and much-loved Kenya settler, stated: 'It was increased from £2000 a year... and you don't starve on

£2000 a year, do you?' But in fact it was something less than half that sum (about £750) and inflation had reduced its value to a level which, with the greatest care, might provide for the running costs of a modest car.

The arrangement did not cease on any subsequent marriage entered into by Beryl, and it was for the entire period of her life. No formal conditions of any kind were imposed, though it is possible that some verbal promises were made. At any rate it meant that Mansfield was absolved from maintaining Beryl ever again.

When shortly afterwards, the Prince of Wales arrived in Kenya for a second royal safari he told Cockie von Blixen (formerly Birkbeck) that he was delighted by the affair between his brother and Beryl. Until then, Prince Henry had been held up by the king and queen as a shining example, and he himself was seen as the black sheep, so far as his relationships with the opposite sex were concerned.[71]

Beryl herself, when I interviewed her in 1986, did not wish to discuss this matter, although she was completely frank about other aspects of her life story. She said she did not remember anything at all about the arrangement, only that she did receive money from 'some nice person in England'. However she was happy to talk about Prince Henry. 'He was *such* fun. I think he liked me because I was so different to all the others' – an understatement of classic proportions! When Beryl's remarks were repeated to a friend in England who knew the couple in 1929, the friend retorted, 'God bless her! Is that really what she said? No wonder he liked her if she thought he was fun. She was probably the only person who did... He was a frightful bore.'[72] But actually Beryl was not the only person who thought so. Beryl's executor recalled being told by a fellow officer of the prince that as a young man 'Prince Henry was full of charm and fun. He was very popular with the ladies, not because of who he was, but because of what he was.' He certainly cut a popular figure among the hunting fraternity at Melton where his dashing riding and open friendliness is remembered to this day.[73]

Presumably some pressure was brought to bear. Both parties would have no doubt been advised that their relationship, if it were allowed to continue at all, must become more discreet. In

February 1930 Beryl returned sadly to Kenya – not, apparently, at her own wish. 'Beryl came out here on Friday,' Tania Blixen wrote on 28 February, '... she had arrived in Nairobi the day before and was very unhappy and depressed. I can hardly believe that everything is as she describes... Anyhow she is stranded out here now, parted from her child and with hardly any money, in a kind of exile, and feeling very lonely and miserable, even though she is so young and light-hearted that I am sure, sooner or later, she will find something to live for. I have invited her to stay here during the races, she is obliged to come down here as she has several horses running, and she says people glare at her and are so unpleasant in Nairobi that it is frightful for her to be there. In spite of all her experience she is still the greatest baby I have known, but there is more in her than in most of the people who pretend to be so shocked at her now.'[74]

From this letter it is clear that Beryl's version of the events of 1929 absolved her of any responsibility for the divorce. Patently this is a biased view. Mansfield had been suspicious for some time of her relationship with the Prince and after the royal safari he could have been in no doubt that his worst suspicions were confirmed. It is hardly surprising that he had subsequent doubts about the paternity of his son. Did Beryl really not know that in behaving in such an irresponsible manner she was putting her second marriage in danger? Surely she must have realized that Mansfield could not tolerate such a situation. It seems, from Tania's comments, almost as if she was surprised at his reaction, and thought he had behaved irrationally.

For two months Beryl worked at the training establishment which was gradually being taken over entirely by her father, and moped around Kenya. To Tania's surprise she received a telegram on 30 April asking her to meet Beryl for lunch at Muthaiga. 'When we met I heard to my astonishment that she was on her way back to Europe, had to leave the same day for Mombasa to catch the Italian boat on the 1st. Considering she only came out on the 1st of March [sic] this seemed an extraordinary plan, but unfortunately a stupid man came up and asked to join us for lunch so I couldn't find out what made her take this step. Perhaps it is the Duke of Gloucester who cannot do without her any longer, and in itself I suppose it is a better idea for her to be at home in England than out here. If he is going to support her for a lifetime, the way her miserable husband has arranged things, then they can at least enjoy each other a little.' One shares with Tania annoyance at 'the stupid man' who has robbed us for ever of the chance of discovering what Beryl obviously wished to confide.

During the summer the friendship between Beryl and Prince Henry flowered again, but despite the disquiet that had been caused, he was never a major figure in her emotional life. Beryl liked Prince Henry for himself, and probably also enjoyed the privileges that went with the position of a royal mistress; and when the affair finally ended she was sad and rather lonely, but not heartbroken. In fact, so far, she had never enjoyed a relationship with a man who 'really mattered' to her. Even her marriages to Jock and Mansfield never achieved the importance that she later gave to much shorter-lived relationships, because neither man gained her whole-hearted respect. In some indefinable way they failed to measure up to her personal view of the ideal man, which was her father.

Late in 1930 Beryl returned to Kenya. Friends claim that she subsequently told them she had been advised that she would forfeit her annuity if she continued to live in England, though she would be allowed reasonable visits to see her son. This may or may not be true. It seems unlikely, but I have found no evidence either way.

Beryl was now twenty-eight years old. Sophisticated and elegant, she had other less definable qualities including her appealing smile: halfway between a brave boyish grin and the shy half-smile of a little girl anxious to please. Throughout her life, this apparent vulnerability awakened protective instincts in those around her.[75] She was at the height of her magnetic charm and the man who was attracted to its full force was Denys Finch Hatton.

CHAPTER FIVE

[1930-1931]

For some years, whilst she had been friends with the now immortalized couple Tania Blixen and Denys Finch Hatton,[1] Beryl had hero-worshipped Denys.[2] She was a constant visitor to Tania's house, drawn to the couple's intelligent, mercurial fantasy world and their sensual enjoyment of music and literature. Perhaps because Beryl had been little more than a child when they first knew her, Tania never saw her as a threat to her relationship with Denys. It is clear from the tone of Tania's letters that until 1930, at least, she and Beryl were friends, indeed they had considerable affection for each other.

Ingrid Lindstrom, possibly Tania's closest friend in Kenya, has been quoted as saying that 'Tania did not really like women.'[3] During research for this book, the same thing was repeated about Beryl. Yet despite these reports it seems that Tania and Beryl were able to find a level of friendship and there is almost a maternal perception in Tania's remarks about her.

During interviews in the spring of 1986 Beryl remembered only that Tania '... was very difficult to get to know. She kept herself very private. But she had lovely things... I enjoyed going there, but not at the end.' Of Denys she said, 'He was a wonderful man, quite brilliant. Intelligent and very well educated. He was a great hunter and a great, a tremendous personality.'[4] Here *was* a man who measured up.

Accusations have been levelled that Beryl was responsible for breaking up Tania's now much publicized love affair with Denys. This is highly unlikely. It is now well known that things between the couple had started to go wrong as far back as 1928 as a result of Tania's jealousy and possessiveness, and Denys's desire to remain free. The situation had come to a head when

Tania discovered that her former husband Bror and his second wife Cockie had accompanied the royal safari which Denys had organized. There were fierce arguments which Tania described briefly in her letters home, where she justified her stance saying that it was 'against the law of nature' for Denys to be friendly with Bror Blixen in the circumstances.[5] Obviously much was said which was not reported, for according to Tania's biographer, Judith Thurman, it was from this moment that the relationship between the couple began to cool.

Beryl's return from England occurred when Denys and Tania's love affair was to all intents and purposes at an end. Denys had moved into a friend's house in Nairobi and Beryl rented a small bungalow at Muthaiga which had once been shared as a pied-à-terre by Denys and Lord Delamere and was only a short walk from Muthaiga Club.[6]

Denys has been described as having a catalytic effect on the lives of those who came into contact with him. In his relationship with Beryl however, he played a pivotal role for he shaped the child-woman, and encouraged her to educate herself. Nevertheless their relationship was not limited to that of teacher and pupil, any more than his relationship with Tania had been when he taught her mathematics and Greek. When Beryl arrived back in Nairobi – sent home it would seem, from what she told friends, almost like a naughty schoolgirl – she was ripe for a love affair with the man she had admired for so long. 'She wasn't just in love with Denys, she was mad with love for him . . .' a friend stated. Her relationship with Prince Henry had been 'a playful one' – a romp that both had enjoyed. But her feeling for Denys was far removed from her light and skittish affection for Prince Henry. For the first time she felt the passionate stirrings of the greatest emotion. The suffocating surges of blood; the heart literally missing beats; and the heady surge of joy at knowing her feelings were returned, at least in some measure, by the adored Denys.

Tania (Karen) Dinesen had arrived in East Africa in January 1914 at the age of twenty-eight to marry her cousin, Baron Bror von Blixen-Finecke. She had previously been deeply in love with Bror's twin brother Hans but her feelings were not reciprocated and in order to escape the unhappiness of constantly seeing Hans she spent two years travelling around Europe. In

1913 after her return to Denmark, and in the teeth of family disapproval, her engagement to Bror was announced. The family liked Bror; indeed with his open friendliness he was a man it would be difficult to dislike. He was handsome and rugged, with fair hair, strong features and fierce blue eyes, but 'He looked down benevolently and lasciviously upon woman-kind and had been raised to believe that the entire world existed, as did the fish in his streams and the game in his woods, for his pleasure.'[7]

The couple decided to emigrate to East Africa after a family syndicate was formed to finance a farm there, based on the enthusiastic reports of Tania's and Bror's mutual uncle Mogens. 'A well-run farm in East Africa just now ought to make its owner a millionaire,' he had told them. In his memoir *African Hunter,* Bror explains that his only anxiety was '. . . how I should be able to put all the money in the bank. The gold mine was ours, all we had to do was extract the rich ore.'[8] Originally a 700-acre dairy farm was purchased by correspondence, in British East Africa but Bror went on ahead to reconnoitre and quickly decided that the best prospects lay elsewhere. 'Gold could not be made out of stockbreeding,' he concluded shortly after he arrived in Nairobi. Whose tin-roofed huddle he described as 'more like an empty old anchovy tin than anything else. The houses were a collection of scattered, rather shabby tin boxes, among which goats, fowls, and all kinds of other domestic animals led a pleasant rustic life... but what did it matter? I had no objection. I was after gold, not smart hotels.'

Disposing of the 700 acres, he bought 4500 acres near Nairobi, and about the same acreage near Eldoret, on which he planned to grow coffee. 'Gold meant coffee. Coffee growing was the only thing which had any future; the world was crying out for coffee from Kenya.' Recognizing the amount of labour required to turn the land into a coffee plantation, he set about hiring a workforce of Africans so that by the time Tania arrived at the farm a thousand workers were lined up to meet the memsahib.

Bror and Tania were married at Mombasa immediately after her arrival. Then the pair travelled to Nairobi in the highlands by a special train which had been laid on for Prince Wilhelm of Sweden who, by a happy coincidence, was visiting the country, and who had been able to support Bror as his best man at the wedding.

Within a year Tania found she had contracted the venereal disease syphilis.[9] Substantiated reports of Bror's infidelities were numerous, although it must be said here that neither of Bror's subsequent wives believed he had ever suffered from the affliction. 'And I should know if anyone does,' said Cockie, the second Baroness Blixen. Nor, despite his renowned promiscuity, were there reports of any other woman making the same charge,[10] and friends of many years' standing state that Bror never displayed any outward signs of succumbing to the complaint.

The farm did not prosper. Bror was often absent, initially due to his service in the war against German East Africa and later on his game-hunting exploits. The social benefits enjoyed by the holder of the title Baroness meant a great deal to Tania, but she was nevertheless a thoroughly unhappy and disillusioned woman by 1918 when she first met Denys Finch Hatton at the Muthaiga Club.

In 1920 the finances of the coffee farm were chaotic, and the Blixens' marriage was in dire trouble. The original mistrust of Tania's family for Bror '... now turned into frank and righteous abomination ... on financial as well as moral grounds'.[11] While Tania was visiting them in Denmark, Bror, in an attempt to raise money for the farm, pawned her silver, 'had her furniture attached by creditors and was ready to sign over the house and park to anyone who would negotiate a loan for them'.[12] A year later Bror was summarily dismissed as manager and Tania was appointed to run the farm in his stead. The Dinesen financial syndicate were insistent that Bror was to have no further involvement with the farm, and he was forbidden even to set foot there. Later they were divorced, much against Tania's will, but Bror had by then fallen in love with Cockie. Tania never forgave Cockie for taking Bror, but this seems oddly dog-in-the-the-mangerish considering Tania's own situation. Long before Bror officially moved out of the farm, Denys and Tania were lovers and Bror customarily introduced Denys as 'my wife's lover, and my best friend'.

Having invested and lost his entire wealth in the virtually failed venture, Bror was penniless. However it was not in his nature to whine about his misfortune. He simply carried on as before, sometimes staying with friends, sometimes camping out in the bush; scratching a living where he could. He was a man who always enjoyed life to the hilt, a man's man, a lovable, impossible, improvident rascal. Bunny Allen described him as 'far too rough for her... [Tania] was a very sweet girl, like a lovely-looking piece of beautiful china. He was never gentle with her, he was rough and ready and always ready to have a party with the boys. He drank a great deal and he wasn't fussy who he went to bed with... He was nice enough in every way, but the difference between him and Denys Finch Hatton was the difference between chalk and cheese.'[13]

Bror's godson Eric Rundgren remembers him as a tall man with a kind, aristocratic face and a wonderful capacity for enjoying himself. 'He was always in a good humour, enthusiastic and prepared to attempt any scheme. His personality captivated people. My father used to say that he could talk anybody into anything.' He recalled the first time he had met Bror in the Norfolk Hotel surrounded by a dozen admiring fans – mostly women – and thinking, 'This is the only life for me, such glamour, such opportunity and such fun.' This impression was never displaced even when later Bror came to the Rundgren house to borrow money and Eric's father told him, 'There goes a man who in twenty-odd years must have made £200,000 out of hunting and now literally hasn't a cent.'[14]

Tania meanwhile had fallen deeply in love with Denys. She was intelligent, sensitive, imaginative. Denys was polished, gentle, intellectual and a man of such blinding charm that fifty years after his death that elusive quality is instantly recalled by his friends as his greatest asset. Most people found extreme difficulty in analysing his magnetism. A friend describes him as a leader, quick-thinking and decisive, but paradoxically he moved and acted with unstudied nonchalance, which may have been taken for indolence were he not well known as an achiever. Despite his scholarly appearance there was 'a suggestion of an adventurous wanderer, of a man who knew every hidden creek and broad reach of the upper Nile, and who had watched a hundred desert suns splash with gilt the white-walled cities of Somaliland'.[15] Many people agreed: 'He was exactly like one of the old Elizabethan courtiers – courtly on the surface, but underneath he was basically a man who would undertake any venture successfully.' In short he was a man who wished to enjoy every experience life had to offer, be it physical, intellectual, aesthetic or sensual. Finch Hatton could never be described as handsome – he had too thin a face, a crooked smile and was almost totally bald – but he was immensely fit and so physically powerful that he once lifted a car out of a ditch unaided.[16]

In common with his friend Berkeley Cole, Denys was deeply attracted to the life that Tania created in her house at Ngong, where she had assembled a comfortable and aesthetically pleasing collection of furniture, paintings, china and crystal. It was an oasis of cool, quiet civilization, where Denys could indulge his intellectual propensities and be assured of admiring and indulgent company. It was an ideal resting place for him between his adventures and unexplained business affairs and for as long as he could feel untrammelled by the relationship, he loved Tania. He moved his belongings into her house and for six years they were idyllically happy.

Together the couple achieved a separateness from their companions and surroundings, so that even in company they seemed locked in their own shining world. Their love was tender, poetic and intense, on a plane that even their close friends found difficult to reach or to identify. They both adored the mysticism of Africa, the velvety soft nights under the vast canopy of stars, the hot dry days when they explored together the bush country, their senses heightened by passion. Tania has written in beautiful prose of their times together, without ever acknowledging the full force of her idolatrous love for Denys.

Denys Finch Hatton had no other home in Africa than the farm. He lived at my house between his safaris, and kept his books and his gramophone there. When he came back to the farm, it gave out what was in it; it spoke – as the coffee plantations speak, when with the first showers of the rainy season they flower, dripping wet, a cloud of chalk. When I was expecting Denys back, and heard his car coming up the drive, I heard at the same time, the things of the farm all telling me what they really were. He was happy on the farm; he came there only when he wanted to come, and it knew, in him, a quality of which the world besides was not aware, a humility. He never did but what he wanted to do, neither was

guile found in his mouth. Denys taught me Latin, and to read
the Bible, and the Greek poets . . . he also gave me my gramophone. It was a delight to my heart, it brought a new life to
the farm, it became the voice of the farm – 'The soul within a
glade the nightingale is.' Sometimes Denys would arrive unexpectedly at the house while I was out in the coffee field . . .
He would set the gramophone going and as I rode back at
sunset the melody streaming towards me in the clear cool air
of the evening would announce his presence to me, as if he
had been laughing at me, as he often did . . . He liked to hear
the most advanced music. 'I would like Beethoven all right,'
he said, 'if he were not so vulgar.'[17]

Beryl Markham is on record as saying that she doubted
whether the love between Denys and Tania was physically
consummated.[18] She did not repeat her claim when I
interviewed her and the suggestion itself is difficult to accept; for
although there can be no actual proof, the couple's closest
friends scoff at the suggestion. There are also two separate and
well-documented occasions when Tania believed herself
pregnant by Denys. In 1922 she appears to have suffered a
miscarriage, almost certainly due to her fragile health following
the brutality of early treatments for venereal disease.[19] In May
1926, convinced that she was pregnant again, Tania cabled
Denys who was in England visiting his family. She used the
code-name Daniel in her cable; obviously a name they had used
for an imaginary child in discussions, and one which she knew
he would recognize and understand.[20]

Denys's curt reply – 'STRONGLY URGE YOU CANCEL
DANIEL'S VISIT' – is breathtaking in its casual offensiveness.
Tania's cabled response to this is lost, but the subsequent cable
to her from England explained, equally coolly: 'RECEIVED
YOUR WIRE AND MY REPLY DO AS YOU LIKE ABOUT DANIEL
AS I SHOULD WELCOME HIM IF I COULD OFFER PARTNER-
SHIP BUT THIS IS IMPOSSIBLE STOP YOU WILL I KNOW
CONSIDER YOUR MOTHER'S VIEWS DENYS.' Injured pride
speaks in every syllable of Tania's final message in this
sequence. 'THANKS CABLE I NEVER MEANT TO ASK ASSIST-
ANCE CONSENT ONLY TANIA.' In the event this pregnancy too,
ended in miscarriage, although it is possible she mistook the
signs.[21] Certainly after the second occasion she could have been

in no doubt at all that her love for Denys would ever culminate in the marriage she craved.

Eventually Tania was unable to contain her desperate urge to possess Denys entirely, even though she clearly recognized that it was destroying the relationship. It was as if she could not help herself. The dissolution started after the first royal safari in 1928 and her anger at Cockie's inclusion among the guests. She was ultra-sensitive to the fact that there were now two Baroness Blixens moving in the tight social circle, and angrily tackled Denys about it. Ingrid Lindstrom thought that the quarrel 'left a reserve of bitterness in both of them, to be tapped later'.[22]

In 1929 Tania spent six months at the family home of Rungstedlund, near Copenhagen, where her mother was recovering from a serious illness. Denys too went home, took flying lessons, obtained a pilot's licence and bought a D H Gipsy Moth aeroplane.[23] For him this was a reintroduction to flying, for he had first learned to fly during the First World War.

Whilst in England he met several old Kenya friends including Rose Cartwright and Beryl Markham. Rose was in England working as a social correspondent for the *Daily Express* and recalls being violently airsick when Denys took her flying – though not until after they had landed. Beryl, separated from Mansfield, was in the joyful throes of her 'mad little gallop with Prince Henry'.

At the beginning of October Tania visited Denys and his family in England. Earlier that summer Tania had appealed to him for financial assistance to save the farm, which had been visited by the twin afflictions of a July frost and a swarm of locusts. He had complied out of his slender funds but his solicitors, presumably acting on instructions, had written formally to Tania making it clear that there were limits to their client's will to assist, and furthermore that she was to be responsible for the legal fees concerned in the matter which revolved around a debenture on the farm in the amount of £2000. Denys's family did not, at first, take to Tania. They mistrusted her and her motives and were antagonistic. One relative declared, 'I don't like that woman. She is trying to take possession of Denys. It won't work.'[24] After the visit Tania returned to Denmark to spend Christmas with her family.

Denys returned to Kenya at the end of 1929 in time for the

second royal safari, which the Prince of Wales had insisted upon
to compensate himself for his earlier, interrupted one. When
Tania arrived in Nairobi Denys was already deeply involved in
safari preparations. The spectre of Bror's and Cockie's close
involvement with this event loomed over everything Denys and
Tania did, placing a further strain on their relationship, though
they went flying together in the Gipsy Moth,[25] an experience
which Tania described as 'the greatest, most transporting
pleasure of my life on the farm.'

> You have tremendous views as you get up above the African
> highlands, surprising combinations and changes of light and
> colouring, the rainbow on the green sunlit land, the giant
> upright clouds, and the big wild black storms, all swing
> around you in a race and a dance... when you have flown
> over the Rift Valley and the volcanoes of Suswa and
> Longenot, you have travelled far and have been to the lands
> on the other side of the moon.
>   One day Denys and I flew to Lake Natron, ninety miles
> south-east of the farm and over four thousand feet lower...
> The sky was blue, but as we flew from the plains in over the
> stony and bare lower country, all colour seemed to be
> scorched out of it. The whole landscape below us looked like a
> delicately marked tortoise-shell. Suddenly in the midst of it
> was the lake. The white bottom, shining through the water,
> gives it, when seen from the air, a striking, an unbelievable
> azure colour so clear that for a moment you shut your eyes at
> it; the expanse of water lies in the bleak tawny land like a
> bright aquamarine. We had been flying high, now we went
> down, and as we sank our own shade, dark blue, floated
> under us upon the bright blue lake. Here live thousands of
> flamingoes... At our approach they spread out in large
> circles and fans like rays of a setting sun, like an artful Chinese
> pattern on silk or porcelain... We landed on the white shore,
> that was white-hot as an oven, and lunched there, taking
> shelter against the sun under the wing of the aeroplane.

Often they flew around the nearby Ngong hills close to the
farm to see the buffaloes feeding, or to visit the eagles.

> Many times we have chased one of these eagles, careening
> and throwing ourselves onto one wing and then to the other,

and I believe the sharp-sighted bird played with us. Once when we were running side by side, Denys stopped his engine in mid-air, and as he did so I heard the eagle screech.[26]

But despite these brief periods of happiness, Tania's misery knew no bounds when Bror and Cockie stayed as guests at Government House in February and she was excluded from the civic celebrations surrounding the prince's visit. She quarrelled violently again with Denys, over what she saw as his disloyal acceptance of her isolation, and to try to make amends he arranged for the prince to dine at her farm. Clearly this quarrel precipitated the fracture of their relationship; Tania felt that if only she could call herself 'the Hon. Mrs Finch Hatton' all would be well, but Denys would not indulge her to this degree.

The royal safari ended in the late spring of 1930, and for much of the year Denys was busy taking clients on safari. His visits to Tania were now infrequent and he called at her house more as a casual friend than as her lover. Though he was sympathetic to her problems regarding the farm, which were many, he refused to allow himself to become involved in her despairing attempts to put back the clock. To keep their meetings light and happy, he often mis-quoted a stanza from Shelley's 'Invocation' to her:

> You must turn your mournful ditty
> To a Merry Measure.
> I will never come for pity,
> I will come for pleasure.

In its original form it is a poem which Tania herself could have written to describe her feelings at Denys's rejection of her need.[27]

At the end of the year Denys left on safari with clients called the Marshall-Fields, and this coincided with Beryl's return to Kenya following the end of her liaison with Prince Henry. She could not live with her beloved father because of her antipathy towards her stepmother, and instead she rented the small cottage in the grounds of the Muthaiga Club, where Denys also spent a great deal of his time when he was in Nairobi. When Denys returned from the Marshall-Field safari in the spring of 1931 he removed his belongings from Tania's farm and left them at the house of a friend – Hugh Martin, a government official living in Nairobi. Denys claimed it was more convenient for him to be living in Nairobi, and that he did not like living among the packing cases which now littered Tania's house.

A friend of Tania's, who does not wish to be named, claimed that this occurred only after Tania had flown into a rage because she had heard that Denys had been seeing Beryl since before the time he went on safari, and that the relationship between the two had been anything but platonic. It was during this quarrel that Denys took back the ring of 'soft Abyssinian gold', which he had given her at Christmas 1928, and which she had worn on her wedding-ring finger ever since.

Rose Cartwright, a staunch friend of both Tania and Denys, is on record as stating that Denys confided to her that he had moved out of Tania's farm after much thought. Tania's jealousy and possessiveness were such that it seemed the only solution, and it was done in an attempt to preserve something of the relationship they had shared.[28] There are many small indications however that at the time Denys and Beryl had their short love affair, his feelings for Tania were merely those of concern for an old and cherished friend going through a bad time. Tania's farm was sold by then and though, by agreement, she remained on the farm as manager until the coffee harvest came in, she recognized that her time in Kenya was moving to a close. Denys's notes to Tania at this period, when above all she needed love and understanding, are gentle but cool: 'Let me know anytime you would like me to run out, if you have anything to arrange in your own plans in which I could help. I have a book here I want you to read. I will bring it out . . .' And again: 'I feel you are looking at the very darkest side of things. I would like to see you before you go and shall try to get out later.'[29]

In the very short space of time between his safaris, Beryl and Denys became lovers. It was a brief, prematurely ended, but infinitely sweet interlude for Beryl. Denys filled the role of lover, brother, mentor, friend.[30] He took her flying, which she loved, though unlike Tania she saw it as an adventure with a practical side to it. Once they flew down to his house at the coast, which he had purchased in the winter of 1926–27. At the end of her life Beryl could only remember that it was a small place near the sea. But in *Out of Africa* the reader is given a full description:

> ... thirty miles north of Mombasa on the creek of Takaunga.
> Here were the ruins of an old arab settlement, with a very
> modest minaret and a well – a weathered growth of grey stone
> on the salted soil, and in the midst of a few old mango trees ...
> The scenery was of a divine, clean barren marine greatness,
> with the blue Indian Ocean before you, the deep Creek of
> Takaunga to the South, and the long unbroken coastline of
> pale grey and yellow coral rock as far as the eye reached.
> When the tide was out you could walk miles seawards from
> the house, as on a tremendous, somewhat unevenly paved
> Piazza, picking up strange long peaked shells and starfish.
> The Swahili fishermen came wandering along here in a loin
> cloth and red and blue turbans, like Sinbad the sailor come to
> life, to offer for sale multi-coloured spiked fish, some of which
> were very good to eat. The coast below the house had a row of
> scooped out caves and grottoes where you sat in shade and
> watched the glittering blue water. When the tide came in, it
> filled up the caves to the level of the ground on which the
> house was built, and in the porous coral-rock the sea sighed
> and sang in the strangest way, as if the ground under your feet
> was alive ... The beauty of the radiant still nights was so
> perfect that the heart bent under it. You slept with the door
> open to the silver sea; the playing warm breeze in a low
> whisper swept a little loose sand, on to the stone floor.[31]

Denys found Beryl's untutored intelligence a stimulating challenge. He encouraged her to read good books. She had always been an avid reader and now he guided her towards poetry, the classics, the Bible. He habitually read from the Bible and could quote it by the hour, but it was because he saw it as a good story, not because he was a believer – indeed if Beryl had any religious belief at all, Denys put paid to it by intellectual debate.[32] He introduced Beryl to good music, which she loved, and she took a strong and lifelong dislike to Beethoven, simply because Denys expressed his disapproval of him.[33] He particularly liked the poetry of Walt Whitman and read to her constantly, though he was able to quote much of it from memory.

Beryl could never have been the companion to Denys that Tania had been. There was no true meeting of well-educated minds, but Beryl's long-standing 'schoolgirl crush' now turned to mature passion. This, twinned with her unconventional nature which was untinged by any hint of jealousy or possessiveness, must have come as a refreshing relief to Denys. She was very different to his previous lovers who had been small, quiet, artistic, refined, well-read women.[34] Beryl, nearly six foot in her tawny magnificence, and with her mind receptive to his tutoring, must have been an intoxicating combination. She was certainly a match for him physically, as athletic as he.

They rode together, picnicked, listened to music and sang together, went to parties and danced, and Beryl was never happier. She still had Melela, the farm bought by Mansfield where her father was living and training. Most of the land they used was leased, but the house and gallops were owned by Beryl and referred to often in her log books as 'my farm'. Sooner or later, she felt, she would return to horses. Denys flew her to Melela several times, landing on the gallops, and they dined in front of huge log fires while Denys read to her, and she listened quietly, her china-blue eyes fixed on his intelligent face. Beryl always had this ability to create an aura of calm. It was one of her most captivating assets.

Their love of Kenya was a shared passion, though Denys's feeling for the country was that of an onlooker compared to that of Beryl who had grown up within its many cultures. A safari with Beryl was a new experience even for Denys, for she was as much a part of the untamed bush as the animals who wandered through it, and she taught him to see it in a different light.

Denys has been called selfish, and his attitude to Tania was undoubtedly so, though he had probably never given her even the remotest grounds for hoping that he would ever become her husband. To him, marriage – even an acknowledgement that a formal relationship existed – would have been a cage. It is more than a possibility that during their relationship he had taken other lovers, briefly. Tania too, it seems, had indulged in brief relationships.[35] Beryl never saw the selfish side of Denys for their affair ended tragically, while it was still at its peak. She never looked further than the day that existed. 'Live each moment to the utmost and never look ahead,' she advised me.

After flying a few times with Denys she, predictably, wanted to learn to fly herself. The advantages of being able to reach remote parts of the colony in minutes rather than hours, and hours instead of days, made a great deal of sense to her, but she also saw it as a fresh and exciting challenge. Denys, sensibly, refused to teach her; he was too new at it himself. So she turned to an old friend, Tom Campbell Black, now Managing Director at Wilson Airways in Nairobi, and with him as instructor she began taking lessons in April 1930.

Tom Black, who had known Beryl on and off throughout the 1920s,[36] mainly through horse racing, had recently made headlines in the world's press by rescuing the famous World War One German air ace Ernst Udet, who had been a leading light in the Richthofen Flying Circus. In March whilst Tom was on his way south from Europe to Nairobi he had stopped to refuel at Malakal in the Sudan and heard that the airman was lost somewhere in the desert. He set out on a careful quartering search of the area and after many hours located the man's position. He had been in the desert for over forty-eight hours with no supplies and was nearly dead from thirst. Tom dropped a message to tell him to make some sort of clearing and, after flying back to Malakal to report Udet's position, Tom returned but was unable to make a landing. He dropped wet towels and a leather water bottle to Udet and landed some way off. Then he found his way on foot to the stranded airman and together they cleared enough distance of scrub to make a take-off practicable.

Under Tom's tuition Beryl proved an apt pupil, and after only eight hours of dual tuition she made her solo flight. But in the meantime a tragedy occurred.

With Tania's impending departure for Europe, and wanting to provide himself with a fixed base for his belongings, Denys had decided that he would build a larger house on his land on the coast and plant mango trees there.[37] However he was due to leave on a photographic safari with another professional hunter, Donald Seth-Smith, in June, so in early May he decided to fly down to Takaunga Creek, returning via Voi to investigate the possibilities of scouting elephant from the air. This had not been done commercially before, and he thought that he could provide a good service to safaris by giving the precise position of herds of game, rather than them spending days tracking it. However he was aware of the potential dangers. An engine failure – common in aircraft at that date, though not usually disastrous near 'civilization' – could mean trying to land in inhospitable country, and a suitable landing place might not be available.[38]

Tania asked to accompany him on this trip, and at first he agreed to take her, but later he changed his mind and told her it would be too rough because of the possibility that he might have to land and sleep in the bush, and that he would need a boy with him, presumably to help clear a bush strip for take-off. Although she does not say they quarrelled over this, Tania's comment – 'I reminded him that he had said he had taken out the aeroplane to fly me over Africa'[39] – leads one to suspect that even their last meeting may have been clouded with the stormy results of her jealousy. After Denys had said goodbye to Tania he spent a few days in Nairobi.

Over dinner at Muthaiga on the night before he left, he asked Beryl if she would like to accompany him down to the coast.[40] He thought she might particularly enjoy the return journey which he had told Tania would be 'too rough' for her. Beryl was 'thrilled at the idea' but she had arranged for some dual-flying instruction with Tom the next day and said she would have to clear it with him before she left.[41]

Denys took off on 9 May with his servant Kamau. Earlier that morning Tom had dissuaded Beryl from going with Denys because he had a premonition of some kind. Also he reminded Beryl of her lesson and the fact that she needed only another hour or so before she could 'go solo' – plenty of time later on to go flying with Denys. It is a tribute to the respect that Beryl felt for Tom's opinions that he was able to persuade her not to accompany her lover on what promised to be an enjoyable and fascinating trip. Perhaps Tom was recalling the condition of Udet, or even two men he had rescued earlier that very week. They were employees of the Shell Oil Company whose plane had come down near Marsabit. The plane he used for the search was a D H Leopard Moth and he could not land it in the scrub, so dropped supplies of tinned fruit and meat to them, as well as a message that he would return next day with a Gipsy Moth which had a slower speed and was able to take off and land in a shorter distance. When he found them they were almost 'delirious with hunger, thirst and sunstroke', and unquestionably he saved their lives. In the event he could not even land the

Gipsy Moth safely and the two men were eventually brought out on camels.[42]

As Denys landed at Vipingo he chipped the propeller on coral, and he cabled Tom asking for a replacement to be sent down. Meanwhile he stayed at his house and put things in order as he had intended. The new propeller was duly dispatched with a mechanic, and by 12 May the aeroplane was ready to fly again. The next day Denys took off for Voi. En route he saw the elephant herd he had hoped to spot and so when he arrived at the home of friends with whom he was to spend the night, he was feeling pleased with himself.[43]

'Denys and I were entertained at a party given by the District Commissioner,' wrote fellow guest and friend J.A. Hunter who was there with a safari client. 'Denys told us he was flying up to Nairobi in the morning . . . to make arrangements for a safari of his own. We left fairly early, for we wanted to be away without any delay in the morning. Denys came and waved us off. The District Commissioner's wife had given him a great armful of oranges and he stood at the door of the bungalow with the light reflected brightly from the fruit.'[44]

On the morning of 14 May 1931, shortly after taking off at Voi, Denys's Gipsy Moth crashed and burst into flames, killing both pilot and passenger instantly.[45] After taking off it had circled twice, presumably to signal goodbye to his hosts who had come to see him off, and to gain height. As it came back across the airstrip at about two hundred feet it appeared to sway and spun in, apparently out of control. Hunter was ready to leave as planned at 8 a.m., when his attention was drawn to clouds of black smoke rising from the aerodrome. 'Fearing the worst we hurried to the scene. We were too late: Denys had crashed during his take-off, the plane was a blazing inferno, and as we watched in horror, held off by the intense heat, a few blackened oranges rolled out from the wreckage.'[46]

Tom Black immediately flew down to investigate the cause of the crash but reached no firm conclusion. Finch Hatton's biographer raised two possibilities. The first was the effect of down-draught, an ever-present problem in hot conditions, particularly around hills, and the second was cramp – a condition which had been causing Denys some annoyance during the previous weeks.[47]

Beryl has never spoken of her personal reaction to Denys's death, but she wrote fleetingly of him in her memoir. Friends say that it was a catastrophic event to her,[48] and it does not require much imagination to picture her distress. The news was broken to her by an old friend at the Muthaiga Club – the same friend who said that Beryl 'was mad with love for him', and their love was still at its very peak when Denys was killed. Interviewed in 1986 Beryl was certain that she accompanied Tom Black down to Voi as soon as the news came through, but Tom took aircraft accident investigator Major C.A. Hooper with him to inspect the plane, not Beryl. It is of course possible that, knowing of Beryl's attachment to Denys, in order to console her and to convince her that Denys was indeed dead, he flew her down there later that day or on the following morning to look at the wreckage. Years later she confessed her love for Denys to her friend Doreen Norman in terms which led Doreen to believe that he had been the only man in Beryl's life who could have competed with her father.

Because of the climate, the funeral had to be arranged hastily for the next day. Tania remembered that Denys had expressed a wish to be buried in the Ngong hills, on a ridge overlooking the vast Athi plains, and from where Tania's house could be seen in the distance. On one occasion the couple had been there at sunset and from the spot Denys had picked for 'his grave' they had seen both Mount Kenya and Mount Kilimanjaro. The body was transported back to Nairobi by train for burial in accordance with Denys's wishes.[49]

The *East African Standard* reported the funeral sadly: 'A few hundred yards off the Kajiado road in the Ngong hills, overlooking the game reserve that stretches for miles, the Hon. Denys Finch Hatton was on Friday, laid to rest in a simple grave in the presence of friends and fellow hunters...'[50]

The rains which had stayed away for years, and the absence of which had undoubtedly been a major factor in the failure of Tania's farm, were heavy that spring. On the morning of the funeral Tania and her friend Gustaf Mohr went up into the hills to organize the digging of the grave. The site was enveloped in cloud and in a matter of minutes they were both drenched and cold. Tania recalled that there was an echo in the hills, and when the boys began digging 'it answered the strokes of the spades, like a little dog barking'.[51] Her grief was terrible to behold. From the moment when she had been given the news by Lady MacMillan after a luncheon party on the day she had expected Denys to return to Nairobi, Tania had appeared like an emaciated old woman, her face a mask of suffering.

Beryl's memory of the funeral, at a distance of fifty-five years, was less poetic, but none the less strong. 'He was buried in the hills at Ngong. It was a lovely death – no, not death – what is it you have when you die? Funeral! That's it. I never go to funerals because I hate them. His was the only one I've been to in my life. Everyone knew about how close we were and they let me stand right next to the place. Tom took me out there. It was very sad for me and for everyone, he was so well thought of, you see, there was no one like him...' Her own tribute to Denys in *West with the Night*, as eloquent as any of Tania's writing, subtly betrays the depth of her feeling for Denys.

There was a large crowd of mourners, including many people who had heard of Denys's death by cable and had driven long distances overnight through the sodden bush to be there to say farewell. Tania was spared the sight of Bror and Cockie at the funeral – they were at Babati in Tanganyika. By the time they got the news the funeral had already taken place. 'Dearest Tanne,' Bror wrote, 'It is terrible for all of us with Denys's death but worse for you who always had such great support in him. It was a great loss for Kenya... a great sorrow to all his friends. When I got the news I thought I would fly to Nairobi to see if I could do something for you – but when one has no money one is so helpless. Can I do something for your boys or your dogs?'[52]

Tania received the sympathy normally allocated to a widow, and few offered comfort to the stunned Beryl, whom many thought, once again, had 'acted badly'.[53] Her predicament was desperate. Separated from Mansfield, and full of grief at the sudden death of her lover, she was in despair. I was told that she contemplated suicide. It is important to recognize that Denys had filled for Beryl not only the role of lover but that of the all-important supporter which she needed all her life. Her inbuilt insecurity and lack of faith in herself and her ability, was assuaged only when she had the support of a strong personality on whom she knew she could rely. Her extreme anguish when her father left for Peru was a parallel of her anguish when Denys died. She tended to regard those who fulfilled this need of hers as infallible beings.[54]

Friends rallied around, however – Beryl's lost-child appeal could almost always occasion assistance. Tom was a prop during these days, flying her to her farm because she needed 'to be alone'. Later she stayed with her father for a while at his neighbouring farm and there in the country she had loved and had embraced so wholeheartedly as a child, she sought to work out her grief among the horses and the familiar sights and sounds.

It was nearly a month later that she returned to Nairobi to take up flying again, and now there was a new determination about her attitude. Tom noted it and approved. She worked hard to learn the rules of navigation. Grief had sloughed off that veneer of sophisticated insouciance she had adopted in London. It was a turning point in her life.

CHAPTER SIX

[1931–1933]

Beryl had already received some six hours of flying tuition in one of the Wilson Airways Gipsy Moths when she returned to Nairobi in June 1931. After a further two and a half hours Tom decided she was ready to go solo. This does not mean she became a fully fledged pilot – far from it. Dual instruction continued as before in a process all pilots have to endure, even today. The student follows the instructor through the various points of flying – take-off, turning, banking, climbing, stalling and landing – whilst paying particular attention to the actions of the different control surfaces upon the aeroplane's flight – ailerons, elevators, rudder and flaps. This was basic instruction to give the student the feel of the aeroplane.

In common with all student pilots Beryl had spent most of her initial training on 'circuits and bumps', for it was not until Tom was absolutely sure that she was capable of handling this procedure that he could allow her to solo. It involves taking off, circling the aerodrome in the correct pattern, and landing. It sounds simple and indeed in today's modern aircraft it is not difficult. But in 1931 at Nairobi things were not quite so easy. The runway – a dirt track – was subject to the sudden appearance of pig-holes and ant-hills and it was not unusual to have to clear it of wild animals who had wandered on to it from the Athi plains in search of water.[1] The landing technique involved executing a perfect three-pointer in which the two wheels of the undercarriage had to make contact with the ground at the precise moment that the tail skid touched down. If the aeroplane came in too fast, when the control column was pulled back to stall the machine bounced up into the air and came to rest after an embarrassing series of bumps always watched with great interest by spectators. If the speed was too slow the aeroplane would pancake heavily, often breaking the tail skid.

Gradually the instructor hands over control of the aeroplane until, confident that the pupil is able to take off, circle the aerodrome and land safely, almost casually he utters the awesome words: 'I think you might be ready for a solo now, you know. Would you like to take her around?' Of course the student has been waiting for just this moment, but when it happens, the stomach tightens, and the heart turns over.

Beryl would not have been sent up alone one second sooner than Tom felt she was ready. He was an extraordinarily careful pilot and she could not have been more fortunate in having him as an instructor. He was probably one of the best pilots in the world at that time. A modest man, with a delightfully puckish sense of humour, he was precise, well educated and kind; and he believed implicitly in the future of civil aviation. While many of his generation who had learned to fly in the war now saw aeroplanes as toys, and flying as the smart thing to do, Tom had a broad vision of future civil aviation which was subsequently borne out almost exactly.

Born in Brighton in 1898, the son of an Australian who became mayor of Brighton, Tom was educated at Brighton College and at the Royal Naval College, Greenwich. Writing of his schoolday interests he recalled, 'When Bleriot flew the Channel there was intense excitement. We all set to work to construct models . . . It was this early toying with models and the opportunity which the war gave to so many of my generation that created in me the urge to fly.' He was seventeen when the war broke out but he immediately enrolled with the Royal Naval Air Service, adding a year to his age in order to be accepted. Later he transferred to the Royal Flying Corps[2] and at the end of the war he led the first British squadron into Cologne.[3]

He remained in the RFC after the war ended, and then, after an inconclusive period studying law, in the early 1920s he went out to Kenya with backing from an uncle. With his brother, he started a coffee farm at Rongai. By now, though, flying was in his blood, and he spent less and less time coffee-farming and more in the air. Eventually his brother returned to England.

Tom hired a full-time manager to run the farm, which was not self-supporting, got himself a commercial licence and did freelance flying work from a landing ground at the side of the Langata Road, which was later to become Nairobi West Airport (now Wilson Airport). He opened up air routes for mail deliveries in East Africa, and he saw it almost as a personal mission to establish a commercial air service there. Without any doubt his level-headed approach to flying was responsible for Beryl's competence later on.

In 1928 Tom met Mrs Florence Kerr Wilson, then nearly fifty years old and recently widowed. In the spring of 1929 Tom flew 'Florrie' to England in a Fokker Universal aircraft belonging to John Carberry, taking Archie Watkins along as the engineer. He had made the flight several times before and indeed was partly responsible for establishing the air route for civilian traffic. There were no airfields as such, for flying was not an established occupation, and proper facilities for aircraft did not become available until the African service of Imperial Airways was formally established in the early 1930s.[4] When Tom made his flight in 1929, the best one could hope for was a level piece of ground, suitable for landing and taking off, located near a refuelling depot. The Shell Oil Company were of tremendous assistance in the early days of flying, particularly over the Sudan, and would usually provide a representative with a fuel supply to hang around and wait for a pilot on a given day. If an aeroplane didn't turn up, the representative would assume the worst and instigate a search – if the pilot was lucky.

At the end of 1924 captains Tony Gladstone and Tom Twist had pioneered air transport routes by making a journey up the Nile from Cairo to Kisumu on foot to establish landing stages for the first flying-boat services,[5] and for many years civilian pilots used landing strips adjacent to these staging posts when flying between Europe and Africa. There were no proper flying maps, merely charts which had been put together based on the few flights made by pilots over the territory. Tom, Florrie Wilson and Archie accomplished their flight to London in eight days, a record time for the journey which lasted only briefly. Tom broke it later that same year.

In Florrie Wilson (who later became a pilot of no mean accomplishment), Tom found an enthusiastic backer for a

commercial air service in East Africa, and on 31 July, with a
capital of £50,000 and a Gipsy Moth aircraft, Wilson Airways
was born,[6] with Tom as managing director. Later that year
Tom flew the Gipsy Moth, loaded with a seventeen-and-a-half
stone passenger (Mr H. White of the Chicago Field Museum)
and his baggage, to Croydon in under a week, a sensational time
for those days when the journey by sea took up to a month.
Whilst in England he purchased an addition to the Wilson fleet
– an Avro Five, which he flew back laden with two passengers
and an engineer; the Gipsy Moth was piloted by Tommy
Woods. In the first full year of operation the company flew more
than 150,000 miles at a cost to passengers of one shilling and
threepence per mile, and by 1931 – when Beryl was learning to
fly – the company had three pilots and a fleet of two Avro Fives,
two De Havilland Puss Moths and three De Havilland Gipsy
Moths.[7]

On the second royal safari, in February 1930, Tom acted as
pilot to the Prince of Wales, operating from a hastily cleared
bush airstrip near the camp. He flew the prince and his aide
Joey Legh across the Rift Valley in a Puss Moth; Legh sat in the
fold-away auxiliary seat. Later Tom flew Bror Blixen over Voi
to spot elephant – anticipating Denys's idea that this might be a
feasible way of locating herds. In March Tom took the prince
over Kilimanjaro in a Gipsy Moth. In his diaries the prince
recalled:

> The view was very wonderful. Below was Lake Amboseli,
> about it a vast area of swampy shallow pools and dense bush
> which stretched away eastward to the Tsavo River.
> Westward was to see, ridge upon ridge, the Great Rift Valley
> where the Athi goes punctuated always with diamond falls.
> And forever ahead of [us], rose the huge pile of the Great
> Mountain, cloud capped Kilimanjaro. And into the blanket
> of clouds the Moth went too and when it sailed out of them,
> far below in the sun dazzle, the great domed peak of Kibo
> glittered in a mail of snow and ice. Glacier after glacier lifted
> as the Moth soared and circled among the great peaks. It
> seemed another world after the green tropics.[8]

Tom's memories of the time he spent flying the prince are
more prosaic. After he flew Blix down to Voi to locate the

elephant he took the prince there and when they were over the herd, the prince, who had his rifle with him, shouted to Tom, 'Go down, Black, let's have a crack at them.' Tom pretended not to hear and flew on. A little later on the return journey the prince spoke to him and Tom answered. When the prince asked him why he had not landed when they were over the elephants, Tom replied, 'I couldn't hear you, sir.' 'Well it's damn funny you can hear me now,' the prince retorted.[9]

In his early flying days in Kenya Tom had accompanied a safari party into the bush, where, with an early cine-camera, the fearless hunters hoped to get live pictures of a lion kill. One of the men shot a lion and the eager cameraman moved in for his pictures before Tom could warn him to wait. The lion, who was in fact wounded and not dead, attacked the cameraman, and the camera, which was still switched on, recorded the scene. Tom then killed the lion but not in time to save the man. The dead man's wife, who had witnessed the whole thing, was prostrate with shock, and became hysterical when told she could not ship her husband's body back to the United States for burial because they were so far from civilization and because of the heat. Instead Tom and the other members of the party conducted a hasty cremation and placed the ashes in the only available container – a tin biscuit box, an item that Tom never flew without. Tom then flew the widow and the biscuit tin back to Nairobi.[10]

In April 1930 Tom made the first non-stop flight from Zanzibar to Nairobi, in five hours and twenty minutes, a journey which normally took two days. It is believed that his was the first aeroplane to land on Zanzibar.

One can imagine the scene at the embryo airport as Tom and Beryl finished their landing run at Nairobi on 11 June 1931. As the Gipsy Moth VP-KAC rolled to a halt amid clouds of red dust, Tom climbed out on to the wing. 'Why don't you take her up now,' he shouted to her, leaning towards the rear cockpit to enable her to hear over the noise of the engine. 'Just climb to about eight hundred feet and make one circuit. All right?' Beryl grinned, holding up her thumb in acceptance, and Tom jumped to the ground.

He stood clear and watched as she taxied to the end of the runway and turned into the wind. Then he shaded his eyes, appraising her performance as she started her take-off run. 'Good girl, hold her down, hold her down, let her build up speed...' Beryl could hear the words repeated in her head. Wilson airport is over five thousand feet above sea level, a height which significantly affects the performance of light aircraft, particularly in hot weather; a pilot needs to be sure of sufficient speed before pulling back on the stick. Taking to the air without sufficient speed will cause the aircraft to stall and Tom had repeated these words so often in his quiet, confident way that she would never fly again without hearing them in her mind.[11]

When she landed after a brief five-minute hop into the air, he smiled. 'Good. That was fine, Beryl. Now let's go round again and see if we can't improve on that landing technique. I noticed that as you came in you flattened out too early...'[12] On the next day she managed a fifteen-minute solo flight, entered in a neat feminine hand in the new pilot's log book.[13]

She could not then fly for a week because Tom was involved in a venture in which he hoped to prove the value of commercial flying in East Africa. In one day he planned to link the four East African territories by flying from Nairobi to Entebbe, Kisumu, Mombasa, Zanzibar and Dar es Salaam, and back to Nairobi. During that week he flew to each in turn, ensuring that there were sufficient petrol supplies and essential spares should he need them. Having announced the flight, he could not allow anything to go wrong. If he failed for some mechanical reason this would set back his dreams of a regular commercial air service for years. In the event he successfully achieved this feat, setting up a world record by covering the 1600 miles in a single day in a De Havilland Puss Moth.[14]

When he returned on 19 June Beryl began her tuition again, each day gaining some new experience. She remembered those early flying lessons with great affection: 'He would wait until the very last minute and then say, "Beryl – do you really want to die – because you'll never get over that mountain"... or he'd say, "Where are you going?" And I'd say, "Nairobi." And he'd say, "You haven't a chance of getting there on this course."' He always waited until she could actually see where she'd gone wrong, and then in his calm professional way he'd correct her.[15]

A month after her first solo on 13 July, with five and a quarter hours in her log, she took her 'A' licence tests and passed. Now she could take off and fly whenever she wished, without the sanction of her instructor. But she still had a lot to learn, for even with her dual instruction, she still had less than fifteen hours of experience. She had not even made her first solo cross-country flight.[16]

She speedily rectified this on 17 July by flying to Nakuru, the nearest landing ground to Njoro. No doubt she took time to fly over her father's farm to waggle her wings at him.[17] Later she said of her early aviation experiences:

> I'm afraid Tom found me rather a trying pupil... distances are long and life is rather lonely in East Africa. The advent of airplanes seemed to open up a new life for us. The urge was strong in me to become part of that life, to make it my life. So I went down to the airport. My people and my friends, of course, shrugged their shoulders as if to say: 'She'll get over it.' They didn't know I'd already decided to take up aviation as a career. By solid application on my part and superhuman efforts by Tom Campbell Black I was flying solo after eight hours of instruction. How zealously did I enter up my hours in my log book. That book is more precious to me than any diary. Every minute jotted down there meant a step nearer my A ticket. It is beside me now as I write. I obtained my A ticket when I had fifteen hours to my credit. I was a fledged (not fully) pilot![18]

Even Tom could not fault her application. Her log book tells the whole story. Special occasions and milestones are recorded in the column entitled 'Remarks'. In mid August she made her first bush landing at Machakos. Later that month she flew to her farm Melela and landed on the gallops. In September she took her first passenger up – it was Tom. During October she added a new type of aircraft to her repertoire. Tom had told her that if she seriously wanted to take up flying as a career in East Africa (and by this time she was considering an aeroplane of her own), she could not do better than buy an Avro Avian. One had recently arrived from England and still bore the English markings GA-BEA.[19] It was an Avion IV, powered by a Gipsy II 120-hp engine. She leased the machine in early November and flew it until the following February when she bought it from Wilson Airways for about £600.[20]

Advanced dual instruction followed, and a spell of blind flying, then 'Passenger M. Cottar'. After thirty hours her confidence was such that she could take up a non-pilot for a local flight.[21] On 13 November Beryl, along with the entire colony, heard with grief and shock that Lord Delamere had died. Delamere went back as far as Beryl's very earliest memories; he had been present at her marriage to Jock, stood in as protector during the break-up of her first marriage, and had given her away on her marriage to Mansfield. Clutterbuck attended Delamere's touching funeral on a rocky outcrop overlooking the lake at Soysambu. Beryl would not attend, but it is certain that her sorrow was sincere and went deep.

In December Beryl's flights became more wide ranging. She flew to Njoro and landed on the polo ground, then on to Nakuru where she stayed for the races; from Nakuru she flew to Naivasha where she stayed with the Errols at Oserian. Other neatly-written notes in her log book reveal that she 'dropped a message to Crofton', and flew a passenger, F. Darling, to Kajiado and back, and her friend Lilian Graham for a flip around Nairobi. Nothing was wasted, no experience too small to profit by.

In the first days of 1932 she took her young half-brother flying, and a few days later on 9 January flew down to Tanganyika to visit Bror and Cockie Blixen, in company with Tom; he flew a Gipsy Moth and she the Avian. Cockie remembers them as being 'very close'. On the return journey from Babarti they intended to stop at Arusha to refuel, so Cockie begged a lift as far as Arusha. 'Tom never took his eyes off Beryl for a single second as we flew to Arusha. In the end I got a bit tired of this and said to him, "I suppose you couldn't watch where *we* are going now and again?"' He told her there were severe down-draughts and he wanted to be sure that Beryl could cope. When they landed at Arusha he talked to Beryl about this phenomenon, reminding her of its potentially fatal effects.[22]

In fact Tom and Beryl had been living together since his return from a trip to England in the previous autumn, and to Beryl the relationship was far more than a simple romance. Some friends say that Tom was the one man in her life who came anywhere near her father in her estimation, even superseding her feelings for Denys Finch Hatton. Certainly when I interviewed her in 1986 she spoke of both men with great respect and obvious affection, but it was Tom's photograph she kept over her chair.

It is not generally known now that Tom was as much at home in the saddle as in the air. He had raced in the colony on a number of occasions, and in common with Beryl and many of her friends was a constant competitor in the series of gymkhana events around the country. He was a magnificent horseman[23] and nothing could have been more calculated to impress Beryl. Together they rode around the high country on the slopes of the Rongai, and around Tom's ranch. They played polo up country where the teams included as many women as men. In Nairobi the couple were often seen dancing or socializing at the Muthaiga Club and Torr's Hotel. Their relationship was a well-rounded one and, as in her relationship with Denys, it was successful because she was never allowed to become the dominant partner. In a curious way Tom had somehow inherited the role of teacher from Denys, though his subjects were less aesthetic.

These were the good times with Tom. His job at Wilson was a tremendous and enjoyable challenge to him and he enjoyed the constant flights into the interior and to Europe.[24] He was a tender and considerate lover, but stood no nonsense from Beryl and never allowed her to interfere with his work. Beryl's tendency to dominate stemmed from a natural ability to command (although some saw it as arrogance), but it cut no ice with Tom. His firm, almost paternal control of her behaviour was probably the essential recipe for Beryl's happiness, given her obvious father fixation. Oddly enough Tom even resembled Clutterbuck in appearance, with his high forehead, long face and thick eyebrows over humour-filled eyes. 'He could control Beryl,' said a friend, 'with a single look, and she adored him.'

But Tom was far more than a lover, he also helped to get Beryl started on her own as a commercial pilot, something which she craved desperately. Throughout her life when she wanted something she went after it with a single-mindedness almost frightening in its intensity. Nothing was allowed to stand in her way and she used people and friends with breathtaking ruthlessness. The fact that Tom was prepared to work as hard as she at achieving her personal ambitions was an important part of their relationship. There can be no doubt that she had loved Denys Finch-Hatton; her intense grief when he died was very real and recognized by many people, though a few perhaps realized how deep the hurt had gone – she was always very good at hiding personal feelings. But her love for him had grown out of childish infatuation for a seemingly unattainable lover who belonged to another woman. Had Denys lived, their relationship could never have lasted, for many reasons. But Beryl's love for Tom had firmer foundations, and might have lasted through her life. At the age of eighty-three, when interviewed for this book, she referred to Tom as 'my beloved' on several occasions, and she told close friends over the years that Tom was the love of her life.[25]

In 1932 the media hype surrounding the professional and romantic liaison between the aviators Amy Johnson and Jim Mollison was at its extravagant height. From letters between Tom and Beryl it is clear that in idle moments, when they lay back and dreamed aloud their lovers' dreams, or when deep in conversation as they rode together on Mount Kenya, they saw themselves as just such a pair. They talked of record-breaking flights that would set them on the road to fame and fortune. Amy Johnson had made her record flight to Australia and Jim Mollison made a successful solo crossing of the Atlantic in his Puss Moth, *The Heart's Content*. However he had taken off from Ireland, and did not reach his intended destination, New York, non-stop. Mollison desperately wanted to succeed in a crossing from England to New York, because people in aeronautical circles realized that any commercial transatlantic service would have to link the great cities of New York and London, but it still remained to be proved that such a flight was possible going 'the wrong way'.[26]

Tom talked to Beryl about these flights, and about the goals rapidly becoming attainable due to technological advances. Here were challenge and adventure, something to work for. There was no doubt in her mind that she and Tom were linked together and would find fame in the eyes of the world as a flying partnership. It was a glittering goal that floated before Beryl's dazzled vision and she meant to have it. Not for the transitory public glory – that never meant anything to her – but for the satisfaction of personal achievement. She was happy, deeply in love, and the future, with Tom beside her, was promising.

From this time onwards her flights generally had some purpose – they were no longer practice hops. She went to friends' farms up country and stayed overnight, or she ferried passengers – for instance in February she flew Betty Playfair from Nairobi to Mombasa, staying overnight there before returning next day to Nairobi. Her passenger list read like the members' list of Muthaiga, though some complained that after offering a lift up country she asked for a fee when they arrived. They had understood she had been giving them a free flight as a friendly gesture.

In March the pair were openly criticized for living together. Beryl was known to be a married woman with a child, and a past, in England. There was an unpleasant incident at the Muthaiga Club when a gentleman standing at the bar, who had probably had too much to drink, expressed his opinions loudly to the world at large. 'Just the sort of thing that's given Kenya Colony a bad name . . .' Stories of sexual depravity in the White Highlands of Kenya were being given unwelcome publicity in England and there was general touchiness among the colonists at the time, about the bad press. Tom reacted by inviting the speaker outside where he thumped him on the nose, but the damage had been done.

This event coincided with difficulties between Tom and Mickey Wheeler (a friend of Beryl's), who accused Tom of exploiting Mrs Wilson, and using her money to further his own ambitions rather than those of Wilson Airways.

Tom was bitterly angry. He could hardly deny the accusation of his relationship with Beryl, but he had worked like a Trojan for Wilson Airways. By coincidence, he had just been offered the job of private pilot to Lord Furness, who had been in the colony on safari that winter. The offer came with the rider that Tom must accompany him to England in the spring. In the wake of the bad feeling that prevailed in the colony, and when Florrie Wilson did not, as Tom expected, rally to his side, he resigned his position at Wilson Airways in April and took the job with Furness.[27]

A few years older than Tom, Furness was a 'red-headed,

steely-eyed, hard-swearing, high-living peer who had about him an air of scandal transmuted to glamour[28] by virtue of his vast fortune which ran into many millions. The family seat of Grantley in Yorkshire was backed up by three other country residences, one of which was Burrough Court near Melton Mowbray, where Lady Thelma Furness introduced Wallis Simpson to Edward Prince of Wales in 1930 and thereby changed the course of English history.[29]

Marmaduke (nicknamed Duke) Lord Furness was the son of a dynamic man who had started life as a docker at Hartlepool and became a multi-millionaire and 1st Baron Furness of Grantley. When he died aged sixty the former stevedore was head of the Furness Line of steamers, had been Member of Parliament for Hartlepool, and was a JP and Deputy Lieutenant for Durham. The scandal that surrounded Duke stemmed from 1921 when his first wife, Daisy Hogg, died suddenly on board the Furness's yacht *Sapphire*, under mysterious circumstances which have never been explained, and was hastily buried at sea.[30] Duke was given to wild temper, scenes of loud bluster and shouting and swearing when thwarted, but Tom seemed to rub along well with him and enjoyed his new employer's company.[31]

Beryl clearly thought that Tom's new position was a temporary arrangement, for she apparently made no move to dissuade him from accepting it. Whether or not she would have been able to is in any case open to doubt for in retrospect it is obvious that Beryl was more in love with Tom than he was with her. Furness had already indicated that he would be spending the next few English winters in East Africa on safari trips, so Tom knew he would be returning to the colony within six months, perhaps earlier. The work would consist mainly of ferrying the Furness family around England and continental Europe, and was well paid. In addition Furness had agreed to allow Tom to compete in the King's Cup air race in his De Havilland Puss Moth during the summer months. Tom announced that he was flying to England in April.

Beryl had already purchased her blue and silver Avian, now bearing the Kenya registration VP-KAN painted on the fuselage and predictably earning it the nickname 'the Kan'. Without telling Tom, Beryl planned to follow him, and

managed to get in some advanced dual instruction from him
before he left. Tom had often told her of his flights to and from
England, so she had some idea of what to expect. Perhaps she
questioned him more closely about his flights to Europe in those
final days before his departure. Beryl's log book records
intensive lessons in spinning, night flying, deliberately flying
into a storm; and she passed all the tests. At the end of March
Tom and Beryl flew to Naivasha where they spent a few days
with friends. Two weeks later she flew Tom to Nyeri where he
picked up an American Waco bi-plane in which he departed for
England.[32] Beryl returned to Nairobi and set the wheels in
motion for her own trip.

At dawn on 24 April, with 127 hours in her log, she took off
from Nairobi headed for Kisumu on the shores of Lake Victoria
on the first leg of her flight. The mechanics at Wilson Airways
had been aghast when she told them she was flying to England.
No special flight servicing had been done, and there was not
even time to paint out the old British registration, GE-BEA,
from the top of the wings. The flight to Kisumu was uneventful,
other than a low run across her father's farm en route, and took
just under two hours. She refuelled there, and stretched her legs
briefly before taking off for Juba, a four-and-a-half-hour flight
during which she encountered a very bad storm and was forced
down with engine trouble some miles south of the airport – 'Just
clearing a swamp where landing might have meant death,' she
said later. She stayed overnight at Juba and the next day, the
weather having cleared, took off for Malakal – a refuelling stop
and the first point on the Nile, an important navigational
feature of the journey. Here she managed to have some minor
repairs done to the undercarriage which had been damaged in
the forced landing.

At Malakal she suffered doubts as to whether or not to carry
on, for she sent word back to Wilson Airways that she might be
returning. But a subsequent cable from the Shell Oil depot at
Malakal advised that she had continued on her northern flight.
She was forced down again at Kosti, just over halfway to
Khartoum. The Avian's engine had been running rough but
she made a perfect landing in deep sand in the desert on the
western bank of the Nile. 'My aeroplane was soon surrounded
by a crowd of grinning natives. They just stood and watched me

until I got the machine going again,' she told reporters later.[33] But she managed to persuade them to help her push the Avian on to some firm sand, and she took off again, landing at the refuelling airstrip where she 'fiddled about with the engine, trying to find out what was causing it to misfire'. Next morning she left for Khartoum, which she reached only with great good luck. The engine had cut out twice in the two hours taken to complete the distance. Here a mechanic had a look at the Gipsy II engine, and said he thought she had a cracked piston ring. She decided to push on to Atbara where he thought there was some chance that they might have the spares she needed.

There was silence then for a week before her friends, anxiously waiting at Nairobi, received news from an unexpected quarter. Sir Philip Wigham Richardson had landed at Atbara in the Sudan on his way south to Nairobi, and had met Beryl there. 'She had a broken piston,' he reported, 'but a spare had just arrived from Cairo. She was quite well and would proceed homeward when the repair was complete.'[34]

The next stages of her journey were equally troublesome. The engine continued to give problems and at Cairo she was forced down yet again in a dust storm so severe that the sun was blotted out and she was unable to see the ground. This time the Royal Air Force came to her rescue. They flew out a mechanic from Heliopolis to examine and make repairs to the engine. After this the engine ran better, and she continued north to Alexandria where she followed the southern Mediterranean coast via Tobruk and Benghazi to Tripoli. Here she flew across Malta to Sicily and on to London via Naples, Rome, Pisa, Marseilles, Lyon and Paris. She arrived at Heston aerodrome on 17 May.

Her flight was widely reported through Reuter's. 'Dressed in grey flannel trousers, a blue sweater and an oil-stained white mackintosh, Mrs Mansfield Markham, 31-year-old sister-in-law to Sir Charles Markham, startled Heston aerodrome yesterday evening when in stepping out of an aeroplane she announced that she had flown solo from Kenya in seven flying days.' She told the press that she had simply decided to take a holiday in England, which she had not seen for about eighteen months, packed some bags and set out. 'I experienced considerable engine trouble and was held up for days in the Sudan. The worst spots were crossing the desert, where the heat was terrific; crossing the Mediterranean, where I did not feel at all chirpy because of the engine trouble I had had; and from Marseilles to Lyon where the visibility and weather were very bad.' She added that on the long sea crossing from Tripoli she had worn an inflated inner tube around her neck. If those who received her at Heston were startled, it must have been something to have seen Tom's face when she confronted him in London that evening. 'He was a little surprised I think,' she remembered. But he would soon have forgiven her – it was a spectacular achievement under any circumstances, even more so given her lack of experience. Could any man have resisted such a compliment from such a beautiful source? His own flight had been performed in a record five days and he must have blanched when he heard Beryl's story. It was less than five years previously that the very first flights between Kenya and England had taken place and Beryl's aircraft was equipped with only a compass, rev counter, altimeter and a lateral stability indicator;[35] she had no form of direction-finding equipment or radio, not even a way of knowing her airspeed.

Immediately she was sucked into London's social whirlpool. In borrowed evening clothes she danced the nights away in the Dorchester, the Savoy and the Ritz. There were many Kenyan friends in England, including the Carberrys and the Soames, as well as the new circle of friends in Tom's aviation world. She spent her days at the airfield where Tom had arranged for KAN to have a complete engine overhaul. Meanwhile she used a borrowed Avian (G-ABLF) to fly around the fashionable aero-club circuit of Heston, Stag Lane, Brooklands and Croydon. On 9 July her own Avian was returned, and she found to her delight that it flew beautifully, its engine problems repaired. She was also lucky enough to fly one of the brand-new Avro 631 Cadets, a new type added assiduously to her log book, along with a Genet Avian – an Avian with a Genet Major I radial engine specially built for the RAF.[36]

She saw the three-year-old Gervase on a couple of occasions, but she showed no signs of wanting him to be with her.[37] If she saw her old flame Prince Henry, who was stationed in Tidworth with the 11th Hussars, the meeting was discreet and not recorded.

In mid August she made a somewhat mysterious flight to

Coblenz in Germany and had to make a forced landing near
Muendon when she ran out of fuel. She damaged the propeller
and fuselage, was shocked and slightly injured and continued
her journey by car to Coblenz where she was to 'meet friends'.[38]
Her snappy refusal to talk to the press of this mishap was
uncharacteristic; indeed she only entered it in her log book as an
afterthought, out of date-order. Maybe she was not going to
enter it at all, but she had second thoughts – ten flying hours
takes a lot of flying, and she was building up her hours with a
purpose in mind. The flight went into the log book, without any
comment on the problem.

That summer passed pleasantly enough; she saw Tom often,
and flew with him on occasions to the Furness's mansion near
Melton Mowbray where they used to ride together. Whilst
watching the King's Cup air races Tom introduced her to
Antoine de Saint-Exupéry, the French writer/aviator; Hubert
Broad, test pilot for De Havilland and one of the best racing
pilots in the country; and to Sydney St Barbe, formerly an
instructor with the London Aeroplane Club and a pilot of some
distinction. St Barbe had latterly given up flying instruction in
order to exploit the potential of sky writing, which had found
great favour in the United States, although it was slow to catch
on in England. Mary, Duchess of Bedford (known as the Flying
Duchess), was a pupil of St Barbe's and later became famous for
her long-distance flights. On one occasion after she had
completed a particularly praiseworthy feat he greeted her
return to England with the word BRAVO written in huge
letters across the sky.[39] All three of these men were to become
firm friends, and over the next few years each in his way played
a part in Beryl's story.

Tom departed for Kenya in early October with Duke
Furness, and on 22 October, four days before her thirtieth
birthday, accompanied by St Barbe, Beryl took off in her blue
and silver aeroplane for the return flight to Nairobi. No
problems were encountered and they spent a pleasant couple of
days relaxing at the old town of Mersa Matruh on the North
African coast, between Cairo and Tobruk. The journey took
only ten days – eight not counting the two spent at Matruh.
Their arrival at Nairobi was noted by the *East African Standard*,
who ran a large report on the flight, and in the private diary of

an acquaintance: 'Beryl Markham (the Duke of Gloucester's love) has just flown out from England and looking very lovely.'[40]

Beryl spent Christmas with John and June Carberry, flying over to the Prestons' place on Christmas Eve to persuade the outrageous Kiki to join them at the Carberry ranch, Seremai, at Nyeri.[41] Kiki, an amusing and beautiful woman, was quite openly on drugs and carried her silver syringe everywhere, causing the ever-witty Cockie Hoogterp to remark to a friend, 'She's very clever with her needle.'[42] When she ran out of morphine, Kiki used to send her own aeroplane down to Nairobi for a fresh supply.[43]

Over the next few months Beryl was a constant visitor to the Carberry ranch. The Carberrys had been leading members of the Happy Valley set in its mid-1920s heyday, and in the early 1930s their social lives were still interesting enough to annoy more serious-minded settlers. A veritable crop of books and articles, 'mushy stories of loose morals in the Wanjohi valley', had caused much criticism in England and by the early 1930s a visitor to Kenya was liable to be overwhelmed by protestations that the settlers were not sexually depraved, and that Kenya was not the last refuge of the morally lost.[44] One visitor at least thought the whole thing overrated and described the Happy Valley social activities merely as a 'group of highly coloured personalities trying a rather successful experiment in communal family life'.[45] Elspeth Huxley's mother, Nellie Grant, who used to visit Lady Idina, the acknowledged Queen Bee of the Happy Valley set, at her home, Clouds, 'must have been unlucky, for she never struck an orgy; though she did once find Alice de Janze asleep on the floor at four in the afternoon'.[46] Lady Idina changed husbands so often that no one ever bothered to remember her latest surname.

Alice was rival Queen Bee to Lady Idina. Once after shooting her lover in a Paris station she attempted to shoot herself. Following this incident Alice was known in Kenya as 'the fastest gun in the Gare du Nord'.[47] Beryl remembered it all as great fun – but could recall no specific incidents. Her log book remains the chief documentary evidence of her life during that period. Flights to 'Silvers' (this could mean either Jane Wynne Eaton, the first woman to fly solo from England to Kenya and whose showmanship ran to a silver plane and a matching silver flying suit so that she came to be called 'Silver Jane', or Mrs H. Silver who owned a Gipsy Moth), the Prestons, and many Wanjohi Valley notables form the majority of entries in Beryl's log.

The Carberrys' daughter Juanita remembers Beryl's constant visits to Seremai, though she was only eight at the time and Beryl was a glowing young woman of thirty. Beryl used to ride Juanita's pony, the only person apart from Juanita herself allowed to do so. Beryl performed gymkhana stunts for the child, such as picking up a silk handkerchief at the gallop. 'Of course I was filled with admiration but on the few occasions I secretly tried it, I usually ended up picking myself up,' Miss Carberry recalled.[48] There was a reason for Beryl's constant visits to the Carberrys – a practical one. Carberry employed a full-time aircraft engineer at Seremai and had his own small fleet of aeroplanes based at his private landing strip. Beryl could fly to Seremai and borrow an aeroplane whilst her own was serviced.[49]

Until April, Tom was busy working for Furness. But in April he had some weeks free before following Furness back to England. He and Beryl spent all their time together up country at her farm.

'If you're really serious about getting your B licence,' Tom told her, 'you could get it by Christmas. Then perhaps you could get a job as private pilot in England.'[50] Tom left in June and Beryl worked from Melela. She flew at every opportunity to build up her hours, and worked like a demon on aviation theory for her commercial ticket. She was so busy that in the week she had to fly to Mombasa to take her B licence tests, she suddenly noticed that her log book entries were incomplete. Beryl always ensured that entries into her log book were neatly made and she habitually jotted down the details of each flight on a pad for copying later into her log book. On the only occasion that the log book is completed in a hand not her own, her father wrote up the entries from her rough notes.

Beryl took the examination that would make her a commercial pilot. The tests included stripping an engine and cleaning jets, petrol and oil filters, changing plugs and adjusting magneto points as well as written and oral examination on the theory and practice of air law and navigation.[51]

On 18 September the *Mombasa Times* announced that 'Beryl Markham has now been granted her Air Ministry Pilot's "B" licence which entitles her to carry passengers in an aeroplane for hire or reward. Mrs Markham holds the distinction of being the first woman in Kenya, and of being the first Kenya trained pilot to obtain a "B" licence. There are very few women "B" pilots anywhere in the world.' Beryl reported later: 'Heavens! How thrilled I was. "My girl, you are getting somewhere at last," I said to myself.'[52] Her first commercial job, before she left Mombasa, was taking tourists for joy flights along the coast.

After gaining her commercial licence she operated from the rented cottage at Muthaiga, taking any kind of flying job that came her way. Arap Ruta was still at her side, a faithful shadow who learned as much about aircraft maintenance as Beryl. Tom was in Kenya again with the Furnesses, and she saw him as often as his work allowed. He told her of his participation in the King's Cup where in the early rounds he managed second, fourth and eighth places, but this was not good enough to get him into the final round.[53]

Beryl had already started to build up her safari work, taking Blixen and his clients game-spotting, and providing a message service to and from Percival's bush camps. From December 1933 she accompanied safari groups, making the camps her base for up to ten days at a time. Operating from hastily cleared landing strips, she would go off each morning scouting by air for the animal herds, reporting their position to the waiting hunters. Tom was unhappy about this work, and constantly warned her always to be on the lookout for somewhere to land. She got into the habit of spotting potential landing sites where she could make an emergency landing if necessary, but seldom had to use any of them.[54] Throughout that winter while Tom flew for Furness, Beryl flew scouting sorties for Blixen and other white hunters.

Beryl and Tom were still lovers during this period. 'As far as I recall he was her only boyfriend,' a contemporary recalled, and he shared Beryl's delight when she landed her first contract delivering mail. George Edye of East African Airways apparently sent for her one day. 'Want a job?' he asked. Beryl was too excited to speak and just nodded. The job was delivering mail and supplies to miners at the gold mines of

Kakamega, Musoma and Watende. Beryl said, 'It was difficult flying. The airstrips were pocket handkerchief size and a forced landing anywhere en route meant almost certain death from thirst.'[55] Gold mining never became big business in Kenya, but in the early 1930s, when a few nuggets were discovered, there was a great deal of excitement and talk of another Rand. Miners flocked to the 'gold fields' some forty miles from Lake Victoria, and when Elspeth Huxley (then a young journalist) visited Kakamega in 1933, upwards of a thousand men were encamped there in tents and roughly erected native bandas, eagerly panning riverbeds and sinking shafts. What she remembered principally though were the fireflies: 'At night the ridges and valleys around about sparkled with millions of these insects, flashing their signals till the countless stars overhead were matched, it seemed, by another canopy of stars below.'[56]

G.D. Fleming, who was a pilot for East African Airways in 1935, well remembered Kakamega airfield. 'It was 5000 feet above sea level, with two runways at right angles, each about 25 by 700 yards.' On one occasion he landed there in a tropical storm. 'It was coming down in a solid wall, the visibility was less than 25 yards. As soon as I crossed the boundary I closed the throttles and landed about 150 yards inside the hedge. The landing strip [I had chosen] sloped uphill very steeply, with tall trees at the top. We used to land uphill and take-off downhill. As the machine ran along the ground I saw through the wall of water a dim object in my path. As it rapidly came closer I realized that it was a car.' He opened the throttle and bounced over the car but by then he could not stop within the length of the runway and the aeroplane somersaulted over the perimeter bank. He regained consciousness to see the passengers 'hanging from the seat belts like bats and very red in the face'.[57]

Beryl augmented her income from this contracted work by providing a courier service for safari parties, and delivering medical supplies or doctors to emergency cases. Sometimes she flew an accident victim or critically sick patient from distant outposts to hospital in Nairobi.[58] In addition she provided an air taxi service to up-country farms, undercutting Wilson Airways' rates of one shilling and threepence per mile.[59] Often she worked as a relief pilot for East African Airways and a colleague, G.D. 'Flip' Fleming, stated:

She was a fine pilot with great courage and endurance, and with the exception of Jean Batten I think Beryl was the finest woman pilot in the British Empire...

I never saw her tired or 'the worse for wear' even after a ten-hour flight or a party the night before. She always looked fresh and cheerful... her navigation was uncanny, and she could find her way to any spot in the vast open country of East Africa... I never saw her make a poor landing, even in really filthy weather, on bad aerodromes or at night.[60]

When the Furness safari ended in January, Tom made preparations to fly to the Furness mansion near Melton Mowbray in Leicestershire. Beryl was heavily engaged in scouting for Blixen's safaris until March and was busy and happy. The pair saw the forthcoming separation as a temporary one. Tom hoped to compete in the King's Cup air races that summer and would return to Kenya for the safari season as usual. He was also hoping to involve himself in the big air race from London to Australia but this would need sponsorship and a special type of aeroplane, and at that stage it was very much a dream. He had made preliminary contact with Charles Scott, a fellow pilot with whom he was considering teaming up for the race, but their plans were very sketchy. The couple talked of Beryl's flying to England during the summer, and this arrangement suited her.

Neither knew it, but his departure from Kenya signalled the end of their love affair.

CHAPTER SEVEN

[*1933–1936*]

In 1933, Beryl was a woman confident of her ability to fly and earn a living in an exciting new field. If she had failed in this venture she could still have supported herself, for her skill in handling horses would not have failed her. Indeed she still helped Clutterbuck occasionally on his farm at Elburgon where he was again training successfully; by the mid 1930s he had produced two Derby winners.[1] But she was still searching for something. Destiny had not finished with her, she was convinced of that, and she was restless, almost apprehensively anticipating 'something that would happen to change my life – I always knew it would'.[2]

Notoriously fastidious about her appearance, Beryl regularly attended a beauty parlour in Nairobi to have her hair lightened and her nails manicured. She invariably dressed in her famous livery of white silk shirt and cravat and the loose white slacks which fitted snugly over her slim hips and flowed sensuously around her exceptionally long legs. Seeing her fine fair skin, her blue eyes and sheer femininity, but particularly her jaunty manner of speaking, an onlooker might have dismissed her as a society woman playing with aeroplanes. But flying was no game to her, and despite the apparent vulnerability in her shy smile she was always aware of the impression she created. Furthermore she was not displeased with reactions to her unusual combination of stunning looks and somewhat masculine profession. There were other women pilots in East Africa at that time, but none except Beryl earned their living at what was regarded as a rather dangerous sport.

It is interesting to speculate about the feelings of a man, stranded in the bush for days with a broken ankle, waiting for assistance after he had sent a runner for help. He must have been delighted when the tiny blue and silver aeroplane roared over his camp. Anxiously watching the aeroplane land on the prepared bush clearing in the distance, he waited for the pilot to walk to his camp. If King Kong had walked into the clearing with first aid and fresh supplies he would have welcomed him like a brother. Imagine then his feelings when, instead of a helmeted male pilot, a tall Garboesque vision of a girl, dressed in white, with long blonde hair and painted nails, grinned cheerfully and handed over a bottle of gin – Beryl's cure-all for bush-stranded hunters. 'He must have wondered if he hadn't died and gone to heaven,' an old timer recalled when he retold the story, but this is only one of many such stories and it is now almost impossible to separate fact from legend.

Operating from the Muthaiga Club, Beryl conducted her freelance flying business with great success. She was the first person to offer aerial elephant scouting commercially, and fortunately there is a report of the first time she tried it. Colonel Leonard Ropner, a Member of Parliament who visited Kenya for big-game hunting in October 1933, reported that Beryl had found a way of using the aeroplane most effectively for spotting elephant.

> I went to Egypt to study the political situation and finding that I had six weeks to spare before the recess ended, I thought I would go to Kenya. So I flew there from Cairo by the weekly Imperial Airways liner. We flew over lots of game, including elephant. At Nairobi, Baron von Blixen, a Swedish sportsman, joined us. The party consisted of ten Africans, three of whom were expert trackers... they had previously been poachers, and one was a murderer!... One of the most amazing sights is hunting by car, but it is not very sporting, I should not indulge in it. I was trying to get an elephant for three weeks but only on the last day of my stay in the bush did I succeed.

Acting on Blixen's advice, Colonel Ropner sent runners two hundred miles to Nairobi with a message for Beryl. She flew to their camp and undertook to scout for elephant and report to the hunters next day.

This was her first charter of this description. She took up the
Baron to look for elephant. At last the spotted one big bull
elephant with tusks which looked as though they might be
over 150-pounds. There were two others with tusks over 100-
pounds. It took them only half an hour to fly back to camp,
but it took a day and a half to march through the bush to the
position indicated. At dawn the next day [Beryl] flew up and
down at the place where the elephant had been seen, while we
made fires to let her spot us. She returned and dropped a
message which stated that she had seen four large bulls. Even
then it took us five hours to reach the spot.[3]

Sometimes Beryl worked for Bunny Allen. 'She was an
excellent pilot...' the former white hunter recalled, explaining
that Beryl would fly into their camp using a makeshift airstrip
which was as close as the hunting party could make it. Having
ascertained what animal the party were after, whether elephant
or buffalo, she would take off and locate a herd. 'If it was
specified that she should look for a big elephant, she was a girl to
know what a big elephant meant.' A big elephant meant big
tusks – up to 200 pounds in weight. Sometimes she would return
and land at the camp, and perhaps take one of the hunters along
to show him. Or she might drop a note to the party in one of the
special leather message bags she carried in the Avian for the
purpose. To these little bags were attached streamer ribbons in
her racing colours of blue and gold. A leather bag could easily
lie lost in the bush, but the gaily coloured ribbons led searchers
to the message quickly.[4]

'She knew her way about the country wonderfully well...
and was a very good bush pilot. Sometimes we would make an
arrangement to rendezvous with her at a certain point on a
river, or by a certain pond that happened to be left over from
the last rains.' Sometimes when thick bush made a landing
impossible she would indicate the position of the animals by
flying in wide circles over them.[5] During the whole of this period
Beryl had no sophisticated direction-finding instruments and
no radio. Her aeroplane was fitted only with a compass, a turn
and bank indicator and an altimeter. If she had gone down in
the bush she had no way of letting anyone know her position.

In January 1934 Ernest Hemingway visited Kenya and went

on safari with Phillip Percival, the most famous white hunter of them all. He later portrayed Percival as big-game hunter Robert Wilson in one of his African stories.[6] During his visit Hemingway contracted dysentery which became further complicated. 'I became convinced that I... had been chosen to bear our Lord Buddha when he should be born again on earth.'[7] It was not childbirth, but a prolapse of the lower intestine. A rescue aeroplane was hastily summoned and Hemingway was hospitalized in Nairobi. Despite the severe pain he was suffering, he not only took note of the flight over Kilimanjaro but was able to use his memory of it with typical eloquence in his novel *The Snows of Kilimanjaro*.

Whilst convalescing he met Bror Blixen and the pair, alike in so many ways, became firm friends. Hemingway invited Bror to join him at the end of February on a deep-sea fishing trip in the Indian Ocean, an invitation which also included Bror's safari client Alfred Vanderbilt. Bror introduced Hemingway to Nairobi society, including Beryl, who had been contracted to work full time for Bror aerial scouting for the Vanderbilt safari. Hemingway referred to this period some years later when, writing of Beryl's memoir, he said, 'I knew her fairly well in Africa...'[8] He could not have imagined that his letter would be a moving force in Beryl's re-discovery as a writer. Bror Blixen also refers to this Vanderbilt safari in *African Hunter*:

> The first time we went elephant hunting in the country around Voi, but it was a miserable business. We had sight of a big elephant that defied us for two and a half months. We were continually in harness the whole time, wore out many pairs of boots, smashed up an aeroplane and three cars, but all to no purpose.

This aeroplane could not have been Beryl's, for her log book shows no break in the operation of KAN throughout the period; she flew for the Vanderbilt party every day for two weeks, during which time she took both Blix and Vanderbilt up in the Avian to look for animals around Kilamakoy.

When the safari season ended Beryl earned her living ferrying passengers to and from up-country farms, and taking any flying job that came along such as cargo delivery, or flying a Nairobi doctor to patients in remote locations. There were diversions: she still competed in gymkhana events and her name generally appeared in the prize list for jumping classes. In April 1934 a new airstrip called Njoro Landing Ground was officially opened. Beryl flew in, along with well-known aviators such as Carberry, St Barbe, Florrie Wilson and Silver Jane. Beryl won a prize for landing at a time prescribed some days previously by the aviation committee, and later collected the trophy for winning the Aerial Derby. This was a thirty-mile course but 'several of the competitors went astray', and Beryl cruised into a finish some minutes ahead of her rivals. The day finished with joy flights for spectators until dusk called a halt to the flying, whereupon everybody trooped to the clubhouse and dancing went on until the early hours.[9]

In early spring there was news that Tom had entered the forthcoming race from London to Melbourne. Thrilled, Beryl wrote asking him for more news. His reply came almost immediately. Beryl's letters to Tom do not survive (except the one she reprinted in her memoir), but some of his answers do. They are far from ardent, even before he met the beautiful actress with whom he was to fall headlong in love and pursue until she simply gave in and married him. Rather they have an avuncular, almost patronizing tone, though Beryl disagreed with this assessment, saying it was 'just his way', and she had long ago edited them, typing them out and printing the words 'extract from a letter to me from Tom Campbell Black' at the top of the pages.

>The Royal Aero Club
>119 Piccadilly,
>London W1
>
>24th March 1934

Dear Beryl,
Very many thanks for your letter, it was clever of you to understand, so really clearly, what I tried to convey about the definite undercurrent of intense and deadly jealousy which exists in people in East Africa. Purged of many of them the country would blossom out into a land of amazing allurement

and prosperity – a land in which one could find the contented realization of one's dreams.

This London houses and holds the millions, yet here things are a little different; the affairs of neighbours, the jealousies of friends, create less interest than in the little tin-pot land of Kenya.

Yet with the marvellous freedom from condemning scandals, with the complete knowledge that one is free to do with oneself as one wishes, see whom one likes, and live entirely untrammelled if so wishing, yet even so, a ghastly mantle of depressing melancholy turns one's thoughts and ambitions in another direction and makes one long to become a personality again, and so to break away from it all, go back to the individuality and independence of the life in Kenya, even despite the lying, scurrilous thoughts and bitter comments of one's neighbours there.

Perhaps what I have written is senseless and contradictory, but I pay you the compliment of knowing that if you cannot logically follow my reasoning, you will at least understand the theme of what I'm writing, and so I will not re-read this letter, because by alterations one may perhaps become more clear in expression, but perhaps one alters what one wishes to convey.

Those who have been friends to us, and even more, should be included in the list of things for which we should be happy and proud. They form my fellowship of lofty thoughts. And one must keep one's dreams, forgetting nightmares, and grotesque unpleasantnesses of 'never mattering' people.

Here I am, longing for freedom, chained to the monotonous drudgery of a well paid job, chained by invisible bonds, for truly if I broke away from my present occupation I should be breaking up the very things that mean so much to me. I like Furness most awfully. Kind and considerate to me in all his business dealings, he is more outside this sphere and so dependent on me for so much, that to leave at the moment would be an ingratitude! Fancy Tom Black, supposed by all to have exploited Mrs Wilson (*vivé* Wheeler's version) to write like this!!! Just fancy sentiment entering into anything in this astonishing age. And from both you and I!

Anyway I'm always mad, and have been lately, for getting down to some practical details of existence I have taken some most amazing stock market gambles and I think I've lost. I now only exist therefore until October. You ask me to write of the race – there isn't much to tell.

I was determined to enter, as I wish it to be a preliminary opening for my flying ambitions. What these are it is difficult to detail, because as machines and ranges get swifter and bigger, so do one's ideas, and much must depend on how the race eventuates. In idle moments we have talked Atlantic Oceans, of cabbages and Kings, and Cape Flights, and now, if all is well and goes well, perhaps it is all within my grasp, but with a faster, possibly impossible conception. The Race must anyway, thank God, be tackled first.

The machine is being built and will I think be fast and the range long. Scott is a grand man to be with, and both of us thought it better right way back at the early whisper of the Race, to go together fifty-fifty level basis, rather than for each separately to rely on second pilots, one or both of whom would not enjoy our absolute and complete confidence, or anyway fit in as a 100% team.

Then we were each separately offered mounts for the Race, and both unknown to each other refused, because of our past agreement. This left us a team without a machine; but we were optimistic and so at length, after many discussions with various syndicates we accepted the Comet. It will be ready in August and we hope for the best. Without knowing other people's performances it is ridiculous to even hint or guess at our chances.

I leave Furness in August, temporarily until after the Race, when I rejoin him in Kenya, and meanwhile from August till October go into training. We take the Race very very seriously and of course hope for the best. If we can put up a good show and have luck in our favour, perhaps my having left Kenya was for the best and not in vain.

Have been over in Germany during the so-called revolution and I think Hitler's action in facing 200 armed rebels only with his pilot and himself, at night, and during the meeting of rebels, one of the most marvellous pieces of physical courage in the annals of history. He is like that though – a wonderful man, above all considerations of personal weakness.[10]

God bless you Beryl and don't please be bored with my attempts to write my thoughts, however badly they are expressed, because I have tried to keep pace with them, and so, naturally have undoubtedly made many, many errors of both composition, construction and coherence.

Tom[11]

Whilst Beryl must have experienced disappointment that Tom was making a record attempt without her (for undoubtedly she had hoped to be part of any record attempt made by Tom), she was reassured by his statement that he would be returning to Kenya after the race. All would be well then. If he succeeded, she reasoned, Tom would be famous and then they would have no trouble in gaining sponsorship for other joint feats of airmanship. However she badly wanted to be part of Tom's attempt – if only to see him during the build-up to the race.

The idea of flying at once to England became irresistible, but Beryl could not afford it. She must have discussed her thoughts with Blix, for he came to the rescue with a solution to the problem. His nephew Gustaf 'Romulus' Kleen, who was then farming in Tanganyika, was just about to depart for Europe and would undoubtedly be glad to pay the expenses of the trip if Beryl would fly him there. The flight was hastily arranged and two weeks before the planned departure Romulus went to Nairobi where he stayed with Beryl at her cottage at Muthaiga.[12]

A few days before the flight planned for mid April they flew to the Carberrys' farm Seremai, where Beryl's Avian was overhauled by J.C.'s flight mechanic. Torrential rain had submerged the airstrip at Seremai on the day of departure, making a fully-laden take-off inadvisable, so it was decided that the aeroplane should be flown to nearby Nyeri aerodrome by Sidney St Barbe. Beryl and Romulus were to drive there with the luggage which would then be loaded on to the aeroplane while it was receiving its full load of fuel for the trip.

The rainwater which submerged the runway at Seremai also covered an unseen hazard. In the heavy downpour a deep channel had appeared across the runway. On its take-off run the Avian hit this furrow and turned over. Luckily St Barbe was unhurt but the aeroplane was slightly damaged and the propeller broken. A new propeller would take a month to arrive from the UK and to Beryl's dismay the flight had to be abandoned.

'As it turned out,' Romulus told me, 'the accident was a piece of luck, for Beryl went down that same evening with an attack of malaria and had to be taken by hospital plane to Nairobi the following day.' Although very gravely ill, with alternating acute chills and burning fever, sometimes barely conscious and often delirious, Beryl fiercely refused to go to hospital. Romulus and the devoted arap Ruta nursed her back to health in the cottage at Muthaiga and as soon as she was out of danger Romulus departed for Europe by boat. They did not meet again for a quarter of a century.[13]

It was six weeks before she was able to fly again and by then the Avian was still not airworthy. Carberry therefore loaned Beryl a Klemm to get around in the meantime. The Klemm was a low-wing mono-plane of German manufacture. Carberry was very pro-German and his feelings were reflected in his aeroplanes and cars. However the Klemm was powered by an engine of British manufacture – a 90-hp Pobjoy, which enjoyed an almost unrivalled reputation for unreliability. Beryl disliked the Klemm. Its only saving grace seemed to be its ability to glide on its huge wings for long distances. Its engine she described as 'so feeble as almost to require of the pilot the sensitive touch of a pianist to keep it in harmony with the weather and wind'.[14]

She did a few taxi jobs in the Klemm in June and July, but it was not until the Avian was repaired at the end of August that Beryl took up her work again. She made only seven flights between April and August, and probably she had not fully recovered her health, for even after the Avian was returned her initial flights were short hops.[15] It was not until November that she was able to continue her work scouting for elephant. She persisted in this despite the warnings of her friends about the risks, and they were many, for it was lucrative work paying nearly twice as much as other charter jobs.

It is true that had Beryl had a forced landing in such country she would have been in deep trouble. In 1986 David Allen, who runs a flying safari business in Nairobi which is the present-day equivalent of Beryl's, was in no doubt. His work today takes him over much of the territory that Beryl flew over in the 1930s. 'I wouldn't like to do it in a single-engined aeroplane and no radio, landing wherever you could get the plane down. It would take some doing.'[16]

During July and the first part of August Beryl stayed with her father, making an unusually long recovery (for her) from her illness. The month-long convalescence with its recurring ill health, headaches and muscular pains, was purgatory to her. In a way it was a blessing she did not know what was occurring in England, for the purgatory would have become hell.

In August Tom had flown Lord Furness to the races at Le Touquet where he was introduced to the dazzling young comedy actress Florence Desmond. She was relaxing after a successful run in the show *Why Not Tonight* and had been to Paris to buy some clothes. Immediately attracted to 'Dessie', as she was known to all, Tom spent the evening telling her about the forthcoming race to Australia. She thought he was either mad or had been drinking too much champagne. England to Australia in three days? An impossible idea!

Shortly after she returned to England Tom phoned Dessie at her cottage in Hertfordshire and she invited him down for the day. He said he would fly down in Furness's Puss Moth if she would place a sheet in the biggest field near her house so that he'd know where to land. This incident not unnaturally provoked interest in the village, coupled no doubt with some lively gossip about 'that actress lady and her pilot friend'. Even the village policeman got in on the act, pedalling portentously down to Dessie's cottage 'to take particulars. In the weeks to follow,' wrote Dessie in her autobiography, 'it became a regular week-end treat for the village – the arrival of the little Puss Moth. People were beginning to take a big interest in the forthcoming air-race to Australia, and the fact that Tom was taking part in the race added to their interest and curiosity to see him when he landed.' [17]

By October when he took off for the race, Tom's feelings for Dessie ran deep. His letters to her are a far cry from those he wrote to Beryl and it is hard not to make comparisons. Whilst he was in training for the race he wrote to Dessie:

> Mildenhall Aerodrome
> Wednesday
>
> My Darling,
> Because I haven't written to you, nor rung you up don't think for one moment that it is because I haven't thought of you. You are ever with me, by day in the air, by night in sleep, and here in the evenings round the fire I see your reflection in the deep shadows of the room.

I have given to my feelings for you the same concentrated determination which I am putting into this flying race, and I want you to realize just a little more than you do, that somewhere, somehow, and some time you are going to look on me as of importance to you.

Maybe it will only be for a tiny period, one cannot control these things at all, any more than one can be quite, quite certain that the machine will hold together.

I think and hope it will, and we are certainly going 'all out' and if the machine lasts the distance we have quite a good chance of winning, even though the French and American competitors have brought over specially built racing machines too.

The weather here is appalling, but we have managed to do a few of the necessary tests. We only took delivery on Saturday, which doesn't allow much time to put it thoroughly through its complete paces. However, except for a night landing at Baghdad on the first night out, and for the filthy weather conditions over Central Europe which are forecast for the next week, everything else is all right.

Do think a little of me as I am always of, and with you in thought.

Always
Tom

Dessie went to see Tom on the eve of the race. She found the circus that surrounded him with the thousands of avid spectators, press and photographers, aircraft designers, backers and manufacturers, as well as the atmosphere, which was charged with tension,

... rather frightening. These keen pilots, the best the world had to offer, were about to compete in a race which would make flying history. Both Tom and Charles Scott[18] had been training for weeks for the race. They were just about as fit as any two men could be ... Champagne corks were popping, but neither Tom nor Charles took a drink, they had been 'on the wagon' for many weeks. That morning the King and the Prince of Wales had been to Mildenhall ... to wish the competitors God-speed. There were three Comets in the race, one was Jim and Amy Mollison's, the second was flown by Cathcart-Jones and Ken Waller, and the third was *Grosvenor*

House, which Tom and Charles Scott were to fly. It was a beautiful-looking twin-engined, low-winged monoplane. At that time it was the finest aircraft of that particular type which had been produced. In order to achieve maximum range, the machine was literally a flying petrol-tank. They carried petrol in the wings, in the nose and in the tail. The pilots sat one in front of the other in a very small space, their heads almost touching the top cowling. As I looked inside that tiny space which was to house Tom and Charles for the next three days (at least that, if their calculations were in order) I wondered just how two men could stand the physical strain of operating a plane while being cooped up like that for so many tedious hours.[19]

Dessie did not want to watch the take-off, which was at dawn on the following day, and as Tom walked her to her car he asked her to marry him. Emotionally upset at the parting and knowing that in the morning Tom would experience a take-off in the Comet carrying for the first time a full load of petrol, as the preliminary to the flight of over eleven thousand miles, she felt that it was the wrong moment to make such an important decision. 'Tom,' she said, 'I'll tell you when you come back.'[20]

The next days were anxious ones for Dessie. When a reporter called and asked if it was true she was going to marry Tom, she told him she did not know. 'I told him Tom had asked me to marry him before he took off on the flight, and that I would give him his answer when he got back.' Finally the news came through that Tom and Charles Scott had won the race in 2 days, 22 hours and 59 minutes. Dessie's joy turned to outrage when she saw the newspapers: 'Campbell Black racing for a bride. [Miss Desmond says] "If you win the race I will give you my answer."' What if Tom thought she'd actually said that? Tom, when he telephoned her from Australia, laughed at her concern, 'Stop worrying about it. Will you marry me?' But she still didn't give him an answer. She felt that the race had no bearings on her feelings for him.[21]

The welcome given to Tom and Charles when they arrived in England was something seen these days only on occasions such as royal weddings. It was followed by receptions, parties, press conferences, an endless round of dinners where Tom had to speak – he always came up with some amusing little line to offset the more dramatic (though completely factual) descriptions given by Scott. But despite their acclaim and reputation, the two men made almost no financial gain from their flight. They had been backed by A.O.E. Edwards, owner of the Grosvenor House Hotel in London's Park Lane, who put up £5000 to buy the Comet. The prize of £10,000 and the Gold Cup worth £500 went to Edwards, and he received besides an unknown amount of benefit from the flight because the words Grosvenor House were on the front of every newspaper in the world. Tom and Charles Scott received no share of the prizes and Edwards eventually sold the Comet to the Air Ministry for £7000 for research purposes, though Tom pleaded with him to sell it back to him for the £5000 it had originally cost him. The only proceeds Tom received out of the venture were the fees people paid to see the Comet, when it was put on show in London, together with payment for a few newspaper articles and advertising copy, and a cheque from Lord Wakefield in respect of services to aviation. A little while later Dessie came to a decision, and next time Tom asked her to marry him she agreed.[22]

The first Beryl knew of this was a small article entitled 'Air Race Romance' which appeared in the same issues of the *East African Standard* as the reports of the race. A four-page report under the banner headlines 'BRITISHERS WIN AIR RACE' appeared a week after the results were known,[23] but Beryl was shocked to read the succeeding paragraph:

AIR RACE ROMANCE

London 23rd October 1934

A secret romance was associated with the flight to Australia. It is now revealed that Miss Florence Desmond, the British actress was asked by Capt. Campbell Black before he left Mildenhall, to marry him. Miss Desmond informed Reuter that her reply to his question was that she would give him her answer when he had won the race. Before Campbell Black left she gave him a black and gold matchbox inscribed with a message of luck and he placed three of her photographs in the cabin of the machine.[24]

Beryl had been expecting Tom to come flying back into her

life after his marvellous victory. She had been so proud of him, and for him, flying up to Elburgon to tell her father the news as soon as she had heard it. Everyone knew that Tom was 'Beryl's boyfriend'. That stupid newspaper article, she felt, couldn't be true. It must be some publicity stunt. She scribbled a note to Tom, but even before he received it, the latest news broke in the English papers and was subsequently transmitted to Kenya. 'Famous airman to wed Top London Actress.' Stunned, she cabled Tom: DARLING IS IT TRUE YOU ARE TO MARRY FLORENCE DESMOND? PLEASE ANSWER STOP HEARTBROKEN BERYL.[25]

Sadly for Beryl, it was all too true. She told me she thought she had flown to England to see Tom when he arrived back there from Australia. She could not remember what they talked about. Tom never mentioned such a visit to Dessie and Beryl's log book for that period is unfortunately missing. Tom and Dessie married in the spring of 1935. A further letter from him, shortly after his marriage, exhorts Beryl once again to stop scouting in elephant country, even though he must have known she would not pay any heed. Beryl had had a recurrence of malaria and he was concerned about her health. He wrote that with Dessie's help he had managed to buy a Comet of his own. In this aeroplane, he explained, he planned to make an assault on several targets: London–Cape Town and return; London–New York and return; London–Hong Kong and return, all to be done in long weekend hops. If he had succeeded with these plans it would have been sensational.

What Beryl really thought of his letter, somewhat heartless in the circumstances, is not known; her comment to me was that she was pleased that Tom was at last achieving his ambitions which 'were endless, absolutely endless. There was so much he wanted to do . . .'[26] She now threw herself into her safari work. No job was too dangerous or too arduous, and she worked ceaselessly. Now she cast off her restless apprehension, for she had a plan of her own. Partly it concerned Tom, for she needed, more than anything, to prove something to him.[27]

She did not give the impression of being broken-hearted. A visitor to Kenya, who knew Beryl only slightly, met her in Muthaiga one day. She was with Cockie, and both were cool, fashionably dressed, each beautiful in her own way, and self-

assured. The visitor was sad because it was the eve of her
departure for England. 'Why go if you don't want to?' asked
Beryl, puzzled. 'Conscience I suppose,' said the visitor. 'Beryl
and Cockie looked at me askance. It was quite clear that both of
them lived entirely for themselves and would never *dream* of
doing something they didn't want to for such a frivolous reason.
Frankly, I think they were amazed.'[28]

Stories of her numerous love affairs abound, but such fleeting
liaisons meant absolutely nothing to Beryl. They may have been
a simple gratification of her sexual needs, or perhaps a symptom
of her endless search for security.

Tom and Dessie had meanwhile flown to Morocco for their
honeymoon in Lord Furness's Puss Moth. Knowing Tom's skill
as a horseman, Dessie had had some beautifully cut jodhpurs
made, intending that he should teach her to ride so that they
could ride out together. He had told her about his rides with
Beryl in Kenya, though she was not aware at that time that the
pair had once been lovers. On the morning following their
arrival in Tangiers the newlyweds went for a ride. Dessie's horse
was a stallion – hardly an ideal mount for a novice, but Tom
told her not to be nervous, they'd take it quietly. Dessie wished
she could have had her first riding lesson somewhere less hilly
than Tangiers, and heaved a sigh of relief when the horses were
turned for home. Alas too soon – for as another horse and rider
came towards them, Dessie's horse 'gave a blood-curdling
scream' and the two horses rushed at each other. Discretion
conquered valour and Dessie slipped off the horse's back and
ran off to the hotel, leaving Tom holding on to her horse's reins
and joining with the other rider in trying to subdue the two
horses now locked in combat.

Later, when Tom came across Dessie sitting in the bar
enjoying a medicinal brandy, he was annoyed. 'You shouldn't
have got off his back... Never mind – you must ride again
quickly or you'll lose your nerve – we can ride again tomorrow.'
Dessie wondered how she could lose something she'd already
lost, but she needn't have worried; the next morning the owner
of the horse was quite adamant. He would not allow Dessie to
ride his valuable animal.[29]

There were further incidents during the honeymoon which
were frightening to Dessie – on one occasion the Puss Moth

aircraft developed engine trouble. They were over a range of mountains with no possible landing place. Even Tom was disturbed. When they eventually landed after a terrifying flight Dessie's legs were like jelly and she was sobbing with relief. 'What [Tom] said about dirty Spanish petrol one can hardly put into print,' Dessie said.

Tom decided that Dessie had better take the train to Biarritz with all the luggage. The weather wasn't good and he said he could take risks in the plane alone that he couldn't take with her. Eventually he landed safely and the pair flew home to England without further mishap. It is interesting to speculate on what Tom's feelings must have been after these events. Despite his undoubted deep love for the delectable Dessie he could not have helped making the obvious comparisons about how Beryl would have reacted to the horse-riding and flying incidents. Beryl would have coped easily with either, so that in fact neither would have become an incident. Clearly Dessie would have to be cherished in a way that would not have suited Beryl.

On their return from honeymoon, Dessie continued her highly successful stage career whilst Tom made plans to assault various flying records in his new De Havilland Comet, which Dessie christened *Boomerang* in the hope that it 'would always come back'. His first attempt was on the Cape Town record, with Gordon McArthur as his co-pilot. His intention was to get to the Cape within thirty-six hours, stopping at Cairo and Kisumu (where Beryl hoped to see him briefly) to refuel. After a quick turn-around he intended to return to England by the same route.

The men eventually got away, and after an anxious wait Dessie was delighted to learn that they had arrived safely at Cairo in eleven hours, breaking all previous records. However, delight turned to disappointment when it was learned that the Comet had landed with one engine completely burned out. Investigation revealed that the aeroplane had been supplied with the wrong dipstick at De Havilland's, resulting in an incorrect oil-level reading. Tom could only return to England and start all over again. But it was not as easy as all that. He needed a fine weekend with a full moon. It had to be a weekend, for the whole record attempt was built around the theme 'To the Cape and back in a long weekend'.

On the second occasion Dessie persuaded the two men to wear parachutes, much against their will because of the added weight and bulk involved. The factor which decided them was the lower insurance premiums if they carried parachutes. Once again *Boomerang* reached Cairo in record time (eleven hours and ten minutes), after battling through severe thunderstorms. On the second leg, headed towards Kisumu, the Comet developed engine problems, and after leaving it almost too late, Tom and McArthur donned the parachutes and jumped over the bush. They were rescued by Arabs and taken on camels over several tiring stages to Atbara. It was two days before the world learned they were safe. Tom acknowledged that had they not taken the parachutes they would probably not have survived, for there was nowhere to make a landing in the sleek, extremely fast racing aeroplane.[30]

Beryl, continuing her safari and freelance bush piloting work, and reading of Tom's exploits, felt she had been left out of the adventure. There is no doubt that she had loved him and found a deep fulfilment in the relationship which, during the two years prior to his marriage, had continued despite the distances involved. Tom's rejection of her, for Dessie, was devastating. But her hurt was not only at having been denied Tom's love. Just as important was the fact that she was being denied any part of the new and adventurous life that Tom seemed to have made for himself. That her life was equally, if not more, exciting seems not to have occurred to her at the time, and despite her love for Kenya she felt she would have to go to England in order to achieve her ambitions. When Tom's attempt on the Cape record failed it is not unlikely that Beryl thought of tackling it herself.

She promised Blix that she would scout for him during the 1935–36 safari season, and return to England as soon as the spring rains started. Meanwhile, she worked long and hard. Nearly all of her work in these days was scouting, though now Blix often added her to the hunting party, whilst occasionally she worked for other big-game hunters such as Percival.

Soon she became so busy with scouting and charter work that she found it necessary to buy another aeroplane. In September she took delivery of a De Havilland Leopard Moth, a three-seater aircraft, in which two passengers could be carried side by side behind the pilot. It was a high-wing mono-plane, more modern than the Avian, though with a cruising speed of 120 mph and a much higher landing speed, not as suitable for bush work where short take-off and landing ability was a major factor. Beryl used the Leopard Moth mainly for air-taxi and air-ambulance jobs.[31]

Questions have always been asked about Beryl's relationship with Blixen. Interviewed in spring 1986, a few months before her death, she made conflicting statements to questions about this speculation. On the first occasion she openly scoffed at the suggestion that she had had a love affair with Blix. 'Good God no! I knew him very well and we were good friends. I flew him everywhere... all over Africa, to England twice.' On the second occasion when the subject of Blixen was raised in another context she made the surprising statement, 'Of course I made love with him... sometimes when we were out there, there was nothing else to do but make love.' When I reminded her that two days earlier she had refuted the suggestion of a love affair with Blix she said witheringly, 'But I never did have a "love affair" with him... It was just how it was.'[32]

Cockie also believed that Beryl and Bror had some form of liaison, though by that time her own marriage to Blix had already failed. This was nothing whatever to do with Beryl. After the coffee plantation at Babarti failed, Cockie and Bror returned to Nairobi where Cockie ran a dress shop. Beryl was her only bad debt, she remembered without acrimony.[33] Bror meanwhile returned to safari work, and 'resumed his pursuit of attractive ladies'.[34]

According to Cockie, Bror was in turn pursued – a story which is worth the telling. A former film star in her native Sweden, Eva Dixon had heard so many stories about Bror, who was a distant cousin, that she decided to sell everything in order to travel to Kenya to meet him. 'For a while,' Elspeth Huxley reports, 'Blix, African-style, enjoyed the company of one wife in the bush and another in Nairobi; but when a friend invited him to stay and he accepted with the rider: "I shall bring both wives," Cockie responded with the edict: "You will take only one." He took Eva. So the marriage ended.'[35] In time, Eva became the third Baroness von Blixen.

After Cockie divorced Bror she married Jan Hoogterp, a handsome and talented young architect, but she is on record as saying that the happiest years of her life were spent with Bror and had he asked her to marry him again she would have done so without hesitation. This is interesting, for the ever-witty Cockie, with all her intelligence and sophistication, would hardly have made this remark had Bror been the coarse man his detractors describe. After her marriage to Hoogterp the couple moved to Johannesburg and it was whilst she was there that Cockie read her own obituary.

Much later, Eva was killed in a car accident at Baghdad. She was the first woman to drive across the Sahara, a feat she undertook for the reward, offered casually across a bar, of a crate of champagne. A newspaper mistakenly reported the death of Baroness Jacqueline Blixen, and when informed of the error by a highly amused Cockie, the editor apologized profusely. 'Don't mention it... I'm returning all my bills marked "Deceased",' said Cockie. When the editor insisted on printing a correction in Cockie's own words the following notice duly appeared. 'Mrs Hoogterp, the former Baroness von Blixen, wishes it to be known that she has not yet been screwed in her coffin.'[36]

Beryl and Eva Blixen became friends – indeed there was a striking physical similarity between the tall, blonde Eva and Beryl, as well as a shared instinct to go 'all out' for anything either wanted. 'Both Eva and Beryl were not afraid to take risks,' said Bror's godson and biographer Ulf Aschan. They were often seen sitting in the bar at Muthaiga Club 'like a lovely pair of Scandinavian bookends', said an appreciative club member.

The season ended with Winston Guest's[37] safari. In his second book *Letters from Africa*, Bror wrote of this safari in great detail and of Beryl's part in it. He wrote of her professional delight when her scouting led to Guest's first bag, a bull elephant with huge tusks. But for herself Beryl was never interested in killing animals for the sake of trophies. She hunted for the pot when necessary but she, like Denys Finch Hatton, preferred to hunt down animals for the camera. In one of his letters Bror told the story of the day that Guest and his wife went into Nairobi by train to collect the mail and enjoy some 'civilization' for the day. 'Beryl expressed a wish to see the elephant at close quarters, having seen so many from the air. She also wanted to get some photos of them.'

Beryl was operating the Avian from a small strip measuring 45 yards by 770 yards, but asked Bror to increase its length by another 55 yards so that she was not so dependent on wind direction. They decided to fly over the area to locate a suitable subject for Beryl's camera within reasonable walking distance of the camp:

> All we had to do was top up the oil and swing the propeller – three turns backwards, one forward – and the kind engine came to life. Five minutes' idling, a few revving tests and we were taxiing down to the north end of the strip. The sun was just coming up over the horizon when we cleared the tops of the trees against a southerly morning breeze. We rose slowly to an altitude of 1000 feet, circled the landing strip and skimmed over the bush. We followed the railway line eastwards and could watch the ice-blue dome of Kilimanjaro gradually being tinted rose by the rising sun. The air was clear after the cool night and along the riverbeds one could see veils of white mist floating along, finally fading away before the increasingly hot sunshine. We gained height by banking repeatedly, the wind played tunes in the rigging stays, the engine hummed and it was wonderful to be alive.[38]

They located a small herd, fortunately within a couple of hours' walk from the Imperial Airways landing ground at Makindu. After landing Bror hired a couple of Africans to accompany them to carry the rifles, food and water bottles, and they trekked towards the herd until they heard the sounds that they were close – occasional trumpeting, the flapping of ears and the puffing sounds as the elephants blew dust over their backs. Beryl had her Leica with a telephoto lens and they estimated that they should get to within thirty-five to forty-five yards for the best pictures. Once in position they waited for the bull to move from the thicket where the animals were feeding, across a clearing to a small clump of trees:

> He looked majestic as he approached. The big thick tusks caused his head to swing slowly up and down in rhythm with his paces. He was chewing on bayonet grass and was clearly

enjoying the sun on his back. Now he was in the clearing and the Leica clicked. He checked for a moment before continuing, and now he had got our wind. But instead of going back as I thought he would he turned straight for us with ears pricked. He evidently meant business. 'Run back all of you,' I shouted, and at the same time he charged with trunk extended and his small piggy eyes gleaming with rage. I remained by the tree, prepared to shoot if absolutely necessary. Just before he was on to me he stopped, emitted two triumphant, ear-splitting trumpet blasts, and turned round and walked back to his family, leaving behind a comical impression of satisfaction. The enemy had been frightened away and he had done his duty! Beryl was delighted. 'By jove!' she said, 'I've never been so frightened in my life . . .' [39]

By the end of February Beryl had arranged to auction the Avian in order to finance a journey to England where she hoped to persuade Tom to join her in a record attempt on the Cape, or alternatively to find a backer for some other record attempt. She had a little capital and was not going empty-handed for once. In addition there was her annuity from the palace which was paid regularly into her bank account in London. With the old king dead and Prince Henry safely married to the former Lady Alice Montagu Douglas Scott, Beryl would not incur any royal displeasure by returning to England, at least none that need concern her unduly. Before leaving she flew to Melela to visit her father. It was to be some years before she saw him again, for shortly after Beryl left Kenya, Clutterbuck moved to Durban in South Africa to train in the rarefied atmosphere of the top-class racing of the Cape. [40]

It was a particular sadness to say goodbye to *arap* Ruta, her loyal friend from childhood days. Ruta had been at Beryl's side through all the shauries of her adult life. When she had made her first successful sortie into the world of horse-training he had smoothed her path. During her marriage to Mansfield he had looked after the horses in her absence, and eased her way when she returned. When she abruptly dropped training to learn to fly he became an adept aircraft mechanic. Uncomplaining, like an efficient shadow, Ruta was always there, virtually the only unchanging fact in Beryl's life through the trauma of Finch

Hatton's death and Tom's desertion, for that was how she saw Tom's marriage to Dessie.[41]

When she left Kenya to fly the 6000 miles to England in her Leopard Moth, Beryl took Bror as her passenger. Eva had gone on ahead some weeks earlier by boat, and would meet Bror in London, prior to the Blixens' departure for the United States where, among other things, the couple were to visit Hemingway who was in the Bahamas. It was a cool, highly professional woman who piloted Bror to England. Thanks to Tom, she had been offered interviews for several flying jobs in England, but it was not her intention to migrate simply to take a mundane flying job there. A routine occupation did not appeal to Beryl, she always needed a goal. In general terms her goal was to be *the* best at whatever she set out to do. Specifically it appears that she intended to try for a record attempt on the London–Cape–London route, or on the still unpicked plum of London–New York–London. She was setting out to show Tom that she was the best pilot there was.

Beryl's trusty Avian was purchased at auction by African Air Services. Some months later it crashed, killing its student pilot, and was burned out.[42]

CHAPTER EIGHT

[*1936*]

Bror Blixen had been intending to travel to his native Sweden by boat until Beryl had asked him to fly with her. No woman was at that time allowed to fly alone over the Sudan and despite her previous record she had been refused permission. The arrangement suited them both to perfection.

Early-morning mist briefly delayed their departure from Nairobi but they were soon flying over the Kikuyu Escarpment and headed for Kisumu, the first refuelling stop on their 6000-mile journey. Beryl recounts this journey in her memoir, and Blix wrote of it in *Letters from Africa*. There are minor differences in each version – both were written some time after the event – but it was clearly an eventful trip. The Abyssinian War had begun and North Africa was controlled by Mussolini's troops, among whom there was strong anti-British feeling.

Blix emphasized the platonic nature of the travelling companions in a letter:

> At times we followed the Nile and at times we flew over the desert with its scorching sand glowing down there below us. Now in the middle of the day it was getting bumpy and extremely hot and the dust devils mounted skywards for hundreds of yards. A tiresome day and when we reached Luxor at about 5 o'clock we decided to stay the night. We filled up with petrol and oil and parked the plane in a small shed before travelling in to the town by car. It was nice to get a cool drink after this long day, followed by a bath, dinner and early to bed. We had great difficulties in making the hotel staff understand that we wanted separate rooms. Our declaration that we were not married made no impression on them, they just kept assuring us that they had a so-beautiful

double room with a view of the river, a private balcony and a bathroom. I insisted on two rooms with baths, but it was not until I added 'I snore' that I got full understanding and sympathy.[1]

After an uneventful flight to Cairo they ran into problems with officialdom. They had, in any case, decided to stop for a few days to overhaul the aeroplane but in the event were delayed for a week while their papers were examined by 'Il Duce's' beautifully-clad officers. Not knowing that the delay would be so long, the pair settled happily into Shepheard's Hotel, then one of the great hotels of the world. 'As you know spring in Cairo is warm. Beryl had lots of air-minded friends here and she spent most of her time with them.'[2] By the time clearance was given for the couple's departure 'the small aircraft shone and glittered in the sunshine'. Beryl's friends at the nearby RAF aerodrome, Heliopolis, had been hard at work.

They were delayed several times by officialdom on the next leg of their journey which lay westward along the North African coast – on one notable occasion it was suggested that Beryl was a man in woman's clothing – but eventually they reached Benghazi. Here all the hotel rooms had been commandeered by the military and in Beryl's memoir she writes graphically of the brothel in which she and Blix were forced to spend the night. Her distaste for the filthy surroundings and the meal provided for them was tempered only by sympathy for the slatternly madam's pathetic history. Blix however saw it differently: 'Finally,' he wrote, 'we found two rooms, spaghetti, good wine, and best of all a friendly reception with a kind old woman who kept a brothel.' Next morning they were faced with the dilemma of taking off in a blinding dust storm or staying another night at the brothel. Beryl opted to leave despite her qualms that the heavy gravel being blown across the airfield might damage the Leopard Moth's metal propeller.

Beryl accelerated and within twenty-five yards the strong headwinds had us airborne. We swayed over bent date palms that were twisting like human forms in agony before the raging storm, and we were carried skywards at a terrific speed. The clouds became lighter, the sun became visible and underneath us was a carpet of swirling dust. Beryl smiled and took out her compass bearing on Tripoli.[3]

At Tripoli, 'despite Beryl's blue eyes and blonde curls', they were not allowed to continue immediately and the couple were again forced to make an unscheduled overnight stop. 'We had our meals in our rooms in bad humour – spaghetti and chianti,'[4] Blix revealed.

At last they left the North African coast behind them and after an anxious flight across the Mediterranean in thick cloud they reached the French coast – Beryl says Cannes and Blix says Nice. They then travelled on to London without any further delays and found it alive with gossip of Hitler's march into the Rhineland and of the king's affair with Mrs Simpson. With the death of the old king, Beryl's friend 'Edward P' of safari days had come into his own at last, but he was to find his brief tenure of the crown an unhappy period. That first evening Bror and Beryl dined with Tom and Dessie Black.

Dessie had heard a great deal about Beryl from Tom, including the story (which Tom believed) that Beryl's son Gervase had a royal parent,[5] and she was intrigued when Tom telephoned her one afternoon, and asked her to meet him at the Mayfair so that he could introduce her to Beryl who had just flown in from Kenya. From Tom's descriptions of Beryl's horseriding ability and her skill as a pilot, Dessie half-expected to meet a masculine type of woman. Instead the tall, attractive girl, with blonde wavy hair, blue eyes and 'long, thin, nervous hands' took her by surprise.[6]

> Later, when she took me to her bedroom and I saw on the dressing-table a large assortment of face-creams, lotions and perfumes I was even more surprised. Beryl was one of the most feminine women I have ever met. As I got to know her better it was a never-ending source of wonder to me that she was able to drive a car, let alone fly a plane.

Dessie thought Beryl had a dreamy, vague personality and recalled that she was more often late for an appointment than early, and on several occasions forgot the appointment altogether.[7] In fact, of course, the 'vague dreamy' outward

appearance hid smouldering ambition. Beryl, who was now
thirty-three years old, desperately wanted to attack one of the
big flying records and she had certainly already given some
consideration to a transatlantic crossing. Tom was sympathetic
to Beryl's aspirations and even helped her by checking her out
in the twin-engine Dragon aircraft so that she could gain a twin-
engine rating, but Tom had plans of his own. Recently he had
been contacted by a group of Spaniards whom he had met
whilst in Spain with Dessie on their honeymoon. They wanted
to buy some aeroplanes, they said, and they wanted Tom to fly
one of the planes to Spain with an unnamed passenger. Money
appeared to be no object.

Tom knew that the caller was almost certainly a fascist
sympathizer, but he did not allow this to worry him. The
Spanish war was no concern of his. 'At that time,' Dessie said,
'no one knew that the war in Spain would be a dress rehearsal
for World War Two,' and even Hitler, at this stage, had caused
no great concern: most people saw him as a strong, potentially
good leader of the German people. The charter fee offered was
unusually large and Tom needed the money, so he accepted and
set the wheels in motion for his delivery trip. However his
longer-term plan to compete in the Johannesburg Race in late
September was taking time to organize – he had yet to find a
sponsor.

Beryl got a job very quickly. She had several interviews and
quickly accepted one with Air Cruisers Ltd in the position of
chief pilot. This company was owned by François Dupré, a
wealthy French financier who was a good friend of Mansfield's.[8]
He also owned the George V Hotel in Paris and the largest
racehorse stud in France. Beryl and Mansfield met occasionally,
even dined together. He wanted a divorce, he told her. Beryl
would not grant his request.[9] She also saw six-year-old Gervase
and for a while used to visit the Markhams' house to say
goodnight to her son. When Gervase would not go to sleep until
Mummy had kissed him goodnight, his nanny put a stop to it.
'One couldn't always depend on the fact that Mummy would
turn up...'

Beryl enjoyed working for Dupré; the duties were light and
generally involved being on call, for he used the aeroplane – an
eight-seater, twin-engined De Havilland Dragon – only

moderately. Several times a month Dupré needed to fly to Paris and spend a few days there. Occasionally there were internal flights, and sometimes he would fly to Deauville. The aeroplane was very expensively fitted out, and included a bar.

Her life was pleasant enough but it was getting her nowhere towards achieving her ambitions. Tom had introduced her to a wide circle of aviation friends among whom were the Mollisons, and she had her own friends on the fringe of court though she was never invited to the Fort as far as she recalled.[10] She was living at this time in a rented flat in Belgravia and was frequently seen about town throughout May, June and July. Later her landlady was to sue for non-payment of rent,[11] and this was not Beryl's only brush with the law. Bow Street magistrates fined her two pounds for 'causing an obstruction with a motor-car in New Bond Street on June 4th. The car was left unattended for two and a half hours whilst Mrs Markham was at a beauty specialist.'[12] At Woolwich she was fined 'twenty shillings for exceeding the 30 mph speed limit at Rochester Way, Eltham. The Magistrate also ordered her licence to be endorsed. A policeman said in evidence that on July 4th he timed Mrs Markham's car for half a mile. Her speed was 50–55 mph. When stopped she said, "I did not know there was a speed limit. I have never been here before."' A slight, and rather feminine exaggeration.[13]

She considered entering the Cape Race, and one evening dined with her old friends from Kenya, the Carberrys. John Carberry was at the time having his own mount for the race built by Edgar Percival at Percival's Gravesend factory. Beryl hoped that wealthy John Carberry would sponsor an aeroplane for her in the race to Johannesburg. As it turned out his help was directed in an entirely different direction.

John Carberry was an Irish peer, and a pilot of no mean distinction. Born in 1892, he had succeeded to the title Baron Carbery at the age of six, and was educated at Harrow and later at Leipzig.[14] He learned to fly in 1912 (the first man in Ireland to fly) and represented England in the 1914 Schneider Trophy race. He married his first wife shortly before the outbreak of World War One in which he served as a sub-lieutenant in the Royal Naval Air Service. After visiting America in 1918 he was bewitched by the country to the extent that in 1919 he became a naturalized American. However there is a story that his naturalization papers were subsequently withdrawn when he ran foul of the law on bootlegging charges.[15] In 1920 he bought an estate in Kenya called Seremai (meaning the place of death – it was built on an old tribal battleground), renounced his title and took the name John Evans Carberry.[16] His accent became distinctly American. He was among the earliest aviators in the new colony and in 1924 he flew a DH 51 (forerunner of the Gipsy Moth) to Kenya from England. His second wife Maia was one of a handful of early women pilots in Kenya in the mid 1920s, and was killed in a flying accident at Wilson airfield in 1928.[17] Beryl claimed she was watching Maia fly when the accident occurred.

With his wealth, the advantages of birth, education and his undoubted flying ability Carberry should have been a popular figure. Indeed certain women did find the thin, erect, square-shouldered and loose-limbed man fascinating. But it was a deadly fascination, for he was an unpleasant character with a cruel, sadistic streak, particularly towards animals. During nearly a hundred interviews conducted for this book not one person could find a good word to say for him. He was thoroughly disliked, probably with good reason, and Beryl at eighty-three still hated him. But in 1936 she was glad of his help and influence. For many years she had taken advantage of the fact that he kept a full-time aircraft engineer based at the airstrip on Seremai and often had her aeroplanes serviced there, borrowing Carberry's detested Klemm to enable her to continue her work. Carberry's third wife, June, became a hard drinker. During interviews Beryl thought that anyone married to him would need to drink if only in self-defence.[18]

At the dinner party in London Carberry made a surprising suggestion. The talk had been about various record attempts and Beryl allowed her enthusiasm to show. Carberry said that if Beryl would attempt to fly non-stop from England to New York, a flight which no one had yet successfully completed solo, he would lend her the aeroplane presently under construction for his own entry in the Cape race. He stipulated that it would have to be back in England in time for him to compete in the race in late September, and that he would only lend her the aircraft if she attempted that specific record. In her biography Beryl claimed that the suggestion that she should cross the Atlantic came from Carberry as a dare. But her contemporary press interviews make it clear that she had been mulling over the idea for a considerable time before the dinner party. All she had needed was the machine and finance.

Jim Mollison had flown the Atlantic from east to west solo in 1932 from Portmarnock in Ireland, but had not achieved his goal – non-stop to New York. Mollison's aeroplane, named *The Heart's Content* after one of a small group of villages in Newfoundland lying near his flight track, was a De Havilland Puss Moth. His flight, which was described as 'the greatest flying achievement ever', received maximum press coverage and brought him worldwide recognition. He was not the first to fly the Atlantic, of course, but the east–west route was particularly difficult because of the prevailing winds, which were smack on the nose of any prospective flyer. Mollison failed in his bid to reach New York when, after more than thirty-one hours in the air, he took advantage of a temporary break in the thick fog which had enveloped him since he first sighted land, and touched down at Pennington Ridge in New Brunswick, Canada.[19] He later carried on to New York, but despite another attempt with his wife Amy Johnson in the following year, the goal of 'non-stop to New York' floated tantalizingly out of his grasp.

Another attempt on the solo east–west crossing had been made successfully by a young Englishman, John Grierson, but his flight was not non-stop. Grierson never intended to fly non-stop. His original plan was to fly round the world in a series of hops, one of which was across the Atlantic stopping at the Orkneys, the Faroes, Iceland and Greenland. To do this he equipped his Gipsy Moth *Rouge et Noir* (aptly named because one side was painted red and the other black) with floats. No record-breaking was attempted, and the enterprise foundered when the little moth turned turtle in a heavy swell whilst taxiing at Reykjavik. Not disheartened, Grierson made a second and successful crossing in a De Havilland Fox Moth in 1934, again via Reykjavik, where he damaged a float and one wing and had to wait for spares to be dispatched to him. His crossing, which took six weeks, may well have set a record for being the longest east–west Atlantic flight ever made.[20]

In 1936 when Carberry made his offer, no one had made a successful solo non-stop crossing from England to America (the specific target was New York), and no woman had crossed the Atlantic from east to west in a solo flight. Amelia Earhart was indeed the only woman to have flown the Atlantic solo at that time and she had done it 'the easy way', landing in Ireland after a relatively short flight of just over fifteen hours. Several women had perished in the attempt.[21]

Beryl needed no time to consider the offer and accepted on the spot. The Vega Gull under construction for Carberry was expected to be ready by early August and Beryl agreed to undertake the flight in the second half of that month. The remainder of the evening was spent discussing who Beryl could get to sponsor the expenses of the flight.

Throughout the summer Beryl made almost daily flights to Gravesend to see the aircraft taking shape. At the end of July she gave up her job with Dupré 'with great reluctance'. Dupré too was sorry to lose her. 'She was an excellent pilot,' he was later reported to have said, 'about the best I have ever employed.' An impressive compliment, for Beryl's successor was Amy Johnson.

Beryl had hoped to take delivery of the Vega Gull, which had already been christened *The Messenger*, in late July or early August (all aeroplanes involved in record-breaking flights were given names – it helped the image). But it was delivered late. During test flights several minor faults needed correction, and Beryl was in a fever of anticipation by the time she finally got her hands on the controls on 15 August for a ten-minute flight. More minor adjustments were needed: the Vega Gull was a brand-new type of aeroplane. It became clear that she could not hope to attempt the flight before early September, but this would still leave time to get *The Messenger* back to allow Carberry to compete in the Johannesburg Race.[22]

Designed as a four-seat cruiser, the standard model Vega Gull was fitted with a 200-hp De Havilland Gipsy Six engine enabling cruising speeds of up to 163 mph. *The Messenger* had a standard airframe and a standard engine fitted with one of the newly introduced French Ratier, variable-pitch propellers. There were two fuel tanks in the wings, two in the centre section and two more in the cabin, giving a total capacity of 255 gallons and extending the range to an estimated 3800 miles.[23]

No radio was fitted but there were some blind-flying instruments, though in the light of today's sophisticated satellite navigation the instrumentation was very basic: a Reid & Sigrist turn and slip indicator, a Sperry gyro 'direction-finding' compass and an artificial horizon; finally an instrument which measured the rate of climb called, somewhat nautically, a 'fore and aft reader'. There were in addition some Smith's instruments to give engine information, and one fuel gauge which gave a reading on the standard tank only. The auxiliary tanks had no gauges. As each tank became empty it was necessary to switch that tank off with a stop cock, and switch the next on. Percival gave Beryl a schedule of the order in which she should use up the fuel so as not to upset the balance of the aeroplane, and warned her that she must take care to switch the stopcock off, before turning on the next one, or an airlock would be created.

While the Vega Gull returned to the factory for adjustments Beryl was not idle. Tom had organized a gruelling training routine for her. There was to be no drinking, no smoking. He had already arranged a programme for himself at Heatherdon Country Club near Elstree where Len Harvey was in training for his fight with the American boxer John Henry Lewis. Tom worked with Harvey daily in the gymnasium and did long cross-country runs wearing thick white sweaters. Beryl, staying with Lord Aldenham (a friend she had met through Dupré) at his Elstree home, Aldenham House, joined them in the daily workouts of skipping, running, swimming and horseback riding.

She spent hours poring over maps with Tom and Jim Mollison, studying the routes and plans of the successful crossings – and the unsuccessful. Jim Mollison, whom she liked but whom Tom despised, was particularly helpful. His own strategy for crossing the Atlantic had paid off handsomely. In fact he had made the ocean crossing in only nineteen hours and it was only after he sighted land that he ran into trouble. Beryl listened carefully. To simplify navigation, Mollison had flown the whole way to Newfoundland on a constant magnetic track, which – with the changing magnetic variation across the ocean – conveniently took him along a line situated between the great-circle track (the shortest route) and the rhumb line, or track of constant true bearing. He had allowed for drift by estimating the direction and strength of the wind by observing the drift of the long Atlantic waves, and movement of the cloud shadows. For the first four or five hours, flying at only fifty feet or so, he kept *Heart's Content* heading three or four degrees to starboard to counteract the effect of light northerly winds.[24]

Mollison was lucky; with good visibility for the first hours he had been able to check his position with several liners which were marked on his shipping chart. When darkness fell he had judged it wise to climb to 2000 feet, where he remained until he sighted the coast. Although it was cloudy, he had been able to get helpful glimpses of the moon and stars. Beryl's experience in night flying – she had flown over East Africa whenever the call came, day or night – enabled her to fly according to the same plan. She knew that if she could cope with effects of fatigue, and if the engine did not fail her, there was absolutely no reason why she couldn't make it.

In late July Tom received the awaited phone call from his Spanish contact. The supposedly secret trip to Spain, in which he flew the fascist rebel leader Marques Rivas de Linares to Franco's headquarters at Burgos, quickly received unwelcome publicity. Tom and his passenger were recognized at one of the airfields on the flight down through France, and the story ran ahead of him. Warned that his life was in danger, he escaped from the war-ravaged country by car. He suffered many delays, but was cool enough to test his theory that the guards at the numerous road blocks could not read, by presenting papers to them upside-down. Afterwards he returned to England where he wrote his story for the *News of the World*[25] and promised Dessie that he would lead a quiet life for a while. Now he had his sights fixed firmly on the race to Johannesburg and at last he had found a sponsor. He was to fly a Percival Mew Gull owned by Liverpool football pools millionaire John Moores.[26]

Did Beryl have any conception of the amount of interest that her flight would arouse? Possibly not. She said later that she 'simply intended to slip away', but somehow the newspapers got wind of it. On 18 August an article accompanied by an impressive number of pictures appeared in the *Daily Express* under the banner headline

SOCIETY WOMAN PLANS TO FLY THE ATLANTIC
ALONE:

> Non-Stop in a light 'Plane.
> Mrs Beryl Markham, thirty-one [actually she was thirty-three] year old English woman pilot, sister-in-law to Sir
> Charles Markham, colliery baronet, is to attempt a non-stop
> flight from London to New York alone. She will leave
> London in a British light airplane in about a fortnight's
> time... With more than 2000 hours of flying to her credit...
> tall, blonde, athletic Mrs Markham is no erratic chance flier.
> 'Flying is my job. This flight is part of it,' she said. 'It is no
> romantic adventure, but a hard job of work which I want to
> justify. I believe in the future of an Atlantic air service. I want
> to be in on it at the beginning. I have worked hard and
> studied hard for this flight. It is a difficult flight I know – I just
> don't like the look of the map. The blue seems too vast
> between the friendly pieces of land. But I feel I can knock a
> few hours off the record and prove something for British
> airplanes and pilots. I had the Atlantic flight in mind for some
> time, then the chance to undertake it was given to me by a
> Kenya syndicate interested in aviation. They are backing me
> right through.

On the following day more headlines – ATLANTIC HAS
NO TERRORS FOR FLYING WOMAN. A photograph of
her running away from the camera is captioned: 'To fly the
Atlantic, but she flies from the camera.' In fact, on Tom's
advice, she wrote a piece for the *Daily Express* for which she
received a small payment.

> Two weeks from now I am going to set out to fly the Atlantic
> to New York. Not as a society girl. Not as a woman even. And
> certainly not as a stunt aviator. But as a pilot-graduate of one
> of the hardest schools of flying known, with 2000 flying hours
> to my credit. And I have a definite object. It is true that I am
> known as a society woman. But what of it? The only thing
> that really counts... is whether one can fly. I have both [A
> and B] tickets. I can take an engine apart and put it back. I
> can navigate. I am fit, and given ordinary luck I am sure I can
> fly to New York. This is to be no stunt flight. No woman's-
> superiority-over-man affair. I don't want to be superior to

men. I have a son. If I can be a good mother to him, and a good pilot, I'll be the happiest creature alive.[27]

By 1 September Beryl was ready to go. *The Messenger* had finished its tests and had been passed by its exacting designer Edgar Percival. Beryl flew the turquoise and silver aeroplane to Royal Air Force Abingdon. 'I'm absolutely satisfied,' she said. 'The machine is grand. If she doesn't get me over nothing will.' Originally she had planned to fly from Gravesend, but after consultation with Percival she sought and received permission from the Royal Air Force to use the long military runway at Abingdon, which was essential to get that enormous load of petrol off the ground. She had made a test run with only half a load of fuel, and the take-off run was far longer than Percival expected. The Air Ministry was opposed to the flight on principle, warning that it was already too late in the year to forecast a settled period of weather over the Atlantic. Indeed it looked as though their gloomy prognostications were to be proved correct, for from 28 August there was low cloud and scudding rain every day. If she had been able to get away only a week earlier she would have had that rarest occurrence, a favourable easterly wind over most of her route; but on 28 August the weather had deteriorated.

So Beryl waited, day after long day. All the preparations were made. With the exception of fuelling the aircraft, which Tom said should wait until the last moment, there was literally nothing to do except to wait for a good weather forecast. The delay was particularly annoying because she had originally planned her departure to coincide with a full moon which she hoped would light her way over the ocean. The press dogged her every move, and each morning brought a fresh spate of headlines. They were much of a muchness: 'Young Mother Plans Flight Today'; 'Daredevil Society Woman Leaves Today'; 'Beauty to Fly Today'. These descriptions at first amused and later infuriated Beryl. She began to feel that they were presenting a frivolous image of her. Every day she waited for a call from the ministry with the weather report, and tried to hide from the press and the endless questions. 'When do you expect to leave?' 'What does your husband think of the flight?'

'What does your little boy think of the flight?' Really, it was too bad! She tried to pass the time by working out at her gymnastic exercises, and she rode Lord Aldenham's thoroughbred horses around his estate.

There were several telephone calls from New York: one from John Carberry, ghoulishly checking that she had not 'chickened out'; and one from Harry Bruno, a New York public relations man who worked for the firm of 'Personal Managers' whom Beryl had taken on at the suggestion of Mollison. If she was successful in her attempt, Jim cautioned, there'd be money to be made out of it – if everything were handled properly. The opportunity to capitalize on public acclaim would soon vanish, Mollison warned, but Harry Bruno would arrange appearances on radio, lecture tours, official welcomes, and if such a thing were possible, would control the press. Beryl, who never seemed to care whether she had any money or not, but simply spent the same amount whatever her situation, agreed wholeheartedly. Money was not a prime objective but if there was money to be made out of it, well and good.[28]

On 2 September after another long day of waiting Beryl dined with a few friends at the Mayfair. It was a small dinner party: Rose Cartwright, Sir Philip Sassoon, Tom, Beryl and Freddie Guest. 'What I chiefly remember is that Beryl was totally unafraid,' said Rose Cartwright. Rose had known Beryl since she was Mrs Beryl Purves. 'She was always fearless. I've only ever known two people like it in my life. Beryl was one of them. Some people are scared and they hide their fear, but Beryl never knew fear. Not when she rode the liveliest horse and not when she flew the Atlantic. She simply had no fear of anything. The night before her flight when we dined with her ... we were all frightened for her, but she acted as though nothing special was happening. Almost as if she wasn't going. I remember one of the men teased her about her nose job. She'd recently had a small operation to straighten out the bump resulting from an accident some years earlier. She wasn't amused. That was the most response we got out of her.'[29]

On the 3rd there was fog over most of the country but the forecasts were that there might be a break on the way. The *News Chronicle* ran an editorial under the heading 'Atlantic Flights'.

An early picture taken shortly after Beryl learned to fly in 1931. *(North Point Press)*

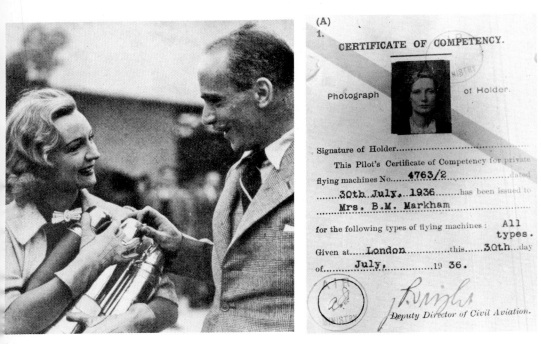

Tom Campbell Black with Florence Desmond.

Page from Beryl's pilot's licence — updated in 1936 to include 'all types'.

Beryl's log book recording her first solo in June 1931 in a Gipsy Moth.

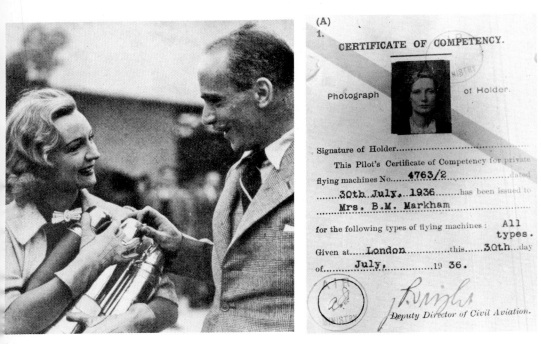

Beryl's Vega Gull 'The Messenger' outside the Percival Aircraft factory's hangar at Gravesend, Kent, August, 1936. *(B.M.E.)*

Beryl riding at Aldenham House a few days before her flight. She said it helped her to relax. *(Photosource)*

Jim Mollison flew Beryl to Abingdon prior to her trans-Atlantic flight. *(British Library)*

THE GREAT ADVENTURE

" I was the last to wave good-bye to Mrs. Markham," writes Henry How, "Daily Mirror" photographer, who in a 'plane escorted her for the first few miles and took this farewell picture. "As our 'plane drew close to hers, we could see her studying maps. Our machines drew closer. I waved my hand, wishing her God-speed. She waved back—and headed for the Atlantic at 130 m.p.h."

Captioned 'The Great Adventure', this *Daily Mirror* front page photo showed The Messenger over Abingdon shortly after take-off. *(British Library)*

Arrival in Nova Scotia: The Messenger embedded in a Balleine Cove peat bog. *(B.M.E.)*

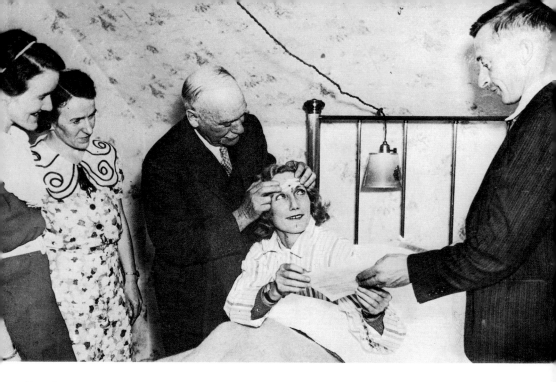

Beryl's own caption reads: 'At Louisburg, Nova Scotia a few hours after I landed.' (*B.M.E.*)

Beryl's triumphant wave on reaching New York. (*B.M.E.*)

Beryl co-piloted the Beechcraft 'Staggerwing' from Halifax to Lloyd Bennet Airport, New York. (*B.M.E.*)

Beryl surrounded by well-wishers at Halifax *(B.M.E.)*

Beryl's own caption: 'Interview with the Mayor in New York.' Fiorello La Guardia offers a civic greeting. *(B.M.E.)*

Beryl waves from the deck of The Queen Mary as she returns to England, September 1936. *(Photosource)*

The damaged 'Messenger' being unloaded from the S.S. Coldharbour at London Docks. *(B.M.E.)*

Beryl's own caption: '. . . at the Commander's Table on the Queen Mary (Comm. Sir Edgar Britain)'. *(B.M.E.)*

Beryl waving from motorcade en-route from Waterloo Station to Savoy Hotel reception. *(B.M.E.)*

Beryl wearing her famous white flying suit, shortly before her trans-Atlantic flight. *(Bettman)*

With Edgar Percival the designer and builder of 'The Messenger'. *(Photosource)*

> Mrs Beryl Markham did not take off yesterday for her
> proposed solo flight across the Atlantic to New York. We
> hope that she will never take off. The time for these 'pioneer'
> solo flights in overloaded radio-less machines has passed. The
> only Transatlantic flights which serve any purpose now are
> those which lay the foundations for a regular mail service. If
> Mrs Markham were to reach New York she would not have
> demonstrated anything worth risking her life for. If she came
> down in the ocean she would cause prolonged suspense to all
> her friends and considerable inconvenience and expense to all
> the ships that would have to search for her. We hope that Mrs
> Markham will think better of it.

Beryl dismissed the article with a wave of her hand and a sniff.
That evening there was yet another party. This time, she
forecast, it was a farewell party. Tom had gone north on
business. Present were Mollison, Percival and Beryl's mechanic
Jock Cameron. 'Before dinner Mollison asked her if she had a
good watch or a mascot. "No," she replied. "Then," said
Mollison unstrapping his own watch, "take mine. It's been
across with me twice. It won't fail you. But mind you it's only a
loan... I want it back!"'[30]

This is the story Beryl and Mollison gave to the press. But
there was a more practical reason. Beryl did have a watch of her
own, but Mollison recommended that she wear two watches.
Her own set to Greenwich Mean Time (London), and
Mollison's recording Eastern Standard Time (New York). She
would be very tired at the end of her flight, he knew. He told her
that to avoid confusion she should make all her calculations in
GMT, and his watch could be used merely as a check on local
time.

The forecast on the morning of the 4th was not promising.
The ministry said there was a possibility of a break in the late
afternoon but it was only a possibility. Before the break – if it
came – there was thundery rain and low cloud. Behind it, and
they did not know how far behind, was a gale. By now Beryl was
thoroughly fed up with waiting. She telephoned Jim Mollison
and arranged for him to fly her to Abingdon, telling him she was
'going this afternoon come what may'. In an interview to the
Daily Express, which they published as a lead story, she

explained why she had not been able to get away as scheduled, what supplies she planned to take, details of food and drink, the amount of fuel. And she finished with:

> People ask me my feelings about this ocean flight. I have become dreadfully fidgety. It is natural. I am still young and while I am supremely confident I am not particularly anxious to die. But if I get across . . . it will have been worth it because I believe in the future of an Atlantic air service. I planned this flight because I wanted to be in that air service at the beginning. If I get across I think I shall have earned my place. Don't you?[31]

Just before five o'clock in the afternoon BST (British Summer Time) Beryl arrived at Abingdon with Jim Mollison. She was dressed warmly and comfortably in grey flannel slacks, blue blouse and jumper, a warmly lined Burberry raincoat and helmet. The first news that greeted them was that they would have to wait. A bomber had overturned on the take-off runway and was being cleared. 'It was the first thing I heard when I arrived,' she complained whilst chain smoking. 'I'm glad I didn't see it, it might have made me feel even more queer inside than I do now. The wind's to blame apparently. Trouble is it's the same wind that I'm taking off into . . . I wish the fire engine and ambulances didn't have to be so obvious.' The press reported that she appeared pale, her face set, her lips drawn. Her friends say she was as casual as usual.[32]

There were puddles lying all over the aerodrome. The latest forecast was telephoned through. Head winds of forty to fifty miles per hour; low cloud over the water, squalls for the next fourteen hours. Both Percival and Mollison tried to dissuade her. But Beryl was now determined to go. 'Neck or nothing,' she said. It was an old hunting phrase, eagerly snapped up by the reporters and used abundantly in the next editions. *The Messenger* was pushed out of the hangar and refuelled.[33]

Tom was not at the airport to see her off. He had gone to Liverpool to see John Moores about his participation in the race to Johannesburg which was coming ever closer. Possibly because of the adverse weather forecasts he assumed Beryl would not make the attempt, and that he would have returned before she took off.

This must have been a blow to Beryl. Despite her assertions that she was attempting the hazardous flight to stake her place in the prophesied transatlantic air service, the truth was that in her mind she hoped that somehow success would win back Tom. 'She worshipped him,' her great friend in later years, Buster Parnell, told me. 'I think she only flew the Atlantic to get back at him after he'd dumped her for Florence Desmond. In a way I think she hoped she'd be killed – just to spite him.'[34] If Parnell's assessment is correct, her great exit scene was missing the principal member of the audience.

The only friends to see her depart were Percival and a number of the Percival works engineers. Jock Cameron gave her a sprig of heather. She refused a lifejacket – she would sacrifice security for warmth, she said. Mollison made a play of being concerned about his watch. 'Don't get it wet,' he said. Beryl asked for the *Daily Express* reporter – he stepped forward and she handed him a letter addressed to his editor. Her basket of food was stowed away – they could hardly find room for it, so confined was the cabin with the huge additional eighty-gallon fuel tank occupying most of the cabin space. She took with her a packet of chicken sandwiches, a 'chewing' mixture of nuts, raisins and dried bananas, five flasks of tea and coffee, a hip flask of brandy and a bottle of water. Now, after some last-minute discussions with Percival, she hopped up on to *The Messenger*'s wing and turned to Mollison. 'Goodbye. Good luck,' she called to him. She grinned shyly – her appealing boyish grin. 'Luck, Beryl,' he replied. 'You deserve the best.'[35]

The runway was a mile long. It was expected that *The Messenger*, with its 1900-pound load of petrol, would take nearly all of that to unstick. Percival himself swung the propeller as Beryl called out, 'Switches on... Contact.' The engine, impeccably tuned, fired first time and roared into life. Immediately, for she did not want to waste a single drop of fuel, she taxied away across the aerodrome in the weak rays of the sun, which appeared through a watery slit in the clouds. The little group of friends, the journalists and the Abingdon workers stood and watched tensely as she sat at the end of the runway performing her flight checks. Then her hand appeared through the sliding side window of the cockpit and waved cheerily.[36] She was off on her great adventure.

One of the biggest hazards faced her right at the start of the flight. Would the aeroplane take off with the enormous load of fuel, within the runway length? Percival and Mollison had previously paced out the runway with Beryl, and placed markers at hundred-yard intervals, with a red flag at the point of no return. One mistake now in the little aeroplane, which was no more than a flying petrol tank, and nothing could have saved her. In the event *The Messenger* needed only 600 yards of the runway. After the tail lifted, the onlookers noted that Beryl coolly held the aeroplane down to gather plenty of speed and was in no hurry to haul it off. Professionalism had taken over from the nervous tension that had overshadowed her through the terrible period of waiting, which all the record-breakers described as 'the worst part of it'.

'She just rushed off,' said Squadron Leader St John who had travelled up from Gravesend with the Percival crew. 'All the pilots at Gravesend have a very great admiration for her. We are all anxious because she is flying a machine with which she really has had too little time to become accustomed. She had only two short flights in it before setting off.'[37]

The following morning the *Daily Express* published on the front page, the letter she had handed to the reporter before her departure.

Sir,

As I am now on the eve of what I believe to be a rather hazardous flight I would ask the usual courtesy extended to the condemned to state some of my views. I notice that I have been frequently captioned in the Press as 'Society Mother,' 'Flying Mother,' 'Bird Woman,' etc.

The phrase 'Society' is repugnant to me. I have no pretensions, and fail to see what bearing an accident of birth has to do with flying the ocean.

I may be 'just another blonde'; but as a professional pilot accustomed to working for my living, and as this flight could not even in my wildest dreams be described as pleasure, I look on it as another job of work. When I am asked my reasons for going I give varying explanations every time. As adequate a reason as any other is that, whatever the result of my efforts, I shall not have laboured in vain as it will give a very real friend

- no other than the bold, bad Jim Mollison - an excellent excuse for a celebration, or the reverse.

In describing my, as yet unaccomplished, but no doubt amazing exploit, please give me the credit of being an ordinary human being without too many of the conventional virtues. I can laugh, love, hate, and occasionally fall in at the off-licence to hear the views of my fellow-beings. I am neither an innocent girl from the country, nor a city slicker, but an ocean flyer, in embryo. If I can dispense with the last two words I am more than satisfied.

I am etc.

Beryl Markham[38]

Tom must have heard the news even before he returned from his trip to the north. When he returned home he told Dessie he'd heard from Percival that 'Beryl had simply gone. Apparently, nothing anyone said could dissuade her.' Jim Mollison had said to Percival with grim flippancy, 'Well. That's the last we'll see of Beryl.' All they could do now was wait.[39]

CHAPTER NINE

[*1936*]

It was a long wait for those left behind. There were headlines in the newspapers on the following morning, reporting Beryl's departure. The stop-press columns carried the news that the aeroplane had been seen off Castletown, Berehaven, County Cork at 10.25 BST. Other than that there was nothing. They could expect nothing. And the day wore slowly on.

The Markham family, literally under siege from the press, rapidly decamped to the country. Speaking on the telephone from his Hurst Green home in Sussex, Mansfield made a statement that he was 'very anxious. I wish my wife all the luck in the world. Our seven-year old son is with me. I think he is too young to realize what his mother is doing.' Later he was to add that he had not been able to sleep and had spent the night pacing the floor.[1]

Just after two o'clock that afternoon a radio message was flashed across the Atlantic. The Radio Corporation of America intercepted the following message from the steamship *Spaarndam* (at 7 a.m. New York Time – 2 p.m. BST), a Holland–America Line freighter headed towards New York from Rotterdam: 'AIRPLANE, PROBABLY MRS MARKHAM'S, PASSED THE SS SPAARNDAM AT 7 A.M. EST., POSITION 47:54 N., 48:22 W., HEADING FOR NEWFOUNDLAND.' This still left her 1500 miles from New York but within a few flying hours of the American coast.[2]

A further sighting by the SS *Kungsholm* confirmed her position and reported that she was heading towards the coast.

At 9.35 a.m. EST (19 hours and 40 minutes after take-off) *The Messenger*, 'flying high', was spotted off Newfoundland, where 'it circled the bay, very likely to fix a position and then headed off to Cape Race, twenty-five miles to the south-west.' Ten minutes later she was seen by the inhabitants of Cape Race, and shortly afterwards above Drook Point in rain and low cloud.[3] Then silence. No word. No sightings. No news.

At Floyd Bennett field where a crowd of 2000 had already gathered to greet Beryl on her expected arrival late that evening, there was an excited flurry of rumours. She had been sighted. She was only five hours away. She'd gone down in the sea off Newfoundland.

And then, over twenty-two hours after Beryl took off from Abingdon, the news came through on the telephone from the tiny community of Baleine Cove, on the eastern tip of Cape Breton, Nova Scotia, that she had crash-landed but was safe. Like Mollison, Beryl had failed to achieve her ultimate goal, but she had safely crossed the Atlantic Ocean from east to west, the first woman to do so. She was also the first person to make a solo non-stop crossing in that direction, from England to America. And she was safe, though tired and suffering lacerations to her forehead.

Now every newspaper in the world wanted Beryl. News of Beryl. Stories of Beryl. Two fishermen had found her struggling through a bog where she had landed the aeroplane, blood streaming from a cut in her forehead. 'I'm Mrs Markham,' she told them. 'I've just flown from England.' They took her to the nearby farmhouse of Mr Alex Burke where she requested a cup of tea and the use of the telephone. Within minutes she was speaking to a startled Edith McGuinness, the telephone operator at the Louisburg exchange. 'I am Mrs Markham. I have just crash-landed my aeroplane. I would like the airport notified and could you also ask someone to send a taxi for me?' She was swiftly whisked to Louisburg where a Dr O'Neil stitched and dressed the cut in her forehead and ordered her to bed. The same doctor had treated Jim Mollison when he had landed near Sydney (Cape Breton Island) in August 1932.[4]

Before she slept, she telephoned Mansfield, Jim Mollison and Harry Bruno, at the expense of an opportunist local reporter, who then contacted his editor with a story which was syndicated around the world. Another speck of human interest emerged, for until then it had not been realized that Beryl and Mansfield were separated. 'Her Broken Romance is not Mended' was a typical headline.[5]

Alert to the potential of his client's publicity value, Bruno said he'd call her back, and did so with a stenographer at his elbow. Hardly a major newspaper in Europe and America failed to carry news of Beryl's success on its front page on 6 and 7 September. Her own version, written for (and paid for) by the *Daily Express*, was cabled to them by Bruno:

> It was a great adventure. But I'm so glad it's over. I really had a terrible time. That's the only word for it – terrible. I knew I was in for it half an hour after I left. I pulled out my chart of the Atlantic and a gust of wind blew it out of my hand. I saw it floating away down to earth. There was nothing on that chart but water... When I saw that chart whisk away I sat back and waited for trouble. It came in plenty. I had rather a bad time after that. There was a 30 mile head wind, a helluva lot of low cloud and driving rain. I almost wanted to turn back, but of course I couldn't do that.
>
> I got my first fright at Abingdon when I saw the trees at the far end of the airfield. I never thought I'd get over them with my heavy load. Then the weather simply went to pot when I got over the sea somewhere near Bristol. It blew great guns, worse and worse. It got darker and darker and darker. It meant blind flying and that went on nearly the whole way.
>
> Once I got over the Atlantic I could see nothing but water, and not much of that. Then an electrical storm popped up to make it all gay and happy. But you know I really welcomed that storm; it was a relief to see something besides cloud and water. The clouds were lying about in lumps, absolutely in lumps, and poor old *Messenger* was so sluggishly heavy. I was flying at about 2000 feet. I wanted to fly lower so that I could keep an eye on the water but bucking winds made that too dangerous. I passed out of the storm, but only into more dirty weather. I've found since I got here that you've all been reading about my having bright moonlight for the first part of my journey. That makes me laugh. I saw the moon only twice and he was a pretty sorry sight. Once, poor old *Messenger* took a terrific toss. I didn't know quite what was happening but she seemed to be behaving in an extraordinary manner. Next time the lightning flashed I took a look out of the window. I was flying upside down. That was a nasty shock... I got so fed

up seeing the sea that I said to myself, aloud: 'If you don't see something besides water you'll go crazy.' I thought about all sorts of things – lots of things about home and Africa, my little boy Gervase and my father in Durban. To help pass the time I made entries in my log book and calculated my position. *The Messenger* should do about 158 mph cruising speed in still air but I reckoned I was doing about 90. Those nasty old head winds were to blame for that . . . I couldn't eat . . . except some coffee and some nuts . . . I got so weary of battling against the icy gale all the way over that I was just about ready to give up whenever I let myself think about it. I never completely lost my bearings, but it seemed so impossible to go on, driving the ship against all the odds, knowing that all the time I was using up far more petrol than I ought. I know I got into a spin more than once. I just went on – on – on hoping for the best but not expecting it, bumping and rocking all over the place.

At a particularly low ebb before dawn, tired, cramped and cold, she reached for her final flask of coffee. A sudden violent lurch tipped the opened flask, spilling the entire contents. She said later that it was the worst moment of her flight and she had been close to tears. Many of the long-distance pilots of the 1930s agreed that the worst part of the flight was the sheer loneliness.[6]

Then dawn broke through the clouds. The wind changed and I stopped being so silly. I wouldn't have imagined that there was an expanse of desolation so big in the whole world as the waste of sky and water I saw go past me from the time I left Abingdon . . . It was fog, rain, sleet for hours on end. If I climbed it was sleet, if I dropped it was rain. If I skimmed the sea it was fog. I couldn't see anything beyond my wingtips.

She had a moment of near disaster when one of her fuel tanks ran dry and the aeroplane dropped to below 300 feet before the new fuel supply reached the engine. The final fuel tank read 'This tank is good for eleven hours.' It was the only one with a fuel gauge. Bitterly she watched the level getting lower and lower. A further moment of anxiety occurred when her engine cut for no apparent reason. This time it was ice in the fuel line – though she did not know that at the time, only heart-stopping fear as she brought the plane in a long shallow glide for a water

landing. As she lost height the ice dissolved and the engine
started up again.

Her hands had been gripping the control column so hard that
they were numb with cramp, but she began to relax again as she
watched the few instruments and saw that everything seemed to
be working well again: oil pressure 42 pounds, RPM 2000;
airspeed 146 mph. Only extreme tiredness and her fuel supply
were now causing concern.

> That tank, on which I was banking my all, didn't last eleven
> hours. It lasted nine hours and five minutes. That's why I
> came down in the swamp. I watched that tank getting
> emptier and emptier and still saw nothing but sea and clouds
> and mist.
>
> When I could bring myself to do it I had a good look at my
> watch. I judged I ought to be somewhere near Newfoundland
> by then. Then I had a good look at my petrol gauge and my
> spine froze. I was nearly out of fuel and I ought to have had
> enough for hours yet.
>
> I thought for a while. And then I reached for my flask of
> brandy. I don't drink much of that as a rule – only for
> medicine. But I took two long swigs of that flask . . . I could see
> nothing could save me. Good old *Messenger* was going to stop
> any moment and I said to myself, 'If I'm going to go, now is
> the time to get ready for it.' The only thing anywhere around
> was fog, great hefty banks of it. And then I saw the coast. The
> beautiful coast. I've never seen land so beautiful. I kept going,
> I wanted to make Sydney Airport, come down, get petrol and
> go on to Halifax. I felt better when I saw land and thought
> perhaps the notice 'This is safe for eleven hours' was right
> after all. But the engine began to go 'put, put, put'.
>
> I knew then that I'd have to come down as soon as possible.
> I watched out for Harbour Grace, the first airfield on my
> route, but could I see it?
>
> I saw that I had to come down and made for the beach. I
> couldn't land there; there was nothing but great big rocks and
> *Messenger* and I would have been dashed to pieces. I went
> inland.
>
> My engine was missing badly now. It was sheer agony to
> watch my petrol gauge . . . I peered around for a field to land
> on. I was still peering when the engine stopped.

Bringing *The Messenger* into the only field that looked suitable, Beryl executed a perfect forced landing. The plane landed into wind, the speed just right. Unfortunately the 'field' was a boulder strewn bog, its green surface covered not in grass but moss. *The Messenger* ran for 40 feet before her weight caused the left wheel and wing to plough into the water-laden peat and the aeroplane tipped up on her nose. Beryl crashed against the windshield and lost consciousness.

I suppose I crawled out somehow. Well, you know the rest. It's been a great adventure. Now it's all over perhaps I'll try it again one day – who knows? I'd have made New York all right if it hadn't been for the miscalculation over petrol. When I came down in the bog on Cape Breton Island there wasn't one drop left in the tanks. I'd been flying only twenty-one hours and I thought I'd enough for twenty-eight. Fifteen seconds more and I believe my aeroplane and I would have gone down on the water and no one would have ever known what became of us.[7]

It was only later she discovered that if she had been higher she would almost certainly have seen Sydney Airport a few miles away and could have glided in.

The photographs of Beryl's stricken plane are an eloquent testimony to the last sentence in her article. The upended machine came to rest only a hundred yards from the ocean. Clearly it had been a very difficult flight, far more so than she had bargained for. At eighty-three she said that it was probably the only time in her life that she had been really scared. After it she hated flying over water.[8]

John and June Carberry telephoned from New York where they had been awaiting Beryl's arrival. She told them about the damage to *The Messenger*. 'She's badly mussed up,' Carberry told reporters later. 'The motor is ripped from its mountings, the propeller broken and the landing gear gone.' To Beryl he had said, 'Leave it there, don't worry about it.'[9]

Tributes poured in:

Mansfield: People might think a woman would be afraid of being alone over the Atlantic. I know my wife's spirit better . . . I am extremely proud of her fine achievement. I think it is magnificent and that she is very plucky. I always had great confidence in her as a pilot. She has done some very good work. I should not have done what she has done for a million pounds – I should have been in a complete funk. When I told our son about it he clapped his hands with joy, but I do not think he fully realizes what has happened. At the moment he is more interested in railway engines than in aeroplanes. The whole world now knows that my wife and I are separated, but we are still very good friends. The reason I did not go to see her off at Elstree was that she did not know herself that she was going until very shortly before. I spoke to her by telephone and wished her good luck.[10]

Jim Mollison: It is a first-rate performance, I am particularly delighted at her success because she went on my advice. I know that Mrs Markham considered this flight as important in her ambition to have a part in the regular transatlantic air service when it starts. On all points; first on navigation, but also on skill in piloting and every other department she has justified her candidature.[11]

C.B. Clutterbuck: Beryl's a grand girl. This is the happiest day of my life. I knew she would triumph, but in spite of my faith in her abilities, yesterday was the most anxious day I have known. It's a devil of a thing for a woman to have done all on her own. All day I have been on tenterhooks and now I shan't be able to sleep for excitement.[12]

Tom Campbell Black: Amazing! I thought she'd do it, but the weather, on what is always a tough crossing, seemed appallingly bad.[13]

Captain Percival: She has shown, in view of the bad weather, a marvellous piece of course-keeping. It has been a very good piece of flying to get through at all.[14]

Amelia Earhart: She did a splendid job. I am delighted beyond words that Mrs Markham should have succeeded in her exploit and has conquered the Atlantic. It was a great flight.[15]

A touching footnote to all the excitement occurred in the offices of the *East African Standard* in Nairobi.

One of the last people in the world to hear definite news of Mrs Markham's flight across the Atlantic was her mother

Mrs Kirkpatrick. The reason was that Mrs Kirkpatrick had been spending a holiday in the Aberdares, far removed from stations and the telegraph line.

Mrs Kirkpatrick, sister-in-law of Sir Charles Kirkpatrick, was in Nairobi yesterday eager for details of her daughter's achievement. 'I think it is a marvellous effort,' she said, 'although I never had any doubt that she would do it. My daughter has always been extremely self-confident and full of pluck from the time that she was a tiny tot.'[16]

All the newspapers made particular mention of the fact that two other transatlantic flyers had delayed their take-off from England due to the inclement weather. Harry Richman, a Broadway singer, and Richard Merrill, a professional pilot, were two Americans who had flown from New York to Britain a few days earlier. Fuel shortages had forced them to land in a meadow near Bristol but they refuelled and flew on to their destination, Croydon, a flight of 221 miles which, due to the strong winds that would have been favourable to Beryl, took them nearly three hours to cover. Much had been made by the papers of the fact that their wings were stuffed with forty thousand table-tennis balls which they hoped would keep the aeroplane afloat should they come down in the ocean. Merrill said they would autograph the table-tennis balls when they got back to the USA and sell them as souvenirs. Now they were waiting for suitable weather for their return trip, but at present were not prepared to risk it. Their aeroplane, the *Lady Peace*, was a much larger, heavier aircraft than *The Messenger*, with an engine of 1000 hp compared to *Messenger*'s 200 hp.

While the world lauded her achievement, Beryl had woken at 4.30 a.m. It was a kind of pre-jet jetlag, one supposes, but she was unable to sleep longer than four and a half hours. She complained that she could still hear the roar of the engine in her head. 'They wanted me to sleep but I couldn't. I was so mad that petrol had stopped me from getting to New York.' She was up and dressed before her host, Captain George Toom, and went out for a walk. Later, after a light breakfast she was driven out to see *The Messenger*, still embedded in the bog. There with Ray Goodwin, the manager of Sydney Airport, the damage was examined. Clearly it would not be possible to continue the flight in the crippled aeroplane, though Goodwin thought it could be

repaired and made airworthy again. Beryl noted with considerable bitterness that the weather was clearing up. It was a fine
morning with light, high cloud. If only . . .

She was depressed, still suffering from mild concussion, the
after effects of the long hours of flight and the seeming failure of
her venture despite an almost superhuman effort. She had then
no idea that her flight was seen as a tremendous success. She was
not to remain long in ignorance as the press descended on
Baleine Cove, an isolated coastal town at Cape Breton which
was once known as 'the Dunkirk of America. A proud fortress,
Cape Breton has the only walled city in North America,
Louisburg, and was reputedly named by early French settlers in
honour of King Louis IV.'

Gradually it was borne in on Beryl that she was being feted.
As more and more people – press and members of the tiny
community – appeared at her side in the bog, it seemed that the
world did not think she'd failed after all. Telegrams started to
arrive in handfuls. One was from Mayor Fiorello La Guardia of
New York: PERMIT ME TO EXTEND MY CONGRATULATIONS
TO YOU ON YOUR EPOCHAL ACHIEVEMENT IN BEING THE
FIRST WOMAN TO MAKE A SUCCESSFUL EAST–WEST CROSS-
ING OF THE ATLANTIC. I SHARE WITH YOU YOUR DIS-
APPOINTMENT IN BEING FORCED DOWN BEFORE REACHING
FLOYD BENNETT FIELD YOUR ORIGINAL DESTINATION. I
HOPE YOU WILL FIND IT CONVENIENT TO CONTINUE ON
ANOTHER PLANE AND LOOK FORWARD TO THE PLEASURE
OF SEEING YOU COME TO NEW YORK.[17] After that Beryl's talk
became brighter, flippant. 'What did I think about? Oh, a lot of
unpleasant things – all the terrible things I've ever done . . .' 'I
didn't know whether I was over Lapland or Newfoundland.'
'See this watch. That watch has crossed the Atlantic three
times. It was Jimmy Mollison's. He put it on my arm as he left.
He wore it both times – when he flew alone, and when he flew
with Amy . . .'[18]

When she was told that an aeroplane was waiting at a nearby
airfield to take her to New York, she gave only a rueful glance at
The Messenger, asking Goodwin to try to ensure that not too
many parts were torn off by souvenir hunters, before allowing
herself to be led away. From the local airfield she was flown to
Halifax.

There she was met by A.L. MacDonald, the Premier of Nova Scotia, who headed a civic reception and conveyed congratulations from the Canadian Government. Awaiting her arrival was a US Coastguard Beechcraft 17, *The Staggerwing*, one of the most beautiful light aeroplanes (in the opinion of the author) ever to grace the skies. Harry Bruno had been busy and Beryl was to co-pilot the powerful bi-plane to Floyd Bennett field where crowds were swelling by the minute to greet her.

Like most beautiful women, Beryl thrived on the adulation which was now directed at her. With the dressing still adorning her forehead, she smiled happily at the crowd (estimated at over five thousand people) who cheered as she stepped from *The Staggerwing* which she had piloted for most of the trip down from Halifax. Her clothes, which had been grey when she left England, had apparently changed colour overnight, for when she arrived in New York she was unaccountably described as 'the beautiful lady in blue'. Perhaps she had borrowed some clothes in Nova Scotia. 'Hello Blondie...' the crowds were reported to have shouted to her. 'Hello, hello,' she called back, and later she is supposed to have said, 'America is jolly grand.' The same newspaper reports that she chewed gum – an equally unlikely event. Much more likely was the report that in the airport building Beryl had asked a girl if she could borrow her compact, whereupon she hastily applied lipstick and a dusting of face powder before she faced the reception committee. 'I haven't a stitch of clothing except what I'm wearing, nor a toothbrush, comb nor a pair of stockings. That's hard on a woman you know,' she told reporters. Within days she was swamped with offers of clothes.[19]

Among the first to greet Beryl were the Carberrys. 'It was a very sporting thing that Beryl did,' said June. 'We are delighted over her success. It's a shame she was not able to reach New York non-stop, but we are very happy to have her with us after such a remarkable trip from home.' John Carberry would not give interviews, but described the trip somewhat dismissively as 'purely a sporting proposition'. The others in the smiling committee, adroitly handled by Bruno, were representatives of the Coastguard, New York Aviation Committee, the police commissioner, airport manager and, inevitably – the customs inspector.

After a short interview with the press she was driven off amidst the deafening sound of 'the hooting of thousands of motor car horns' in her first experience of a motorcade, escorted by police motorcycles with sirens wailing, to New York. On arrival at the Ritz-Carlton Hotel, where a suite had been booked for her, she bounded up the steps to the cheers and applause of a waiting crowd. In the foyer she was asked, 'How about a drink of orange juice?' Beryl burst into peals of laughter, apparently sharing some private joke with her party. 'Oh I think I'd like something stronger,' she said, stifling her laughter. 'I'll have a champagne cocktail.'[20]

After a short rest she appeared on the stage of the Avon theatre in West Forty-fifth Street for a radio interview with Milton Berle in which she laughed and joked, but said she'd rather fly the Atlantic again than appear on radio. 'I am so very glad to have got here,' she said, serious for a while. 'I only wish I could have done it in my own machine.' Later still, interviewed for the newsreel, she clasped her hands tightly behind her back, hung her head and smiled her sweet, shy smile. '. . . and did you have anything to drink, Mrs Markham?' 'Yes I did . . . I had a drink of brandy.' 'Just one?' 'No,' she replied, irrepressible laughter bubbling up, 'Two swigs, I'm afraid.'

The following day was Labour Day. She enjoyed a quiet morning in the hotel with friends, and the inevitable few journalists. Several fans managed to invade Beryl's suite asking for kisses and autographs. Bruno put a security guard on her door and later took her in an open-top car into the countryside around Westchester. That evening she attended a celebration party given by the Carberrys and other friends. Someone loaned her an evening dress. 'I am waiting for the shops to open tomorrow,' she told reporters, 'so that I can do a lot of shopping. I am also looking forward to seeing New York.'[21]

The days that followed were a whirlwind of interviews, luncheons, dinners. On Beryl's behalf Bruno had been in touch with Goodwin in Nova Scotia about *The Messenger*, and subsequently contacted Wing Commander Edwards of the Royal Canadian Air Force, at Halifax. After a survey he reported to her that it was structurally sound, though souvenir hunters had stripped the fabric from one wing and stolen the sparkplugs.[22] The engine needed major repairs too so there was no question of her making the return trip to England in the aeroplane... or at least not for some considerable time. She had mentioned this possibility to journalists, and it may be that Carberry was insisting on her fulfilling her part of the bargain to get the aeroplane back to Britain in time for him to participate in the Johannesburg Race. Now, it was obvious that Carberry's participation in the race would have to be abandoned.

Bruno cabled Wing Commander Edwards: WOULD AP-PRECIATE CHEAPEST AND BEST METHOD PUTTING SHIP FLYING CONDITION BILL SHOULD COME OUR OFFICE ADVISE COST BEFORE REPAIR STARTED BELIEVE ESSENTIAL GET SHIP UNDER SHELTER EARLIEST MRS MARKHAM AND I APPRECIATE ALL YOU HAVE DONE TO HELP STOP HARRY BRUNO.

There was a civic reception where Beryl met the popular, rumpled little mayor, Fiorello La Guardia. She towered over him, svelte, happy and confident in her new clothes. 'It's hot, isn't it?' he said, mopping his forehead. Looking as cool as a cucumber, she agreed. The two clasped hands so often for the hordes of cameramen that in the end Beryl said with exasperation, 'Look! Do you mind...?'[23]

Congratulatory cables and letters poured in. In 1986 this writer ploughed through more than forty which Beryl had kept in her old tin trunk. It was an astonishing selection. People wrote to say that they'd stopped work to pray for her, had sent drawings of her. One letter was supposedly written and signed by a dog, yet another was from a man named Markham who sent her the Markham family history dating back to the Battle of Hastings. There were cables from the firms who had sponsored petrol and parts, and from friends: MARVELLOUSLY DONE BERYL LOTS OF CONGRATULATIONS EVA VON BLIXEN; THANK GOD YOU SAVED MY WATCH JIM MOLLISON; and from people she had never heard of: I HAD FORGOTTEN HOW TO PRAY UNTIL I HEARD OF YOUR MAGNIFICENT ATTEMPT. I PRAYED THAT GOD WOULD GIVE YOU COURAGE AND KEEP YOUR INSTRUMENTS TRUE AND LAND YOU SAFELY. CON-GRATULATIONS ON YOUR MAGNIFICENT VICTORY. ENGLAND DARES AND PERPETUATES BRITISH SPIRIT. HURRAY FOR THE WOMEN OF ENGLAND. HARRY O'HEARN 2746 HAMPDEN PORT, CHICAGO; there was even a cable from a theatre producer of a show in England, *Broadway Rhythm*, offering her £500 a week to appear in the opening scenes representing the arrival at Croydon of the first transatlantic passenger aeroplane.[24]

During the busy, exciting days that followed Bruno tried to arrange a lecture tour of the United States. Beryl could fly from city to city in *The Messenger* if it could be repaired, or even another aeroplane would do. Things looked great, he assured her. She relaxed and started to enjoy herself but told him that she was returning to England in time to see the start of the Johannesburg Air Race, and then she intended to fly down to South Africa herself. But she would return to the USA later to take up some of the offers.

On 14 September, a week after her own arrival, came news that Merrill and Richman had also landed in a swamp after running out of petrol. They had failed in their objective of a New York–Croydon– New York round trip, but they had broken the east–west record, taking 17 hours and 44 minutes for the trip. They had encountered headwinds, though not as strong as those Beryl met, and the papers were quick to point out that Beryl had gone nearly 400 miles further than the two men, despite the fact that her aeroplane and engine were smaller. There were said to have been 'disagreements' between Merrill and Richman during the flight, especially over the dumping of fuel whilst over the ocean.[25]

Immediately Beryl heard the news she offered to fly up to rescue the two stranded pilots. This created further headlines but Eddie Rickenbacker – the famous American air ace of the First World War, and Merrill's employer – would not allow her to take any further risks. Richman and Merrill waited for rescue by a light aeroplane in the same way that Beryl had done. It was still not proven that man in his puny machines could successfully make the crossing, and a commercial transatlantic passenger service was a long way from becoming a reality.

Meanwhile, some of Beryl's friends were busy furthering their reputations. Eva von Blixen was planning a non-stop flight from New York to Stockholm with a countryman, K. Bjorkvall. The flight eventually took place on 7 October, but at the last minute, to Eva's fury, 'Bjork' refused to take her and took off on a solo attempt. He made a forced landing near the Irish coast and was rescued by a French trawler. The baroness had some acid comments to make to journalists on her countryman's performance.[26]

Jim Mollison, who still hoped to take the London–New York record, travelled to New York, arriving on 25 September, to take possession of the Bellanca aeroplane in which he hoped to make the flight to London and return. It really was too late in the season to be thinking about transatlantic crossings, but the record was now so close to falling that those in the running hardly dared delay. In the event Mollison was forced to land at Harbour Grace, Newfoundland, where he was delayed by bad weather. In the end he took off, like Beryl, despite the conditions. He then flew to Croydon, establishing a record time of 13 hours and 17 minutes for the crossing from Newfoundland. By this time even he realized that it would be suicidal to attempt the return and Bellanca later repossessed the aeroplane after issuing a writ for its return.[27]

Tom, meanwhile, was engaged in the last-minute preparations for his entry in the Johannesburg Race. The aeroplane which he was to fly in the race was a Percival Mew Gull. This super-sleek little racing aeroplane represented a new peak in perfection of line, but was a 'hairy little beast to fly' in the opinion of many pilots. It was fast and very unforgiving. On Friday 18 September he flew to Liverpool to be present at the naming ceremony of the Mew Gull *Miss Liverpool* at Speke Airport. On the following day he was due to give a demonstration flight for the sponsor Mr John Moores and a large crowd of wellwishers – the Moores' publicity machine had not been idle. The purpose in sponsoring the flight was to publicize the City of Liverpool and Tom Campbell Black was the right person to sponsor, for he would obviously start as one of the favourites in the fastest thing on wings.

Tom waved goodbye to the crowds and slid into the tiny black and white aeroplane, which was no more than four feet off the ground at its highest point. It was a fine, bright day with an autumn sparkle to the sunshine as he taxied out to the runway.

Modern aircraft are fitted with a tricycle undercarriage arrangement which places the aircraft in an upright position when taxiing. The Mew Gull, however, like most aircraft of its vintage, was fitted with a tailwheel, so that visibility was extremely limited until the tail was lifted from the ground on take-off. In addition, the extremely long engine with its faired-in cowl meant that the only way a pilot could see ahead was to fishtail along, looking out of the side windows.

Thus Tom probably never saw the aircraft that killed him.

It was a Hawker Hart – a 'light bomber' in the parlance of the day. Its pilot, a young RAF officer, with equally restricted vision, and landing with the sun in his eyes, could not see anything but the ground thirty or forty yards to the side and front of his aeroplane. He stated that he had checked the runway whilst flying a routine circuit of the aerodrome before landing. Simultaneously, Tom had jumped into the Mew Gull and quickly taxied out on to the runway. At the inquest a woman witness stated that Tom was reading a piece of paper, which may have been a map, seconds before the accident, so that his attention may have been diverted. To the horror of the spectators, the Hawker Hart landed straight on to the tiny Mew Gull, its propeller slashing through the tiny bubble of canopy, and through Tom's left shoulder and lung.[28]

Terribly wounded, he was gently lifted from the plane and taken to the hospital, but he died within half an hour. The only words he spoke were, 'Oh God! Help me, darling! Help me, darling!'[29]

Dessie was on stage rehearsing for an opening night the following week, when news came through that Tom had had an accident. They had had a silly tiff the previous evening over the positioning of some furniture, and Tom had slept in his dressing room, but they had made it up before he left for Liverpool on Thursday morning. Dessie had had the furniture moved back the way he wanted it, but she couldn't help thinking of him. 'How sensitive he was! How quickly he took offence and was hurt! He reminded me of a highly strung, nervous thorough-bred. If anything upset him, his eyes would flash and up would go his head.' After only eighteen months, the exquisite actress was a widow and her grief was accentuated by the thought of their quarrel.

Dessie travelled to Liverpool with members of Tom's family in order to accompany Tom's body back for the funeral. That night she stayed at the Moores' home near Liverpool and never forgot their kindness. During the night whilst Dessie was sobbing her grief into the pillow, her hostess Ruby Moores came into the bedroom, got into her bed and cradled her in her arms. Dessie eventually fell into an exhausted sleep and woke the next morning to see Ruby slipping quietly from the room.[30]

The inquest recorded 'accidental death' and it seemed particularly tragic that Tom, with such outstanding ability as a pilot, should meet his death in what the press described as 'a million to one accident', where all the ability in the world could not have saved him.

Beryl was still enjoying her triumph when Jim Mollison telephoned to tell her of Tom's death. Though she had technically already 'lost' him to Dessie, he was still the man in her life. All through the summer and in the build-up to her flight it was to Tom that she turned for help and guidance. When Denys had been killed, Tom had been there. In this terrible grief there was no one to whom she could turn and all her old feelings of insecurity returned. Later she was to receive a long letter from Percival, but initially, she recalled when I asked her for her reaction, 'It didn't seem possible. You know he was so good... I could hardly believe it was true.'[31]

Her return passage was already booked on the Cunard White Star liner *Queen Mary*, leaving for Southampton on Thursday of that week. She told Bruno to cancel all her appointments. The remainder of her stay in New York was unmarked by interviews or meetings, but she did attend the reception in her honour organized by Bruno and his wife for the eve of her departure to England.[32]

On the journey back to England she was, inevitably, photographed. Wearing a chic white satin evening gown, she smiled out from the photographs, at the captain's table and perched on the edge of the dressing table in her first-class stateroom. But there is no humour in her smiles.

The journey was not uneventful, for a fellow passenger was Jack Cohen, vice-president of Columbia Pictures Corporation. Before the great liner docked at Southampton Mr Cohen was able to cable the following message to his New York office: AFTER MUCH PERSUASION FINALLY INDUCED MRS BERYL MARKHAM TO SIGN CONTRACT APPEAR IN MOTION PICTURE PORTRAYING HER GREAT ACHIEVEMENT FOR COLUMBIA.[33]

Beryl later told a friend that she used to stand by the ship's rails for hours on end, particularly at night, just watching the water, thinking that if she'd first crossed the Atlantic by sea she'd never have dared to fly across it.[34]

So much black water. So much sorrow in her heart.

Shortly after Beryl left New York, work started on salvaging *The Messenger* on behalf of John Carberry. Under Ray Goodwin's supervision, 'thirteen fishermen and two mechanics wearing hip boots' manhandled timber several miles across the oozing peat to construct a platform around the aeroplane. Two rotary jacks were employed in the task and after four days *The Messenger* was 'ripped free from seven feet of mud'.

Inspection disclosed a bent propeller shaft but the propeller itself was, remarkably, undamaged. It was decided to take *The Messenger* to Louisburg by scow, and the seven-mile trip, in the face of strong, shifting winds, took three and a half hours. 'At one point during the journey,' said one of the engineers involved in the project, 'it seemed as though we might have to abandon the scow in the rough seas. That would have meant the loss of the aeroplane, and possibly the lives of the four men on board. But the wind abated and we were able to proceed.' At Louisburg 750 people had gathered to watch the aeroplane's arrival, 'and only one policeman who stood no hope of controlling the crowd. They ripped the fabric of the right wing, took the gas tank covers and loose fabric.' Ray Goodwin had already removed the valuable instruments.[35]

Mr William Fischer, who was responsible for the shipping of the aeroplane to New York and thence to London, said: 'We loaded it on a motor vehicle for the long trip to Halifax and ran foul of the highway authorities before we'd gone twenty-five miles. Although the wings had been dismantled they insisted that it was still too wide for the road. So the freighter *Ulva* was summoned from Halifax and picked up *The Messenger* from Sydney and later transferred its cargo to the SS *Cold Harbour*. Altogether,' Mr Fischer asserted, 'the removal job was just about as difficult as the flight. It took three weeks' labour and cost about $3000.'[36]

CHAPTER TEN

[1936–1937]

When Beryl arrived in Southampton she received a heroine's welcome. 'Trial by press', she called it. She smiled for the cameras, posed obediently by the ship's rail, shook hands with the mayor innumerable times, as she had done in New York, answered the same questions that she had been answering for weeks, and in every way behaved as everyone thought she ought. A civic reception was laid on for her, followed by a ride in an open car through the streets of the old city, passing under the ancient Bargate, but her heart was not in it.

Percival was there to greet her, and to tell her about Tom's accident. Until now she had had to rely on scraps of information sent to her by cable and the crackly transatlantic telephone line. The letter sent by Percival which she had received the day she sailed from New York still left many gaps. She needed to understand how it could possibly have happened that Tom, so careful, so knowledgeable, so calm and precise in everything concerning aeroplanes, had been killed. 'If you want to be good, remember you can't fly on your emotions. It's the harebrained pilots that make people distrust flying, the hero boys full of daredevil nonsense from the last war . . .' he'd once said to her.[1] But her talk with Percival had to wait until she'd said all the right things and pleased all the people.

'Will you make another attempt to fly non-stop to New York?' 'I know I said I would not like to fly the Atlantic again, but that was shortly after I had arrived in the United States and you may imagine what sort of state of exhaustion and fuss I was in just then. But I have great hopes of flying from New York to France next May in an air race which the French government is sponsoring. I may do it solo, but it is more likely that I shall go as co-pilot with someone.' 'You knew Mr Campbell Black well. What have you to say of his tragic death?' 'Mr Black's death is a great loss and a personal sadness.' 'Are you going to watch the start of the Johannesburg Race?' 'Yes, I intend to motor down to Portsmouth tonight, so that I can be there for the early start.' 'We hear reports that you have made a hundred thousand pounds from your flight, Mrs Markham, is this true?' At this Beryl laughed aloud. 'I don't think I've made quite that much yet. I have signed a nice expensive contract to make a film in Hollywood – with flying as the theme. There is an option on both sides.' 'Does this mean you will be returning to America?' 'Not until I've been to South Africa to visit my father.' 'Are you going to South Africa immediately?' 'First I want to see my little boy Gervase – I've brought back a picture of my aeroplane which was painted in New York as a souvenir for him. Then I will probably fly on to South Africa as I want to see the British Empire Exhibition in Johannesburg, but I'll do it in easy stages.' 'Is the cut on your face still giving you trouble?' 'Oh, but it's disappearing. It *is* disappearing, isn't it? There's only a little bump now.'

Endless questions, questions, questions.

Inevitably when the articles appeared she was misquoted. Her son Gervase mysteriously became 'her son Gerald', and she apparently told some reporters that she would never again fly the Atlantic.[2] It was not until they were on their way to Portsmouth in the late afternoon that Beryl was able to talk quietly to Percival and learn the full sad facts – hear with terrible anguish that 'A foot either way would have saved him.' He also told her about Dessie. When Dessie learned of Tom's death she was in final rehearsals for the opening night of a new show, due to open two days later. Because of Tom's death the opening was postponed but on the day after the funeral Dessie received a call from the producer. 'What do you want me to do about the show, Dessie? I need to know.' Dessie, though young in years, was a professional trouper of the old school. She told him to advertise the opening night for the following Monday. 'Don't worry. I'll be ready.'[3]

'It's tonight,' Percival told Beryl.

Beryl was not the only one who cabled her best wishes to Dessie that night. As Dessie sat in her flower-filled dressing room she found one telegram particularly moving. It was from all the pilots taking part in the Air Race – Tom's friends. But for the accident he'd have been with them in that last flurry of preparations prior to the dawn start:

FLORENCE DESMOND VICTORIA PALACE LONDON. WE SEND YOU OUR LOVE AND THOUGHTS AND OUR ADMIRA-TION OF REAL COURAGE. TOMMY ROSE, CHARLES SCOTT, KEN WALLER, MAX FINLAY, DAVID LLEWELLYN, CHARLES HUGHESDON, ALLISTER MILLER, STANLEY HALSE, VICTOR SMITH, CLOUSTON AND ALLINGTON.[4]

Her performance that night, Dessie felt, was not her best. She had to steel herself against the waves of sympathy directed at her across the footlights. Her voice seemed to her to be small and far away. It brought the house down.

'Many film and theatre celebrities were among the audience which enthusiastically welcomed Miss Florence Desmond at the Victoria Palace last night when, just over a week after the death of her husband Captain Tom Campbell Black she appeared in the premiere of *Let's Raise the Curtain*... We only saw her twice but the piquant spot of the evening was her impersonation of Marlene Dietrich who, with Noël Coward, watched from a box. Miss Sophie Tucker and Mr Jack Hylton were also present.'[5]

'Isn't it strange,' Dessie said to a friend in the wings, 'that all that could happen in one week – that Tom could die and be buried and I be back here doing the same things that I was doing last Saturday.' And to a reporter: 'I am just going on with my job as Tom would have wished me to do.'[6]

Beryl was at Portsmouth aerodrome at dawn on Tuesday 29 September to watch the start of the big race. In connection with the forthcoming British Empire Exhibition, South African mining millionaire and industrialist I.W. Schlesinger had offered prizes totalling £10,000 for places in the long-distance race. His intention was to stimulate interest in aviation in South Africa and to publicize the exhibition. It was planned on much the same lines as the London to Melbourne Race, won by Tom and Charles Scott two years previously.

After Tom's death Amy Johnson had come forward to say she would be willing to take his place and fly *Miss Liverpool* if the aeroplane could be repaired in time. Predictably, a great deal of publicity was given to this offer, but Dessie was very unhappy about it, and in any case Percival could not undertake to have the plane repaired in time. Amy Johnson mistakenly thought she would be honouring Tom's memory by taking his place. But many thought she was simply cashing in on tragedy, partly to counteract the publicity being given to Jim Mollison who was in New York preparing for his transatlantic flight to Croydon in the Bellanca. She had recently started divorce proceedings against Jim, charging cruelty, apparently prompted by Beryl's former employer, François Dupré, with whom Amy was currently enjoying a much-publicized liaison in Paris.

With Tom's Mew Gull withdrawn, and Carberry's mount, *The Messenger,* still en route to New York after its extraction from the Baleine Cove bog, together with the withdrawal of several aeroplanes which could not be made ready in time, there were only nine entries on the starting line. These nine left Portsmouth aerodrome at one-minute intervals on their way to Johannesburg via the compulsory check points of Belgrade and Cairo. Because of the Italian–Abyssinian conflict, the route was planned carefully to avoid Italy, against whom Britain had applied sanctions. After Cairo each contestant could take his own line to Johannesburg.

With the technical advances that had taken place since the London–Melbourne race, it would be logical to assume that the race would be a closely fought thing. It was a disaster.

Tom's former partner Charles Scott and his co-pilot Giles Guthrie were the winners in their Vega Gull, the same model as *The Messenger.* Their aeroplane was the only one to finish the course within the allotted time. Arthur Clouston, a Farnborough test pilot, flying a second-hand, open-cockpit Miles Hawk, eventually finished after an astonishing series of misadventures including a complete engine change, a forced landing in a swamp, and a crash landing in some tree tops. But he was too late to be considered for a place. Nevertheless, young and impoverished by his entry in the race, he hoped the authorities might offer him a consolation prize. They didn't. The remaining prize money went to the families of those who had been killed in the race. Max Finlay with his crew of four had crashed in their Airspeed Envoy whilst taking off near Lake Tanganyika. Finlay and his radio operator were killed.

Of the other entrants, Llewellyn and Hughesdon, also flying a Vega Gull, had crash landed near Lake Tanganyika. They were both thrown into the water but were unhurt and spent the night on a sandbank. When dawn broke they saw that what they had taken during the darkness for logs were in fact crocodiles. Fortunately they were rescued before further harm befell them. The undercarriage of the BA Double-Eagle flown by Tommy Rose and Jack Bagshawe collapsed on landing at Cairo. The undercarriage of the BA Single-Eagle flown by Messrs Allington and Booth collapsed when they had a forced landing in Bavaria. Victor Smith in a Miles Sparrow Hawk dropped out at Cairo with oil trouble and Allister Miller, having run out of petrol, damaged his Mew Gull in a forced landing near Belgrade. The final entrant, Stanley Halse, flew himself to a standstill. When eventually forced to land because of fatigue he tried to put his Mew Gull down in a jungle clearing. The little thoroughbred plane, 'a plane that really needs flying',[7] not renowned for its forgiving qualities and with a stalling speed of 76 mph, landed badly, injuring the pilot and having to be written off.[8]

After watching the start of the race Beryl returned to London where a crowd of friends, along with the gentlemen of the press, met her at Waterloo Station. Again she was feted and driven in an open-topped car for a celebration lunch at Claridge's. Later, she contacted Dessie. Beryl could not have known that Dessie was now aware of what Tom had once been to her. Tom's trunk had been sent to Dessie from the Royal Aero Club where he kept his log books and papers. In it she found the telegram sent by Beryl: DARLING IS IT TRUE YOU ARE TO MARRY FLORENCE DESMOND? PLEASE ANSWER STOP HEARTBROKEN BERYL. Dessie recalls surprise rather than shock when she read the message.[9]

When Beryl contacted her to talk about Tom, Dessie found that Beryl had nowhere to live and, as usual, no money either, for the option payment on her film contract amounted to only a few hundred dollars. Dessie immediately invited Beryl to stay with her. Some months before Tom's death, the Campbell Blacks had bought a large house in St John's Wood. Now Dessie was lonely and depressed, rattling around alone in it. 'I was especially glad of her company,' she recalled.

It was a pretty white house with blue window frames; a giant old tree faced the front door. In the sitting room the white walls were hung with a large collection of old maps enthusiastically collected by Tom, whilst on a low table near a large bookcase stood a silver model of the record-breaking Comet *Grosvenor House*. A picture of the Comet in its bright scarlet livery hung over the mantel which was lined with trophies and silver cups, mainly won by Tom on the turf in Kenya. It was a room redolent of Tom's activities. Dessie and Beryl did not use it much.[10]

Because of the interest in Beryl and her flight, and Dessie's theatrical work, the two women were able to come to terms with the loss, which affected each of them deeply in her own way. For Dessie it was the loss of her beloved husband. Beryl mourned the man whom she still adored, though she had already lost him as a lover long before his death; but he had remained her friend and 'supporter' and it was probably the loss of this support that affected Beryl most in the aftermath of her pyrrhic victory. For the next few years she was often reported as entering races and drumming up financial support for record attempts, but all were to come to nothing. The truth was that with Tom gone she had no motivation, no need to prove anything.

She was immediately swept into a round of lunches and dinners in honour of her flight. Tributes continued to fall about her head like April showers. In an amusing speech the chairman of Anglo–American Oil, one of Beryl's sponsors, said, 'Our guest might well be forgiven a secret glow of satisfaction that on her solo flight in her relatively small 200-hp plane she penetrated further into Canada than the two bright American lads who followed her, when the weather had cleared up a bit, in their faster and more powerful machine elaborately equipped with wireless – to say nothing of 40,000 ping-pong balls... Mrs Markham's flight gives an entirely new meaning to the term "the flighty sex" ... I am one of those who think that her name will be handed down among the great names of women in history. And what is most gratifying to all of us is that the machine, like the aviatrix, was British...'[11]

Percival, by now a staunch friend, said that her course-keeping and navigation must have been extremely accurate. He recalled that when her position was reported by the SS *Spaarndam* some 200 miles off Newfoundland, she was exactly on course – no mean feat after 1500 miles with no opportunity to check position. He presented her with a small trophy commemorating the flight. It embodied a silver and turquoise model of *The Messenger* and an engraved plaque stating 'From E.W. Percival. 2656 miles in 21 hours and 25 minutes'. Beryl replied with a short, graceful speech: 'It was windy in more ways than one when I took off...' she began cheerfully.[12] During her speech she commented on the fact that she had counted on a range of twenty-seven hours and had been disappointed when it proved to be under twenty-two. She did not mention the fact that during the recent salvage operations *The Messenger* had been found to contain enough fuel for a further 300 miles' flying.[13] The mechanics involved theorized that ice had formed in the air intake of that last tank of fuel, causing the engine to cut and Beryl to assume she was out of petrol.

She was particularly proud of the telegram she received from the East African Aero Club offering congratulations and making her a life member,[14] and she ought to have been on top of the world. But for Tom's death she would have been. She liked the attention, provided it did not intrude beyond the invisible fence she had erected around her personal life. But she could not see that the attention she was receiving was actually helping her, and in retrospect her victory seemed a hollow one. There was no doubt that her reputation as a pilot had been established, but little in the way of financial rewards had resulted. She was as impoverished as ever, though she dined out most nights in the best hotels and nightclubs in London and was recognized wherever she went. But the offers of appearances on stage did not appeal to her and no serious offers of work, other than that from Hollywood, had been made. The little money she had made from her public appearances in America and her newspaper articles would hardly pay Bruno's bill.

So she went on with the circus. On 18 October *The Messenger* was unloaded from the freighter (aptly named SS *Cold Harbour*) at London Docks. Beryl went to see her aeroplane but she already knew that she'd lost it. Carberry had told her he was shipping it back to Kenya where he would have it repaired. There was no question of her flying it to South Africa, he told her, nor of putting it on display to the paying public. He had held to his bargain, she to hers and the arrangement was now at an end. Perhaps he was peeved at missing the Johannesburg Race, but more than likely it was just another example of what James Fox called 'fun spoiling' – a hobby of Carberry's. It would have meant nothing to him financially to let Beryl have the aeroplane – or even to make it available to her on loan.

Instead Carberry shipped it to East Africa where it was sold for an undisclosed, but almost certainly small sum. Some time later a friend of Beryl's saw it at Dar es Salaam. It was lying derelict outside a hangar. He thought it may have been bought by someone who had wanted to learn to fly: 'I think it wasn't really suitable for local flying, having been built for long-distance flying. I imagine whoever had it just lost interest because it couldn't be flown and possibly couldn't be properly maintained, and it was a rather crumpled heap on the ground. I tried to climb into the cockpit and stepped on to the wing but it just collapsed underneath me and went a bit further towards Africa.'[15]

In November Beryl and Dessie were reported as taking part in a charity darts match where the other celebrities included Lord Semphill, Amy Johnson, Steve Donohue and Jimmie Wilde. But the biggest attraction was His Majesty the King, who was said to 'throw a pretty dart'.[16] Within a month the royal dart-thrower would have abdicated his throne in order to ensure the help and support of the woman he loved.

The King's Secret Matter had now reached crisis proportions. The US papers were running banner headlines speculating on the probability of a 'Queen Wallis'. All society had been discussing the couple's liaison for months (since the king's holiday with Wallis on the yacht *Nahlin* in September, and even prior to that), and now ordinary citizens were becoming aware of it. When British newspapers, previously muzzled by protocol and loyalty, reported the divorce of Wallis and Ernest Simpson, the seriousness of the situation was fully revealed. In December the abdication was announced. Edward, king no more, went abroad. The Duke of York, now reluctantly King George VI, sat on the throne of England. When asked what should be done about the coronation planned for Edward on 12 May, the harassed Prime Minister Stanley Balfour reportedly snapped, 'Same day. New king!'

While Dessie worked at the theatre, Beryl was out every night, dining and dancing until the small hours. 'I loved to dance,' she told me. 'I used to be very good at it.' Mollison was a particular friend with whom she had a casual affair, but Dessie disliked him. He was a rough, hard-edged heavy drinker, aptly nicknamed 'Brandy Jim'. 'He did drink rather a lot,' Beryl said. 'So I started to avoid him after a while. I hardly drank then.'[17]

'He was coarse, boorish and arrogant in his manner,' Dessie said, and this is borne out in his own writing, for a bigger piece of conceit than his memoir *Playboy of the Air* would be hard to find. 'Before the London–Melbourne Race,' Dessie recalled, 'Tom had a piece of grit in his eye. Seeing that Mollison had a neatly pressed handkerchief in his breast pocket he asked if he might borrow it. Mollison took out the handkerchief, blew his nose on it and handed it to Tom. Tom simply let it drop to the ground, he never liked him after that.' Dessie also remembered receiving a call from a friend who managed the Grosvenor House Hotel. 'We've had the most awful night here. Jim Mollison and Amy Johnson had a fearful row and he's beaten her up. The bathroom looks like a slaughter-house...' There were lots of equally unpleasant anecdotes about Mollison from other sources, but he was, undoubtedly, a good pilot and a brilliant navigator.

Dessie was annoyed to come home from the theatre one night to find Mollison and Beryl in the sitting room. 'Mollison was so drunk he could not stand up, but when I came in, Beryl told him he'd better leave. She knew how much I disliked him. Astonished I said to her, "But you can't let him go in that condition – he can't even walk properly!" Beryl simply shrugged and raised her eyebrows. I had a bed made up for him in Tom's old dressing room and he spent the night there. But I was very cross with Beryl for putting me in that position.'[18]

Shortly after this Dessie put the house on the market. The constant daily reminders of Tom were too sharp, and the house far too big. The two women moved from St John's Wood to a flat in Stockleigh Hall. Sometimes, as time went on, when Beryl was at one of her innumerable parties, she would call Dessie after a show and ask her to come and join them. Occasionally Dessie would go along. 'They were always very bright and cheerful parties, and I was grateful because it made me go out and meet people.' One night Dessie was in her dressing room when she received such a call. A voice said, 'You don't know me. My name is Charles Hughesdon. I am speaking for Beryl Markham. We are having supper at the Hungaria Restaurant and Beryl asks if you would care to join us after the show.' It was the same Charles Hughesdon who had crashed in Tanganyika during the ill-fated Johannesburg race. Later, when another friend of Beryl's came over to the table Charles asked Dessie to dance, and went on dancing far longer than politeness demanded.[19]

On the next evening Beryl and Dessie were having supper at the Savoy Hotel with a group of friends. Charles threatened to gatecrash the party and Dessie spent the entire evening anxiously looking over her shoulder. On the following Sunday, Charles went to lunch at Dessie's flat. The two had already fallen headlong in love, but Beryl was hardly to know this when she came in after lunch and sat talking. After a while she got up, went over to the writing table and scribbled a note which she unobtrusively slipped to Charles before leaving them alone. After she'd gone Charles said to Dessie, 'Nice friend you've got!' and showed her the note which invited him to try to get away somehow and join Beryl that evening.[20]

After this incident things began to cool between the two women, especially in the spring of 1937 when Beryl could not raise enough money to pay the increasing number of bills which came flocking in. In order to keep up with the smart lifestyle and constant round of parties, dinners and suppers, she needed a good wardrobe. Milliners, shops, and dressmakers were pleased to provide clothes for her; she was good-looking, well known and wore them so well. Her vitality, deer-like grace and sense of chic ensured that they would be noticed. Dessie had introduced Beryl to her own dressmaker, the young Teddy Tinling, who was not known then for tennis clothes, and he made the two women some beautiful gowns. Likewise Dessie's milliner produced some lovely hats for Beryl – tiny frivolous affairs which Beryl wore at a cheeky angle over her forehead. But when the bills were presented Beryl couldn't pay them. In the end, she simply replied that she was going to declare herself a bankrupt. Dessie was mortified because so many of the creditors had taken

Beryl as a client on *her* introduction. She made it clear how she felt and Beryl moved out of the flat.[21]

No formal bankruptcy claim was ever filed, and Beryl settled with her creditors out of court for five shillings in the pound. This was backed up with a promise to repay the balance when she was able but it remains open to doubt whether Beryl ever seriously intended to honour this offer, for she had a preposterously irresponsible attitude to money. She was almost certain of getting sponsorship for 'The Big Race', she told her creditors, which would enable her to pay them off; she had already been offered an aeroplane, a Northrop Delta IC, registration G-AEXR.

This big race had already been announced in the press: a transatlantic race from New York to Paris. The prize money, put up by the French government to mark the tenth anniversary of Lindbergh's solo flight, included £30,000 to the winner, but with additional prizes for fastest time over various legs of the course, the winner might expect to collect anything up to £50,000. Initially there was to be a mass start, but the rules were changed after protests regarding safety, so that contestants could choose any day in August to make the flight. The winner would be the pilot with the fastest time. Contestants could fly solo or with a crew.

It was too good an opportunity to miss, and every pilot of note was looking for sponsorship. Early British entries included Jim Mollison, Amy Johnson, and Beryl. Howard Hughes, Roscoe Turner and Amelia Earhart entered from the USA, whilst Mussolini's son, Bruno, was a member of the Italian team. 'Every country with an air force is determined to win for the prestige value,' the *Daily Express* announced.[22]

Initially Beryl had an unlikely partner in her bid for sponsorship. This was Jack Doyle, a handsome boxer who had recently broken into show business, having appeared in a film and made several cabaret appearances as a singer. Doyle fell for Beryl and for a few weeks the pair were inseparable. Beryl even gave him a few flying lessons. 'I hope he was a better lover than he was a singer,' a friend of Beryl's said caustically. Doyle's manager was convinced that he could get sponsorship for the pair in the big race, but it all came to nothing. The relationship swiftly ended and Doyle went out of Beryl's life as quickly as he had entered it.

Beryl rented a flat at a smart address off Wigmore Street, and continued living life very much as she always had. She was always beautifully dressed and always in the middle of anything that was going on, yet with her quiet, casual manner she often seemed to be standing back, assessing it, rather than joining in. An acquaintance who recalls her in those days said that there was a sort of bright, pearly luminescence about her. She nearly always wore white, and with her clear healthy skin, fair colouring, blue eyes and blonde hair she stood out, even in a crowd – almost as if she glowed. 'Your eyes were somehow drawn to her. There was a calmness about her, and when you spoke to her she looked you in the eye and listened, as if what you said was the most important thing in the world.'

She saw very little of Gervase. This may have been by private agreement between Beryl and Mansfield. Dessie could not remember Beryl ever visiting her son during the time Beryl lived with her.

The race was due to take place in August, but in late April the Americans requested a postponement, claiming that there was too little time to get machines ready for such a potentially dangerous project. Beryl had already entered in a French aeroplane because she had been unable to get an English sponsor. Eventually, after much argument and dire warnings that the scheme was suicidal, the transatlantic race was called off. A race went ahead but the course was changed to a 4000-mile circuit which started from Marseilles and took contestants down the Mediterranean, over Italy and Greece to Damascus, returning directly over Europe to Paris. The prizes too were changed so that the top prize was £15,000. With these changes the race became almost a military affair between the European nations, each anxious to display aerial superiority. In the event the Italians, who had entered six aeroplanes, took first, second and third places. After the race Mussolini is said to have stormed at the winning pilot for not allowing his son Bruno's plane (which came in third), to cross the line first.[23]

The changes to the race left Beryl out on a limb. Her French backer, a friend of Dupré's, withdrew his support, for with the ocean flight abandoned, he was now able to find a French pilot.

Beryl managed to get a wealthy South African syndicate, including I.W. Schlesinger,[24] to back a new entry, but they too eventually lost interest in the French race. However, they put a new proposition to Beryl and in June she sailed to New York with a mission to find an American machine, capable of at least 200 mph. It was thought, though never confirmed, that her intention was a round the world flight. If so, she had left her attempt too late, for at the time of Beryl's arrival in the States, Amelia Earhart had already set off with Captain Fred Noonan to encircle the globe at the equator. It was her second crack at the record; an earlier attempt in March had failed at Honolulu when the Lockheed Electra plane crashed on the runway and was damaged.

After flying across the country to California with Frank Hawks (the man who introduced Amelia Earhart to flying), Beryl stayed in Los Angeles. Here, she was generally expected to take part in the Bendix Air Races, hotly contested by women pilots as no woman had at that date ever achieved first place, but she made it known that she intended to wait until Amelia returned from her global flight in order to meet her.[25]

Sadly, in early July, the world learned that Earhart and Noonan were lost in the Pacific Ocean between British New Guinea and Howland Island. Amelia had always known that the leg from Lae in New Guinea was the most difficult of the flight. Howland was flat and only two miles long by half a mile wide, and therefore difficult to find, unless navigation was totally accurate. The Electra would be out of radio range for most of the flight and she would have no way of checking her position for 1800 miles. By the time the couple left Lae on 2 July they had flown 22,000 miles and made twenty-two landings. Now as they journeyed eastward their remaining ports of call were Howland, Honolulu and home by Independence Day – 4 July. Their last message was relayed by Amelia. She was clearly disturbed at having been unable to make a previously arranged radio contact with a US naval ship and her voice was uncharacteristically anxious as she said: 'We are on a line of position 157 dash 337. Will repeat this message on 6210 kilocycles. We are running north and south.' They were never heard from again.[26]

In an unlikely manner, Beryl found herself in the middle of

the press hysteria surrounding Amelia's disappearance, for when the news came through she was staying at the home of Jacqueline Cochran, another blonde aviatrix who broke numerous records. Much later, in May 1953, Cochran became the first woman to break the sound barrier in a North American F-86 Sabre jet.[27]

Like Beryl, Jackie Cochran had had an unconventional childhood. The adopted daughter of a poor family, she had been dressed in sacking and left to run wild and barefoot around the Southern saw-mill towns, without any education, while her adoptive parents searched endlessly for work. Like Beryl she had the reputation for single-minded determination to achieve: 'When Jackie Cochran put her mind to do something she was a damned Sherman tank at full speed,' said a friend. When she grew up she went to work in the beauty business. She worked hard, earned a lot of money and learned to fly. Eventually, having already achieved great wealth by her own efforts, she married a wealthy friend and despite a series of hazardous, largely unsuccessful early record attempts, she eventually became one of the most respected women pilots in the United States.[28]

At the time Beryl visited her, Jackie and her husband lived in sybaritic luxury on a thousand-acre ranch with an olympic-sized swimming pool, private golf course, stables of thorough-bred horses and an army of servants. In addition to the other facets of her overwhelming personality Jacqueline Cochran claimed to possess extrasensory powers. There was some evidence for this, well known among their friends who knew that Jackie was often able to tell them precisely what her husband Floyd was doing at a given time, even though he may have been hundreds of miles away.[29]

After Amelia disappeared an immense search for her by the US Navy, authorized personally by President Roosevelt, was instigated. Jackie was simultaneously contacted by George Putnam (Amelia's publisher husband) in a desperate hope that her clairvoyant powers could assist the search for her missing friend. The press clustered around Coachella Ranch like flies around a honey pot while its chatelaine willingly provided what help she could.

The aircraft had come down in the water and was still afloat, she said. Both Amelia and Fred Noonan were still alive, though Fred had suffered a fractured skull and had been unconscious since the accident. She mentioned the US Coastguard cutter *Itasca* and a Japanese fishing boat, both of which were in the search area. She even provided a precise position for the wreck, though the navy were not able to find anything when they eventually reached the spot. For two days Jacqueline claimed to 'know' that Amelia was alive, and gave details of the aeroplane's drift on the water. Then she sensed her friend was dead.[30] Since the aeroplane was never traced these claims could not be proved, but Jackie was so shaken by the experience that she never again publicly used her clairvoyant ability.

One person who would not have been surprised by this performance was Beryl. She was in the habit of consulting clairvoyants from time to time, having absorbed the African's belief in magic during her upbringing. When the reporters, who only gradually drifted away from the ranch, realized that Beryl was a guest, she too was interviewed. She told them that she was very distressed at the news, but more determined than ever to continue her own aviation career. 'I've always wanted to meet Amelia Earhart,' she said, 'this time I'd hoped to see her in Los Angeles on her return. Miss Earhart's loss is all aviation's.' Asked what she would have done, had she been in Amelia's position in the South Seas, she replied, 'I'd have probably tried to land in the water with the wheels folded into the wings. The plane would stand more chance that way than on a jagged reef. Then I'd have taken to my emergency lifeboat.'[31]

Beryl remained in the United States for five months. She made many friends and travelled extensively in the west. Because the motion picture offer from Columbia was still open, she inevitably visited the studios and as a result she made contact with people who were part of the movie scene. She was often taken to the sets of films and on one occasion she was taken by the prominent screenwriter Anita Loos[32] to the set of the movie *Conquest*, where she was introduced to the star Greta Garbo who was playing Marie Waleska to Charles Boyer's Napoleon.

At the time, Garbo was just about to enter upon her much-publicized love affair with Leopold Stokowski, the brilliant and flamboyant conductor who was later to become a great friend of

Beryl's. Anita Loos, author of the best-selling *Gentlemen Prefer Blondes*, seems to have been a busy hostess, for she introduced Garbo to Stokowski at a dinner party and claimed that 'Stokie' had decided in advance of their meeting that he was going to have an affair with Garbo. According to other guests at the dinner, Stokowski turned on such mesmerizing charm that Garbo was hypnotized by the man with the hawk-like face.[33]

At first the gossip columns merely noted that the pair were often seen together; however they discounted a romance since it was known that Stokowski motored a hundred miles north every Friday evening to spend the weekend with his wife and children at their Santa Barbara home. All through that autumn the press continued to hound the pair, who both shunned publicity. It was not until the following spring that the real storm broke when they spent a holiday together in Europe. Later Beryl, who was very much a part of the circle of people in which they moved, was to say of Garbo that the star's avoidance of publicity was no pose. 'She is a very timid person who sincerely shrinks from meeting crowds of strange people.'[34]

Beryl spent some time looking at the powerful new aeroplane engines developed by Al Monasco Incorporated for the Ryan Aircraft Company specifically for air-racing. She even discussed the possibility of purchasing a Ryan STA, but the matter was left in abeyance pending a meeting with her backers. Undoubtedly her main reason for making the trip to California was to take up the offer from Columbia to make a motion picture of her transatlantic flight, with Beryl in the starring role. But within weeks of her departure from California Beryl told a woman reporter that 'the bargain with Columbia had been declared off'.[35] For a while she let it be thought that the studios had lost interest in the story because so much time had elapsed since the time of her flight that public interest had waned. But much later she told friends the real reason. She had not photographed well in the screen tests.[36] She was bitterly disappointed. In December she sailed for Africa.

CHAPTER ELEVEN

[*1937–1941*]

Beryl spent Christmas on the ship she had boarded in San Diego. On 27 December she arrived at Sydney in New South Wales where she stayed for a week before boarding the *Mariposa*, bound for Melbourne. Interviewed there for the newspaper *Truth* she was described effusively as 'Pretty as a talkie star, and utterly feminine, from her aureole of golden hair to her lacquered toenails. Her eyes are clear china blue. She has a flawless complexion and is as slender as a willow wand.' She was surprised by her noisy welcome at the little port of Balmain, she said.

> She wore slacks, the acid test of a woman's figure – of royal blue linen, immaculately creased and zippered on the hips. On her feet were sketchy red sandals and on her blouse was a fluffy scarf with red, white and blue whirligigs, fastened with a small aeroplane brooch of the soft gold that one finds in Kenya. About her wrist was a double chain linked with tiny enamelled flags spelling her name in morse code. Round the other . . . a wide silver bracelet, made in Arizona. In it is set a wide sensible watch flanked by two turquoises . . .

The reader also learned that Beryl's favourite colour was blue, that she disliked green. That she was not superstitious. That she was not a teetotaller though she disliked cocktail parties. That she never gambled and unless it was unavoidable never played bridge. 'Tea is her favourite drink.' Beryl must have been playing with the lady journalist. The article went on to divulge that horses were Beryl's favourite animals:

> Dogs come next. Cats are not in it at all, and she doesn't care

for children in the mass, just an individual child here and
there appeals to her . . . She takes great care of her complexion
with cleansing creams . . . She is five foot nine and a half,
weighs nine stone, takes size five in a shoe and $6\frac{1}{2}$ in a glove.
Her mother is Irish and her father an Englishman who gives
her her head in flying exploits but asks her now not to do it
any more over water.[1]

On 17 February aboard an Interocean Lines cargo boat
which had left Perth three weeks earlier, Beryl returned to
Africa, and was reunited with her father who was living in
Durban. She stayed with him for only part of the three months
she spent in South Africa. Her relationship with her stepmother
was still difficult and it was impossible for Beryl to spend any
length of time there, no matter how pleased father and daughter
were to see each other. During these few weeks, however, Beryl
happily slipped back into the daily routine of a top-class racing
stable; but her purpose in visiting South Africa was not solely to
see her father. She also had meetings with potential backers, a
syndicate headed by Schlesinger.

A record flight of some kind was still very much in her mind
and she was able to provide details of the latest advances in
civilian aircraft in the United States. The only information
Beryl ever gave to journalists regarding these discussions was
that 'it was the only major flight not yet done'. Although it was
never confirmed, the newspapers who wrote about Beryl were
almost certainly correct in their assumptions that she had a
'round-the-world' attempt, or possibly a stratosphere flight, in
mind.[2]

In May she boarded an Imperial Airways flying boat and
headed for England by way of Kenya. Her discussions with the
potential sponsors had been inconclusive, and, interviewed in
Mombasa where she broke her journey, she informed the
journalist that 'any future attempts at records are in the lap of
the gods. I have no settled plans in the meantime, but I long to
be back in Kenya,' she continued, 'I have such happy
memories.' The *East African Standard* concluded that her
journey to Britain was in connection with another record-
breaking flight.[3]

Here something of a mystery occurs. The stamps in her

passport reveal a fast journey (21 April, Sudan; 22 April, Yugoslavia; 23 April, Brindisi and Bracciano; 24 April, Lyon and Paris), and one would assume from this that she flew to London by the scheduled airliner. But Beryl stated to me that she flew with Blix to Europe on that occasion and suffered some apprehension during the flight: 'Europe was a rather dangerous place to be just then . . .' Initially I was inclined to assume that Beryl had merely confused the dates with the flight that she had made with Blix in the spring of 1936. However a further piece of information revealed that her memory might not have been at fault.

In Bror Blixen's *Letters from Africa* he too wrote of their flight to Europe. He mentions no dates but, despite small differences, the flight he describes is clearly that which Beryl also writes about in her memoir. In *West with the Night* she states that the date of that flight was 1936; however, Bror ends his version with the following passage:

> . . . it was getting dark as we approached the town at low altitude, in spite of regulations. Now we could discern the Eiffel Tower against the horizon and a little later we landed at Le Bourget. We taxied along the deserted hangars till we reached one that Beryl recognized. A surly old man, who was in a hurry to get home, opened the sliding doors. *Voila!* and we pushed in the plane. 'Customs?' '*Non, non, monsieur,* it is too late for that.' I put my suitcases in a shed only taking out what I needed for the night. There was another man in the shed, fiddling with his luggage, and as he was leaving, I thought I recognized his gait – however, it could not very well be that person, as he was in Spain. Yet, who else would walk in that particular way with the great trunk slightly bent to the right and with those long arms like a gorilla's? 'Ernest!' I shouted, and sure enough, it was Ernest Hemingway, unshaven and dirty, but him, without a doubt. 'What are *you* doing here?' he asked in astonishment. I could ask the same, I from Africa and he from the Spanish Civil War.[4]

The trio drove together to the Ritz. Both men were unwashed and Hemingway had a week's growth of beard. Beryl left them to have dinner with a friend '. . . some duchess or other', Blix wrote. Blix records that the trio spent the following morning enjoying the sights of Paris, particularly 'the chestnuts in blossom' before continuing to London.[5] This raises intriguing questions, for Ernest Hemingway never left the USA in 1936 but he was known to be in Paris on the very day in 1938 that Beryl's passport reveals was the day she arrived there. The flight that both Beryl and Blix describe, with its delays and tribulations, could not have been made in 1938 for – as Beryl's passport reveals – that journey took her only days from Kenya. Undoubtedly the meeting in Paris between Blix, Beryl and Hemingway took place. Perhaps it was Blix who telescoped several events into one. He arrived at the Ritz Hotel in Paris on a number of occasions unwashed and unshaven. On one of these he was accompanied by Sir Charles Markham and both men were dirty and dishevelled, having had their luggage stolen. An angry commissionaire tried to evict them from the hotel steps as undesirables until Bror's wife Cockie came to their rescue by explaining that one of the 'tramps' was her husband.[6]

Beryl found a different London from the one she had left a year earlier. Now the talk everywhere was of war, though there was a brief respite in September after Chamberlain's return from Munich declaring 'peace in our time'. For a month or so there was almost a return to the old carefree days as relief flooded through the country, but soon came the first news of Hitler's persecution of the Jews and the murmurings in Europe refused to be stilled. Before long fears of war were again uppermost in people's minds. It seemed a long winter, mitigated by parties drenched in enforced gaiety. Sensitive to atmosphere, Beryl became unhappy and restless. She did some riding and hunting, renewed some old friendships, and spent most of her time in aviation circles. In the spring, lonely and depressed, she was named in the papers as the respondent in a divorce case.

Mansfield had been pressing Beryl for a divorce for some years because he wanted to remarry, but she had always refused. In February 1938 at roughly the same time as she arrived in Natal, she had been mistakenly named by the British press in a divorce case with a co-respondent she had never met, a Mr Geddes. Later an apology was printed – the Mrs Markham in question was Sir Charles Markham's wife.[7] But Mansfield did file for divorce in the spring of 1939, naming

Captain Hubert S. Broad as co-respondent. Mrs Broad also filed naming Beryl as co-respondent.[8]

Hubert Broad, whom Beryl had met through Tom many years earlier, had been chief test pilot to De Havilland for a number of years and was a well-known and universally respected figure in British aviation. In 1925 he had been second in the Schneider Trophy and in 1926 he won the King's Cup Air Race in one of the very first Gipsy Moths. Clearly a certain amount of evidence must have been available – the pair had spent a lot of time together that winter, according to witnesses – but the case was defended strenuously by both Beryl and Broad, and no divorce resulted.

The court case with its attendant unwelcome publicity, lack of money and, more importantly, lack of any real love and support made Beryl very depressed. In addition her son Gervase, always inclined to delicate health, contracted meningitis that winter and was very ill. She saw him several times, and she worried about him, but of course she was virtually a stranger to the child.[9] She was thirty-seven and felt that her life was leading nowhere. She had tried for some time, unsuccessfully, to get news of arap Ruta and in April she wrote to Roddy Hurt, an old friend, asking him if he had heard anything of Ruta, requesting news of Kenya gossip and pouring out her troubles. Roddy's lengthy reply mirrors Beryl's feelings at the time she wrote to him, as well as his obvious affection for her.

Internment Camp,
ISIOLO, N.F.D.

19th May 1939

Beryl my dear,
Thank you so much for writing to me, and I've been meaning to write back for nearly six weeks now, but somehow it didn't become *un fait accompli*. I'm afraid I've been very slack – but I'll try to make up for it now. My dear I loved getting your letter, and hearing from you again after a long time. I'm most awfully sorry to hear about all your troubles – poor Beryl – and you sounded so depressed and alone when you wrote. I wished I could suddenly find myself in England and have taken you out to dinner, and made you really tight in true

Nyeri form. I haven't seen or heard of the case at all. I wonder did Markham drop it at the last moment, or did it come off? Anyway if it did I hope you won all the way – and got a lot of damages. You deserve a lot of luck and happiness Beryl my dear, and don't seem to get it which is so unfair. If I can help you *in any way at all* my dear, please, please do let me do so. Write to me, put any idea up to me, and let me see if I can be of any help to you. I don't want to throw bouquets at you, they may be, and probably are – unwanted – and I've never told you this to your face – but I admire everything about you my sweet. I admire your personality, your terrific guts, your looks, your figure, and all the rest of it. I hope I am a friend of yours Beryl dear, and so, as such please tell me if I can ever be of any help to you.

You ask me for Kenya news. Actually I am a bad source from which to seek information, gup or titbits, because, like you, who say you have buried yourself away and practically gone into retirement these days – I too prefer to live 80% of my time in the NFD [Northern Frontier District] and as far away from the chitter-chatter, gup – scandal and 'fetina' as I can get. I go to Nyeri for a weekend, where I've a small cottage on Schofield's farm behind Seremai, about once a month, and see the chaps and have a party. I've been to Muthaiga only twice in the last ten months, and when I go I'm afraid I find it so boring these days. The place is monopolized by Joss,[10] who lives there, and by Mary who is too drunk to get up before afternoon, and then slowly appears in order to get tight again. She looks quite frightful these days. Brandy has practically closed up one eye completely, and the rest of her is covered with spots. She's as round as the Albert Hall too.

No, I infinitely prefer the Aero Club, for my drinking, parties and friends. Nigel is being divorced and is going to marry Gladys Gooch – and the poor old chap has been kicked out as Secretary of Muthaiga. He goes on October 1st. Dina[11] is out here again looking wonderful. She brought a Portuguese boyfriend with her from Europe but threw him away when she got to Nairobi, he fell for someone else and I don't remember who is Dina's chap now... June and JC [Carberry] left Nyeri a fortnight or so ago for England and America. Blix I haven't seen or heard of for literally years... Kenya is a damn fine place... I've been here in Isiolo for two and a half years now and in the KAR for nearly six and I love it as much as ever. They made me a Captain a year and a half ago and gave me command of this Company, and the Internment Camp – and £750 a year.

I tried to trace your boy *arap* Ruta for you, but Alice was first ill and then went home, and no one else knew him, so I'm afraid I drew blank... Won't you come back to us in this country Beryl dear? There are lots of people who think of you and say nice things about you, and we all miss you a hell of a lot. Do write to me again meanwhile, my dear. Snap out of your depression and loneliness, and please tell me if I can be useful to you in any way. Bless you and the very best of luck and everything to you.

Roddy[12]

With the divorce case out of the way Beryl's spirits lifted, but now she was bored with London. Her friends had only one topic of conversation. Was there going to be a war? No one was interested in anything but the possibility of war. Record-breaking flights had already become a thing of the past, frivolous amidst the earnest military preparations. Beryl could raise no interest from anyone for her proposals. Many of her friends, anxious to secure their positions in the forthcoming fracas, were already wearing Royal Air Force blue. After a year she had still not found a job which offered fulfilment, creditors were pressing and her allowance from Prince Henry was already pitifully inadequate to support her lifestyle. She did not feel part of the groundswell of nationalistic pride and she hated the idea of war. As soon as she could get on to a ship, she booked a single passage to New York. Interviewed on her departure for the United States aboard the SS *Manhattan* she was still telling reporters that her journey was to look for an aeroplane in which to make an attempt on one of the big aviation records.

On 23 June she arrived in New York, breezily telling journalists that she had returned to America 'just because I like it better than any other place'. She also told them that she intended to divorce Mansfield by the end of the year and to become an American citizen. She did neither in the event, but readers learned that in contrast to her last visit following a crash landing in Nova Scotia, when she had needed to borrow a dress from a friend, Mrs Markham came equipped with 'ten daytime outfits and several billowy evening gowns in her trunk'.[13] It was almost certainly too late to cash in on her flight of three years earlier but Beryl was desperate enough to take anything – even demonstration work. First she needed to get an American pilot's licence and she had already arranged through correspondence with Jackie Cochran to travel to California in order to do just that. Jackie put her in touch with the Ryan Aircraft Company which was looking for a demonstration pilot, but this came to nothing. In the spring of 1940 Beryl did do a significant amount of flying in the Ryan SCW[14] but she never obtained her American licence.[15]

Within weeks of her arrival in California, Beryl received an offer of work from Paramount Studios. They had a motion picture called *Safari* on the stocks, in which the hero scouted big game from a small bi-plane. Beryl was offered the job of technical adviser. She rented an apartment near the studios and went to see the Paramount chiefs. *Safari*, she learned, was the story of an African hunting expedition and marked the third picture in which Edward H. Griffith had directed Madeleine Carroll. In those previous movies, *Café Society* and *Honeymoon in Bali*, Miss Carroll had appeared opposite Fred MacMurray. In *Safari* she would co-star with Douglar Fairbanks Jr. Coincidentally, Madeleine Carroll's first movie was financed and directed by Mansfield in England during the early 1930s. It made Miss Carroll's reputation but almost bankrupted Mansfield.

Fairbanks was to play the lead part of Jim Logan, white hunter to the safari party which consisted of Linda Stewart (Madeleine Carroll) and Baron de Courland (Tullio Carminati) and others, but Fairbanks, Carroll and Carminati comprised the inevitable love-triangle which also included several familiar angles. The beautiful, but disillusioned heroine whose only love had been an aviator, killed in Spain, was now determined to find security and peace of mind as the wife of the rich titled sportsman financing the expedition. No one was surprised when at the end of the film the girl walked out on the despicable baron for the handsome adventurer, who at one stage in the film explained that prior to coming to Africa as a hunter, he had been an aviator with the Chinese army. Topically, he went on to tell the wide-eyed heroine, 'I enlisted because men must fight to defend their freedom.'[16] It was all good stuff, no shocks, very entertaining escapism. That was what moviegoers wanted!

Beryl was delighted. She was not only to assist in the flying sequences. It was her job to make the natives' Swahili sound authentic, and to ensure that Miss Carroll's wardrobe was suited to Africa rather than one of the many beaches near Hollywood. 'Authenticity. That's what we want,' Beryl was told. She thought it was all going to be the most enormous fun. And so it turned out to be.

The studio had established two locations to shoot the film. One, at Baldwin Lake, was on a ranch once owned by a gentleman called 'Lucky' Baldwin. The ranch was east of Hollywood, not far from the Santa Anita Racetrack, and the small lake, surrounded by jungle-like growth which flourished in the Californian climate, had last been used to film *The Road to Singapore* starring Bing Crosby, Bob Hope and Dorothy Lamour. For *Safari*, an African trading post (something which amused Beryl immensely because she'd never come across one quite like it in Africa) was built on the banks of the lake, complete with a huge warehouse and wharf.[17]

The other location was Sherwood Forest, west of Hollywood in the Santa Monica Hills, so-called because the leading man's father had once made his memorable version of *Robin Hood* there. In and around Sherwood Forest several sets were built, including a complete African village, a safari base camp, and a landing strip.

Beryl was not the only expert on the film. Ever anxious for authenticity, the director had also hired Prince Modupe, scion of an unnamed African tribe, to teach the extras Swahili and the art of drumming. In addition, the chief set designer had lived in West Africa for many years prior to the First World War and had been Supervising Architect for the German Imperial Government there. As if this were not enough, reality was further provided by a small herd of elephants which grazed loose in the Santa Monica Hills location, and a tame leopard called Nissa, whose only foible was to refuse to work with any actor unless he or she had been drenched in gardenia perfume.[18]

Shooting started in August. The studio carpenter had built a practical seventy-foot stern-wheel boat. The first time out, it sank with all hands, including the two stars – however it was sailing in only four feet of water so no lives were lost and no damage done, except to the electric motor. It transpired that the turning of the ship's wheel had caused the seams to spring, but after rapid repairs the boat was able to proceed in a dignified fashion around the lake.[19]

There were a series of further minor accidents during the shooting, but no serious delays resulted. Griffith, the film's director, walked into a camera boom and cut a three-inch gash in his forehead on the first day's shooting. The portable dressing room occupied by one of the supporting players, Muriel Angelus, (who filled a highly decorative but superfluous part in the story), caught fire and burned part of her wardrobe. A fire extinguisher broke loose from its moorings on the boat and hit Carminati on the head. The DH Gipsy Moth used for flying scenes backfired one day and started a small bush fire which stampeded the elephants. Apart from these diversions everything went well, and Beryl thought it 'was the most tremendous fun'.[20]

Safari was finished by 22 December, well within its production schedule and budget, and everyone went off to celebrate Christmas, feeling pleased with themselves. The single exception to this was Douglas Fairbanks Jr. A few weeks before shooting had ended on 9 December, a birthday party had been thrown for him. It had been a brilliant and enjoyable affair attended by the entire cast and the star's friends and family, including Doug Jr's father Douglas Fairbanks accompanied by his third wife, the former Lady Sylvia Ashley. Doug Senior appeared tired. Two days later the man who had become a Hollywood legend died of a heart attack. It was a tremendous sadness for Doug Jr. When I asked for his memories of the filming of *Safari* his reply was, understandably, that his father's death overshadowed all other memories of that period.[21]

In December, whilst working on the set of *Safari*, Beryl was recognized by a visiting British journalist, Molly Castle (known as the Hollywood Spy), who wrote an article on her for the *Daily Mirror*.

> I've known Beryl Markham for years and years . . . but as long as I've known her I've hardly ever heard her talk about

herself. She's one of the most modest and self-effacing girls I've ever met. That's unusual in most places but fatal in Hollywood. None of the local press has uncovered the story that she could tell – if she would. She is tall, slender and has long golden hair which I've never seen covered except by a flying helmet. Her legs are very long and she is one of the few women who really look good in slacks which she wears most of the time. She speaks Swahili as well as she speaks English which I found out only the other day when I heard the director of *Safari* asking for the pronunciation of a sentence. She rides perfectly but mostly as a method of transport rather than for the sport of it . . . She once earned her living on safari by elephant spotting for Freddie Guest's outfit. Actually the picture on which Mrs Markham is advising, though full of thrills is by no means as exciting as some of her own adventures.

Asked by Ms Castle why she didn't write a book about her adventures, Beryl said she didn't think she could, but she might one day tell her adventure to someone who could make them the basis of a screenplay.[22] The final paragraph of this article does seem to support the case of those who – many years later – argued that Beryl was not the author of her memoir. However Beryl's statement on this occasion was made in the aftermath of a period of success at a time when she had no financial worries. After almost a year had passed without work she was to change her mind.

In Europe war had been declared. Initially it caused only minor ripples in the Hollywood community. Life there went on much as before except that the studio writing teams were told to start working on plots with a war theme. Soon, however, even Hollywood was affected when leading actors with English affiliations such as David Niven and Douglas Fairbanks Jr deserted the community 'for the duration'. This was serious![23]

Beryl loved California, with its smart, pleasure-bent, luxurious lifestyle and perfect climate. She soon had a host of friends, mostly – inevitably – of the handsome male variety, at least one of whom called her by her nickname 'Toots'.[24] Anita Loos introduced her to many useful contacts through whom Beryl hoped to get work on another picture; but meanwhile she was content to live a leisurely existence. She had enjoyed a good salary from the film, she was overwhelmed with invitations and in general she quickly became as much a part of the Hollywood scene as she had previously been part of the London one.

She enjoyed beach parties at Malibu – then unspoiled by the shack-like buildings which now litter the Pacific Coast Highway – and horseriding in the hills on the ranches of her friends. She spent lazy days around swimming pools and fun days of riding in open-topped Cadillac convertibles along wide palm-lined boulevards with Glen Miller music streaming out from the car radio; evenings at never-ending parties, a-glitter with stars of the silver screen.

From time to time her name appeared in tit-bits of gossip, usually noted as a guest at the parties which were reported in the columns of writers such as Hedda Hopper. But as time went on, when no other film job was forthcoming and as no serious relationship developed, Beryl became anxious again. Among her circle of friends at the time was the French writer Antoine de Saint-Exupéry.

Beryl and Saint-Exupéry had a lot in common. Born in Lyon in 1900 into a wealthy French family, he was educated first by Jesuits until his unruly behaviour proved too much for them. Then he was sent to Switzerland where he was thoroughly grounded in the classics. Near his childhood home was an airfield and as he grew to manhood, Saint-Exupéry was fascinated by the aeroplanes, stating to his outraged parents that he wished to become an aviator. After some setbacks he persuaded them to agree to this unusual career and went to Strasbourg for a formal military course in flying.

In 1926 Saint-Exe (as he liked to be called) became a commercial pilot making regular trips on the Toulouse–Dakar run. Later he established the first airmail routes in South America from Brazil to Patagonia, and from 1932 to 1935 he flew airmail from France to the Sahara. In 1935 whilst on a long-distance flight over Africa he was forced down in the desert. Lost for three days he and his companions almost died of thirst before a timely rescue. He enlisted as a captain in the French Air Corps Reserve and when France fell, he disappeared after being captured by the Germans. It was feared that he had been executed, but he turned up again in Portugal, after escaping from his captors despite having his aeroplane shot from under him. He spent the early 1940s in America and, already established as a writer, through the classics *Night Flight* and *Wind, Sand and Stars,* he published the charming fairy story *The Little Prince*; this was followed by his last book *Flight to Arras,* which was published in 1942. He then returned to Europe and was killed in mysterious circumstances whilst engaged on a wartime flying mission over the Mediterranean.[25]

But in the winter of 1940 the lanky poet – for his own works are nothing if not poetic – with his round, good-natured face and bright eyes set under drooping eyelids, was living in Hollywood.[26] Beryl had first met Exupéry during the summer of 1932, when he flew in the King's Cup Air Race, achieving a fourth place, and she was there with Tom following her first solo flight to England. Exupéry was also a good friend of Sydney St Barbe and Hubert Broad[27] whom, a year earlier, Mansfield had cited as Beryl's co-respondent in the divorce case. Beryl told friends that it was Saint-Exupéry who encouraged her to draft an outline for her autobiography,[28] and on his recommendation she sent it to Ann Watkins a New York literary agent. Work began on early chapters of her book and my personal feeling is that Saint-Exupéry did more than merely encourage her; that he may have shaped the book for her and helped her to establish a style.

There are unmistakable similarities between Saint-Exupéry's writing and Beryl's autobiographical work. It is not the purpose of this book to put forward a detailed literary assessment of the styles of these two writers, but a short example will illustrate the similarity in phraseology and even tempo which occurs in many places throughout both authors' works. In the following extract from *Wind, Sand and Stars,* which had been published shortly before Beryl started working on her memoir, Saint-Exupéry describes a room and a character:

> In one of these [workman's houses] Sergeant R— was sleeping fully dressed on an iron cot. When he had lighted a candle and had stuck it into the neck of a bottle, and had drawn forth out of the darkness that funereal bed, the first thing that came into view was a pair of clogs. Enormous clogs, iron-shod and studded with nails, the clogs of a sewer worker or a railway track-walker. All the poverty in the world was in

those clogs. No man ever strode with happy steps through life in clogs like those; he boarded life like a longshoreman for whom life is to be unloaded.[29]

In chapter twenty-two of *West with the Night* Beryl describes her arrival with Blix at a brothel – the only accomodation they were able to find in Benghazi on their journey from Kenya to London in 1936:

> A door opened down the yard and a woman came towards us. She had a lighted candle and she lifted it close to our faces. Her own face held the lineage of several races, none of which had given it distinction. It was a husk with eyes. She spoke but we understood nothing. Hers was a language neither of us had ever heard.
> ... She showed us two rooms not even separated by a door. Each contained an iron bed that cowered under a sticky blanket and had an uncovered pillow at its head... Everything lay under scales of filth. 'All the diseases of the world live here,' I said to Blix.[30]

Even in these small extracts there is more than a vague similarity. In both cases the author is struck with the poverty of the room which coincidentally includes an iron bed. And the two phrases 'All the poverty in the world was in those clogs' and 'All the diseases of the world live here', are surely the result of something more than coincidence. Beryl was to continue writing in this vein long after Saint-Exupéry had gone from her life, even after his death in 1944, but it seems certain that it was he who taught her how to find her literary voice.

By December 1940 Beryl's financial problems had escalated because the income from her annuity could only be paid into a sterling area due to wartime currency restrictions. Her solicitors, Withers and Co. of London, suggested that Canada or the Bahamas would be a convenient place to make the monthly payments, but she would not be able to transfer the money from there into the United States. Coincidence occurred at this point, for the Duke of Windsor had recently been appointed to the governorship of the Bahamas, and friends of Beryl's who were going to Nassau for a holiday in the spring of 1941, learning of her friendship with the former king, invited her to join them.

In March 1941 Beryl travelled to the Bahamas by way of New York, where she met publisher Lee Barker of Houghton Mifflin. Barker told her that he was certainly very interested in the outline for the proposed memoir which the literary agent (Ann Watkins) had shown him, but he needed to see a chapter or two before he could offer her a contract. Beryl had already left two chapters with Ann Watkins for appraisal, and prior to her departure for Nassau, she arranged for these to be forwarded to Houghton Mifflin.

Beryl's friends had rented a property called The Retreat at Nassau, and the long lazy days of sun worship and swimming in the warm blue sea off white beaches were punctuated by Beryl tapping away on a portable typewriter in the corner of a shady veranda.[31]

It is known that Beryl re-established contact with the Duke of Windsor whilst she was on the islands. The extent of their friendship is not known, but Beryl certainly visited Government House on a number of occasions and she could also remember dining with the duke and duchess.[32] It is not unlikely that in Beryl the duke saw a charming reminder of happier times, and, in her concern for him, Wallis too made her welcome often at Government House. The couple's situation was anything but an idyllic sinecure.

The duke's appointment as Governor of the Bahamas was an unprecedented and extraordinary solution to a bizarre problem. No member of the British royal family had ever served as governor of a crown colony. This would have been quite unthinkable, for the royal family were constitutionally required to remain totally aloof from political alliance and any controversy. Furthermore at that time the royal family were not accustomed to expect public criticism nor to have to reply to such. As governor, the duke had to face all these ills and was responsible to the Colonial Office for the running of the colony. It was an intolerable situation for a man who had been groomed for the supreme role of constitutional monarch, but he took it on, undoubtedly fully aware that it was the best he could hope for, and hopeful that it might form a stepping stone to better things after the war. As governor he was held to be popular among the white population (for his presence attracted a great number of American tourists), and among the islanders who referred to him as 'de King'.[33]

He had, at least, the help and support of the woman he loved, and this help was not inconsiderable. HRH had arrived to take up his post in August 1940 (a month of 'searing humidity and mind-destroying temperatures),[34] and for a while the duke and duchess were brittle and understandably cautious about striking up friendships. But by the time Beryl arrived the initial nervousness had worn off and the duchess was accustomed to entertain often. With her quick, bright energy she had transformed the formerly gloomy residence, overfilled with heavy late-Victorian mahogany pieces, to a bright and comfortable, well-furnished home filled with light and flowers.[35]

The duke's aide, Gray Phillips, was a close ally of the duchess and he also became a friend of Beryl during her stay in Nassau.[36] Six and a half feet tall, the Old Etonian classics scholar was charming, resourceful and witty. A bachelor with a strong artistic streak, he was Beryl's dinner partner on several occasions at Government House and elsewhere. The duchess's dinners were said to be extremely amusing for she was very clever and funny and tried always to ensure that her guests were equally entertaining.[37]

By the end of June Beryl had sent four batches of typewritten manuscript to her publishers in Boston, totalling 110 pages. On 26 June 1941 the following internal memorandum was sent by Houghton Mifflin executive Paul Brooks in Boston:

Mr LeBaron R. Barker
New York Office,
Dear Lee:
Bob entirely shares my enthusiasm for Beryl Markham's project. He says: 'This is first-rate stuff and I'm all for publishing it.' I gather from you that there is no need to make a contract now, but I think you're safe in giving her a good deal of encouragement. Meanwhile I look forward to seeing the new chapters that you told me are on the way. May we keep the manuscript for the time being?

Yours
PB[38]

The reply to this reads:

Dear Paul,

Here's a letter from Beryl Markham which pretty well sews up the manuscript. At the same time, as soon as you reach a decision the better. I should advise a small advance on signing and an additional amount on completion: something like $250 and $250. Note the reference to 110 pages and to a brief outline. Is this all on hand at Boston?

As ever

Lee[39]

The memorandum was accompanied by the following letter from Beryl:

'The Retreat'
Nassau, Bahamas
29th June 1941

Lee Barker Esq.
Houghton Mifflin Co.
New York City

Dear Lee:

It was indeed a great pleasure to hear from you. Having had to move from place to place and work hard at the same time, it made me very happy to know that you like what you have seen of my book.

The fourth, not the second batch of material went to Ann Watkins some time ago – the whole totalling one hundred and ten pages. Have you read this last bit?

As to where I expect to finish it, my preference would be somewhere in New York State or Connecticut. On the other hand, I came here only because of the Sterling Area – and can get no part of my very meagre income (now horribly reduced by war taxes) into the States. I must therefore make the best deal I can on the book (the sooner the better) but naturally you would have first crack at it without even asking! You have been so very helpful and believe me, I appreciate it. I certainly promise you that I will accept no other offer without getting in touch with you first.

The weather is due to be unbearable in about two weeks and all my friends are leaving, and so I can't help hoping that some kind soul will give me a contract before the heat wave falls! Luckily, I have my re-entry permit and am still on the quota.

In the mean time the work goes on day by day and will be shipped to New York as long as the postage holds out!

Kindest regards,
Beryl[40]

The series of letters went on:

'The Retreat'
Nassau, Bahamas.
July 23rd 1941

Dear Lee,
Very many thanks for your encouraging letter. The contract arrived the other day; I signed it and sent it off to my Attorney in New York with instructions to hand it over to Ann Watkins, she must have it by now. My Attorney Eddie Eagan, takes care of everything for me in the States. I was not concerned about your company's part of the contract, but since I have never had a working arrangement with Ann Watkins, as to commission, I thought Eagan might take a look at it, though I know the normal rate is ten percent.

The work is coming along fine, I will let you know as soon as I have settled in the States – because of expense, I may not be able to make New York until a little later...[41]

The tourist season was coming to an end as the temperature soared into the nineties, and with the accompanying high humidity it was difficult to work. Her hosts had left in mid June, but Beryl had nothing to hurry back for and was enjoying a liaison with a Scandinavian journalist.[42] By late July, however, not only had the weather become unbearable, but with the Government House party's departure on a tour of the out-islands there was absolutely no one, including her journalist friend, left in Nassau. Beryl returned to the United States.[43]

CHAPTER TWELVE

[*1941–1944*]

Beryl's declared preference for New York State or Connecticut as a place to continue her work may have been prescribed by Saint-Exupéry's return to the East Coast, but she obviously changed her mind, for after leaving the Bahamas she travelled directly to California. In Los Angeles she stayed with friends for a few weeks whilst she looked for permanent accommodation, having given up her old apartment before her departure to Nassau. Shortly after returning to California she was introduced to Raoul Schumacher at a party.

The writer Scott O'Dell had for some time been working at Paramount Studios and knew Beryl through her work on *Safari*. He told me, 'I invited Raoul along because I thought she might like him. He was very entertaining, extremely handsome and fair-haired – no picture I ever saw of him did him any justice.'[1] Another friend told me, 'Raoul was very well-read and remembered anything anybody had ever written, he was a sort of walking encyclopedia.'[2]

Schumacher was thirty-four years old, five years younger than Beryl (though for some years Beryl had been hiding her real age, even in formal documents).[3] At the age of twenty he had inherited some money with which he bought a small ranch in New Mexico. This venture was successful, and when he eventually sold out he made a considerable profit. After an extended trip to Europe where he had relatives, he returned to the USA in 1936 and spent some months in New York working as a free-lance journalist. When this proved unsuccessful he spent two years ranching in Mexico before moving to Santa Barbara, California, in 1939, and Los Angeles in 1941.

When he and Beryl met in August 1941, Raoul was living in

South Spalding Drive, Beverly Hills.[4] Several people recalled Raoul's claims to have been working in Hollywood at the time on one of the anonymous writing teams employed by the major studios, but no record exists of any such employment. An item in the *Santa Barbara News Press* some years afterwards also stated that Raoul 'was for some years actively engaged on scenario writing [in] Hollywood',[5] but he is not listed on any studio employment register or other studio records of the period. He was not registered as a scriptwriter, nor did he belong to a writers' union. Scott O'Dell said he had never heard that Raoul worked for the studios.

Another well-publicized rumour is that Raoul was a ghost-writer. There is no proof of this activity prior to his meeting with Beryl, although in 1945 he told a magazine journalist: 'I once ghost-wrote a full-length Western novel on the dictaphone in seven days.' Adding disarmingly, 'It was a worst seller.'[6]

His greatest asset was charm and Beryl fell deeply in love with him. Scott O'Dell told me about their meeting: 'There was an instantaneous attraction between them – almost a conflagration. It must have been purely physical because she knew nothing at all about him. Next thing I knew they'd disappeared together and it was about four months before they surfaced again.'[7]

During these months Raoul acted as Beryl's editor. The few pages of manuscript for *West with the Night* which survive reveal editing in Raoul's handwriting which certainly added polish, but cannot be regarded as major changes to her own words. It was almost certainly at his suggestion that the design of the book was altered so that it became a series of remembered incidents with no strict chronological order. Pages have been re-numbered and chapter headings revised. Small episodes were discarded and the entire manuscript was 'tightened up'. 'Cut school at Nairobi – use Balmy story instead,' he scribbled across one page.

It is impossible to overstress the importance to Beryl of this type of practical support. A close friend of many years standing said, 'Help and encouragement have always been very important to Beryl. She was always able to do things for herself but she needed to know that there was someone to whom she could turn if she needed guidance.'[8] This need for a prop, created by a basic insecurity and a lack of confidence in her own ability, had initially been filled by her father, and subsequently by *arap* Ruta, Denys Finch Hatton, and Tom Campbell Black. Since Tom's death there had been no man in Beryl's life who filled this important role of supporter, until she met Raoul.

Houghton Mifflin were enthusiastic about the work she had so far submitted to them:

September 19, 1941

Dear Miss Markham,
I have just heard... that you are back in California. I also gather the book is nearing completion. All this is very good news. As you know we are very enthusiastic about as much of the manuscript as we've seen so far. The last batch we received through Ann Watkins' office was Pages 110–132 on July 16. Is there more manuscript on the way?
... When may we hope to see the complete manuscript? To do a proper promotion job, we like to have a manuscript about six months before publication. So you see, there is no time to be lost.

Sincerely Yours
Paul Brooks[9]

12340 Emelita Street
North Hollywood,
California
23rd September 1941

Paul Brooks,
Houghton Mifflin,
2 Park Street
Boston
Dear Mr Brooks:
Very many thanks for your letter, which cleared up a lot of things in my mind. I hope I can maintain your present enthusiasm for the manuscript in the succeeding chapters.

My moving here from Nassau took up a certain amount of time, but in spite of this, I have managed to complete about fifteen thousand words since arriving in California. Ann Watkins has had a good part of this for some time and will receive the remainder shortly. I am, of course, sending her a first and second copy – one for your office and the other for her own use. Margot Johnson suggested that I send the material in large batches, rather than a chapter or so at a time. I would be willing, however, to send it along as I turn it out, should you prefer it. Naturally, I would like to have your opinion of it, as it progresses.

I was interested in your information concerning publication dates in general. I knew very little about any of these things when I was writing to Lee, and I realize more than ever that there's no time to lose.

As to when it will be completed, I hope to have it on your hands by November 1st – at least not later than the fifteenth. That was the approximate date I gave to my agent when I signed the contract.

By the way, I asked Lee if my book had any chance of being considered for one of your fellowship prizes, but so far have had no reply, or is this type of thing not eligible.

My Best Wishes
Beryl[10]

Brooks replied that he would prefer the manuscript in 'large chunks... or complete, rather than chapter by chapter' and telling her that it was too late to consider the book for a Literary Fellowship. 'Fellowship projects have to be considered as such from the very beginning. In any case, I doubt whether this is just the sort of book to come under that plan.'

By October Beryl had found a more permanent residence in North Hollywood.[11] This was a single-storey house, not large but roomy enough for Beryl and her friend Dorothy Rogers, with whom she shared. The costs of travel and house moving may have been responsible for a request to her publishers for a further advance. An unsigned memo dated 17 October in the Houghton Mifflin files has an interesting addendum. The original typewritten script reads: 'Mr Linscott would like the Beryl Markham blank back before next Tuesday.' Scrawled on this memo are two short handwritten notes. The first: 'Drawing prepared. Author wants money', is capped by a terse query written in another hand. 'Or what?'

MEMORANDUM
To Mr Greenslet   From RNL   Date Oct 20 41
Last June we signed up a non fiction project entitled WINGS OVER THE JUNGLE written by Beryl Markham and sent

us through Ann Watkins, with a contract calling for $250 on signing and $250 more on receipt of a satisfactory manuscript. The author has now written us, through Lee Barker (who strongly seconds her request) asking if she can have $100 more at the present time in view of the fact that she has now sent us 199 pages of manuscript and expects to send us the rest next month for publication early in 1942.

Beryl Markham is a famous aviatrix who was brought up on an African ranch, become a professional horse trainer, learned to fly, and for years operated a sort of air taxi service for African hunters during which time she had innumerable adventures. This book is the story of her life, written with really extraordinary vividness and dramatic quality. We gave her a contract on the basis of the first chapter and the material received since more than lives up to our expectation.

Beryl Markham is now in this country, has put aside all other work to finish the book promptly, and has apparently, run out of funds and needs this small amount to tide her over for a month while she completes it.[12]

October 23rd 1941

Dear Miss Markham,
Hearing from Lee that you need some small further advance immediately, I have mailed a check for $100.00 to Margot Johnson at Ann Watkins. We continue to like the manuscript better and better. When may we hope to have the whole thing ready for press?
Paul Brooks
Managing Editor
P.S. We all feel that the present title WINGS OVER THE JUNGLE, does not do justice to the book. It applies to only a small portion of it and is also rather conventional. Will you rack your brains and send me some alternative suggestions within a day or two? We want to prepare a selling sample but are stopped until the title is decided.[13]

Probably the suggested title originated in the offices of Beryl's agent, Ann Watkins. One can almost sense Beryl's delicate eyebrows being arched in the second paragraph of her reply.

October 25th

Dear Mr Brooks,
Thank you so very much for your letter and your kindness in

sending Margot Johnson a cheque for me. I wouldn't for a moment have bothered you, except that things became just a bit difficult in the last couple of weeks.

I am very much encouraged by your comments regarding the latter part of the manuscript, but where in the world did you get the title WINGS OVER THE JUNGLE? It surely is not mine and was never suggested by me in any letter to anybody – it sounds like a title chosen by a protégé of Osa Johnson! (Not to be unkind).[14]

The title that I have selected is: THERE FELL MY SHADOW, taken from a line out of the book. It seems to me appropriate in more ways than one, but if you think not, let me know and I will try again.

Yours very sincerely,
Beryl Markham[15]

October 27th 1941

Dear Miss Markham,

I don't know where the title came from either, but I had every intention of changing it. THERE FELL MY SHADOW is certainly better, though I'm not sure it's perfect. Could you put on your thinking cap and produce a few alternatives?

Yours sincerely
Paul Brooks[16]

October 31 1941

Dear Mr Brooks,

I am still in search of a perfect title, at your suggestion, which I must say is quite a mark to shoot at. I understand that it must be appropriate to the book, and at the same time have appeal to the buying public.

Here, after wearing myself to a thin white centre, is all I am able to offer. If you find none of these to your liking however, please let me know what angle I ought to aim at.

1. STEPS TO THE SKY
2. ONCE IN THE WIND
3. CATCH THE QUICK YEARS
4. KWAHERI MEANS FAREWELL
5. KWAHERI! KWAHERI!   (Swahili)
6. ERRANT IN AFRICA
7. STARS ARE STEADFAST
8. NO STAR IS LOST

Sincerely yours,
Beryl Markham[17]

November 4th 1941

Dear Miss Markham,
In the absence of Paul Brooks I am writing . . . to say that our
own title preference is for 'There fell my shadow', with a
second choice, 'Once in the wind.'
                                    Sincerely,
                                    R.N. Linscott[18]

November 12th 1941

Dear Mr Linscott:
Thank you for your letter. I am glad that your choice of a title
is the same as my own, though from Paul Brooks' last letter, I
gather he thinks a better one might still be found. At this
point, however, I have no further suggestions. THERE
FELL MY SHADOW seems to apply all through the book –
also, the title appears in a line from one of the later chapters
which I think adds to its authenticity.
    Meanwhile the work goes on and I hope to have it ready for
you shortly.
                                    Sincerely
                                    Beryl Markham[19]

November 18th 1941

Dear Miss Markham,
You're right – I'm still far from content with THERE FELL
MY SHADOW. It seems a little pretentious, and the *double
entente* [sic] is not evident until one knows a little more about
the book. The perfect title would suggest that you are writing
about Africa, not as a traveller or an explorer, but as one who
has lived there and grown up there. It has been suggested that
AFRICA IS MY HOME, while very simple and literal, gets
this idea over very well. How does it strike you? . . . We must
decide immediately. I wish that you would send me a day
letter, at our expense, giving your opinion of the title
mentioned above and suggesting other alternatives which
accomplish what we have in mind . . .
                                    Sincerely yours,
                                    Paul Brooks[20]

COLLECT DAY LETTER NOV 22ND 41 NORTH HOLLY-
WOOD
PAUL BROOKS. MOST ANXIOUS CO-OPERATE BUT
FEEL SUGGESTED TITLE NON INCLUSIVE COLOUR-

LESS AND HAS MISSIONARY FLAVOUR. OFFER FOL-
LOWING ALTERNATIVES. RETREAT TO FLIGHT. THIS
TOO IS AFRICA. AFRICAN MOSAIC. PAGE OF A LIFE.
STILL TRYING HARD IF UNACCEPTABLE. BERYL
MARKHAM.[21]

Brooks replied that THIS TOO IS AFRICA was the best so
far, but that she should come up with more ideas if she could. He
was worried about getting the complete manuscript and asked
her to cable him collect with a definite date.

COLLECT OVERNIGHT TELEGRAM NOV 29TH NORTH
HOLLYWOOD
PAUL BROOKS. MAILING ADDITIONAL 15000 WORDS
TOMORROW STOP EXPECT FINISH BOOK DECEMBER
15 BUT MAKING EVERY EFFORT TO FINISH EARLIER
STOP STILL THINKING ABOUT TITLE MEANWHILE
FOLLOWING MIGHT BE CONSIDERED STOP NO OTHER
AFRICA = BERYL MARKHAM[22]

PAID TELEGRAM DECEMBER 5 1941 BOSTON
BERYL MARKHAM. FEEL CERTAIN WE HAVE FINALLY
DISCOVERED PERFECT TITLE QUOTE I SPEAK OF
AFRICA UNQUOTE USING TITLE PAGE LINE FROM
SHAKESPEARES HENRY FOUR QUOTE I SPEAK OF
AFRICA AND GOLDEN JOYS UNQUOTE PLEASE WIRE
COLLECT YOUR OKAY SELLING SAMPLES UNDER
WAY REGARDS. PAUL BROOKS[23]

COLLECT NIGHT TELEGRAM DEC 5TH. NORTH
HOLLYWOOD
PAUL BROOKS. DELIGHTED WITH YOUR TITLE AND
LINE FOR TITLE PAGE FULL MARKS TO YOU AND
WILLIAM SHAKESPEARE REGARDS BERYL MARK-
HAM.[24]

PAID TELEGRAM DEC 22 1941
BERYL MARKHAM. GLAD TO HAVE FOUR MORE
CHAPTERS AND EAGER FOR BALANCE WHEN MAY WE
EXPECT TOTAL. PAUL BROOKS[25]

COLLECT NIGHT TELEGRAM DEC 23 1941 NORTH
HOLLYWOOD

PAUL BROOKS. HAVE HAD BAD ATTACK OF FLU
HOWEVER MORE MATERIAL IN MAIL AND LAST TWO
CHAPTERS UNDER WAY XMAS WISHES. BERYL
MARKHAM[26]

The final work was delivered before the end of January and
the book was produced for a June 1942 release. In the event, the
title became *West with the Night*. It is not known who was
responsible for this title; no correspondence exists and Beryl
could not remember, but she did recall that she had suggested
the title *Straight on Till Morning*, from which the eventual title
evolved. The line: 'I speak of Africa and golden joys. Henry IV,
Act V sc. 3' appeared on the title page and the book was
dedicated to 'My Father'.

In addition there was an acknowledgement: 'I wish to express
my gratitude to Raoul Schumacher for his constant encouragement and his assistance in the preparations for this book.' Beryl
could never have imagined how controversial this short
dedication was to become some forty years on.

While she waited for her book to be released, Beryl
surprisingly decided to throw in her lot with the war effort,
which, after Pearl Harbor, had escalated dramatically. In 1986
she told me that Raoul was overseas with the US Navy at the
time and she was lonely, so she wrote to the California wing of
the Civil Air Patrol, enclosing a résumé of her flying experience
and asking if she could be of any help.

3 March 1942

Dear Mrs Markham
Your kind letter of February 27th is at hand and we were
indeed very glad to hear from you and your offer of assistance
in the Civil Air Patrol is greatly appreciated. You may rest
assured that we will be very happy to see you and may I
suggest you call my secretary . . . for an appointment at such
time as may be convenient to you.
        Yours very truly

        Bertrand Rhine
        Wing Commander for California
        Civil Air Patrol[27]

Until that time women had not played any sort of flying role in the CAP and though Beryl had a meeting with Wing Commander Rhine to discuss the matter, nothing ever came of it.[28]

Years later she told friends that she spent some time during the war training pilots, but that she hadn't enjoyed it.[29] There is also a story, widely believed, that she flew look-out patrols along the Pacific coastline, but neither of these stories can be verified by official service records, and such service, if any, must have been very short, for from early June she was fully occupied with other interests.

When *West with the Night* was released at the end of May 1942 it was acclaimed by the critics. Not renowned for generosity, they were almost effusive in their praise, and in literary circles at least Beryl was lionized for a time. A selection of reviews is printed below:

> When a book like Beryl Markham's *West with the Night* comes along it leaves a reviewer very humble. Words of praise used for other works seem trite and thin. For *West with the Night* is more than an autobiography; it is a poet's feeling for her land; an adventurer's response to life; a philosopher's evaluation of human beings and human destinies. To say that Beryl Markham captures the spirit of Africa would be presumptuous and ridiculous; Africa has captured hers, and she speaks with eloquence close to enchantment of the things it has meant to her.
> Rose Field, *Books*, 5 July 1942

> [Miss] Markham has made a real contribution to the literature of flight. Her background is more romantic than Ann Lindbergh's, her perception as delicate. Here are the jungles and excitements of Osa Johnson... At a moment when our constant thought is of danger and destruction in the heavens it is good to read some of the poetry of flight, to experience secondhand the wide solitude of the sky.
> E.M., *Boston Globe*, 17 June 1942

> Here is more than a mere autobiographical work. Here is an interpretation of Africa – A scrutiny into its age-old secrets and a glance into its future. As for the stylist, he will find Miss Markham's writing distinguished. It has strength, it has the precious quality of unexpectedness; it is unfailingly intelli-

gent, like the mind of the woman who shaped it. For her thinking is bold, original and challenging as her life has been.
M.W., *Christian Science Monitor*, 8 August 1942

A book quite unlike anything that has been written by any other woman or about Africa, its natives, its hunting and its future by anybody. It is written as a book on such a subject should be, straight out of experienced knowledge. Its thought was born in the long, wide-spaced African silences. Its opinions are those of a woman who has always from childhood been very much a person in her own right, and by reason of a country where cut-to-pattern people do not belong. And it is written with exceptional simple beauty in a style that, without aiming at distinction achieves it unquestionably.
J.S. Southron, *New York Times*, 21 June 1942

The Chapters on flying over Africa are unusually thrilling...
Her descriptions of the strange country over which she travelled are sensitive... and a little rapturous about the 'feel' of Africa.
Clifton Fadiman, *New Yorker*, 20 June 1942

Beryl Markham does more than tell of Africa. With admirable modesty, she offers us a thrilling as well as appealing saga of a very valiant and very human woman, philosophically pitting her skill, bolstered by limitless faith in herself, against relentless Nature in all her multifarious disguises, in the dank jungles, the desert wastes, and the boundless skies.
Linton Wells, *Saturday Review of Literature*, 27 June 1942

One of Houghton Mifflin's most popular and productive authors of the period was Stuart Cloete, a South African who from time to time reviewed the work of other authors. He and his writer/illustrator wife Tiny were to become friends of Beryl and Raoul, who moved in the same literary circles in New York. At the time Beryl's book was published Cloete had not met her, but he was sent the book to review by Dale Warren – Houghton Mifflin's publicity agent.[30] Cloete liked it very much and Houghton Mifflin used his neatly written praise in their own publicity releases.[31]

The book should have been a great success. It was not.

Timing is everything in publishing. With the United States firmly committed to the war effort the public taste for works of a poetic nature seems to have waned. The royalties provided Beryl with a modest income for a year or so and then the book vanished.[32] No reprints were ordered. An edition was published in England by Harrap & Company, on the very poor quality paper allowed to publishers at the time, but sales were limited and before long that version too, faded from sight.

However, encouraged by the book's initial success Beryl had moved to New York. Later Raoul joined her. By now their relationship had deepened and they decided to marry. Beryl contacted Mansfield, at last agreeing to the divorce which he had sought for the past decade. It is difficult to understand her previous reluctance to formalize her separation from Mansfield. Perhaps it was pique at his refusal to support her, or perhaps she felt a measure of security in technically remaining a member of the aristocratic Markham family. In August she moved to Wyoming where she rented a house in order to establish a ten-week residency, which would enable her to obtain a fast severance of her existing matrimonial ties.[33]

On 5 October she filed her plaint, charging that Mansfield had subjected her to 'intolerable indignities'. Her case was accepted and the divorce was granted on 14 October. Raoul and Beryl were married in Laramie on the following Saturday and left Wyoming immediately for a month's honeymoon in Virginia at the home of friends.

In a letter to Dale Warren in November, shortly after the couple's return to New York, Stuart Cloete reveals, 'I saw Beryl and Raoul yesterday. Funny they should [have been] staying with a cousin of mine in Virginia – the grand-daughter of Lady Northey who was Evangeline Cloete and one of the most beautiful women I ever saw . . .'[34] Beryl had previously written to say she had 'more or less been brought up by [Cloete's] cousin Lady Northey in Kenya when Major General Sir Edward Northey was Governor there'.[35] This is an obvious over-statement of the facts. Beryl did know Lady Northey well at a social level, but she was already married to Jock during the Northeys' years in Kenya (1919–22). If Lady Northey helped the young bride on matters of social etiquette this was probably the sum total of her influence.

Back in London, Mansfield was experiencing difficulties with the validity of Beryl's divorce papers. He eventually had to go through the English courts since they would not accept the American judgement. It took him a year to obtain a Decree Absolute which was granted only after he was able to produce 'proof of adultery' which consisted of a letter from Raoul admitting that he regularly slept with his own wife.[36] Mansfield was at last free to remarry and his second wife Mary took over as stepmother to Gervase who was then at Eton.

Through the winter of 1942–43 Beryl lived alone in New York and the Cloetes 'saw a lot of her'.[37] 'What happened to the cowboy she married?' Cloete scribbled at the foot of a letter to Dale Warren. Raoul returned in January 1943 and shortly afterwards the couple departed for a small ranch in New Mexico.[38] It was no more than a piece of arid land with a small wooden shack, but they made it their base for about six months. Beryl hated the cold and bleakness of winter in New York and had gone with alacrity towards the sun. Her friend Stuart Cloete wrote sadly to Dale Warren at Houghton Mifflin:

> Dear Dale,
> . . . I have no favourite blond now that Beryl has gone with the wind and the shoemaker West into the snowy night . . . about the silliest thing I ever heard of as there is no food, no servants and damn few houses from what I hear . . .
> Yours Stuart
> (Cloete)[39]

Despite Cloete's condemnation the move was not merely whimsical. The Schumachers were already experiencing the first of their persistent financial problems and could no longer afford to live in New York in the style which Beryl had adopted on the expectations of her book's success. The royalties from rapidly diminishing sales of *West with the Night* and the rent she received from her Kenyan farm Melela would hardly have covered the couple's drinks bill. In addition there was her annuity from Prince Henry, but she continued to experience great difficulty in having this paid to her in the USA during the war years, due to sterling transfer restrictions. Raoul's contribution to the couple's budget is hazy but this does not necessarily mean that it was non-existent.

Melela had been leased since Beryl left in 1936 and she now wrote to her agents in Nairobi asking for advice about whether or not to sell the property. It seemed highly unlikely, then, that she would ever return to Kenya permanently and at the time she wrote it was far from clear who would win the war. The agents' advice was to sell while she could. Beryl took the advice and subsequently received the sum of £400. Ten years later, when Beryl was in Kenya and virtually destitute, Melela was sold again for £40,000.[40]

Beryl spent most of the summer of 1943 running the ranch and raising turkey poults. Her remarkable affinity with all animals enabled her to keep the chicks alive through a long spell of wet weather to which they are particularly susceptible.[41] When I interviewed her in 1986 she repeated claims previously made to others that Raoul was often absent and that she did a little writing, mainly to help overcome boredom and loneliness.[42] It is difficult to explain these regular absences of Raoul's. Despite almost a year's research with the assistance of the US Military Personnel Records Office I was unable to locate any record of service for him during this period, although he did serve with the US Coastguards for while, later on. Scott O'Dell too was puzzled. 'I never heard of Raoul serving in the Navy.'[43]

Beryl's first short story, 'The Captain and his Horse', appeared in *Ladies' Home Journal* in August 1943. This magazine had previously published a chapter from *West with the Night* under the title 'Wise Child' which had proved popular, and Beryl had no difficulty in placing another story with them. Interestingly the basis for the story was several discarded paragraphs from the manuscript for *West with the Night*, but she appears to have borrowed the idea from her friend Stuart Cloete according to the following letter:

September 7th 1943

To Dale Warren
Houghton Mifflin

Dear Dale,
Many thanks for your note. I'm glad you find the [cough mixture] good for a hangover. I had never heard of it being

drunk for pleasure before but you are a great innovator.

Yes I have read Beryl's magnificent horse story, and you will find my equally magnificent horse story in a forthcoming *Colliers*.[44] I wrote mine some time before Beryl wrote hers and read it to her when she was in New York.

Hon Y Soit Qui Mal Y Pense...

> Yours
> Stuart[45]

By September when Houghton Mifflin wired her to ask if she would speak at a forthcoming book fair in 'the East' the Schumachers had left New Mexico for good and were living on a small ranch at Lake Elsinore in Southern California where she wrote 'Something I Remember', another short auto-biographical story. Houghton Mifflin also wanted to discuss her future writing plans.

'Something I Remember' and 'The Splendid Outcast', both written in the winter of 1943–44, were written in the same style as *West with the Night,* and are based on actual incidents in Beryl's early life. Her success in publishing these short stories provided the Schumachers with a potentially lucrative source of income and Raoul was not slow to recognize the marketability of Beryl's name. However it was almost certainly Raoul who wrote the next two stories which appeared under the name Beryl Markham. Both 'Your Heart will tell You' and 'Appointment in Khartoum'[46] rely heavily on Beryl's flying experiences in Africa for the story-line, but they are purely romantic fiction and are written in a totally different style to that of Beryl's book and her earlier stories. This style is clearly repeated in 'The Whip Hand', a short story published under the name of Raoul Schumacher which appeared in *Collier's Weekly Magazine* in June 1944.

Although in later years Raoul claimed to friends that he had been a writer during the early 1940s, 'The Whip Hand' was the first time his name had appeared in print. His writing style was smart and snappy, contemporarily popular with the readers of a whole range of periodicals who lapped up escapist fiction at an astonishing rate. It is unlike Beryl's more poetic, sensitive style of writing though it is known that she co-wrote these stories to the extent that she told Raoul of her experiences and provided background information about Africa. It seems that she was not able, or was not prepared, to write popular fiction to order.

Another story, 'Brothers are the Same', writter in 1944 and published in *Collier's* under Beryl's name in February 1945, was almost certainly also Raoul's work although, again, Beryl must have provided much of the detailed background information on the Maasai and Africa. Not enough it seems, for Raoul was driven to researching in a reference library for tribal customs of the Maasai which Beryl could not provide.[47] Nevertheless there is more of Beryl in this story than in the previous two and the Schumachers obviously felt they had found a successful formula. Raoul, who had been a frustrated writer, could be relied upon to turn out fictional stories based on Beryl's adventures and experiences whilst Beryl herself could occasionally write a short autobiographical episode. In this connection Raoul's subsequent claims that he had been a ghost writer appear to be true, although these activities seem to have been mainly confined to those stories he wrote under Beryl's name with story-line help from her.[48]

Scott O'Dell visited the couple whilst they were at Elsinore and found them working in the basement, the coolest place in the house during a heatwave. In a letter to *Vanity Fair* in March 1987 he recalled: 'Beryl [was] dictating, Raoul copying; [they were] writing a short story and stewing in the torrid heat. A New York editor sat on the doorstep.' The New York editor was almost certainly Kyle Crighton of *Collier's Magazine*, who was known to have been in regular contact with Beryl at the time. Interviewed for *Collier's*, Beryl admitted to being unsure as to whether the adventurous life she had led was a hindrance or a help to her as a writer. 'That old adage "Truth is stranger than fiction" is so correct for me,' she told Crighton, 'that any inventive power I might have is stifled.'[49]

The statement that Beryl was seen dictating to Raoul is an important one, though when I questioned Mr O'Dell later he revised this, saying that Beryl was merely 'telling stories to Raoul and he was putting it into readable prose'. Unfortunately O'Dell could not recall the substance of the story on which they were working, but he did recall Beryl and Raoul's relationship at this time, more than a year after their marriage: 'They were deliriously happy and went about hand in hand, dressed in

Levis, concha belts and matching calico shirts and hats. Modern lovers out of ancient times. Beryl had a horse, a cat and two Nubian goats to remind her of her African days. How I envied them and their Arcadian lives.'[50]

Beryl too remembered this time for she had already told me that she and Raoul used to ride out 'dressed as cowboys', but she could provide no further details. She was promised a series of lecture tours and Raoul, having had 'The Whip Hand' published, now felt he could write under his own name. To all appearances the couple's future as a writing team looked set to flourish and in the summer of 1944 Beryl and Raoul moved to a much larger, rented house in Pasadena, north-east of Los Angeles.

That winter Scott O'Dell noticed the first snags in the fabric of the once idyllic relationship. The couple were known for throwing numerous parties. O'Dell attended one of these parties and was sitting on the sofa next to Beryl when Raoul carried in a tray of martinis. Somehow Raoul spilled a drink and Beryl meaningfully whispered to O'Dell that this clumsiness was becoming a habit. It was a clear hint about the heavy drinking that was later to become a real problem for Raoul, and O'Dell was startled by the glint in Beryl's eyes as she spoke. Later he spent some time alone with Raoul and they talked about writing.

> I asked what they were working on . . . he said he was doing a novel about Africa. I said, 'Why are you writing about Africa, you've never been there?' He replied, 'Are you kidding? I've lived there through Beryl and all her stories.' He was quiet for a minute and then he said to me, 'You are my best friend and I want to make a confession. I want you to know that Beryl did not write *West with the Night*, or any of the short stories. Not one damn word of anything.'

But did Raoul actually claim to have written them all himself? 'Yes I'm sure of that, Raoul wrote them all,' O'Dell stated. 'But anyway that was when everything started to go wrong for them, when they were in Pasadena.'[51]

Some years later Roual was to make a similar statement about his authorship to another close male friend, but the evidence does not substantiate his claims. I have no doubts that Raoul wrote three – or perhaps four – of the fictional stories published in Beryl's name. They were clearly based on Beryl's own experiences and it is obvious that she must have provided the background, probably in just the manner that Scott O'Dell witnessed. But I believe Raoul's claim to have written *West with the Night* was a weak attempt to bolster his own ego when he was feeling the first icy vibrations of Beryl's disapproval.

Certainly he had edited the manuscript, maybe he even became involved in the writing of the final six chapters, and this might well have led him to assume a closer identity with the work than was justified. He may have genuinely felt that his contribution entitled him to some claim to authorship. But there is nothing to corroborate his reported statement that Beryl wrote 'not one damn word'. On the contrary, all the surviving documentary evidence points to Beryl having been the book's author. According to the correspondence between Beryl and her publishers, Houghton Mifflin had already received one hundred and thirty-two pages of manuscript by July 1941, and a further sixty-seven pages had been sent to Ann Watkins before Beryl left Nassau for California. Yet although she wrote the final six chapters (of twenty-four) after she met Raoul, there is nothing in *West with the Night* which even hints at a change in writing style.

Saint-Exupéry's death had been announced only weeks before O'Dell's visit to the couple in Pasadena.[52] Could it be that in making his surprising 'confession' Raoul felt that there was no possible danger of it being refuted?

These first signs of strain in the marriage that had at first been so happy also marked a new characteristic in Beryl. Where there had once been a childlike appeal, there now appeared a hardness in her manner bred out of a great disillusionment. There was a peremptory edge to her voice and the look in her eyes when she watched Raoul was now more often jaundiced than adoring. What had gone wrong for the couple in the months since O'Dell had last seen them? Was it only because of Raoul's increasingly heavy drinking, or had she already discovered at this stage that he had male lovers?

O'Dell did not know the real cause behind the small manifestations of approaching disaster; he saw the Schumachers too seldom, he says, even to hazard a guess (though Raoul's statement, 'You are my best friend,' sits uneasily in this light). He saw no evidence of homosexuality in Raoul. 'To the contrary, I thought he was rather like me in that respect – too much the other way, and I knew he had earlier enjoyed several affairs with some high-flying women in New Mexico and Arizona,' Mr O'Dell added.

But Raoul had been found lacking in some way, of that there is no doubt. The idol had feet of clay. He did not measure up. Perhaps at this stage in their relationship, it was merely Raoul's failure as a provider that forced Beryl to recognize some disappointing reality in his make-up. That year of 1944 was the most prolific time for the couple as writers, but even then they only produced five short stories between them. Beryl's short lecture tour had provided a much needed boost to the couple's income and according to O'Dell she had received a large advance to write a book on Tod Sloane, the celebrated jockey, though if this is so it was from a source other than Houghton Mifflin and Beryl's agent was never aware of the contract.[53]

Perhaps, once again, Beryl's marital problems were caused by her own promiscuity. Few men would have been tolerant of her attitude towards casual sexual encounters. But this seems unlikely, for almost imperceptibly Beryl now began to assume a dominant role in the relationship. Raoul was the underdog, (which hints that he was the wrongdoer) and nothing could have been more fatal for the surivival of the marriage. Essentially Beryl needed support from a partner, someone she could lean on in times of stress and who could assuage her own deep-seated insecurity. Clearly she did not receive the support she needed from Raoul and anything less was almost guaranteed to earn only her growing contempt.

CHAPTER THIRTEEN

[*1944–1948*]

In April 1945 Raoul was placed 'on general reserve' (without pay) with the US Coastguard 'and released from active service duty' (though beyond Beryl's statements on the subject there is no evidence that he ever saw any).[1] With the war virtually over, Beryl and Raoul started to think about a permanent home. Both wanted to remain in California, preferably on a small ranch, somewhere quiet where they could write but not too far from social contacts. Milly Kelleher, a friend of Raoul's from Santa Barbara, provided the answer.

Milly ran one of the four real-estate agencies in Santa Barbara and she had on her books a small 'avocado ranch' which had previously been the country retreat of Leopold Stokowski and his former wife Evangeline. Beryl had known Stokowski since her trip to the West Coast in 1937, at the beginning of the maestro's affair with Greta Garbo, but had already returned to South Africa in February 1938 when their romance burst into public gaze courtesy of the world press and culminated in the famous, wistful remark, 'I only want to be left alone.'[2]

Stokowski married Gloria Vanderbilt in April 1945 and in strange ways strings were pulled that jingled echoes in Beryl's earlier life, for Gloria was the niece of Lady Thelma Furness (the former wife of 'Duke' Furness who had been Tom Campbell Black's employer in the 1930s). Thelma had also been the acknowledged mistress of Edward, Prince of Wales, who bestowed upon her the nickname 'Toodles'. For five years the prince had enjoyed a sophisticated liaison in which matters were always satisfactorily arranged to ensure that he and Lady Furness could spend weekends together at Fort Belvedere, the prince's home in Windsor Great Park.[3] Their personal idyll was ended when Thelma, about to depart for a holiday in America, naively suggested to Wallis Simpson, 'I'm afraid the Prince is going to be lonely. Wallis, won't you look after him?'[4]

As a child Gloria had been the principal character in a legal battle that captured world headlines in which she was dubbed 'poor little rich girl' and in which her widowed mother, also named Gloria (the twin sister of Thelma Furness), fought a vicious battle for custody of 'Little Gloria'. The child who had inherited millions of dollars had an unhappy upbringing for which she never forgave her mother.[5]

When 'little' Gloria married Stokowski, a man forty-two years her senior, the press conjectured that she was seeking the father she'd never known. Publicly she cut off her mother's allowance, declaring through newspaper interviews, 'My mother can go to work or starve.' When her Aunt Thelma castigated her – again in the papers – for 'her bad example to the average American girl and her inhuman treatment of her mother' Gloria answered with a broadside: 'Lady Furness need not criticize and be so anxious about the American Girl. The average American girl lives in a happy home and receives Mother Love. My mother gave me neither of these blessings. Let her Ladyship go back to England and tend to her own affairs.'[6]

Gloria's petulance even affected Beryl, for the new Mrs Stokowski did not like the Montecito ranch in the hills at the back of Santa Barbara. Possibly this was because Stokowski's previous wife Evangeline had lived there, but it was also locally notorious for having been the hideaway of Stokowski and Garbo during their harried love affair some years earlier.[7] Stokowski loved the seventeen-acre ranch, and it was probably at Gloria's pre-marital request that he put the property on the market, but he could never bring himself to sell it.[8] He had more or less built it to his own specifications, or at least had personally designed and supervised much of the building, and he even claimed to have personally planted some of the avocado trees.[9]

Throughout the years that he owned the property, despite long absences he maintained a regular correspondence with the handyman Robert Lopez who looked after the house and garden from 1942 to 1957. Stokowski's letters were full of minute instructions for the garden, down to the precise site for, and after-care of, the rare and exotic trees which regularly found their way to the ranch. Often when the maestro made an overseas tour he would be asked what gift he would most like to commemorate the occasion, and he always requested a tree for his Montecito ranch. The ranch, having been unlived in for some time now found its way onto the books of Milly Kelleher.

Milly, the mutual friend of both the Schumachers and Stokowski, at once saw a solution to the dilemma and Beryl and Raoul moved into the property in Toro Canyon in the late spring of 1945. They paid no rent and lived there as guest-caretakers rather than tenants. Stokowski continued to visit the house whenever he returned to the West Coast.

Like Stokowski, Beryl adored the ranch. In 1986 she told me it was the loveliest house in the world. 'Lovelier than Njoro?' 'Mmm... different,' she said. Indeed in its setting it was remarkably like Njoro. Nestling high in the foothills of the Santa Ynez mountains which form an impressive backdrop to Santa Barbara, the rustic timber house overlooks sunbaked slopes of red-earthed groves of fruit trees. The climate is, like Njoro, seemingly eternally sunny and the views from the house are equally spectacular, for whilst in Njoro the views across the fabled Rift end with the Aberdares, in Toro Canyon the views across the hills terminate in palm-fringed beaches and the glittering, blue Pacific Ocean.

The house itself, single-storeyed with large cool rooms, is U-shaped and built into the hillside so that one wing is higher than the other. It is not an ostentatious residence, but it is well-designed, comfortable and typically Californian. The large living area which forms one side of the building is on the lower level and the bedrooms form the higher wing, so that from every room the views are spectacular, and each window has a clear prospect. In the centre of the horse-shoe are a swimming pool and a patio, both built at the same time as the house. All the rooms open on to the pool and patio; bougainvillea tumbles everywhere in bright red and pink confusion. The windows of the house, generously shaded under overhanging eaves, have always been flung open to the gardens basking in the California sunshine and cool ocean breezes.

Even today in the uncultivated hills which lap the edge of the ranch, wildlife abounds – deer, foxes, bobcat and rabbits roam the quiet hills of the canyon.[10] There is an ever-present hot dry scent of eucalyptus and pine, and a sweet elusive perfume from the creamy flowers of towering yucca plants. Wherever you walk you hear constantly the quick scuttling sounds of lizards, disturbed from basking, as they scurry across dry undergrowth. Bluejays screech in the trees and bustle in the flowerbeds, buzzards hover constantly on the air currents of the surrounding hills.

Beryl loved to ride out alone in these hills, she was totally at home here and despite the problems she was experiencing in her marriage was probably never happier. Initially the move caused a cessation of hostilities and the Schumachers rapidly became a popular addition to Santa Barbara society. Beryl – now aged forty-four – was stunning and her writing success had added a new dimension, an aura of self-confidence. She was still a minor celebrity in her own right and Raoul was a charming man. 'In those days anyone who had a black tie and knew how to hold a knife was welcomed with open arms,' said a friend. 'Raoul was a very entertaining guest – before he started to drink heavily that is...'[11] There were also a number of people in the town whom Beryl knew from her past, including Thelma Furness who stayed there for a time, and Gabriel and Rhoda Prud'homme, whom she had first known in Kenya where the wealthy couple had owned a lavishly equipped farm in Nanyuki. Rhoda and Beryl were alternately close friends one week and at loggerheads the next. Rhoda loved to entertain often and on a grand scale from her Pacific Coast house and Beryl was not above turning up at Rhoda's impressive parties wearing her riding clothes, to the annoyance of her hostess.[12]

As usual Beryl did not have many women friends. 'The other women tended to keep a tight hold on their men when Beryl was around,' Warren Austin said. 'Men really liked to be around her and she liked to be around them. She didn't especially work at it but she had such charisma, and she was so interesting that it just happened that way. She couldn't help shining in any kind of gathering and the other women didn't particularly like always being in her shadow.'[13]

A typical day for Beryl and Raoul started with a ride in the hills before breakfast. During the morning they would work independently; each had their own typewriter and Beryl preferred to work in her room.[14] Several times a week Beryl would visit a beauty salon in nearby Santa Barbara with its white Spanish-style buildings and red-tile roofs. Cool court-yards with splashing fountains provided pleasant meeting places for lunch with friends. Afternoons were spent around the pool, and in the evenings the couple often dined out or went to the casino. In the colder months they sat in the pleasant sitting room around a spitting log fire, and read, or invited friends in to play bridge, a game which Beryl disliked but played moderately well. Stokowski had installed at one end of the room a grand piano for his work. Beryl recalled playing this piano, though how good she was is open to conjecture.

Maddie de Mott, who became a peripheral member of the same social set in those years, first met the couple in 1946 at a cocktail party.

> I was very impressed at how dashing everyone was – well-dressed and cheery. I particularly remember Beryl as being tall and really quite lovely-looking with blonde hair. Raoul appeared to be less socially minded in a way. He didn't seem to have quite as flashy clothes and was rather a friendly, simple person. They moved about in a group I knew quite well. They were independent, working for themselves... Both were writing short stories and were, I gather, making quite a bit of money. I think they also used to sometimes go up to a ranch in the hills behind Santa Barbara and help with the cattle... and they particularly liked picnics. I remember one picnic that I went on... Beryl was riding in a car, it was a red convertible and her blonde hair was streaming out behind her. She had dashing young men with her, plus Raoul. Sometimes she enjoyed driving herself. Raoul was a bon vivant who really enjoyed life. He used to say that work was the curse of the drinking classes and was suspected of spending more time drinking than working. His drinking though was rather jovial, and his greatest asset was his overt friendliness and witty humour.[15]

It was about this time that Warren Austin met the Schumachers. For some years Dr Austin had been personal physician to the Duke of Windsor during the duke's period as governor of the Bahamas. He arrived on the islands some time after Beryl's visit there in 1941 so had never met her, but he had heard of her. Austin was running an army hospital when the prince's ADC, Major Gray Phillips, came in with a broken finger, suffered in a bicycling accident. The two men became firm friends and this led to Dr Austin's appointment as physician to His Royal Highness.

The doctor's most colourful memories of his time in the Bahamas revolve mainly around the constant 'security exercises'. From the beginning there had been concern that the Germans would try to kidnap HRH, and given this forewarning it would be reasonable to assume that security would have been appropriately strict. However Dr Austin recalls that whenever the army staged one of the frequent 'mock kidnap' attempts, the stand-in prince was always captured, and once during a major fire, all the fire hoses were found neatly cut into slices.[16]

Dr Austin and the duchess were frequently the only two Americans present at dinner parties and often partnered each other for bridge. 'A lot of the English people were really good and in fact more or less made their living out of bridge. The duchess was always terribly worried that she might make someone lose who couldn't afford it, and I was her able partner in ensuring this did not happen.' He heard of Beryl through his great friendship with Major Gray Phillips and his frequent meetings with the Duke and Duchess of Windsor. And when, at the end of his service in Nassau, Dr Austin dined with His Royal Highness and Major Phillips, they discussed their personal plans for the future.

> When I said I was going to California they said, 'But you must look up our good friend Beryl Markham and give her our regards.' That was the main reason that I headed for Santa Barbara. I went to the house in Toro Canyon and lived there with Raoul and Beryl for a while. It hadn't been my intention, but they insisted that I stay there and simply wouldn't hear of me going anywhere else. They lived a typically laid-back existence; socially both were very popular and fun to be with. I thought Beryl was a most marvellous woman, but she just couldn't credit why I had to go off each day and work for a living.[17]

In 1946 Beryl's son, Gervase, then aged sixteen, came over

from England to stay with her for six months. Mansfield had
provided the fare to grant the boy's natural wish to spend some
time with the mother whom he had seen so infrequently, but of
whom he was immensely proud. Gervase's age seems to have
taken Beryl by surprise. 'She was terribly upset,' said Warren
Austin, 'she didn't want people to know that she was old enough
to have a son that big...'[18]

When Gervase arrived in Santa Barbara his wardrobe was
unsuitable for the Californian climate and Dr Austin was
dispatched to clothe the new arrival – Beryl would not be seen
out in Santa Barbara with him. 'She wasn't at all like a mother
to him and left it to me to make sure he had proper food... I
remember the poor boy seemed to have one cold after
another... I think Beryl saw this as a sort of weakness of
character. She more or less kept him hidden away up at the
ranch,' the doctor recollected. Nevertheless Gervase enjoyed his
visit to his mother. He admired her lifestyle, so colourful after
the drab war years in England, and in particular he was
impressed that she was a friend of Stokowski, who paid several
visits to the ranch whilst Gervase was there.[19]

Gervase never appeared to resent the lack of maternal
demonstration by his mother, and when in subsequent years he
spoke of her to his wife Viviane it was only in the most
affectionate terms. To his children he never spoke of Beryl at
all.[20]

Stokowski was very attracted to Beryl, whose looks have often
been described as Garboesque, so her physical appearance was
probably to his taste. The two enjoyed a brief flickering love
affair which mellowed into a mutually rewarding friendship,
though it flamed occasionally over the following years.

Dr Austin soon discovered that all was not as it appeared on
the surface. 'I hadn't been at the ranch for long when I realized
that things were very wrong between Beryl and Raoul. It was
difficult for me because I liked them both. It was all rather
unhappy and they had lots of personal problems which they
didn't seem able to resolve.'[21]

Raoul's drinking was initially the chief cause of their
arguments, but Beryl's promiscuity also became an item of
contention after Raoul returned home unexpectedly one day
and discovered her in *flagrante delicto* with a close friend of the

couple.[22] Violent conflict ensued. Beryl had now discovered that Raoul's own sexual preferences were bi-sexual and had been prepared to ignore this foible only whilst her own extra-marital activities were not questioned. Indeed their large circle of friends included many from Santa Barbara's gay community and Beryl had none of the contemporary aversion for what was still considered to be sexual deviation. Dr Austin thought that whilst Beryl may not have been happy about Raoul's occasional homosexual activities it did not initially constitute a funda-mental factor in their conflict. She was far more concerned that Raoul's excessive drinking was causing him to become seriously overweight, and – perhaps more relevant – unable to produce stories that were acceptable to publishers. The couple's relationship deteriorated into bitter, bickering recriminations on both sides.

Scott O'Dell told me about an incident which he also wrote about in his letter to *Vanity Fair* in March 1987. He had only seen the couple once since they moved to Montecito and on that occasion Beryl was very rude to him. He did not elaborate, and was probably unaware of the reason, but it was at a time when Beryl was suspicious of all Raoul's male friends. Some months after his visit, O'Dell told me, he received a telephone call from Beryl to say she thought that Raoul was dying. 'Come and get him!' she demanded. Why she should have contacted O'Dell in this way is something of a mystery for he had only seen the couple four or five times in as many years. He lived a three-hour drive away from Montecito and there were – and still are – many people in Santa Barbara who claim to have been extremely fond of Raoul. O'Dell arranged to meet Beryl at a convenient half-way location on the three-hour drive between his home at Pomona and Santa Barbara. 'She drove up and stopped outside the Beverly Wilshire Hotel. She just looked at me and never said a word. She got out of her car and opened the back door and what was left of Raoul fell out onto the pavement. She got into her car and drove off without saying a word to me and left Raoul lying there with all the cars going by. When I had last seen him he had been about my height and conformation, I suppose about one hundred and ninety pounds, but the hospital said he weighed under a hundred pounds.'[23] In her book Beryl admits to being 'pathologically' afraid of sickness. Her treatment of her son's minor ill-health, which she wrote off as a weakness in his character, further supports this. It is no excuse for her callous behaviour on this occasion but together with the background of open conflict between the couple it does, perhaps, provide an explanation.

O'Dell claims that Raoul's illness, which involved other unpleasant symptoms as well as weight loss, was psychosomatic, although this was not immediately recognized. It took three complete changes of blood before there were any signs of recovery. It was only after Raoul told him how his relationship with Beryl had deteriorated that O'Dell realized the reason for his friend's illness. Raoul claimed that after they moved to Montecito he had told Beryl that since she called herself a writer she had better start writing. Beryl had flown into a rage, he said, and had locked herself away for a month working on a book about Tod Sloane which she then sent to Houghton Mifflin. Schumacher claimed that Houghton Mifflin had returned it with the comment, 'This story doesn't sound remotely like *West with the Night*, as if it had been written by a different person.'

This damaging claim is not substantiated by archive records. Houghton Mifflin's indexes show no evidence that Beryl had ever been commissioned to write the supposed book on Tod Sloane (though they do show another commission at that time to Raoul and Beryl as co-writers), and there is no record of any such correspondence. Allowing for the passage of time since his conversation with Raoul, Mr O'Dell might have been recalling a similar incident which occurred at a later date.

O'Dell states that Raoul then told him how Beryl had 'worked on him ... subtly and unsubtly, until [O'Dell] picked him off the street'. She locked herself away at nights. At parties she would introduce him as a 'beginner' writer, 'Raoul writes for the pulps, he's quite successful, you know.' It is difficult to know why this remark could cause offence for that was surely exactly what he did, but Raoul claimed that Beryl's constant, vengeful domination was responsible for his illness. In view of this it is somewhat surprising that immediately he was able, he returned to Montecito, despite Mr O'Dell's pleas to him not to do so.[24]

Raoul had two further stories published under his own name: 'Peaceable and Easy' and 'Sucker for a Trade', both Westerns in the style of 'The Whip Hand'. Another story was published under Beryl's name entitled 'The Transformation', but the style betrays the fact that it was ghosted for her by Raoul. Although the Schumachers paid no rent for the ranch, their income from writing during 1945 and 1946 must have been minimal. Only five stories in total were published and when she was unable to goad Raoul into work Beryl tried seriously to write a short fictional story herself. It was returned.

'At one point Beryl was particularly concerned because after a quarrel Raoul refused to help her by editing her writing,' Warren Austin confirmed. 'The story she had written had been rejected but she got her writer friend Stuart [Cloete] to help her, and then it was published.'[25] This editorial assistance by Cloete enabled Beryl to produce a story called 'The Quitter', written in 1946, which provided the only income earned by the couple for nearly twelve months. Without doubt this is the incident to which O'Dell referred. 'The Quitter' does have horse-racing as a background, but there is no mention of Tod Sloane.

[Kent] remembered the long ago days when Sheila had been trapped in a loose-box by an angry stallion. It was a stallion the tawny haired girl had loved with courageous passion – but not with understanding.

She had loved his smooth amd massive beauty, but all the while there was fear in her, and this she fought because of him, but she did not know how to keep evenly burning the flame of his spirit. In those young days she thought that love and admiration were enough, and she offered both. She went boldly one morning into the stallion's loose-box and closed the door behind her.

It was not a new thing; she had done it before – timidly, at first, and then with greater ease. But on this morning the stallion was at his feed, and she entered too quietly. Startled, he turned on her and his fright blazed into fury. He whirled and tried to reach her with his teeth and hoofs. For long and terrifying minutes, she cringed under the feedbox, beating him off with her tiny riding hat, weeping – for fear, and for his faithlessness.[26]

'The Quitter' is important for several reasons. It was the last story known to be written by Beryl that was published and it indicates that she *was* personally able to produce fictional work even though it was not, in itself, of a finished quality. The editorial changes made by Cloete to this story provide yet another writing style; less informal than Raoul's, but more prosaic than Beryl's early autobiographical writing. It is reasonable to assume that Beryl produced this story out of financial desperation rather than an urge to write and Cloete helped further by personally submitting the story to the editor of *Cosmopolitan*. He was a regular contributor to this magazine and his own story 'The Son of the Condor' appeared in the same issue as 'The Quitter'.[27]

The claims and counterclaims concerning Beryl's authorship only received public attention after *West with the Night* was republished in 1983 and belong later in her story but there is a further piece of evidence which is worth mentioning at this point. In Houghton Mifflin's contracts file is a copy of an agreement for 'An African novel by Beryl Markham and Raoul Schumacher', for which an advance of $2,500 was paid. This is clearly the book to which Scott O'Dell referred in his report of the conversation he had with Raoul in Pasadena, when Raoul told him he was working on a book about Africa, for the date on the contract was January 1944. No chapters were ever submitted to Houghton Mifflin in respect of this advance. Journalists Barry Schlachter and James Fox saw pages of an incomplete manuscript when they visited Beryl in Nairobi in 1984; the subject was Somalia, and Schlachter now believes that the pages they saw were written for this commissioned novel.[28]

If Barry Schlachter's theory is correct then some work was done on this novel, but it was never finished. Despite their financial problems Beryl somehow raised enough money to visit Kenya in 1947 to gather material for it and during an interview in Mombasa she told a reporter that she had given up flying totally and was now a full-time writer.

She is a short story writer of some standing in America and is about to start on her first novel. Her visit to Kenya will not be a prolonged one, as she has to be back in the United States by mid-March or she will need a re-entry permit. 'Of course I have come back to see my mother and brother mainly, but I am anxious to collect local "colour" for my book at the same time. I have been away so long and I feel it is essential to return to get the atmosphere back in my mind again.' Her mother who lives at Limuru is Mrs [Clara] Kirkpatrick, and her brother who is in Nairobi is Sir James Alexander Kirkpatrick, baronet, squadron leader in the RAFVR.[29]

The reporter obligingly added the information that Beryl had been brought up in Kenya and educated mainly by governesses, but had spent three years at a Nairobi school. Asked if there was any chance of her returning to Kenya Beryl replied that America was very much her home now as she had so many friends there and couldn't stay away for long. In the event Beryl saw very little of Clara or her half-brother Alex, for most of the three months was spent in Somalia. She found Kenya hauntingly beautiful and full of ghosts, for many of her closest friends were dead (she had only recently learned of the death of Bror Blixen in a car accident in Sweden in 1946), or had left the country.

Unfortunately, the manuscript Messrs Fox and Schlachter saw was subsequently mislaid and could not, after Beryl's death, be traced. Nor was it among her papers when I was allowed access to them in the spring of 1986. The reasons for the trip to East Africa had been two-fold. Research was one, but both Beryl and Raoul hoped that the separation might provide a breathing space and ultimately enable some form of reconciliation. During Beryl's absence Raoul promised to work on short stories, but when she returned to California she found no improvement in the situation. Raoul's heavy drinking had not decreased and the work he had promised to do in her absence had not materialized. He became particularly annoyed when, in an attempt to help him to lose weight, Beryl worked out a course of exercises. 'She wanted me to jump [a skipping] rope,' he told a friend indignantly.[30]

It was only a matter of time before he moved out of the house and their separation was irrevocable. Beryl told Doreen Bathurst Norman that Raoul had cut her out of his life completely, and ignored all her letters to him in later years. Beryl stayed on alone at Toro Canyon for a short time before she too, moved out. Warren Austin had left the ranch some time previously, and was deeply involved in setting up his medical practice, but sometimes he saw Beryl socially.

She was very glad of invitations towards the end for she really hadn't enough money to live on and welcomed being fed. But she was still the same imperious Beryl. I remember once taking her to a dinner party. The hosts were very nice – what you might call nouveau riche, but very nice. In the centre of the table was an enormous flower arrangement and in the centre of this was a sort of fountain. A bit showy but quite attractive. After the meal one of the guests felt obliged to comment on the centrepiece, and the host, who had obviously been waiting for just such a prompt, proudly announced that he had made the table himself incorporating the mechanism from a barber's chair into the centre of the table.

He pressed a button and the centrepiece slowly ascended, the fountain playing and flowers turning on the revolving pedestal. Beryl took one look at this apparition, said, 'Oh my God. I can't stand any more of this! I'm going...' and got up and left.

Dr Austin could do nothing but mutter his apologies and follow her.

As on previous occasions of emotional stress, during this time when her marriage had broken up and her future was uncertain, she was very depressed and confused and seemed totally unable to cope. There were other problems too. Dr Austin recalls that the last time he saw Beryl in Santa Barbara she was worried whether, in view of the impending divorce, her United States resident's visa would be renewed in the following year. In addition there was the question of money. Deeply affected by the intense emotional stress, she was apparently unable to write and therefore had no income other than her annuity. Neither Beryl nor Raoul had any work published after their separation, but for Beryl the almost surgical incision terminating her career as a writer was typical. In 1931 when she had decided to take up flying she gave up her successful racing career with scarcely a backward glance. When her writing overtook her interest in flying, she gave up flying as though it had never been of any real significance. And after 1947 her writing too was consigned to her previous life. 'Never look back!' Beryl told me. It was a precept by which she herself lived.

After she left Santa Barbara she went to stay for a while with an old friend, Sir Charles Mendl, who was then living in Beverly

Hills. Beryl probably first met Sir Charles in 1928, when Mansfield took her to Paris during their honeymoon. Sir Charles had been press attaché at the embassy since 1926, and was a friend and colleague of Mansfield's. On his retirement in 1939 he moved to California, and was known to be very kind to Beryl especially when she was in financial difficulties towards the end of her marriage with Raoul. The break-up of her marriage coincided with Sir Charles's own marital problems. His first wife (an American writer) renounced her title and regained US citizenship in 1946, and the couple were living apart when Beryl stayed at the Mendl house in Benedict Canyon. She seems to have regarded him very much as a father figure and kept his signed photograph to the end of her life.

During her remaining time in the United States, Beryl enjoyed a romance with a well-known folk singer. She left Santa Barbara and went to live in one of the small villages which dotted the Southern California coast. There in a timber cottage, she told a friend,[31] she spent her days beachcombing while her lover produced a chain of hit songs which are world famous. It was a lazy, languorous period, unreal in many ways for it was a 'between times' interlude. She still maintained contact with her many friends and among her papers some years ago were many letters dating from this period, including a friendly letter of encouragement from Frank Sinatra. It is the letter of a considerate friend to someone who is having a rough time. There was a friendly letter too from Joseph Kennedy, confirming a conversation in which he advised Beryl on her financial affairs.[32]

Raoul returned to the Toro Canyon ranch after Beryl had left it. A friend who accompanied him on the day he moved in recalled that despite her own personal fastidiousness Beryl had 'lived like a little animal. The floor in her bedroom was thick with dust with sort of game-tracks leading from her bed to the bathroom and to her dressing table. No housework had been done for a long time and there was a lot of clearing up to do. Her typewriter was thick with dust and had obviously not been used for months.'[33]

Raoul continued to make a show of being a writer. For a while he made a determined effort to succeed. The actor Joseph Cotton and his wife Lenore had been friends of both Beryl and

Raoul for some years, and now in an effort to help Raoul, Mr Cotton secured a contract for twelve radio 'playlets' which Raoul was to write for him. Only two were ever finished. Raoul lapsed good-naturedly back into bouts of heavy drinking and though he sat each day at his typewriter he never again produced anything that was published.[34] He spent some time helping a young writer friend by editing his work and generally providing encouragement, but was not himself able to write. A likeable man, he was very popular in Santa Barbara and everybody felt a great deal of sympathy for him. There was general relief when in 1952 he seemed to gain a new lease of life. With the help of a woman friend, Mary Lou Culley, he reduced his drinking and founded a company to make food-vending machines which enjoyed a brief success, but he lacked the application to maintain its progress.[35]

He divorced Beryl in 1960[36] and married Gertrude Chase Greene in July of the same year at her family home, Hope Ranch, Santa Barbara. Scott O'Dell, himself newly married, saw Raoul again for the last time. 'I was there to autograph copies of my latest book and Raoul came into the bookshop. He had recently married and was looking good and had put on all his weight again. He told me he had run a bar in Mexico for a while but nothing else as I recall. He was a listener more than a talker.'[37] Raoul's stepson, John B. Greene Jr, who lived with the newly-married couple, recalled him with affection. 'He was a smiley sort of guy. He used to sit and pound away at the typewriter for hours...'[38] But Mr Greene's sister, the elder of the former Mrs Greene's children said, 'I didn't like him. I don't think he ever wrote anything that was published after he married my mother – he didn't have to.'[39] Gertrude was independently wealthy and seems to have cared a great deal for Raoul.

John Yabsley, an Englishman who worked first as major-domo for Mrs Greene's family and then for the newly-married Schumachers, said, 'Schumacher had the right sort of air about him, he could go anywhere in any company and be accepted. He never had any money and I don't think he owned any property, but people were glad to loan him places to live. He was liked by everybody in Santa Barbara. Until he married

Gertrude Chase he had nothing, but he was very good for her and they were happy together.'[40]

Raoul was very overweight and in poor health when the marriage took place, and within two years, at the age of fifty-five, he died of a heart attack.[41] All his papers are believed to have been destroyed when his widow died a few years later.[42]

Long before the divorce, Beryl had informally reverted to the surname Markham. Not surprisingly in the circumstances, this caused a howl of protest from the Markham family. However Beryl reasoned that her main claims to fame – her transatlantic flight, and her writing – had been done under that name, and her son's name was Markham. It seemed a logical and perfectly moral choice to her.

Spring 1949 found her in England to watch Gervase's passing-out parade in the Life Guard Regiment during his two-year period of compulsory National Service. She never returned to the United States although she always, for the remainder of her life, talked of doing so.

CHAPTER FOURTEEN

[*1949–1960*]

Beryl gave as her reason for her visit to England the fact that she wished to attend the regimental ceremonials for Gervase's passing-out parade, but there was more to it than that. She could see no future for herself in California. She was forty-seven and her health was – unusually for her – not good; she was apparently unable to write and had long since given up flying. She had therefore metaphorically kicked the dust of California from her feet, and what she wanted to do more than anything else was to return to Africa, her spiritual home. She had no money as usual, but rescue came in the form of an old friend, Tom, Lord Delamere, who provided her fare to South Africa.[1]

After spending some months in London with friends, she travelled to the Cape where she went immediately to call on Stuart and Tiny Cloete. They had recently returned from the United States and were surprised one day when Beryl 'just turned up. She seemed at a loose end and stayed with us some two months,' Tiny Cloete recalled. The Cloetes had both liked and welcomed Beryl, having felt an 'immediate bond' early on in the relationship due to Beryl's mendacious assertion that 'her mother had died when she was a child and she had been brought up by Lady Northey', a cousin of Stuart's.[2]

Beryl was penniless – living entirely on the Cloetes' goodwill and, as usual when she was desperate, on her wits regardless of any possible consequences. Beryl told a friend that Cloete 'wrote by the moon, in the way that some people garden by the moon' and often worked through the night at his work. On occasions, Beryl claimed, she did some nocturnal typing for him.[3] Her involvement went further than typing. In an apparent attempt to raise money quickly she sent off some of

Cloete's short stories under her own name, to the literary agent they shared, and when a short time later, Cloete also sent the same stories to the agent 'there was a very awkward situation'. Beryl consequently left the Cloetes and they never saw her again, but after her departure Tiny found that many of Stuart's hand-made silk shirts and scarves had also left, and that Beryl had charged numerous items of cosmetics, expensive French perfumes and clothes to their charge accounts. 'She had charm, but no warmth and was completely amoral,' was the opinion of her hostess.[4]

On many previous occasions Beryl had abused the kindness of friends by obtaining credit in their name. She lost many friends because of her complete lack of integrity regarding financial obligations, and she seldom repaid loans. But she could not have hoped to keep her breathtakingly blatant attempt at plagiarism hidden, so why had she attempted such an outrageous fraud? The only explanation seems to lie in a deteriorating health condition which seriously affected her judgement. The same condition had also possibly affected, for some time, her ability to write. But I think that writing had never been an 'easy' thing for her and that whilst she was able to cope with writing personal reminiscences (in the way that many people are capable of writing an autobiography but never attempt other works) she could not write to order. She did not possess the sort of imagination that could invent plots; indeed Rose Cartwright – an old Kenya friend – was forthright about this lack of imagination. 'She had no imagination whatsoever, it had never developed in her as a child and I think that this was why she was often brave to a foolhardy extent,' she told me.

After leaving the Cloetes, Beryl spent a period in Durban with her father, who had enjoyed considerable success as a trainer in South Africa.[5] This was no mean accomplishment, for racing in South Africa is a far cry from Kenya. The Cape horses were international class and the competition for the huge prize money was fierce. It was one thing to succeed in prewar Kenya among trainers who were for the most part amateurs, but quite another to emulate that success in the racing world of the Cape.

But what Beryl really wanted was to get back to Kenya. She was at a crossroads in her life and could not see where her future lay. It did not lie in staying with her father for she could not

share him with Ada, her barely tolerated stepmother. She was
bad-tempered and abusive towards Ada and created total
disharmony in the Clutterbuck household. Eventually, Beryl's
ill-natured behaviour irritated Clutterbuck to such an extent
that he told his daughter to leave. Again, her appalling
behaviour seems to have been partially caused by her physical
condition. Clutterbuck gave her enough money to buy a
second-hand car, an old Sunbeam Talbot saloon, and to pay for
the petrol and oil for her proposed journey to Kenya, and she
left South Africa to drive alone to Kenya via Rhodesia. When
she arrived in Nairobi in April 1952 she was destitute[6] and
entirely dependent on the generosity of old friends. But in her
usual way she managed, living on her wits and credit, and was
seen often in smart night spots such as the New Stanley Grill,
always immaculately turned out and looking very glamorous.

She stayed for some time with a friend in Nairobi and
subsequently on an up-country farm, but they were stop-gap
solutions to the long-term problem of finding somewhere
permanent to live. It was no time for a peripatetic existence.
Kenya was beginning a period of great trauma, the result of
growing nationalism among the Africans, and a desire for self-
government. At its extreme this flared into anti-Europeanism in
the shape of the terrorist movement known as the Mau-Mau,
which involved secret oath-taking ceremonies where initiates
(often unwillingly) swore to kill Europeans and those who
supported them.[7] It was the grisly, ritualistic manner of the
murders which followed – of men, women and children of both
races – that was so frightening. In the general fear and panic a
State of Emergency was declared by the British and the leader
of the nationalist movement, Jomo Kenyatta, was sentenced to
life imprisonment. It took five years to bring the situation under
control, and it was to be a further five years before the Kenyan
Africans achieved independence with Kenyatta as the first
president. Meanwhile inhabitants of up-country farms lived in
trepidation, and servants who had once been thought of as
friends were necessarily treated with suspicion. It was not the
Kenya that Beryl remembered.

Everything changed for her one evening in Nairobi when she
met Charles and Doreen Bathurst Norman at 'some formal
function or other. She was all dressed up and looking fantastic –

I'd heard of her of course, she was very much part of the old-Kenya legend...' Doreen recalled. When Beryl told the couple how worried she was at not having anywhere to live and no money, they did not hesitate. 'Our guest cottage is empty at the moment – you can use that!' they told her. At first Doreen silently half-regretted the hasty invitation and wondered what it was going to be like with that 'blonde bombshell' around all the time, but the next day Beryl turned up at the farm at Naro Moru wearing an old mac and wellington boots. The women became friends from that moment.

The Bathurst Normans were an exceptionally close-knit family and one of the happiest things about this period for Beryl was the Bathurst Norman children, George and Victoria, who were aged twelve and ten. Active and self-confident, they attached themselves to Beryl, and much to her surprise they liked her and enjoyed her company. Equally to her surprise, for she had never been closely involved with children, she liked them in turn. 'Victoria would carefully put her head around the door of the guest house in the very early morning, and if there was a welcome, she would jump into Beryl's bed with her.'

Over the next few years, many were the evenings they spent listening to Beryl's collection of Burl Ives records, with which they would all join in. Beryl taught them to play card games such as poker and backgammon, with matches as stakes,[8] as her father had once taught her. They were fascinated by her stories of horses and people and places, and impressed by her horsemanship but, as they recalled years later, she never spoke to them of her own exploits. Beryl was essentially modest, and never discussed her adventures or successes. Possibly these children knew 'the real Beryl' better than anyone else, for she was relaxed in their company.

Forest Farm, the Bathurst Normans' property at Naro Moru, was situated on the grasslands which intersected with belts of forest on the slopes of twin-peaked Mount Kenya, immediately below the perpetually glistening Diamond Glacier. Park-like grasslands were bordered by primeval forests of cedar festooned with curtains of lichen. *Podocarpus* of airy green, bushes of sweet-smelling, evergreen witch-hazel, and clumps of cedar dotted the grass, edged with the enchanting limuria bush, smothered in beautiful little jasmine-like flowers, at least as sweetly scented and which turned into a wild berry - delicious when fully ripe. Among the grass grew a profusion of wild flowers such as the wild gladiolus and the lovely *Acidanthra candida*, locally thought to be a freesia because of its scent. The air itself was crisp and thyme-scented 'like the Sussex Downs', Charles Bathurst Norman used to say.

Through the forest rushed and bubbled a mountain stream, careering downhill like a Scottish burn. Born in the glacier and flowing through peatlands before it reached the forest, it provided an endless source of delicious uncontaminated drinking water, filtered through hard black basalt stone thrown up by the last earthquake which had left its core in the mountain's peaks. The brook became a branch of the Naro Moru River (Naro Moru being Maasai for Black Stone), which had been stocked with trout that could be seen where sunlight hit the water, glimmering in pools overhung with flowers and ferns.

The Bathurst Normans had bought a tract of this paradise to remove their children from the coast where Charles was stationed as district commissioner (Mombasa), and where their son George 'had shown every inclination of trying to die of malaria'. The choice of district for them was therefore dictated by the fact that 7000 feet was the lowest altitude guaranteed free from the malaria-carrying anopheles mosquito.

'It was wartime then, and by no means certain who would win the war, and as Charles could not leave his post the matter was becoming extremely urgent,' Doreen related, but a friend suggested they should consider the western slopes of Mount Kenya and arranged that Doreen be taken there by a land agent. She fell in love with this enchanted country at first sight, and so – a short time later – did her more cautious husband. They bought a completely undeveloped piece of land which had previously been used by its owner only on rare occasions to graze a dry herd. The die was cast and thereby several people's lives were changed – including Beryl's.

The land had no house on it and was approached by a rough track, occasionally used by the forestry officer who had built a camp higher up. What was more, nobody could be found to build the house. One day Charles said to Doreen, 'I think you'll have to go up and build it,' to which she simply replied, 'All right.'

The train carrying Doreen's station wagon arrived late, but it was unloaded instantly and she set off for Naro Moru over appalling roads. At last, blinded by dust and desperately tired, she stopped at Fort Hall for a drink, where a party of the British Army was doing the same. She collected a young officer as co-driver, and they joined the army convoy which provided better lights than her car – blacked out for use in Mombasa. Eventually they reached Nyeri where, thinking enough was enough, Doreen booked into the White Rhino Hotel for the night.

Next day she proceeded to instal herself in a mud hut at the bottom of the farm, below a small belt of forest which lay between her camp and the site chosen for the house – both sites chosen for their proximity to the river. There at night herds of elephants could be heard watering, and the magical night sounds of an African forest lulled her to sleep, the odd screech of the hyrax being the last thing she heard. The African gang, which consisted of carefully selected old retainers, erected the house in five months. The children transferred there and George never suffered from malaria again.

The couple were encouraged to think, quite erroneously as it turned out, that the farm would be suitable for Jersey cows, so cattle, a few fodder crops with maize shambas for the labour force, together with their own vegetables and fruit, became the mainstay of the farm. The milk was turned into cream and sent off to the creamery to be turned into butter. Doreen made soda bread from the butter milk. This is how things were when Beryl first arrived.

When she first went to stay at Naro Moru, Beryl was often unwell, unusually for her; but initially she refused to see a doctor because of her aversion to hospitals. At times, her condition made her difficult and argumentative and Doreen was particularly aware of Beryl's feeling of 'total insecurity'. Charles was a barrister by profession, and had a successful and busy up-country practice with offices in Nanyuki.[9] When her hosts discovered that Beryl could not only type, but type extremely well, an obvious solution to some of Beryl's problems occurred to them. Beryl became legal secretary in Charles's law practice, and she was thus able to earn some pocket money. 'Her typing was fast and accurate and her spelling impeccable,' Doreen stated, adding that she had always treated the gossip of Beryl's rumoured illiteracy as utter nonsense, and adopting a course of 'never apologize and never explain', along with Beryl. The work also gave Beryl something with which to occupy her mind, but her health continued to deteriorate.

As the condition (fibroid tumours in the womb) worsened, Beryl became increasingly perverse and her temper extremely volatile, probably because of a hormonal imbalance accentuated by her approaching menopause. 'At times she seemed almost mentally out of control, banging doors, and breaking things,' Doreen recalled. 'Sometimes when she sat and talked after dinner her voice would go up a tone and she would rave at us for hours about nothing in particular.' On one occasion after the Bathurst Normans had retired to bed, they heard a noise, and when Charles got up to investigate he found that Beryl had broken the sitting-room window and wrenched it off its hinges in order to get in to see them; she was incredibly strong for a woman despite her illness. On another occasion, after a row over nothing in particular, she struck Charles, but he promptly hit her back, telling her she would have to leave the farm if her behaviour did not improve. She threatened suicide and once ran away without telling the Bathurst Normans where she had gone. She eventually turned up at a neighbour's house where to the astonishment of her hosts she treated them to a tirade lasting several hours. It was all very disruptive and worrying for the Bathurst Normans, who had more or less adopted Beryl and were extremely concerned for her.

Eventually Doreen was able to persuade Beryl to see a doctor who diagnosed probable cancer of the womb, and had her admitted to hospital at once. It wasn't cancer, but the condition (probably worsened by several incompetently performed abortions in earlier years) was serious enough to require a hysterectomy, which in the early 1950s was still regarded as major surgery. 'Beryl told us she hated hospitals and wouldn't stay there to recover from the operation, so the next day we brought her home and put her to bed in the cottage,' Doreen recalled. 'She wasn't supposed to be moved and she did, actually, look awful. The next morning there was a fearful racket in the yard and I looked out of the window to see my dog and a strange dog having a fight. Then Beryl's boxer dog Caesar joined in the fray. I was on my way out to put a stop to it when the door of Beryl's cottage burst open and Beryl erupted into the yard in pyjamas. She strode over to the dogs as if there was nothing wrong with her, and taking each by the scruff of the neck she hurled them aside. Then she grimaced at me, wiped her hands together as if to say 'That's that then!' and strode back to bed without a word.'

To the Bathurst Normans' dismay Beryl's behaviour showed little sign of improvement as she gradually recovered from the operation. Eventually, Charles felt he could no longer tolerate the upheavals in his home, and said Beryl would have to leave; but Doreen would not allow it, for Beryl had nowhere to go and no money. Leaving Naro Moru would not resolve Beryl's problems. Charles himself then became ill with what turned out to be an infected bile duct, which eventually required surgery. At times he felt very unwell and found Beryl's tantrums particularly trying but because Beryl had virtually become part of their family they agreed to tolerate her behaviour.

George and Victoria were then taken back to school in England as the Mau-Mau troubles grew in intensity and Charles refused to allow Victoria to stay on the farm. One day Charles and Beryl visited a local farm owned by a white hunter called Eric Rundgren[10] who was in the process of selling up. They had gone there to buy some chickens from the young Dane, Jørgen Thrane, who was in charge of the farm whilst Rundgren and his wife were away on safari.

They stayed talking, Jørgen expounding the profits that could be made from growing wheat in the area and adding sadly that he would be leaving when the farm was sold. Charles asked, 'Would you come and grow wheat like that for me?' 'Yes,' said Jørgen without hesitation. On the drive home Beryl said to Charles, 'I suppose you do realize that when that chap said Yes he meant just that?' According to Beryl, Charles looked dumbfounded but immediately made plans to see Thrane again. He wrote about it to Doreen who was in England on the 'school run'. 'I'll tell you all about it when you return. I call it "last chance in Africa" . . .' the letter said. Doreen came back to find Jørgen Thrane installed, and was instructed by Charles to get to know him better and let him know what she thought. Asked to describe him at that time Doreen said

How can you describe someone who after thirty years you regard as one of the greatest friends you have ever had? I'll do my best. Jørgen had originally arrived in Kenya with two words of English – 'Yes' and 'No' – and ten shillings[11] in his pocket. On the recommendation of a friend he had obtained a job in the Trans Nzoia before leaving Denmark. His lack of English and Swahili got him the sack, and he arrived by way of another job at the Rundgrens where he became involved in growing wheat. The district was swarming with Danes, Charles used to call it 'the last of the Norse Sagas'.

Jørgen quickly became a friend and was delighted to be at Naro Moru. He was one of six children, the youngest of whom was Gudrun, who had gone blind at the age of thirteen but this had not prevented her from becoming a famous organist in Denmark. To obtain a farming diploma, Jørgen had worked in a plastics factory to earn the money to pay for the course. His sport was rowing and he had formerly been an inter-Scandinavian competitor. He also loved horses and riding and had owned a beautiful hunter in Denmark.

He was essentially very easy to get on with, 'gemütlich' to a degree (there is no English word for this quality). Always full of laughter, we all loved him. Very shortly after he came to the farm, Charles offered him a full partnership. Jørgen had already saved a little money and this he put into the farm, with the remainder of the risk covered by Charles, and the farm was then registered as Norman and Thrane Ltd. He quickly became devoted to Charles whom he treated as a mixture of father and elder brother. He is intuitive and shrewd rather than clever, but he will work very hard to acquire any knowledge necessary to the success of a new project. To look at he is very tall and slim, very fair and with blue eyes crinkled round the edges. Jørgen and Beryl quickly developed a close relationship. Somehow he managed to provide the strength and support that Beryl always needed, and from the time he arrived at the farm, she was able to pick up the threads of her life and go on.

The oddest thing about Beryl was that although she could ride any horse, anywhere, fly the Atlantic, and was unafraid during activities such as game-spotting, over mundane things she was indecisive and needed to have her hand held, metaphorically speaking, all the time.

Doreen Bathurst Norman thought that after Clutterbuck left for Peru in the early 1920s, Ruta had filled this role, followed by Denys Finch Hatton (whom Doreen always regarded as the greatest love in Beryl's life), possibly because his detachment made him somehow unattainable. When Beryl had a 'supporter' – and this person did not have to be a lover, but just someone on whom she could trust and rely, and whom she respected absolutely – then 'her insecurity took time off'. Jørgen was following in the footsteps of Clutterbuck, Ruta, Finch Hatton, Campbell Black and Schumacher, who were the major figures in Beryl's life; between them came shorter periods of supportive help from Lord Delamere, and numerous others.

Although Beryl's behaviour improved after Jørgen's arrival at Naro Moru, she was still restive. The secretarial work gave her an interest, but what she really wanted was to get back to horses. During her convalescence a friend gave her a broken-down racehorse to use as a hack. The animal 'looked like a coat hanger when it arrived. It had been overdosed with worm tablets and quite ruined for racing – or for anything else really.' It was the best thing that could possibly have happened. Beryl decided to work on the animal and in time it was not only fit but was able to race. 'It never won, but I think it managed to get itself placed a couple of times,' Doreen recalled. This episode was a turning point in Beryl's life and set her on the track of her next great triumph. She decided to start training again and there was some talk of her training for Tom Delamere whose stable was not doing too well at the time. Beryl went to Soysambu to discuss the proposal but it came to nothing and she eventually decided, with Jørgen's enthusiasm to bolster her resolve, to train publicly.

The problems were immense. Firstly Beryl had no money to buy horses and nowhere to train from. Secondly she had been out of training for thirty years, and had no current reputation or contacts. She was already approaching her mid fifties, an age when most women would not contemplate taking on a new and stressful career, particularly after major surgery. Predictably, none of these difficulties occurred to Beryl – or if they did she paid no heed to them. She managed to raise £1500, the most likely sources being Mansfield, who helped her financially on a number of occasions, and Clutterbuck. Probably it was a combination of both.

At the bottom end of the Bathurst Norman property was a small piece of land consisting of a small house and twenty-five acres, which providentially came on to the market. Originally it had been part of Forest Farm but it had been sold separately, some years before the Bathurst Normans arrived. Beryl put up her capital, the Bathurst Normans underwrote a bank loan and the small farm – heavily mortgaged – became Beryl's. Twenty-five acres could never in normal circumstances have provided an adequate basis for the establishment she had in mind, but fortunately the Normans were happy for her to use some of their land, and their farm machinery and labour were at her disposal for gallops and the maintenance of paddocks. Equally important, she had the personal support of Charles, Doreen and Jørgen:

Jørgen was tremendously excited and keen about the whole thing. She could never have got started again if it hadn't been for his enthusiasm and hard work, he was an enormous help to her. He was detailed by the local 'security committee' to live at Beryl's farm. The Mau Mau troubles were at their height and they would not countenance Beryl living there alone. Just before Beryl left we had an African visitor to the farm. He showed me a card which stated that he was a communicant of the Church of Scotland and that he could hold services on farms. I replied that I should make inquiries as to whether any of the farm workers would like him to do so, as several were skulking around looking at our visitor and appeared frightened. I got a lot of flak . . . Surely I would not prevent the workers from hearing God's word, and so forth. I asked around and got the distinct impression that he wasn't wanted but as it was nearly dark I grudgingly allowed him to stay the night. He did, and held a very different kind of ceremony – a Mau Mau oathing ceremony.

We lived in a very vulnerable position, and deliberately did not have Kikuyu house servants. One night all our cattle were driven off. Having checked that Beryl was all right, Charles sent Jørgen off to the police at Naro Moru. Believe it or not we had no telephone until just near the end of the emergency! The result was that they caught the gang sitting around a fire drying their clothes and cutting up the meat from one of our cows. The police shot at them, killing one and wounding another but the rest vanished into the night. All the cattle broke back except about seven and we got one that wandered in from goodness knows where – possibly as the result of another farm raid.

We heard later that it was considered that Charles, whom they referred to as Mzee (a mark of respect as well as of age), was considered to know all about them and they were reluctant to touch us as they believed they would certainly be caught. They never tried anything again. We all carried revolvers or automatics all the time...

Beryl had *arap* Ruta to help her on her farm. She had tracked Ruta down when she visited Kenya after the war, and she never subsequently lost touch with him. Soon after arriving at Naro Moru, she suggested to the Normans that they should give him a job. He'd be very good, she told them. 'In fact he was quite good, though by then he'd started to drink a lot and at times was rather a nuisance because of it,' Doreen recalled. During her illness Beryl had also begun to drink quite heavily, but she managed to ease up after her recovery and disapproved of other people drinking to excess.

Not long after her move to her own farm, Beryl was visited by her son Gervase and his heavily pregnant wife Viviane. They were en route to Europe after spending the first year of their marriage in India. The couple had met when they were lunch guests of a mutual friend at the Cavalry Club in London in 1951. Viviane, who was on holiday from her home in France, was instantly attracted to Gervase and the feeling was mutual, but by a strange quirk of fate Gervase was leaving on the following day for a holiday in France. He was not due to return until Viviane herself left for France. 'A case of ships that pass in the night you might say,' chuckled Viviane. However Gervase managed to return earlier than planned, and the pair had a day together before Viviane went home.

They wrote to each other constantly. 'We more or less fell in love by letter. After our marriage, shortly after he came down from Oxford, Gervase had the opportunity to work in India – a country that I had passionately wanted to visit all my life. Our

time there was a great happiness to us both, but it was almost a
spiritual homecoming for me.' On their way home to Europe
they stopped over in Kenya to visit Gervase's grandmother,
Lady Markham, who had virtually raised Gervase, and who
had remarried and moved to the colony. However, hearing that
they were in Nairobi, Beryl telephoned and asked the young
people to stay with her at Naro Moru.

'Beryl was very sweet to us,' Viviane recalled. 'She was not at
all what I expected – she seemed very quiet and ordinary, not
the sort of person who had lived the adventurous life that I knew
she had.' The couple liked Thrane and enjoyed the happy
atmosphere that prevailed on the farm. Indeed the entire visit
was a very successful one. Beryl did not behave 'like a mother',
but then she never had. Her relationship with her son is an
intriguing one, for she undoubtedly cared for him in her own
way, but she had no strong maternal need to see him or have
him around her. She talked of Gervase occasionally to close
friends but somehow did not feel it necessary to make any
contact with him, or indeed his family when he later had two
daughters. Interviewed in 1986 for this biography she spoke of
'my little kid' in a way that would have suggested to a stranger
that she had enjoyed the most intimate maternal relationship.
But in fact that brief visit in 1955 was the last time that Beryl
ever saw her son, and she never met her two granddaughters.

Interestingly Gervase never spoke of his mother to anyone
but his wife. 'He was extremely proud of her achievements but
of course he had never really known her as a mother.' His two
daughters, Fleur and Valery, grew up with a very hazy and
confused picture of their maternal grandmother.[12]

In the mid 1950s Beryl suffered two bereavements. Firstly her
half-brother Sir James 'Alex' Kirkpatrick was killed in a
shooting accident. Beryl had liked him, though her affection for
him was always tinged with reflected dislike of their mother,
and she disapproved of his drinking. Doreen Bathurst Norman
recalled that between the two there had been 'the mutually
critical attitude that is very common between brother and
sister'.

Then, in 1957 Clutterbuck died in South Africa. It was a deep
and lasting sadness for though she had not seen much of her
father during the previous twenty years, Beryl still retained her

hero-worship of him.[13] Clutterbuck was still successfully training horses until shortly before his death and told his daughter that although he would leave his estate to his wife Ada, he would leave Beryl his 'best horse'. He did so, and Beryl would have loved to have taken the horse, but South African horses could not be imported to Kenya and Beryl hadn't the resources to cope with the problem. So she had to let the opportunity go by.

With Beryl's drive and ideas, and Jørgen's herculean assistance, the establishment started to take shape. There were horse-boxes, feed stores, tack stores, exercise yard and gallops to be built, and in 1956 Beryl took delivery of her first crop of horses, all from Kay Spiers' Lolchorai Stud. Mrs Spiers is remembered as one of the greatest horse-breeders in Kenya, and until her death in 1977 she produced consistently good racehorses. Title Deed was initially owned by Kay Spiers and trained by Beryl. Ulysses, whom Beryl 'bought', was her first good horse. However, she had little or no money with which to pay for the horse, 'so Kay supplied her more or less on HP terms', Doreen Bathurst Norman recalled.

Ulysses was a particularly good-looking horse and Beryl loved him. He was not only a racehorse but had won prizes in the show ring – the perfect, and rarely found, all-rounder. Title Deed, a two-year-old, was a marvellous little bay horse with a big heart, who flicked his ears forward as he passed the winning post. He was particularly good over middle distance, and gave her her first win, a two-year-old plate in September 1958. He was a sound, honest and consistent horse who in six seasons won thirteen races, and was placed nineteen times.

Beryl's own colours of blue and gold had long since been re-allocated when she started training again, so she re-adopted the old Clutterbuck colours of black and yellow. Soon they were seen in pole positions at race meetings.

One day Beryl went to look at a horse called Little Dancer. She immediately recognized the horse's potential but this gave her a problem, which she took to Charles Bathurst Norman. 'Look, I've bought this horse but I can't afford to pay for it,' she told him. The Bathurst Normans characteristically bought the horse for her. On New Year's Day 1959, thirty-three years after she had won the same race with Wise Child, Beryl's second brilliant career in training took off when Little Dancer won the Kenya St Leger.[14]

Her next horses were Niagara and Snow Goose, both bought as yearlings. Once again Kay Spiers sold them to her on hire-purchase terms. Something about Niagara particularly attracted Beryl, and she had to have the little filly. Curious to see this horse about which Beryl seemed so anxious, the Bathurst Normans went down to see her. 'She was an extraordinary little grey thing, still with her fluffy foal coat – she didn't look anything out of the ordinary,' Doreen remembered. They were perhaps understandably doubtful about Beryl's confident prediction that 'this horse is going to win the Derby for me . . .' Niagara was by a horse called Toronto out of Propaganda, and as Beryl started to train the youngster, she knew she'd made the right decision. Niagara was very fast indeed.

The 1959–60 racing season belonged to Beryl. She was selective about her horses and the races in which they ran. The leading trainer and owners are positioned not by the number of races won but by the value of stakes. With her small stable she took on the big trainers and Niagara obliged by winning the Kenya Guineas, the first race in the Kenya Triple Crown series. The East African Derby was Beryl's next goal.

There was a great deal of rivalry between the syces in Beryl's stable and those of the then leading trainer Gladys Graham, whose farm and training establishment marched with the Bathurst Normans' land. At times, as Beryl's success grew, the rivalry sparked into open confrontation. 'You can imagine how popular Beryl's success was, can't you?' Doreen asked with a smile. Beryl's employees were absolutely convinced that Mrs Graham's syces would be out to sabotage Niagara, who was entered for the Derby, and they took no chances. The horse was never left alone for a single minute.

'Of course Gladys would never have allowed anything like that but the boys were convinced and nothing would dissuade them. A few days before the Derby, Niagara travelled down to Nairobi by train accompanied by Beryl's childhood playmate Arthur Orchardson who packed a revolver just in case, and insisted on sleeping with the horse in its box,' Doreen recalled. The syces' anxiety was catching! Arthur rode for Beryl on a number of occasions and although he was then getting towards the end of a brilliant racing career (which included riding countless winners including – in 1936 – the winner of the East African Derby), he was extremely fit. After Niagara had been loaded up and sent on her way, Doreen casually asked Beryl, 'You are insured I suppose?' and was shocked when Beryl replied: 'Well actually no...' Doreen immediately telephoned the insurance company.

This inattention to administrative detail was typical of Beryl. In later years nearly all her problems were caused by her lack of concern for the form-filling which is an essential task of the trainer, but while she had Jørgen to take care of this side of things for her everything ran smoothly. Like Ruta, Jørgen smoothed all the rough edges and left her free to concentrate on the horses. Beryl was even reluctant to make the commitment of declaring a horse for a race. She always procrastinated, and usually would not even name the rider until the very last minute.[15]

On the eve of the Derby, Beryl and Doreen travelled down to Nairobi and went to the race course. 'We found everyone in a fearful flap. Niagara had cast one of her racing plates and had worked herself into such a highly-strung state that she would not let anyone near her to replace it,' Doreen told me. Beryl listened with mingled disbelief and exasperation to the complaints poured into her ears. Without a word she stumped into the box and picked up the horse's leg. Turning around she said to the suddenly silent little crowd, 'Well! What are you waiting for? Get on with it!' Beryl had the knack of making even a highly excited horse quiet simply by touch.

On 3 August 1959 the *East African Standard* racing correspondent declared, 'The Miller will stay when others have had enough,' covering himself by adding: 'The only three-year-old that has proved herself to be in any way outstanding is Niagara, winner of the Kenya Guineas over a mile. I am not sure that she will stay the extra half mile, although there are very few... that I would choose to beat her.'

Riding Niagara was Tony Thomas, a jockey recently brought into the country by Beryl. 'He was a gentle and totally unsophisticated man, much at a disadvantage with the tougher Kenya jockeys, whom he feared. The week before the Derby he had made a mess of a race and Beryl had told him that if he made a mess of the Derby he would be sent home on the next aeroplane,' Doreen Bathurst Norman said. 'He therefore took Niagara right round the outside, going yards further than anyone else, and then let her go. She needed no urging – in fact she stopped if hit – and went like an arrow. Tony was a gentle rider with beautiful hands, and all problem horses went well for him.'

On the following day the racing correspondent of the *East African Standard* reported the race under the headline 'Niagara wins Derby by eight lengths'.

> ... ridden by Tony Thomas who, a newcomer, took the Derby in his first season ... It was a very easy victory gained in record time. Mrs Beryl Markham had got the horse into splendid condition, not surprising in view of the fact that she is the daughter of the late C.B. Clutterbuck, Kenya's outstanding trainer of former years ... Half a mile from home Thomas took Niagara to the front and the filly made the rest of the field look as though they were standing still as she drew away and, never challenged, won by eight lengths with the greatest of ease ... in the record time of 2-minutes 38.6-seconds.

The race was the most valuable ever in Kenya to that date, with a stake of £835 going to the winning owner. Beryl was ecstatic. There had never been any doubt in her mind, and she was well aware that when Niagara shot past the winning post she wasn't even being hard pushed.

On this performance Niagara started favourite for the Kenya St Leger, which – if she won it – would earn Beryl the coveted Silver Plate awarded annually to the leading trainer. The horse's winning performance in the classic race was afterwards described as 'a walk-over'. It was the filly's fifth successive win and she was the first horse to take Kenya's Triple Crown, consisting of the Derby, St Leger and Guineas.[16]

The *East African Standard* reported in January 1960.

> Continuing her winning career in Kenya, Mrs Beryl Markham's grey filly Niagara won the Kenya St Leger yesterday with the greatest of ease to give her owner a classic double. This owner also duplicated, some quarter of a

century later, the feat of her father the late C.B. Clutterbuck, by winning two St Legers in successive years. Niagara, odds-on favourite, won on a tight rein far more easily than the official verdict of two-and-a-half lengths indicates, making most of her rivals look little better than hacks.

A month later Niagara also walked away with the Delamere Gold Vase, and Beryl achieved her ambition to top the leading trainers' list. It had taken her only two seasons and she held the position for a further six, until she chose to abdicate by leaving Kenya. She subsequently said that Niagara's victories that year had given her the greatest thrill in her career.[17]

Niagara had an inherent weakness in one knee and was not easy to keep sound. As a four-year-old, she ran only twice and on one of these occasions won the Civil Service Gold Cup. If she had been able to run more often, her career would have been even more outstanding, but her easy victories meant that she carried successively heavy weights as penalties and the gallant little mare was eventually 'weighted-out'.

Success breeds success. Owners now beat a path to Beryl's door, and she had her pick of the best horses and the wealthiest owners in Kenya. Through determination, hard work and talent she was back at the top. She was never satisfied with anything less than perfection. A perfectionist herself, 'she had no time at all for second-raters and was hyper-critical of anything of which she did not approve,' a friend said.[18]

As her establishment grew she built her team around her – *arap* Ruta and Arthur Orchardson were an integral part of it. Jørgen was her mainstay. He played a heroic part for he took all Beryl's imperiousness with laughter, and her commands with grave respect. 'Her gallops were kept in immaculate order,' one of Beryl's former jockeys told me, 'and when Beryl said, "I'd like a gallop just along here," it was like one of the ten commandments. The next day there'd be machinery in place and within days a new gallop would emerge, picked clean of stones by a mini force of Africans. If Beryl said, "Paint that door blue will you?" it was painted blue, although shortly afterwards she might say, "Oh God! Not that shade of blue – can't you see it's wrong, you fool?"' Jørgen could take this tyranny with amusement, and he was the perfect foil for Beryl's brilliance.

Charles and Doreen Norman also remained tremendous supporters, and jockeys Tony Thomas, George Price, Alec McAleer and Derek Stansfield all contributed over the years to Beryl's legend.[19]

In July 1960, Jørgen went home to Scandinavia for a holiday. While there, he watched the Irish jockey Ryan Parnell – known to all as Buster – riding at Copenhagen. At the age of twenty-six, Buster had already ridden 280 winners and had been champion jockey of Denmark in 1957, and of Scandinavia in 1959. On Wednesday afternoon in the last week in July, Jørgen telephoned Buster to ask if he would fly to Nairobi and ride for Beryl the following weekend. 'It's a bit difficult,' explained Buster. 'I'm supposed to be getting married on Saturday...'

'Sunday will do!' said Jørgen obligingly.

CHAPTER FIFTEEN

[*1960–1964*]

When Buster Parnell arrived in Kenya before that August Bank Holiday weekend, he could hardly have suspected that he was at the beginning of a partnership which was later to be called 'invincible!'[1] Leaving his bride of one day to follow him in a few weeks, Buster was still unsure of whether or not he had acted wisely in leaving Copenhagen, where his career and reputation were well established.

'I'll never forget the first time we met,' Buster said. 'Beryl came into the room and her presence was overwhelming. There was about her a waft of scent – a freshness like going into a field of new-mown hay.' After the usual preliminaries she said, 'I've got eight horses running at the meeting over the weekend. I'll put you on two of them.'

Taken aback, Buster said firmly: 'I ride the eight or I go back to Denmark tonight!'

Her eyes did not flicker as she replied, 'Yes sweetie . . . that's what I said. You ride the eight.' Buster rode the eight horses, won six races and was second twice.[2]

After the races Beryl took Buster to the Muthaiga Club. On their arrival she explained: 'You'll have to stay on the veranda – professional sportsmen are not allowed into the club.' In another piece of straight talking Buster told her that 'just this once' he would wait for her, but she was *never* to bring him there again. She never did. Afterwards they drove up to Naro Moru.

'It was a very isolated place up in the bundu – the back-of-beyond wasn't in it – there was *nothing* there, absolutely nothing, but Beryl's place. I remember thinking, I left my bride of twenty-four hours for this?' Buster told me.

'We dress for dinner,' Beryl warned as she left him in one of the guest cottages. Buster showered, changed into a smart suit and sober tie, and went up to the house. When Beryl swept into the room he knew he'd made a mistake. He had never heard of the old Kenya custom of dressing in pyjamas and dressing gown for dinner – a relic from the pioneer days.[3] Beryl was dressed in white silk pyjamas and dressing gown. 'Oh sweetie,' she said apologetically. 'You look so uncomfortable...' Buster hastily acquired expensive pyjamas and a dressing gown which satisfied the requirement for correct evening clothes.

The following weekend was the East African Derby meeting. Buster rode nine horses for Beryl, winning eight races (four winners on each day of the two-day meeting), and creating a racing record in Kenya. On his other ride he managed only a third place![4]

Beryl had no runner in the Derby that year, but with this single exception she monopolized the race from 1959 until she left Kenya, to train in South Africa, in the mid 1960s. Her winning horses were, in 1959: Niagara; 1961: Speed Trial; 1962: Cutlass; 1963: Lone Eagle; 1964: Athi.[5]

Beryl herself always rode on the dawn workouts. Buster recalled how each day she would appear in the yard, looking as if she'd stepped off the front cover of *Vogue*. Silk shirt, perfectly cut jodhpurs, shining leather boots, little kid leather gloves. A broad-brimmed hat and a leather whip tucked under her arm completed the ensemble. Buster dressed correctly too – glistening boots, shirt and tie, cap, whip – 'exactly as if we were at Newmarket, there were no blue jeans and dusty boots at Naro Moru, it was first class all the way with Beryl. That was all she knew,' he said.

'Tell them to bring the horses around, will you sweetie?' she would say when she was ready.

The strings of thoroughbreds on these early-morning rides would number up to forty, and they were taken to the gallops on the slopes of Mount Kenya, which Beryl referred to as 'the top gallops'. On the way they were always sure to see elephant, troops of colobus monkeys and buffalo. Beryl always rode at the head of the string with Buster following at the rear riding shotgun. He recalled their morning rides:

'It was breathtaking in more ways than one up there at 8000 feet. After a gallop the string would pull up with horses and riders gasping for air and sweating... all except Beryl. She'd sit serenely cool, delicately fluttering a tiny pocket handkerchief in front of her face. The views from up there were unbelievable. Twice a year – for we used to get two harvests in Kenya – you could look out across Cole's Plains and see a thousand acres of gold. When the sun shone on that wheat it was like looking down on a huge ribbon of molten gold, stretching away down to the Aberdares. The air was like champagne. There was a different clarity to it, a different smell. The water in the streams was glacially cold, but so soft that if you put your hands in it you could work up a lather, just from the oils in your skin.

'They simply don't make 'em like Beryl any more. She worked me like a dog, but I gained something from her that money couldn't buy. Confidence, knowledge and a different dimension to life. Everything I've done since, all my personal success has its roots in what I learned from her. Her way of handling any problem was to say, "Now what would my father have done?" and she'd sit with her head in her hands thinking it out until she came up with an answer. She didn't love her father – she *idolized* him. He was the one great love in her life. No other man ever measured up to him. I think Tom Black came closest and she worshipped him too.[6]

'I've ridden for the best trainers in the world, people like Prendergast and other greats, but I can tell you she was *the* best. She could have taken on the world and won. Mind you, we had two syces to every horse! She never made any money out of all her successes, because for every thousand pounds she charged, she spent twelve hundred on the horses. She spent money like water, but she was a bit like the queen and never carried any with her...'

Instead, with a delicate wave of one of her long thin hands, she would say to whoever was with her, 'Just pay the man, will you darling?' or 'Put it on the account!' Personal accounts such as her Muthaiga Club bill went unpaid for years, but she kept nothing for herself during those years of success. It all went back into the horses.

'The boxes were *absolute* luxury, nothing was too good for the horses. Each box was eighteen foot by eighteen foot. They were lined with teak, and had banana-leaf roofs. They weren't placed in rows or blocks like conventional stables, but dotted around like a little African village. [Beryl insisted that horses were gregarious and needed to satisfy their herd instinct by looking at each other.] After gallops every morning we would have breakfast and discusss work. They were really pukka breakfasts with avocado pears, haddock or trout, cereals, kedgeree, cod's roe, caviare, freshly baked bread and chunky marmalade. The table was always set with silver and best china.

'One of the other jockeys, Tony Thomas, was a great fisherman. He used to toddle off to the river every morning with a bamboo pole to which was attached some line and a rusty old hook. Without fail he was back within half an hour, always with four lovely little fresh trout for breakfast. Tony wasn't the brightest chap around so I thought, this must be easy, and went and invested in some expensive fishing gear and accompanied him on some of his morning jaunts. I never caught a thing! He could sit twenty yards from me and pull out four trout before I had got my fly into the water. I threw the fishing gear into the river one day in a fit of pique! Beryl told Tony rather unkindly one day that he was such a good fisherman because he understood the fish. "Your brain is about the same size," she said. She could cut a man's legs from under him with three words.'

Beryl kept stocked up with the best of everything, all on credit. 'We might die tomorrow,' she was fond of saying, and she ran up huge accounts all over Nairobi. Once someone gave her, or she won, a crate of champagne. It wasn't what she was used to, not Dom Perignon or Krug, but some lesser brand. 'Sweetie,' she asked Buster thoughtfully, 'who do we dislike enough to give this jungle juice to for Christmas?'

'After breakfast we used to walk around the stables, there wasn't much to do of course, the staff did all the stable work but she'd stop and look at each horse . . . perhaps to give a carrot here, a sprig of lucerne[7] there, and give instructions to the syces. By eleven o'clock we'd be ready to go up to the house for our first drink (which she habitually called 'a pinkie') of the day. She had a phenomenal capacity for alcohol in those days, but you never saw her the worse for it.'

Buster Parnell told me frankly that he had loved Beryl. 'But,' he stressed (patently realizing that I must have heard of Beryl's reputation), 'it was an unconsummated love affair. The only time I ever kissed her on the lips was the day Lone Eagle won the Derby. It was a totally unnatural relationship; at times I hated her guts but by God I respected her. Now over twenty years later, though I haven't seen her for years, I still love her like a lover.' Spare, tanned and supremely fit, with greying hair and eyes that crinkle at the corners when he smiles, Parnell has the typical figure and stamp of the professional jockey. But the resemblance ends there.

For our first interview I met Buster Parnell over informal drinks, and could not help noticing that his understated silk shirt had the distinctive Dior symbol on the pocket. There is a confident swagger to his walk which was noticeably accentuated when, dressed in racing silks, he walked across the parade ring to greet the owners for whom he rode that weekend in Denmark and Sweden. It was difficult to rid oneself of the impression that he was somehow riding for them as a special favour![8]

He is an immensely colourful and entertaining character who mentions as an aside: 'As of today I have won two thousand and sixty-three races.' One can imagine that with Beryl and Buster around life could never have been dull.

'At times she was a first-class superbitch who never gave a damn about anyone but herself. She had a fantastic ego, unbelievable talent and a capacity to work that you wouldn't credit. She wasn't in the game for the old English motto of being in it for the pleasure of competing. Oh no! Win. Win. Win! She didn't care how; she worked us like dogs, and she worked harder than all the rest of us put together. She was the epitome of Africa. Hard as nails! But she had great *class* – in the way that a Derby winner has class – it's a sort of presence. Her success was due to the fact that she had more talent than all her competitors put together and she fed her horses better. That was her "secret". It was just good feeding and hard work. That slight sheen that Mervyn Hill and Robin Higgin[9] wrote about, that everybody put down to some magic formula she'd learned from the Nandis as a child... all nonsense – that was the superfit sheen you do get on really fit horses. She never fed any secret formula to her horses – she didn't need to fake it – she was too good.'

Buster's first impressions of Naro Moru were soon forgotten

and it became 'God's own country', both to Buster and his young bride, Anna. They stayed during that season, returning to Denmark for the summer, but they were soon back in Naro Moru the following autumn for the next season. Everything was as before. Every night they dressed for dinner and dined formally 'as if we were at Buckingham Palace'. There was always a huge log fire for it gets very cold at night at Naro Moru. After dinner they would sit talking before the fire. About ten Beryl would suddenly say to Anna, 'You look very tired, sweetie. Why don't you run along?' Anna used to be furious at this summary dismissal – especially as Beryl used to keep Buster talking, sometimes for another hour or two. Then she would say to him, 'I think you ought to run along to that nice little wife of yours. You really oughtn't to leave her alone so much...'

When it rained at Naro Moru they were totally cut off, because the farm was surrounded by black cotton soil which made movement by ordinary vehicle impossible.

'Jørgen had a four-wheel-drive machine, and even after he moved off Beryl's place in about 1962, he used to come and keep us in contact with the outside world. Beryl would wait two days and when she ran out of some luxury item, she'd shout for Jørgen. We might have absolutely everything, but she'd perhaps run out of Beluga caviare and she was on the telephone immediately: "Jørgen, sweetie. I have to get some supplies. Can you help me?" Her cook could produce anything at all to cordon bleu standards and it was all done on a dirty little black, old-fashioned stove. The kitchen was filthy, you never went out there. After I saw it for the first time I didn't eat for three days, for fear of food poisoning. After that I took good care not to go and look!'

In 1962 Buster flew down to Rhodesia with Beryl where they raced Speed Trial in the Castle Tankard race, and stayed in Salisbury. She had considered the possibility of moving there but she didn't like the atmosphere, and was uneasy, although it seemed like paradise to him. 'This won't last,' she told Buster. 'We won't come here.' Events proved her right. 'She was like that sometimes, not clairvoyant, but there was something uncanny about how she sensed things that were to happen later,' said Buster.

Shortly before Uhuru[10] Beryl's farm at Naro Moru was sold

to the government for African settlement. Before this, one of her owners, E.R. 'Tubby' Block, had discussed the imminent problem of new premises with her. He had some land by Lake Naivasha and suggested that she might set up a training establishment there. 'I had a piece of land but I had no accommodation for her establishment. However there was a neighbouring piece of land which was up for sale, which consisted of a house with about a hundred acres.' Much of it was lake frontage of soft volcanic sandy soil, unsuitable for viable farming purposes (although there was experimentation going on for the growing of asparagus), and so it wasn't affected by the African settlement programme. He told Beryl that if she bought the adjoining property and needed more space for training, she would be welcome to use part of his land for this purpose. Apparently interested, for she wanted to move closer to Nairobi, Beryl asked the price of the property. 'Three and a half thousand!' Block told her. 'I'll think about it,' she promised. It was a very reasonable price, and he thought she would probably accept. Shortly afterwards he went off to Europe for a holiday lasting over two months, but when he returned it was to find a new house and stables, in advanced stages of building, on his land. Block explained:

> Beryl had used her persuasive powers on my manager and told him I'd agreed to let her build a house on my property. She had turned down the idea of buying the property next door and got away with using my farm. Well, I let it carry on. There was no point in doing anything about it then because the place next door had been bought – snapped up by somebody else. Quite rightly, it was a real bargain! Anyway, her establishment was soon completed and she moved in with her horses.[11]

Tubby was the son of Abraham Block, a pioneer who had arrived in British East Africa in 1903 from South Africa, at the time when it was proposed that the protectorate could provide a homeland for the Jews. This scheme did not materialize, but Block stayed on, and although he had no money he was befriended by Lord Delamere. Over years of immense hard work and sacrifice he became involved in many business activities 'usually profitably', but on one occasion at least, he

was reduced to his last span of oxen. His experience must have
been akin to that of Beryl's father, though Block would not have
had Clutterbuck's initial advantages of birth and social
position. Tubby was born in 1919, and was still a small child
when his father acquired the Norfolk Hotel through a shrewd
piece of wheeling-dealing. Abraham gave up his other interests
to concentrate on the hotel business, founding Block Hotels, and
in the process creating a dynasty.[12] Tubby, like Beryl, was a
child of Africa. They dealt well together.

Beryl's house at Naivasha was at the edge of the lake on the
way to Hell's Gate, the district adjacent to the Maasai Reserve.
It was the best house she ever had in Kenya, and the one she
most liked. The number of birds was almost incalculable and
the area was once described by Sir Peter Scott as the finest bird
sanctuary anywhere in the world. 'One was always awakened
by the cry of the sea eagle, and a boat trip on the lake was like
stepping into a Disney film. There were quite incredible birds
everywhere,' Doreen Bathurst Norman recalled. 'From the
giant goliath herons and countless kingfishers, to lily trotters
dashing across the lily leaves. The early-morning haze on the
water reminded one of a painting by Turner – it was a world of
magic.' Tubby Block continued Beryl's story:

> After Beryl moved into Naivasha, Aldo Soprani and I gave
> Beryl quite a few horses. She used to tell us which horses to
> buy. She always did us extremely well in that respect – we
> were leading owners for three years running. We had four
> Derby winners and won every other classic – every other race
> there was to win on the Nairobi race course.

Buster Parnell told me of some of the horses that Beryl had
located for Block and Soprani:

> Mountie was one of them. He was a mountain of a horse but
> pound for pound he was the best horse we ever bought. Beryl
> was in the hairdresser's when she heard the asking price,
> £1000. That was two arms and two legs in those days. She said
> she'd take him. 'Tubby can afford it,' she said airily. He won
> eleven races and was never beaten. Spike was another good
> horse she found for Tubby. Money (other people's,
> especially) was no object to Beryl. When we went to buy

Spike, she watched him gallop down the paddock then she turned to Noreen Kidman and said, 'Yes, we'll have him.'

'Hold on,' said Noreen. 'You don't know how much I want for him yet.'

'I said we were buying him, sweetie,' said Beryl. 'Not paying for him. You'll have to discuss the price with Tubby.'

A constant source of annoyance to Block and Soprani was Beryl's habit of running several of their horses in the same race. She was never sure which was the best horse on the day. If she told them X was best that day, they could almost be sure that Y would romp home.

> In the 1961–62 Derby she ran two of our horses, Rio Grande, which was the favourite ridden by the stable jockey, and Speed Trial, ridden by veteran jockey Arthur Orchardson who was then sixty-three years old. Needless to say Speed Trial won![13]

Beryl always regarded Speed Trial as 'the most brilliant horse I have ever trained, until he went wrong'.[14] Buster Parnell explained that the horse was once frightened by pigs, had reared up and fallen over, damaging his spine. 'He was never quite the same after that.'

Arthur Orchardson had grown up with Beryl at Njoro, and technically – through his mother's marriage to Clutterbuck – was Beryl's stepbrother. As well as being a good jockey (he won many East African classics), he was a first-class shot, and took a third prize at Bisley in the mid 1960s using the old 303 rifle. Arthur donned his boots and silks – and had his skull-cap tied on – before eleven o'clock. Then he walked nervously around the race course for hours before the race, and was stunned and delighted by his unexpected win. He bought a sports-model racing bike out of the proceeds.

On the weekend after his Derby win, Anna and Buster Parnell passed Arthur on the main road and stopped to talk. He was cycling from Nairobi to Nakuru. Anyone who knows this road will be impressed, for it consists of a series of significant undulations and under the heat of the equatorial sun at heights of over six thousand feet, it was not a ride to be undertaken lightly at any age.

Despite her owners' complaints Beryl continued to run several horses together, and Buster Parnell particularly remembered one race. It was not a classic or even very important, but all races were important to Beryl. Buster was riding the favourite who had been backed down to four-to-one on; Tony Thomas, the second stable-jockey, was on a fifteen-to-one outsider. 'Look,' Buster said to Tony before the race, 'your horse is only here today for the outing. Tuck him in behind the others and take him round. If you can get a place, let him go, but whatever you do, don't pass me!' As the field came round Cemetery Corner at the Ngong Forest course, Buster suddenly found Tony was up alongside him, sawing at his horse's mouth. 'What the hell are you doing here?' he asked angrily.

'I can't hold him.'

'Well he can't win, you'll bloody well have to hold him.'

'What can I do?'

'Fall off the bloody thing if you have to!' Buster said, and kicked on hard to pass his colleague. As Buster flashed by the winning post, an empty horse shot past him – it was Tony's mount. Buster looked around and asked the other jockeys if they'd seen Tony fall, but no one had seen anything. But retribution was just around the corner, for over the loud speaker system came the instruction, 'Will Buster Parnell please report to the stewards.'

Buster entered the room shaking like a leaf and looked around at the grim faces of the stewards, and then at Tony who was holding his head at an odd angle and gazing at Buster with mute appeal in his eyes.

'Parnell. I understand that as you came around Cemetery Corner you instructed Thomas to fall off his horse because he looked like overtaking you. Is that right?'

Buster thought for a moment, then said, 'Yes, m'lord.'

There was an interested shuffling of bodies in the seats in front of him. 'I see. Can you give us your reasons?'

'Well, my lord. It occurred to me that if the number one stable-jockey on a horse backed at four-to-one on was beaten by a horse from the same stable, ridden by the second jockey carrying odds of fifteen to one, the crowd might not to be too happy about it.'

There was silence. Then, 'Wait outside, Parnell. Thomas, you can go.'

Ten minutes later the senior steward came out. 'All right, Parnell, you can go. But tell Mrs Markham not to run two horses in the same race if there's likely to be a repetition of this situation!' Fortunately Beryl was amused when he told her.

Her undisputed reign over the Kenya turf continued, and by the mid 1960s she had won the Kenya St Leger four times (including her win in 1926 with Wise Child) and the East African Derby five times. With Parnell as her stable-jockey, Beryl changed the face of racing in Kenya, and set standards for performance on Kenya turf. Parnell thinks she could have done this anywhere in the world. 'No matter where you are you have to beat the competition. That's what she set out to do and she could have done it anywhere. She proved that when she went down to South Africa with her Kenya countrybreds and won there, against top-class horses...'

I asked Buster to tell me about some of Beryl's owners and he obliged, characteristically:

That whole period was a fusion of talents and coincidence. Beryl, Soprani, Block and me. In particular Block and Soprani provided the money for Beryl to really show what she could do. She never could have done it all without them. Between 1962 and 1964, Block and Soprani had something like sixty-five horses with us – Soprani was a coffee baron up at Thika. She gave them what they wanted in the way of winners, but she certainly got her money's worth in return. She used to sit outside the Stanley [one of Block's hotels] in the Thorn Tree café[15] and say to the manager, 'Send that funny little thing out to me to do my nails.' And then, while holding court like the Queen of Sheba, she'd have her nails manicured by one of the girls from the beauty shop. 'Send the bill to Tubby would you?' she'd call out as she left.

Sir Derek Erskine was another owner. He was a wonderful old boy; a charming man. He had a lisp and couldn't sound his Rs. He built a huge swimming pool on the first floor of his home and when asked why, said, 'To keep the fwogs out of course.' He was immensely wealthy and owned a rather lovely Bentley. Once at the race course he ran out of petrol. 'Lend me ten shillings would you old chap?' he asked. Him

with all that money and me on a jockey's pay! 'You must be
joking,' I said. 'Ten bob's worth of petrol in that thing won't
get you far.' 'No, but it will get me to the gawage, where I
have a cwedit account.' I never got the money back! He had
the best string of polo ponies in the country, but he wasn't a
great player. He used to gallop up and down all day wearing
them out and not scoring goals. Sometimes, when you won a
race on one of his horses Sir Derek would give you a present in
kind. He had a grocery/greengrocery wholesale business
(which was why we called him the Galloping Greengrocer),
and usually you got a case of something which had been
'sticking' in the warehouse. Once I was the lucky recipient of
a case of tinned prunes. I thanked him, not quite sure of my
luck, and he peered at me, saying earnestly, 'They're warver
good for you, you know. Only twy not to eat them all at once.'
When he got his knighthood I congratulated him. 'Yes,' he
said brightly, telling me he had to go to London to be touched
on the shoulder by Her Majesty. 'Fwightfully nice of her
wasn't it?' I loved him, and so did everyone else.

Living in isolation sometimes had its drawbacks, such as the
time Buster recalled when one of the horses developed a hernia.

It was Rio Grande, a big colt who showed a lot of promise. We
called in the vet but he was a new chap. Had never even
castrated a horse, let alone operated on a hernia. We had no
electricity, just candles . . . There wasn't enough *pinker, pinker,*
to get electricity out to the stables. Beryl got John Pettifer on
the phone from Limuru. He gave instructions by phone and I
ran between Beryl and the new vet with instructions and
questions. It was a total success and a month later at Nairobi,
Rio was the biggest certainty of the day.

Mickey Migdoll, a great chum of Beryl's, had put a very
large bet on him, the biggest bet he'd ever had on a horse in
his life, and now he was sweating on it. When we started Rio
jumped out of the stalls in front, really full of himself, but
when we got to the first corner he became confused and ran
the wrong way up a slip road. The rest of the field put on a
spurt, and by the time I turned Rio and set sail after them,
they were a couple of furlongs ahead of me. Mickey Migdol
was furious. He took off his hat and slammed it down to the
ground. 'What a fix!' he said with understandable bitterness.
'That's the biggest swindle I've ever heard of. I'm never

coming near this place again.' And he got into his car and drove to the gate. As he reached the gate he heard the crowd cheering. 'Who won after all?' he asked the gateman. 'Rio Grande won, bwana.' Hardly believing him, Mickey rushed back into the stands to find that Rio Grande had won by three lengths. There was no stopping him. When I caught up with the others I gave Rio a little push and he sailed past them as if they were standing still.

Mickey also recalled this race but his version is as follows:

It was a race where Rio Grande was in such company that I thought the only way he could be beaten was if he fell down (he started at odds of one to three on), and that it would be a mere formality to pick up one hundred pounds, which was a lot of money in those days. So I laid the odds; three hundred pounds to win one hundred pounds. Sitting in the box and watching the race, I saw that Rio Grande was last by twenty lengths and appeared to be going further back. I turned to Paddy [Mickey's wife] and said, 'You see that horse at the back of the field, I have three hundred pounds on him!' Anyway he maintained this position as they turned into the straight and I really thought I had lost my money, when all of a sudden Rio Grande took hold of the bit, and before you could say Jack Robinson he had hit the front and went on to win by over three lengths.

Undoubtedly Mickey lived through some anxious moments; Buster's more colourful version was probably born in the after-race release of tension and high spirits. He is a born raconteur and was happy to tell me another story about racing in Kenya.

Peccadillo was a fantastic miler that Beryl trained, and he could not be beaten over that distance. Once though, he was beaten. A farmer from up country had gone bankrupt just before this particular race. He was a very well-liked man and his syces and some of the jockeys had clubbed together, putting the entire amount of money they collected on a rank outsider in the race at fifteen to one. This horse, a mare, couldn't touch Peccadillo under normal circumstances of course, but when I got down to the start I noticed that she was foaming with sweat and literally jumping out of her skin. Doped to the eyeballs – this was in the days before mass dope testing. I mentioned the mare's appearance to her jockey who put me firmly in the picture. 'This horse wins this race. Don't get in my way!' he warned me grimly. Not that I had any choice. When the machine opened, the mare shot out in front leaving a stream of bubbles behind her. I pushed Peccadillo for all I was worth but the best I could manage was a poor second. When the horses were led into the winner's enclosure one of the senior stewards stepped forward. 'I say!' he said, 'I know that horse and I think she's been d . . .' He didn't get any further. All I saw was a hand come out of the crowd with a brick in it. It hit the speaker on the head and down he went. By the time he came round both horse, owner and prize money had gone. We never saw either of 'em again.

Buster was champion jockey five times in Kenya. He won the title each time he contested the championship and was never beaten. When, in the mid 1960s he was offered a good post in Ireland, Beryl was very unselfish. 'Of course you must go,' she told him when he expressed doubts. 'It's a marvellous opportunity!' It was, for he became champion jockey there. This might be considered surprising in view of the fact that for some years he had been riding in Scandinavia and East Africa, areas not noted for prominence in first-class racing circles. However it indicates the level of performance that he and Beryl had jointly presented in Kenya.

At the height of her success, Beryl was like an eagle. No one and nothing could touch her then, and after a successful race meeting she was as high as if she had been on drugs. On the day Lone Eagle won the Derby she went to dinner in the New Stanley Grill. She timed her entrance just right – everyone had just finished their fish course. As she entered the room everyone rose to their feet and gave her a standing ovation. She was like a queen as she swept to her table, amidst cries of, 'Well done Beryl!' 'Oh thank you darling!' she'd say, smiling and blowing a kiss here and a giving a little wave there. 'So kind of you, sweetie,' she'd say as she patted an admirer's cheek. It was almost as though she had a hundred-watt bulb in her head and the rest of us had only seventy-five.

As always, in social matters she was unreliable. She would accept dinner invitations and just not turn up. 'Silly little man, he must have made a mistake!' she'd say, when her host complained. This was a well-entrenched habit noted by Florence Desmond twenty-five years earlier. Probably it stemmed from her upbringing; East Africans have the same disdain for time. But if a horse was involved Beryl was always punctual and was never late with a feed or a poultice.

Once in the 1963–64 season Beryl won forty-six races in twenty-six days' racing; her stable won everything that year except the Leger. 'Horses came first, second, third and fourth with her. That's why we got on so well together,' Buster said.

> Once every fortnight or three weeks we'd drive down to Nairobi, singing our heads off, and make for the New Stanley or the Norfolk. Tubby paid for everything, we always went first class at the Block hotels.
>
> For weekend meetings the horses were loaded on Thursday night, after an eight-mile walk to the station. Then we'd take off for Nairobi. The horses would arrive Friday night and then there'd be a boozy party. When I went to dinner with her on my arm I was a proud man. Even though she was thirty years my senior, she was a knockout. When she got dressed up to go out, there wasn't a woman in Nairobi could hold a candle to her . . . Races were on Saturday and Monday – no Sunday racing then. Monday nights there was always a terrific party. On Tuesday we would get all the supplies we needed to last until the next race meeting, and then we'd drive back to Naro Moru again – singing at the tops of our voices, because now we were glad to be going back. We lived in a different way up there. It was pure fantasy land.

'Banks are robbers with a licence,' Beryl used to grumble when she owed them thousands. By the mid 1960s she was running everything herself, for Jørgen had bought his own farm at Nanyuki in partnership with the Bathurst Normans' son-in-law. She was hopeless at administration and budgeting and at times, despite her huge success, was so broke that Buster had to scratch around to pay the horses' feed bills. 'But the horses never went without the best, no matter what. I remember one night our dinner consisted of potato soup, followed by baked potatoes, and we drank crème de menthe all evening. It was all there was, and that's bloody desperation! The week after that we had eight winners and two seconds in a two-day meeting and we were back on champagne again.'

When the Markham stable went down to a race meeting they often used to take twenty horses: twelve which were to run, and eight reserves. The reserves hardly ever ran. Once, the railway track was washed away at Thika and the horses were walked from Thika to Nairobi, but even so Beryl got six winners at that meeting.

Beryl and Buster often fought noisily. Times without number Buster walked out. 'Right! That's it. I'm leaving,' he'd storm.

'When?'

'As soon as I can book a flight out to Denmark!'

'What are you waiting for, then?'

And he'd stump up to his cottage and pour out his grievances to Anna. Two days later there would always be a knock on the door and one of Beryl's houseboys would be standing there with a package. 'From the memsahib. She says will you come up to the house?' Often the parcel would contain a couple of silk shirts, or a nice tie. 'By then my temper would have cooled off anyway, and I would go up to the house to find Beryl fluttering about. She would never discuss the quarrel – instead she'd say, "How about a little pinkie, darling?" and everything would be back to normal.'

One of these stormy scenes was enacted on the day before the Oaks. 'This time,' Buster told Anna, 'I really mean it. Pack up, we're definitely going this time. I can't take any more.' Without telling Buster, Anna went up to Beryl's house, taking the racing silks as an excuse.

She found Beryl in tears and drinking heavily. 'Please send him up to me ... don't let him go ...' she said. On the following day Blue Streak won the Oaks and no more was said about going home – until the next time![16]

'She really didn't know how to take me. At first, like the other jockeys, I called her madam, but later I called her Beryl. I was the only one allowed this privilege. Once Tony Thomas called her Beryl inadvertently. She looked over her shoulder to see who he was talking to ...'

Beryl used to hold weekly court sessions for the employees on pay days, with a 'Fines and Advances book' very much in evidence, for minor misdemeanours such as poor work and drunkenness. Beryl spoke fluent Kipsigis, Kikuyu, and – of course – Swahili. She also spoke Luo and a little Maasai, though she pretended not to. 'If we had any trouble I couldn't cope with she'd have the culprit in, and sit and question him for hours,' said Buster. 'They could hide nothing from her for she spoke their language and also, more importantly, she knew how their minds worked. She could be just as devious as them and she had the advantage of superior intelligence. She always got the truth in the end. For major crimes like robbery, the man would be put off the farm, and if he didn't go quickly she'd set the dogs on him! But there wasn't much of that, and nor did she have any trouble during the Mau Mau because she knew her people. We had eighty staff on the place – syces, riding boys, shamba [garden] boys, house servants. If we needed sixty people to run things, Beryl would have eighty – that was her way.'

'Beryl never gave me an on-course instruction in all those years I was with her,' Buster told me at the end of his three-day interview. 'On the gallops, or over dinner we'd discuss tactics, but never on the course. If I won, she'd always say, "Well done, sweetie. I knew you'd win." If I lost she'd say, "Never mind, darling. You did your best." If there was ever a problem about a horse she'd have the first choice at solving it. If she was wrong, I got my crack next time round.'

A short time after Beryl moved to Naivasha, 'Romulus' Kleen returned to Kenya and visited her. She had last seen him nearly thirty years earlier, in 1934 when she was ill with malaria after their abandoned flight to England. One evening he dined with Beryl, Jørgen and Charles Norman. When the other two men had left, they began to talk and Romulus told Beryl a story he'd kept to himself all the intervening years.

When Romulus had arrived in Nairobi in 1934 before the proposed flight to England, a mutual friend of theirs, considerably older than both of them, took Romulus aside and said to him: 'Now my boy, I am going to give you some fatherly advice, and it is this. You have very little money, so do not get emotionally involved with Beryl, because if you do, you will be put in an awkward position should anything go wrong with the aircraft during your journey, and you have to make prolonged stays in hotels on the way. As neither of you is exactly a tee-totaller, when the moment comes for you to pay the chits (which you will naturally have signed), you may – to put it mildly – pale beneath your tan.' Romulus thanked the well-meaning friend for his kind warning, and accordingly, when – on most nights that he was her guest – Beryl had appeared at his bedroom door to wish him goodnight (sometimes repeated several times), he had merely responded with a cool and formal, 'Goodnight, Beryl. Sleep well.'

Beryl was highly amused at his confession, and told him, 'Well, I do admit to having wondered at the time if you could possibly have been gay! Oh dear, now you will never know what you missed!' The incident was not finished, however. Over dinner that evening Romulus had told Beryl that he had to ride a race in Nairobi the following week. Since he had been with the UN Force in the Congo he had not been on a horse for a month. 'Could I ride work for you tomorrow morning to get my muscles back in shape?' Romulus asked, adding hopefully that his first mount should be a quiet and steady sort. 'No problem at all . . .' Beryl assured him.

Next morning after the gallop he dismounted with buckling knees. He was received by a grinning Beryl, and her two amused male companions of the previous evening who had obviously been invited to rise early in order to come along and watch the fun. 'He ran away with you, didn't he?' Beryl asked with obvious delight. Romulus admitted that the pace had been considerably faster than he had intended. He did not add to her obvious satisfaction by revealing that his shins were bleeding, and his entire body felt as though it had been put through a mincing machine. Later Buster Parnell told him that the horse he had been given to ride was Speed Trial, the Derby winner of the previous year and known to be the fiercest puller in Kenya.

At times Beryl's humour had a slightly sadistic side to it, Romulus recalls, and he had noticed this even in the 1930s. On one occasion when he was flying with her she suddenly started circling over broken country. After about half an hour of this he couldn't help asking if she had a problem. She replied that everything was fine but she had to wait for the clouds to clear over her intended landing strip. 'Why?' she asked, grinning wickedly at his discomfort, 'were you getting frightened?'[17]

One of Beryl's greatest moments on the track was in the 1963–64 season, when Lone Eagle won the East African Derby.

With Jack Doyle, former heavyweight boxer turned singer. *(Topham)*

Beryl with her white convertible, 1936. *(Topham)*

With Douglas Fairbanks Jnr on location for *Safari*, Hollywood, 1939. *(B.M.E.)*

San Diego, 1937: Beryl discusses plans for an aeroplane suitable for attempt on unspecified record. *l. to r.* Beryl; Tex Rankin, Al Monasco. *(B.M.E.)*

Beryl at a New York literary luncheon in 1942. *(B.M.E.)*

Cover of Beryl's copy of
the first edition of *West
With The Night.*

Raoul Schumacher,
Beryl's 3rd husband,
taken in New Mexico,
1943. *(British Library)*

settler, nor of a veteran of the Boer War, nor of an
American millionaire who went there and shot Zebra and
Lion, but of an Africa true to each writer of each book.
Being thus all things to all authors, it follows, I
suppose, that it must be all things to all readers.

Africa is mystic; it is wild; it is a sweltering
inferno; it is a photographer's paradise, a hunter's
Valhalla, an escapist's Utopia. It is what you will and
it withstands all interpretations. It is the last vestige
of a dead world or the cradle of a shiny new one. To a lot
of people, as to myself, it is just "home". It is all
these things but one thing - it is never dull.

From the time I arrived in British East Africa at the
indifferent age of four and went through the barefoot
stage of early youth hunting wild pig with the Nandi,
later training race horses for a living and still later
scouting Tanganyika and the waterless bush country between
the Tana and Athi Rivers, by aeroplane, for big game, I
remained so happily provincial I was unable to discuss the
boredom of being alive with any intelligence until I had
gone to London and lived there a year. Subsequently I flew
an aeroplane across the North Atlantic to America and
added a line to the second of my log books.

Boredom, like hookworm, is endemic.

I have lifted my plane from the Nairobi
airport for perhaps a thousand flights and I have never
felt her wheels glide from the earth into the air without
knowing the uncertainty and the exhilaration of first
born adventure. — Break —

The call that took me to Nungwe came about one o'clock
in the morning relayed from Muthaiga Club to my small
cottage in the Eucalyptus grove nearby.

It was a brief message asking that a cylinder of oxygen
be flown to the settlement at once for the treatment of
a gold miner near death with a lung desease. It was signed
with a name I had never heard and I remember thinking that
there was a kind of pathetic optimism about its having

Page of original manuscript for *West With The Night* showing edits in Raoul
Schumacher's handwriting. Other pages show edits in Beryl's handwriting.

Beryl with her dog in the Avocado Orchard at the Santa Barbara ranch, 1946. *(V. Markham)*

Ditto — taken by Gervase in 1946. *(V. Markham)*

The ranch at Santa Barbara which was formerly the romantic hideaway of Stokowski and Garbo.

Niagara winning the Derby in 1959. *(B.M.E.)*

Beryl with her own horse 'Blue Brook' c. 1960. *(B.M.E.)*

'Daddy 1946' — The picture that Beryl kept at her side until her death. *(B.M.E.)*

Beryl, Gervase and Beryl's favourite dog Caesar, Naro Moru, 1955. *(B.M.E.)*

Beryl with winning owner, Nairobi, 1977. *(B.M.E.)*

Beryl's house at Naivasha c. 1963. *(B.M.E.)*

With George Gutekunst during the filming of *World Without Walls*, the televised documentary of her life. *(G. Gutekunst)*

Derby Day, Nairobi Racecourse, 1986, a few months before her death. *(Author)*

Like her little filly Niagara, Lone Eagle was by Toronto out of a mare called Xylone, which Beryl had bought in-foal, for Norman & Thrane Limited, at the Nakuru horse sales. Lone Eagle ran first in their colours: farm companies were allowed to own horses but they had to be run as though they were privately owned. As the date for the Derby drew close it was obvious that Lone Eagle stood a very good chance and another of Beryl's owners, Lady Kenmare, bought the horse from the Norman/ Thrane consortium 'because she dearly wanted to lead in the Derby winner', Doreen Bathurst Norman said.[18]

With justification Block and Soprani were annoyed when Lone Eagle walked off with the Derby trophy. Their own horse, Mountie, had been a fancied Derby prospect, and Beryl had not run him. This caused a bitter row. Beryl had run Lone Eagle to please Enid Kenmare and because she loved Lone Eagle, whom she had delivered as a foal, and reared from that day on. In addition to the Derby winner that season, Beryl trained Fair Realm to win four races including the Spey Royal Cup and Kenya Guineas, and Spike (an outstanding two-year-old by Kara Tepe out of Harpoon), who won races with style and grace: '. . . but once Spike, a beautiful mover, was called upon it was all over,' enthused the *East African Standard*. 'He is a fine colt and it will be interesting to see if he can stay, and become an E.A. Derby winner in the traditions of Niagara and My Realm.'[19]

All that spring, however, Beryl's winners were becoming harder to find, and in the summer of 1964 it was realized that a mystery illness had attacked all but the older horses. It was a strange sort of lethargy, which Beryl later attributed to an excess of fluoride in the water. Her horses still looked magnificent but the muscles were affected in some unexplained way which prevented their expanding in exercise, and they could not gallop. No matter what she did she could not cure the problem, and in particular Lone Eagle, Mountie and Spike were affected by what Beryl called 'fluorescent poisoning'.

One of Kenya's most respected journalists, the late Mervyn Hill, visited Beryl at this time and asked her over lunch how the thrills of flying and racing compared. She told him, 'In flying you are handling the plane yourself and no one can interfere for good or bad. In racing you can produce a horse in the paddock

as fit as you think it can be. After that it's up to the jockey.
Within minutes, even seconds, months of planning and hard
work can be undone.' She was emphatic about the greatest gift a
trainer could have. 'Infinite attention to detail. Your
judgement grows over the years, but you can never afford to let
up. Flair alone will not win races.'[20]

Beryl never let up for a moment. 'In mechanical terms she
was born with a super-charger and no governor on the
accelerator,' Doreen Bathurst Norman said.[21] Beryl's appalling
behaviour to the Bathurst Normans in the first year after she
returned to Kenya had not only been caused by her illness,
which was real and serious, but also a frustration which drove
her at times to the edge of madness. Now, successful and fulfilled
despite her problems over paperwork, she could stand back
subjectively and cope with them. Jørgen often spent weekends
at the Naivasha training establishment to help with such
matters, and the mere fact that he was available was enough to
maintain Beryl's confidence in her ability.

CHAPTER SIXTEEN

[1965–1980]

Enid, Countess of Kenmare, was Beryl's wealthiest owner. Her oblique links with Beryl stretched back into the past, for Lady Kenmare had previously been married to Lord Furness after his marriage to Thelma Morgan ended, and Beryl had first met the countess in the mid 1930s when Tom had worked for the couple as private pilot. One day, Beryl flew in to Burrough Court with Tom, and the then Lady Furness told her nine-year-old daughter Patricia, 'Today you are going to see a very beautiful lady.' 'And I did – I shall always remember the first time I saw Beryl. She was dressed in a white flying suit and looked so glamorous and beautiful – and she remained so as long as I knew her,' Patricia (now Mrs O'Neill) told me.[1]

Raised in Australia, Lady Kenmare was the daughter of Charles Lindeman, who introduced vines to New South Wales and thus pioneered a great industry there. Her own interest in horses was, like Beryl's, a life-long one. Much married and widowed, she was reputedly fabulously rich after an astonishing run of bad luck had dispatched her four husbands early to their respective graves, providing Lady Kenmare with a series of inherited fortunes. Her first husband, Roderick Cameron of New York, whom she married in 1913, died in the following year leaving her with a baby son, also named Roderick, who ultimately became a writer. Her second husband, General Frederick Cavendish, whom she married in 1917, died in 1931 leaving the beautiful relict with two further handsome children and his considerable worldly wealth. In 1933 she married Lord Furness. He died in 1940, again leaving her 'a fortune'. Finally she married the 6th Earl of Kenmare in 1943, and he died within a matter of months of the wedding.

Her serious interest in racehorses stemmed from the period of Lady Kenmare's marriage to 'Duke'[2] Furness when the couple owned famous stud farms in England and Ireland. After Lord Furness's death, these were acquired by the Aga Khan. Lady Kenmare bought a property in Kenya some years after the war, in which she lived during the winter months, when not at her villa in Cap Ferrat in the south of France which her son Roderick made his permanent home. Her son by General Cavendish inherited the title Baron Waterpark and lived in England and her daughter Patricia Cavendish, another horse-lover, accompanied her mother to Kenya.

At the time of Uhuru there was general consternation among the relatively newly-arrived wealthy expatriates who owned to massive doubts about Kenya's future as an independent republic. There was a small scale exodus, mainly to Rhodesia and South Africa, but the old-established settlers, in the main, stayed on. Lady Kenmare had no deep roots in the country and was the recipient of constant and mixed advice about her financial situation in Kenya. She had a friend who was very highly placed in the new government and it is believed that he advised her to get her money out while she could.

Lady Kenmare's concern reached a peak in the summer of 1964, at the very time that Beryl was having her problems with the mysterious illness which had attacked her horses. Beryl was sure that these problems were due to the water at Naivasha, and she knew that to cure them she would have to move. Lady Kenmare's daughter believes that the main impetus for the arrangement which resulted came from Beryl, who badly wanted to train in South Africa. 'She worked on my mother for about six months to get her to agree to the move.'[3] Eventually Beryl and Lady Kenmare came to an agreement that they would move to South Africa together and set up a training establishment there. Firstly, though, there was the question of finding suitable premises.

Beryl always made friends easily. She had contacts all over the world who she was convinced would come to her aid, and indeed she was right. This occasion was no exception, for some friends of Beryl's, Air Vice Marshal Freddie Smart and his wife Doris, had moved to South Africa in the early 1960s due to his ill health. Sadly, even the move to a lower altitude with a temperate climate had not helped, and when Beryl contacted her, Doris Smart had been recently widowed. The letter from Beryl told Doris of her plans to move to the Cape to train, and of the search for a suitable establishment. Money, Beryl said, was no object whatsoever.

Doris accordingly approached appropriate estate agencies and sent Beryl details of various properties, including a stud farm called Broadlands. Having narrowed the choices down to two, Beryl and Lady Kenmare flew to South Africa within a week of receiving the information and had no hesitation in declaring that Broadlands was the ideal situation. The deal was struck on the spot.[4]

In August Beryl announced that she expected to move to the Cape in the following January, as private trainer to the countess. She would take with her a considerable proportion of the best open-class horses. Lady Kenmare purchased Spike, Speed Trial, Mountie and Battle Axe from Messrs Block and Soprani. Despite shipping in large tanks of spring water Beryl was still having difficulties with fluoride poisoning, and Spike, was withdrawn as unfit though he remained Beryl's best hope for the forthcoming East African Derby. In the event Beryl achieved a notable double with a new horse, Athi, who before her departure for South Africa won both the East African Derby and the St Leger in the season of 1964–65. It was Beryl's fifth Derby winner and her fourth victory in the St Leger.

Some time after the new year, Doreen Bathurst Norman had 'a yell for help from Beryl who was in the depths of packing up'.

> I said of course I'd help, so I got the car out – it was an old Holden – and drove down to Naivasha from Thompson's Falls where we were living. Forest Farm had been sold for settlement by then.[5] I remember the drive down to Beryl's place very well, for as I came over the escarpment the brakes failed.
>
> We finally got everything packed but there was a lot of fuss and bother getting exit permits for the horses and in the end they only came through the day they actually left. Jørgen was helping her make the arrangements, and he hadn't bothered Beryl with the details, but actually I don't think the permits had arrived when the horses left Naivasha.

Doreen was as sceptical as many others in Kenya of Beryl's ability to take on the high-class bloodstock of the Cape with her Kenya countrybreds. Beryl, though, was convinced that she could make a success of it and clearly convinced Enid Kenmare, who had 'all the money in the world, and thought that with Beryl as her private trainer she would sweep the boards'.[6]

Beryl had also persuaded Jørgen to accompany them to South Africa to manage Broadlands. It is doubtful that he ever seriously intended to do so as he had only recently invested heavily in his own farm, Kamwake.[7] But he did drive down to South Africa with Beryl in her new blue Mercedes, and Beryl clearly thought he was going there on a permanent basis.[8] Beryl had always had Jørgen around at weekends to tackle anything which was a problem to her. His help during those years cannot be overestimated. She depended on him absolutely and he had never failed her.

The horses travelled by sea to Durban and arrived in very poor condition after a 'terrible voyage' during which the temperatures in the hold reached 120 degrees. It took a long time to get them back into condition.[9] The ménage, including Lady Kenmare's nine assorted dogs and Beryl's two great danes, settled into Broadlands, but Jørgen stayed only until he was satisfied that everything was functioning well. His departure was a very bitter blow to Beryl, though it came as no surprise to anyone else. After he left, Beryl became 'unspeakably rude' to Lady Kenmare.[10]

Broadlands was a lovely place. Sited at Somerset West, near Lowry's Pass on the national road, it was approached through a black wrought-iron gate flanked by two imposing white pillars. A half-mile, tree-lined drive led to a white-walled Cape Dutch house with huge blocks of stables set among 400 acres of green paddocks, orchards and vineyards.[11] The house, which dated back to 1780, was one of the oldest in the area, and the Kenmare finances were put to work even before the new owner arrived, in a gutting and redecoration programme that had locals gossiping for weeks.

Broadlands was the only training establishment in the Cape which was owned and run entirely by women. With Lady Kenmare and Beryl were Patricia Cavendish and a secretary Julie Wharton, 'all of whom are passionately interested in horses and all have fascinating stories to tell', the *Cape Times* reported.[12] Miss Cavendish, whose love for animals was not confined to horses, told reporters the story of her pet lion cub Tana, who slept on her bed until as a four-year-old lioness she was taken to a game reserve. Miss Cavendish stayed with the lioness until she had been taught to hunt and look after herself. She had loved her life in Kenya, where she was surrounded by a collection of 'wild' animals, and initially resented the move to South Africa.[13]

Julia Wharton met Lady Kenmare by accident. She was on holiday in Natal and had been asked by a friend to help unload Beryl's string of horses from the ship at Durban and transport them to Broadlands. She met Lady Kenmare in a railway siding at Bellville and accepted the job as her personal secretary. Later Doreen Bathurst Norman found to her surprise that Julia was a distant cousin.

If skill and dedication were a measure of success then this combination of enthusiasm and money should have been unbeatable. Beryl obtained a training licence, one of only two issued to women trainers at that time, and everything looked set fair. Broadlands did, in fact, enjoy early success and Beryl's name as a winning trainer soon appeared in the lists. She scored a good double at one of her first meetings later that year when Marie Celeste II won the Durbanville Cup and Mountie won the third race of the day. Further victories with Title Deed and Kara Prince, Lone Eagle and Mountie followed, all viewed with a certain amount of astonishment because of their breeding. But Beryl felt that she was following in the hallowed footsteps of her father. He too had gone to Durban and trained successfully. 'What would my father have done?' was still her greatest *aide-mémoire* in times of stress. And the stress came all too soon.

It was scarcely avoidable. Both Beryl and Enid Kenmare were beautiful women with strongly developed characters. Both were accustomed to getting their own way. In fact the combination of Beryl's talent and Enid's money was never enough to guarantee a successful union. Beryl had never worked happily with women, she was more at ease with, and preferred, the company of men. Nevertheless for a while both powerful personalities suffered the partnership to continue for each had her own reward, even from this uneasy relationship.

Beryl was not easy to work for. She was tough and demanding on the staff. One morning on a workout ride, a girl groom was thrown from a horse and broke her arm, and as she lay on the ground in considerable pain, Beryl rode back to see the cause of the delay. Looking at the girl, she said with exasperation, 'Bloody fool!' and rode away again, leaving someone else to take care of the injured girl. 'That's what she was like. Very hard. But if it had been her who'd fallen and broken her arm, she would have said the same thing, "Bloody fool!" and then she'd have got up and carried on, broken arm and all, I've no doubt. She was immensely courageous and stoical about pain,' the former Miss Cavendish recalled.[14]

In June 1965 Buster Parnell flew out from Ireland to ride for Lady Kenmare. His wife Anna had recently given birth to a son, David, and Beryl became the child's godmother. 'Funny little thing, isn't he?' she said when she first saw him, but she became quite fond of him in her own way – and also of his sister Tina. 'She would sometimes say to Tina, "Come along, sweetie, let's go and play," ' Anna Parnell told me, 'and she'd allow Tina to make up using all the contents of her make-up drawer. Tina was only about three years old then and loved it, she used to come home with her face in a terrible mess.' By then Beryl would have tired of the fun. 'What a dreadful little child,' she'd say, handing Tina back to her parents.[15]

Buster saw immediately that Beryl was unhappy. 'One of the main problems was that she simply couldn't get on with the stud-farm manager,' he said. 'He was undoubtedly knowledgeable about managing a stud, but he had no conception of how a training establishment should be run and they were constantly at loggerheads. Beryl often had to back down – being a private trainer isn't quite the same as being a public one.' One of her particular problems was the maintenance of gallops. The manager simply didn't know how to keep the gallops as Jørgen had done. For example Beryl would constantly find that on the eve-of-race workout, a horse would go unsound because it had bruised a foot on a stone. 'This would never have happened if Jørgen had been around – he would never have allowed that sort of thing to happen. Beryl had become accustomed to that level of back-up. She didn't get it at Broadlands.'[16]

The truce between Lady Kenmare and Beryl was thin on occasions, as Buster observed:

> Lady Kenmare threw lots of parties, luncheons and dinner parties – they were marvellous fun. There'd often be anything up to eighteen or twenty of us – a real mixture too, dukes, archbishops – you never knew who was going to be there. Beryl was always the last to arrive and she'd sail in, usually after everyone else had sat down, looking marvellous with her two boxers, Circe and Caesar, trailing her. She never consciously made an entrance, but it happened that way. Enid habitually allowed her two pugs to join her at dinner and the four dogs caused absolute havoc. It would always start well, but after a while there would be stirrings and murmurs from under the table. Then little growls. Eventually the diners would be politely holding on to their wine glasses and politely pretending they hadn't noticed that the whole table literally shook from the minor war occurring around their feet. Eventually Beryl would say plaintively, 'Enid, I do wish you would control your dogs, darling.' Enid would smile sweetly and raise her glass – which never contained anything stronger than water or Coca Cola.[17]

Anna Parnell remembered a similar incident: 'Once at a particularly important luncheon Enid asked Beryl not to bring her dogs into the dining room. All went well until there was a great crash and Caesar and Circe leapt through the open window. All conversation was stopped, and I looked at Beryl who sat quite unperturbed, continuing her meal – I thought she was rather pleased.'[18]

Buster stayed through 1967, but he found the situation almost intolerable. He had gone there to do a job of work and found himself in the middle of the constant squabbles. Matters did improve when the old manager left and a younger man was recruited from Kenya, but tragically he had not been there long before he was killed in a car accident outside the gates of Broadlands.

Finally, Beryl could take no more. If she couldn't manage the stables as she wanted, then she really couldn't be expected to turn out winners. A final quarrel over stable management led her to leave, taking the few horses she herself owned – Niagara,

Title Deed and Kara Prince. Responsibility for the break-up lay on both sides. Beryl had been for years a public trainer and therefore responsible to no one, except for the individual performance of a horse to its owner. But as a private trainer she was, ultimately, the paid servant of Lady Kenmare, and the silken chains weighed heavily. Lady Kenmare was then well into her seventies, and although she was only ten years older than Beryl, she looked and acted as though there were more than that number of years between them. She had suffered a back injury some years earlier and had (according to Beryl at least) begun to act in the cantankerous way of the elderly. 'She could never make up her mind exactly what she wanted to do with the farmland. One minute she would plan to plant vines, and the next she would have them all ripped out for another crop. Beryl felt it was all very unsettling,' Anna Parnell stated.

'Enid was getting very old and difficult. She couldn't understand what I needed, and so I left,' Beryl told me.[19]

Lady Kenmare, who originally thought she had been buying into Broadlands in a partnership arrangement, with Jørgen Thrane taking all the administration and management off her hands, found instead that she was the sole owner, and having to take full responsibility. She had no help from Beryl, who was uncooperative and embittered by Thrane's departure.[20]

Hoping to set herself up as a public trainer, Beryl managed to find a temporary home for herself and the horses with a friend, Belinda Black.[21] The new stables were in the Flats, a rather poor area and not at all what Beryl had been used to. But she couldn't afford to set up properly, and despite her successful years she had no savings. Buster and Anna Parnell used to go out to see her during this time, before they too became discouraged and returned to Europe. 'It was a really dreadful place she had there. You had to walk miles over sand to get to Beryl's place, it was quite awful – and of course she had no money. She never really stood any chance of succeeding there. Oddly enough I became very good friends with her during that period. At Naro Moru she had never paid any attention to me, but at the Cape when she was unhappy and needed someone to talk to then I got to know her and liked her very much...' Anna said.[22]

Finally, after a row with the stewards at Cape Town, Beryl moved briefly to Natal, but after a few months decided to move permanently to Rhodesia.[23] At sixty-six she was no youngster to be thinking of starting afresh in a new country where her reputation was unknown. However, few people would have guessed her age, for physically she was as slim and lovely as ever and looked at least twenty years younger than her true age. She always dressed in slinky, silky materials, and there was always some little item like a silk scarf, or some other accessory which added chic to her outfits. She moved with extraordinary lightness 'as if she had wings on her ankles', and it was as if age had passed her by. She settled on Inverness Farm at Ruwa near Salisbury, and at first she was confident that she could succeed there despite the lack of a 'supporter'.

Interviewed shortly after her arrival, she said, 'I wish now that I'd settled here when I left Kenya . . . I would have been well established now. I have been very impressed with the standard of racing here . . .' Asked about her flying career she replied, 'I can't remember how many hours I've logged – it must be about three thousand – but horses have always been my first love. I can't wait for my first race, it beats flying every time for excitement.'[24] In fact it was nearly thirty years since she had last piloted a plane, but the trails of her glamorous flying career still clung to her and whenever she could, she used them to get publicity for her training establishment.

Peter Leth, an old friend from Naro Moru, where he worked for a while culling buffalo at Soysambu, was living in Rhodesia when Beryl arrived. He recalled, 'She was taking a hell of a gamble when she went to Rhodesia. She had no contacts, she couldn't get anyone to send good horses to her to train and she couldn't get any jockeys to ride for her. I used to drive out to her place about ten miles from Salisbury to ride fast work for her. She was certainly in a mess financially and a friend of mine, a solicitor, tried to help her. But she never really had a chance there, the odds were all stacked against her.' The odds included constant rows with the stewards, while concerns about her establishment revolved mainly around her doubtful financial ability to run a training yard. In addition Beryl could never accept handicaps allocated to her horses. In Kenya during her youth the stewards had all been family friends and to argue the handicap was all part of the game. In more formalized racing circles such arguments were viewed more seriously.

'She was such a character you couldn't help being fond of her, but she had a shocking temper,' Leth told me. 'On one occasion I rode a morning workout for her. When I got back to the stables, I slipped off the horse and turned to Beryl, expecting to be thanked or at least to discuss the performance of the horse. Instead I turned to get a bucket of cold water thrown over me with great passion. "You slowed that horse up," Beryl stormed at me. Apparently there were prospective owners looking on and they hadn't been impressed. I got the blame.'[25]

Tired, dispirited and once again penniless, Beryl soon realized that she would have to return to Kenya. A wealthy friend helped her by buying her beloved Niagara for breeding. Part of this bargain was that Beryl should keep the resulting foal from Niagara's visit to the top South African stallion, Ships Bell. Ships Bell had done little on the race course, for he damaged his knees and had to be pin-fired as a comparative youngster. He had been sold out of training for only 300 guineas. However his breeding was impeccable, being by Doutelle out of Belle of All (winner of the One Thousand Guineas at Newmarket), and he could get very good progeny. The result of his meeting with Niagara was the lovely little colt Water Boy, whom Beryl reckoned would be 'a really great horse'.

When in 1970 Beryl returned to Kenya she knew that she would need quick success. But the task was not so great as she had faced in Rhodesia. Here she was known, indeed was a celebrity, almost a legend. Her reputation and contacts were immense. When she found some difficulty in regaining her trainer's licence she approached the (then) vice president, Daniel *arap* Moi, who was sympathetic and personally saw to it that she was registered as a trainer. Once again Aldo Soprani helped her by giving her his best horses to train. Tubby Block thought better of returning to her, and risking the constant *shauries*, but she immediately persuaded a few other influential owners, and she set up her establishment at Thika on Soprani's coffee plantation.

Her house was situated in the middle of the plantation, on the slope of a hill with railed paddocks at the side, and there were good stables. The disadvantage was that there was no jockey's house nearby and jockeys had to travel by motorbike each day along seven miles of appalling tracks which were impassable in wet weather.

Soprani's trust in Beryl was not misplaced. Only weeks after the opening of the 1970–71 season she provided him with winner's trophies. Using the recess between seasons to prepare the horses, she planned carefully and brought on two new purchases for Soprani, Heron and The Sultan. With Heron, a grey yearling bought from Jack Ellis for Soprani's string, Beryl once again carried off the coveted Kenya Triple Crown of the East African Derby, Kenya St Leger and Kenya Guineas. With the brilliant two-year-old Sultan (winner of the Derby and St Leger) she also won the Futurity Stakes and the Champagne Stakes, and four others. In all, during that season of 1971–72 she helped to lead in twenty-three winners and became firmly entrenched in her usual position at the top of the leading trainers' league table.

After considerable difficulty she was able to import her own Water Boy into Kenya. The horse's South African parentage was against him, however Beryl had powerful allies and she was not afraid to use them occasionally. In this instance the allies were patrons Peter Kenyatta, son of the President of Kenya, and the equally well-connected Hon. Charles Njongo. Whatever it took, Water Boy was imported and, despite inevitably heavy handicapping, bore out Beryl's initial hopes.

As a three-year-old he won four races including the important feature races Delamere Gold Vase, Italian Challenge Cup and the Summer Handicap. After his 'surprise win' in the Delamere Gold Cup, under the headline, 'Red Faces after Water Boy's win', the *East African Standard*'s racing correspondent conveys Beryl's attitude with precise humour:

> 'I wish Water Boy was in the Derby,' was the sentiment expressed somewhat understandably by the colt's trainer after racing on Sunday – understandable for Beryl Markham that is, but a line of thought likely to put Mr Michael Cunningham-Reid off his cigars. For on Sunday [his horse] Devon Lad ... had run a really tremendous race to finish six lengths clear of the whole Delamere Gold Vase field bar Water Boy.
>
> Mrs Markham seemed to gain a good deal of amusement, after the race, even if not before it, from my conclusion last

Saturday that Water Boy did not have the class for such a contest.[26]

Water Boy never went on to achieve the greatness that Beryl predicted, although he won a total of ten races. 'He was weighted out of it,' she said matter of factly to me, 'his breeding, you see.' Nevertheless his speed was impressive, and his time over 1400 metres of 1 minute 26.2 seconds remained a course record for many years, vindicating Beryl's faith in him.

In 1971 Beryl received news that Gervase had been involved in a car accident and was critically injured. Mansfield flew to France to be with his son during the weeks that he hovered between life and death. 'During that time I really got to know him,' said Gervase's wife, Viviane. 'He was so kind to us and so sweet to the girls. It was the first time since our marriage that he had behaved as I thought a father, and a grandfather, should. That was a terrible time for us all. Gervase was in great pain but he was, like Beryl, immensely stoic. The bravest person I have ever met in that respect.'[27]

Following their visit to Beryl in Kenya in the mid 1950s Gervase and Viviane lived in London for twelve years with their two daughters Fleur and Valery. For most of that time Gervase worked for the *Financial Times*. In December 1967 they moved to France where Gervase launched an English weekly edition of *Le Monde*. A disagreement over advertising policy caused his resignation and he subsequently worked for a while at the International Chamber of Commerce in Paris. Beryl could not afford to travel to Europe. She was distressed when she heard that her son had died in hospital, but she had never been close to him. Many of her recent friends were not even aware that she had a son and the sensitive, introverted man had made little claim on the mother he saw as an unattainable figure. Gervase's body was taken to England for burial in the Markham family tomb and within months Mansfield too was dead.[28]

In the years between 1972 and 1978 Beryl continued to win races with a gradually shrinking string of horses, though no further classics came her way in those years. Now over seventy, she retained her lissom good looks and rode out every day despite having suffered a broken leg in 1972 which kept her in plaster for months. 'She was stunning even then,' recalled Ulf

Aschan, a friend in Beryl's latter years. 'Her walk was that of a young woman, she wore her hair long and ash blonde, her figure was still fantastically good and from the back you would easily take her for a bird of thirty.'[29]

The late Robin Higgin, an expert on Kenya's racing history, who died suddenly whilst the last chapters of this book were being written, told me, 'She was unquestionably the most brilliant trainer Kenya has ever known. I would really love to know what Beryl's secret was. I remember that there was always a very faint sheen of sweat on all her horses, so faint that it was a sort of bloom . . . I've never seen it before or since on any horse anywhere in the world, and I don't know why it was there. Her horses always looked absolutely magnificent. I feel sure she gave them something, perhaps some herb known to the Africans which gave them a little extra something . . . perhaps she got it from Clutterbuck. He also did extraordinarily well as a trainer, even when he went down to the Cape. But I think Beryl was better. She was an absolute sod about declaring jockeys. She was apt to change her mind on the morning of the race – she used to do that sort of thing all the time. You never knew who was going to be up until the last minute. It made her very unpopular in certain quarters.'[30]

There are many in Kenya who truly believe that Beryl had a secret formula, and if so it has died with her, but those closest to her during her greatest success scoff at the theory. Buster Parnell, who accompanied her on countless evening stables, remarks simply, 'She didn't need to fake it . . . she was too good.' The nearest approximation to an elixir was described by Doreen Bathurst Norman.

Beryl always had a little mixture made up which she carried round with her. There was nothing special about it, it contained the usual additives that one gives horses – salts, vitamin supplements and that sort of thing. As she worked her way around the horses she would add some of this mixture to the horse's feed. One horse might get one handful, another three handfuls, and another none at all. She seemed to know exactly what the personal requirements of each horse were, but there was no magic about it. It was just skill and a unique and intimate knowledge of the individual horse's needs.[31]

The writer Martha Gellhorn, the former wife of Ernest Hemingway and a prize-winning war correspondent, met Beryl briefly during the early 1970s. Invited by a mutual friend to drinks at Beryl's rented house, she wrote, 'I had never heard of Beryl, and so arrived ignorant . . . Beryl received me in a typical sitting-room, "settler" furnishings, big chairs covered in chintz, a stalwart piece to hold drinks and glasses. No books; it is a professional deformation always to notice books'[32] – incorrectly as it turned out, for Beryl had a large and impressively varied collection of books, though these were not on public show.

> Beryl wore tight black trousers and a high-necked silky pullover; exotic clothing for upcountry where khaki prevailed. She looked very glamorous, fair hair, tanned face, splendid lean body; certainly not the least horsey as I would have expected. I jumped to instant wrong conclusions; this obvious darling of the Muthaiga Club, the ancient boring centre of Nairobi social life, trained racehorses, whatever that meant, for amusement. Two admirers were visiting her, one older, one younger, and I was impressed by the way they leapt to be serviceable about drinks while Beryl waited gracefully to be waited on . . . I took her to be a striking woman of forty.[33]

Beryl continued to attract admirers – even, it was rumoured, lovers. However care must be exercised in this matter of Beryl's reputed love affairs for if the stories repeated to me were all true, Beryl would never have risen from a reclining position between the ages of fourteen to eighty-four. They are part of the sea of rumour, gossip and speculation which forms Beryl's legend. Beyond any doubt she was promiscuous in her sexual relationships with men, but her affairs were not totally indiscriminate, for she retained an inbuilt fastidiousness where her body was concerned and took a great pride in it. Doreen Bathurst Norman, probably Beryl's greatest woman friend, said that Beryl's attitude towards sex was more like that of a man than a woman. 'I don't think Beryl ever thought how her behaviour must have appeared to the people of the real world, and if she had thought, she would have said it was stupid and would certainly never had let it worry her for a minute.'

Typical of the way in which gossip clung to Beryl without any foundation were stories told me by a number of people regarding meetings that Beryl supposedly had with Prince Henry, Duke of Gloucester, when he visited Nairobi in the late 1950s. In these stories Beryl had disappeared for days with the prince. In another version she was 'actually seen' being smuggled out of a car into the back entrance to the Muthaiga Club to meet him. The third was that Prince Henry borrowed the governor's car to visit Beryl on her farm and crashed it on the return journey (this latter story at least, is partially true for HRH did crash the Rolls-Royce and His Excellency, Governor Mitchell was understandably upset about it). But what actually happened was that Beryl spent the entire period of the prince's visit with the Bathurst Normans, and never left the farm. Prince Henry never visited her there. Doreen stated, 'She did in fact write to him but he did not answer.'

In 1975 Beryl invited the Irish jockey Dennis Leatherby to Kenya to ride for her. He found her very tough, but an excellent trainer. Once, when they were riding back to the stables at Thika his horse, an uncut colt, tried to mount Beryl's horse. Beryl fell off and Leatherby immediately got off to help her. 'No, no, sweetie,' she told him firmly, 'I'm fine, leave me alone thank you.' 'That was Beryl,' he said. 'She didn't accept help from anyone and she was very, very tough.'[34]

Buster Parnell, Beryl's partner in the 'unbeatable combination of talents' which formed the true peak of her racing career, returned to ride for her at the New Year meeting in 1976, and the *Standard* reported the event.

> Highlight of the meeting was the return of Buster Parnell who rode three winners out of five rides for Beryl Markham. First winner was on P. Kenyatta and Samson Mirithi's Greenacres. Buster made ground fast on Greenacres and his challenge was beautifully timed as he was twice headed. His second win was a close-fought victory on Sun Queen and his third win came when War Chant, belonging to Mary and Colin Haynes, cruised along calmly in front... beating the field by seven lengths.[35]

Robin Higgin considered Parnell to be the best jockey ever to have ridden regularly in Kenya. 'His natural exuberance and wit did not make him the most popular jockey in the eyes of the racing authorities, but Kenya racing and Beryl in particular benefited from the flair which he so consistently displayed.'[36]

Buster returned to Kenya for the seasons of 1977, 1978 and 1979. But in 1979 he was deported. His natural exuberance had led him to be 'rather naughty with the wife of an influential man. That wasn't the reason given of course – but it was the real reason,' Buster claimed with a grin. According to Romulus Kleen, Beryl had always stood up for Buster with the racing authorities, no matter what trouble he got into, and showed enormous loyalty to him; but on this occasion even she couldn't help.

In 1977 the Aero Club of East Africa celebrated its fiftieth anniversary with a golden jubilee dinner at which Beryl was the guest of honour. One of Beryl's closest friends in her last years, Paddy Migdoll, recalled: 'She was terribly nervous – she hated crowds and making speeches. I think it was probably the one thing that she *was* afraid of.'[37] The Aero Club presented her with a commemorative souvenir, a large canvas on which were screen-painted the signatures of many aviation friends spanning fifty years. It hung in Beryl's sitting room until her death.

The same year, F.D. Erskine, nicknamed FD and son of the Galloping Greengrocer Sir Derek Erskine, inherited some horses from his father when that vastly popular knight died. 'I inherited Beryl along with them,' he recalled.

> At that time she had about sixteen horses in training but her financial affairs were in a terrible mess. She was wonderful with horses but her administrative ability was zero. She didn't even have an oat crusher – I bought her one but within weeks it was stolen. I think some of her syces were dishonest – they can be like that with the elderly out here when there is no one to keep an eye on them. I tried to get her to take on a young lady as a sort of understudy. This girl was frightfully keen and greatly admired Beryl, but I'm afraid Beryl wouldn't, at that time, have anything to do with ladies. She loved to have men around her.[38]

FD arranged for his accountant to take care of Beryl's administration and for a long time Beryl would drive into Nairobi once a week, with all her paperwork. This help must have made a great difference, for in the 1978–79 season her count of wins doubled from twelve to twenty-four, and at the age of seventy-seven she trained Aldo Soprani's Sailor Beware to win the Kenya St Leger – an incredible fifty-two years after her first victory in the same race with Wise Child. Her second horse, Indian Dancer, took second place. Some years earlier she had ceased to be Soprani's sole trainer, but he remained loyal and always sent her a few horses. He relied on her judgement but they had an irascible relationship. 'Beryl treated him shockingly,' reported one of his friends. 'He was frightfully rude to her,' said one of hers. It was a typical example of Beryl's relationships with many of her owners. Her statement to Parnell – 'Horses are never any trouble – it's their owners I can't stomach'[39] – is a precise summing up of her attitude.

After two years, supervising Beryl's administrative affairs became 'too much' for FD. Beryl never cooperated and he was reluctant to accept the inevitable responsibilities involved in declarations and bookkeeping. But he remained steadfast to her as a friend. The good friends always did so, despite all the difficulties.

> What I remember most about her was that she was a very gracious and beautiful person. The jockeys adored her, in fact they were proud to ride for her and I was most impressed by the way that the horses loved her – she had a great affinity with them. They went very well for her – in spite of the fact that she worked them very hard – they had to be good horses to stay with Beryl's training schedule. She had three of my horses and she was marvellous with them. One especially, Clean Sweep, won the Dewars White Label Trophy and led from start to finish and at one point was seven or eight lengths clear of the field. Clean Sweep won that trophy two seasons running for me, with Beryl training. She also trained Kaa Chonjo for Peter Kenyatta – it means Always Ready. I really loved that horse and bought it from him and am now using it for breeding. Unfortunately the foal born of Kaa Chonjo and Clean Sweep was stillborn but I would dearly love a 'Beryl' foal so I will try the combination again.[40]

Mr Erskine's comment – 'horses had to be good to stay with Beryl's training schedule' – was echoed by Robin Higgin, who is on record as saying that Beryl's system may have led to the premature retirement of horses which might have had longer, if less illustrious, careers in other hands. But he could recall no horse that had failed to show form in Beryl's yard becoming a success elsewhere.[41]

With responsibility for financial and administrative affairs back in her own hands, Beryl once again allowed these matters to become a hopeless muddle. She had no business sense whatsoever and as a result her tally of successes slumped again, though she did achieve a respectable total of ten winners.

Most of her wealthy owners gradually drifted away and soon she was left with a string of only four horses. When she became very ill with gastric problems, her friends did everything they could to persuade her to see a doctor and finally they enlisted the help of a very old friend and owner 'Lady CB' (Cavendish Bentinck)[42] who, together with F.D. Erskine, went to collect her from her cottage at Ngong, with the intention of taking her to the hospital. Beryl saw them coming and locked every door and window in the house. She would not let anyone near her for two days and told her callers firmly by telephone, 'I hate hospitals. I'm not going anywhere near any doctor or hospital because if they looked inside me they would have pronounced me dead five years ago.'[43] This dislike, amounting almost to a phobia, had always been with her from her very earliest days.

For years Beryl had fought with the stewards of the Jockey Club of Kenya. Her attitude towards them veered from annoyance to outright contempt and she saw them as pettifogging. And her finances were in a mess. Nevertheless when, in June 1980, without warning, she received a letter from the stewards advising her that they were 'not prepared to grant [her] a Public Trainer's Licence for the season 1980–81 or thereafter', Beryl was very shocked.

She immediately engaged a first-class advocate who, writing to Mr Michael Cunningham-Reid, acting senior steward, stated his client's case in admirably clear terms:

> We are aware that under rule 5 (vi)... the Stewards of the Jockey Club have power at their discretion to renew or refuse a Trainer's Licence... However in the case of Mrs Markham you will appreciate that [this decision], communicated to her without warning... amounts to depriving her totally of the

only means she has of earning her livelihood. In addition this decision involves a very serious stigma: the fact of having had a trainer's licence refused in Kenya would undoubtedly mean that Mrs Markham would suffer severe embarrassment in any application for another licence elsewhere in the world. Whether or not the Stewards intended this result when making their decision, the fact remains that by so deciding, the Stewards both gravely injure our client's reputation, and by implication cast grave doubts upon her honesty and her ability . . . With the greatest respect to the Stewards and to the Board, it would seem that a number of charges can be levelled against the decision thus to deprive Mrs Markham of her livelihood. Our instructions are that at no time has Mrs Markham been given an opportunity to hear the charges against her, or of being heard in her own defence, or of bringing evidence to answer any such charges as may have been taken into account by the Stewards. It is a fundamental rule of natural justice that a person has the right to be heard; without this, it cannot be said that Mrs Markham has had fair treatment or proper impartial consideration of her case on its merits.

Our client has already suffered both loss and damage, because in a small community word spreads with frightening rapidity and this matter appears to be already fairly common knowledge amongst the racing fraternity. Mrs Markham, if we may say so, enjoys a hitherto completely unblemished record; she has been Leading Trainer for many years, and it is common knowledge that her horses are always immaculately turned out. She has now recovered from her recent illness, and her doctor confirms that she is back to complete fitness. These facts underline the seriousness of the damage caused by the letter of 10th June.

We request you, therefore, both to withdraw the letter . . . and to hold a proper enquiry into the question of renewal. Both we and our client would be happy to attend any meeting to which we are invited, or to supply any information you require. We trust that this upsetting matter can be resolved in an amicable fashion as soon as possible; we feel sure that there will be no call for Mrs Markham to have to seek redress in any other forum, and that you will ensure that she receives the equitable treatment from you that she has the right to expect.[44]

Beryl had some enemies among the stewards, but she also had many friends. Her licence was renewed almost immediately, and she went on for several years with her small establishment. In the 1980–81 and 1981–82 seasons she won four races each year, when each of her four horses obliged once in each season. Two of these horses belonged to a friend, Freddie Nettlefold, and the other two to Beryl. One of her horses was exceptionally good but she couldn't keep him sound.[45]

'During that entire period the effort of simply continuing was very tough for her,' Buster Parnell told me. In 1982 Buster Parnell managed to 'slip into Kenya for two hours whilst changing flights en route to London from India'. It was illegal for him to enter the country of course, but Buster was not the man to allow such a small consideration to weigh with him unduly. He took a taxi to Beryl's cottage near the race course and luckily she was there. 'Beryl was very moved. She took hold of my hand and said, "Sweetie. You just sit there and have a little pinkie. I'm just going outside for a cry and then I'll come back and we'll have a long talk." And she did – she would never have let me see her cry, of course. When she came back she had on fresh make-up and we sat and talked until I felt that if I didn't get out the police would be in to pick me up.'[46]

Buster, to whom letter-writing is a chore, kept in touch by postcard until Beryl's death. They are brief and to the point: from India, 'Won the Derby today!'; from Denmark news of another important win and the message, 'How are those bastards at the club behaving? Don't let them get you down!'

But she was struggling against the overwhelming odds of insufficient money, her own lack of administrative ability and, despite outward appearances, old age. Horses were never declared and so missed races in which Beryl intended them to run. She had virtually no income other than her annuity from England and the little her two training fees brought in, and though her horses continued to have the best of everything, Beryl was deeply in debt and living very simply. The end of her racing career was inevitable.

Her social life was as full as ever. She retained the ability to make friends and her personal magnetism, together with her reputation as a celebrity, ensured invitations, which she usually promptly forgot. Long-term invitations with old friends she always kept, and every Tuesday for many years saw her blue Mercedes wending its way to Muthaiga, the district around the Muthaiga Country Club. There she had a standing lunch appointment with her friends 'CB and Lady CB'.

The CBs' home was small but one of the oldest and loveliest in Muthaiga, built entirely of wood. The L-shaped sitting room had a chapel ceiling and the walls and ceiling were lined with beautifully ageing Kenya timber. The grounds were several acres of indigenous and imported trees and plants, much of it informal, completely screened from neighbouring properties and the road by trees and high banks of bougainvillea. The house was virtually unchanged since the earliest days of Kenya's European Settlement and totally unmodernized, apart from the provision of electricity and modern plumbing. The servants still dressed and were treated as they were in the old colonial days. Behind the high screen of trees was an oasis where one could experience the life of decades earlier and the 'old' Kenya where Beryl felt at home.[47]

The CBs expected Beryl every Tuesday, no matter who else happened to be visiting, and immediately she reached the verandah she always kicked off her shoes. Throughout her life she had gone barefoot by choice whenever possible, and in old age was still proud of her feet, which were tiny and beautifully shaped. Lady CB (now the Duchess of Portland) recalled that even though she had known Beryl since the early 1950s, and had seen her sometimes two or three times a week over lunch:

> I never really knew her well. In fact I wonder how many people did really know her. Perhaps it was because Beryl never spoke about herself. Without prior knowledge one would never have realized she knew anything about flying. Moreover, she never mentioned her son or granddaughters. It was a long time before I knew she had a son. Somehow one had the feeling that she was entirely detached from people, not that she disliked them – they were just not important to her. Not so with animals. Going round her stables with her was a revelation of her love for horses. She was entirely dedicated and devoted to them – as she was to her dogs. My husband knew Beryl when she was young and she trained one or two horses for him. I remember him saying that she moved like a beautiful animal.[48]

Even in the late 1970s and until 1980 Beryl was fit and active. She rode every day and told friends she was now happier on a horse than off. Her stance was upright and relaxed, and she still walked with the light springing step she had learned as a child, poised on the balls of her feet as though ready to take off at any moment; her movement was part of her legend. When she lunched every Sunday at the Muthaiga Club, newcomers and visitors would look up and watch Beryl with interest, as her story was whispered to them.

It must be said that Beryl was not concerned about her poverty. She had always lived as best she could. When there was money she spent it, when times were difficult she lived on credit. It was her ability to persuade local merchants to allow her credit that brought Jack Couldrey into her life.

CHAPTER SEVENTEEN

[*1980–1986*]

'I got involved with Beryl some years ago when I was asked to serve a writ on her, on behalf of a local shopkeeper,' said Jack Couldrey, a Nairobi solicitor. When he visited Beryl he found her living in genteel squalor, and he immediately wanted to do something about this for although he had not known Beryl personally, his family had known hers. The godson of Jock Purves – Beryl's first husband – Jack felt a certain obligation. 'My father had known Beryl's father in the old days. I just couldn't leave her to live in those conditions.'[1]

Jack Couldrey contacted Ulf Aschan, a friend of Beryl's,[2] and between them they contacted many aviation and racing people who agreed to subscribe a certain amount each month to a fund to meet Beryl's expenses. From that day until Beryl's death in 1986, Jack managed Beryl's affairs. When first he went through her papers he knew nothing of her personal life and thought she probably had no income whatsoever, so he was surprised to learn that she had once written a book, and that there was evidence of a regular though small annuity from London, which he assumed came from the Markham family. Jack Couldrey could in no way have been said to have fallen under the spell of Beryl's charm, but he nevertheless became the last link in the chain of 'supporters', for once again Beryl had found someone to take on the burden of administration and 'boring details' which she loathed.

In the early 1980s Beryl moved into a cottage in the grounds of the Nairobi race course. Since this move occurred virtually at the time that Beryl's previous solicitor was writing to the Jockey Club regarding her licence, it appears that the difficulty on that occasion was speedily resolved, for Beryl's new home belonged to the Jockey Club and she lived there rent-free until her death. It is a pleasant location and meant that Beryl was able to continue training without the need for daily travelling. The narrow well-kept murram road from her door leads directly to the race course and stables. The cottage, unpretentious and modern, had an airy sitting room, two bedrooms and a bathroom 'complex'. It had originally been intended as living quarters for jockeys. From the sitting room Beryl could look out to see racehorses grazing in the small pasture beyond her fence.

With her servants Odero and Adiambo, she settled in. Early each morning the grooms brought the horses to Beryl's cottage where they received the day's instructions. Later she would drive her Mercedes down to watch the horses working out and to supervise various aspects of stable routine.

On the morning of 19 August 1981 the grooms went as usual to the cottage and waited. Beryl did not appear but they waited for a while thinking that the memsahib had simply risen later than usual. Odero, who had been Beryl's houseboy since the days at Naro Moru,[3] was washing down Beryl's car and he confirmed that she had not been seen that morning. Odero slept a little way from the house in his own quarters, and Beryl usually unlocked her door early so that he could get in to prepare breakfast. He was puzzled but not alarmed at this stage. Eventually the little group of waiting men became concerned enough to go to Beryl's neighbour, the race course veterinary surgeon Mr V.J. Varma – 'VJ' to race course patrons.

'I went across to the house and knocked on the door,' VJ recalled, 'but got no answer. I called out to her but still there was no response. By now I had begun to worry, so I went round to her bedroom window and called out again. Beryl answered me and said she was in a very bad way. She couldn't talk much but said she needed help right away so I went round to the front door and broke in.'

When I went to her bedroom I was very shocked at what I saw. Beryl was tied hand and foot with telephone cord. The bindings were very tight and she had been there a long time, for her hands and feet were badly swollen. She was virtually naked and had bad bruising and cuts about the face and neck.

It was obvious that she had been severely beaten up. She was in great pain due to the bindings having been so tight that circulation had stopped. By this time Mrs Bowden, a friend of Beryl's, had arrived and we proceeded to cut the bindings.[4]

Beryl would have suffered great agony when the bindings were released and the circulation was restored after many hours, but her primary concern was for her dogs. They toured the house looking for the 'corgi-pugs' and Beryl at first thought they had been stolen. Eventually they found the two animals under Beryl's bed, obviously very frightened and sitting quietly in a corner. Only then were her friends allowed to give her first aid and take her to the hospital.

Paddy Migdoll continued the story: 'She was left with *nothing*. Everything was stolen – even her passport and driving licence. She can be a difficult person because she is such an individual, and not everyone likes her, but when we went around asking for help for her we found out how many friends she did have. Everybody rallied around and donated things. Money, clothes, coats, blankets, everything...'[5]

Had Beryl merely obeyed her attackers (for there were several) and 'gone quietly' she would probably have simply been tied up and left, while the burglars ransacked the house. But this was not in Beryl's nature. Her attackers had been able to bind her because they surprised her whilst she was asleep. But as she lay bound on her bed she hurled a constant stream of invective in Swahili at the men, and it appears that the worst of her injuries were inflicted in an attempt to shut her up.

Although in the burglary most of her 'lovely things were stolen',[6] she was, fortunately, left with two of her most prized possessions, the silver and turquoise model of her Vega Gull, mounted on the trophy which Edgar Percival had presented after the transatlantic flight, and the engraved silver cigarette case she had long ago given to Prince Henry and which he had subsequently returned to her.

Sir Charles Markham, who lives at Karen (the Nairobi suburb which is named after Karen Blixen), said: 'I think that beating up was a very great shock to her. She never thought Africans would turn on her like that, and it seemed to age her a lot. A little while before the robbery she had been here for the christening of my grandchild and she was the life and soul of the party.'[7] It certainly seemed to affect her movement, for she walked stiffly after that incident and her sprightly walk was gone for ever.

She went on training, though. David Sugden, who had helped her with her training programme in 1979 (when Beryl still had some of the Soprani horses), now sent a couple of horses to her.

> I remembered what she had been like, and the judgement and experience she brought to training... When in 1982 I had the opportunity to buy a couple of horses, I sent them to Beryl to train because I still felt she had such a lot to give. Her technique was not one of shouting or telling people what to do, but rather of *asking* the horses to do what she wanted. Her feeding and exercising routines were all geared up to the individual horse – she didn't treat the horses as a string.
>
> One good example was a horse with very bad tendons. He was a big horse, yet she managed to slim him down without losing any of the horse's 'physique' in order to make him light enough for the tendons to carry him – and he won races afterwards.[8]

Mr Sugden is on record as having said some years later that he rated Beryl as being still one of the best trainers in Kenya and that given the horses and finance would possibly be *the* best, despite the fact that she was well over eighty.[9]

Beryl continued her habit of driving to the Muthaiga Club each week for Sunday lunch. One Sunday in August 1982 she was surprised, as she approached the front gate of the race course, to find it closed. She asked the askari (guard) why and he said he didn't know, but that he was quite happy to open it for her. So Beryl drove off towards the Muthaiga in her faithful old Mercedes.

What Beryl (and presumably the askari) did not know was that there was an attempted military coup in full swing. As usual Beryl drove through the centre of town, stopping at the New Stanley hotel where she often met friends for pre-lunch drinks. Here she encountered some armed soldiers in the road who demanded money, which Beryl, predictably, refused in a manner which left them in no doubt that they weren't going to get any, by means other than force. Even Beryl must by now have realized that it was dangerous to be on the streets, and she immediately set off for Muthaiga. Before long she came to a road block. 'Where are you going?' came the challenge. 'I'm Beryl Markham and I'm going to lunch at Muthaiga Club,' she answered. When armed guards tried to search her car and her handbag, she accelerated and drove through the barrier. The guards opened fire and several bullets hit the car. 'One of them grazed her chin and she arrived at the club dripping blood. It was quite a mess but she calmly parked her car at the front entrance and walked in with her dogs – which wasn't allowed, though an exception was made in this case. Quite a few people were staying there and they loaned her some clothes as hers were badly bloodstained. She stayed at the club for some days with her dogs until law and order was restored,' a fellow guest at the Muthaiga Club recalled.[10]

Beryl soon recovered from this experience, though Sir Charles Markham felt that 'both the robbery and the coup incidents shocked her very deeply – more than most people thought'. A week after the incident, the *East African Standard*'s correspondent 'Petersfield' wrote about the effect of the attempted coup on the racing community, and reported: 'I looked in at Ngong and was delighted to see the horses, as usual, out for their morning exercise... and there was Beryl as unchangeable as always, asking me, "What's new?"'[11]

Now though, whilst she still trained her small string of horses, there were signs that age had not passed her by after all. Her carriage was still upright but there was the stiffness of age about her movement. Her smile, her humour, were still sometimes those of a young woman, her charm (when she wanted to charm) dazzling, and her temper (to those unfortunate to receive its blast) as fearsome as ever. She might have ended her days in a slow descent to obscurity and indeed her life looked set fair to do just that.

She insisted on keeping her horses, despite Jack Couldrey's advice that they were costing more than she could afford. This of course counted for nothing with Beryl. She never inquired how Jack was able to pay her bills and keep her in pocket money – it simply never occurred to her to ask.[12]

By writing to the firm of solicitors in England who

administered the trust fund set up for Beryl in 1929, Jack had been able to have the annual amount increased, as a temporary measure. Such an increase can only be considered as personal generosity by those concerned.

Christmas 1982 saw the usual delivery of cards from friends all over the world. Among these was an intriguing letter from a man unknown to Beryl:

> December 20th 1982
> San Rafael, California

Dear Beryl Markham,
Two summers ago, driving back to Ketchum, Idaho, after a superb day trout fishing with Jack Hemingway, he said, 'George, have you read my father's letters?' I was startled for, though we have been friends for years, Jack had never mentioned his father to me nor I to him. I said no I hadn't. 'They're very revealing,' he said. That was the end of it but when I returned home I read the letters.

Well, quite an experience and indeed revealing... cruel, kind, hateful, loving, petty, grand, boastful and *never* once humble except on page 541 in a letter to his editor, Maxwell Perkins. On the chance you have not been told of it I quote the following passage:

'Did you read Beryl Markham's book, *West with the Night*? I knew her fairly well in Africa and never would have suspected that she could and would put pen to paper except to write in her flyer's log book. As it is she has written so well, and so marvellously well, that I was simply ashamed of myself as a writer. I felt that I was simply a carpenter with words, picking up whatever was furnished on the job and nailing them together and sometimes making an OK pigpen. But this girl can write rings around all of us who consider ourselves as writers. The only parts of it that I know about personally, on account of being there at the time and heard the other people's stories, are absolutely true. So you have to take as truth the early stuff about when she was a child, which is absolutely superb... I wish you would get it and read it because it is really a bloody wonderful book.'

Such praise intrigued me mightily, coming as it did after Hemingway had cruelly savaged most of his peers and a few of his betters. Further, I was still annoyed by his silly and pompous use of pugilistic metaphor when comparing his work with that of other writers ... i.e. 'I could go the distance with Stendhal for sure and maybe with Flaubert, but I couldn't get in the ring with the Count.' Good Lord, who other than Shakespeare could! What rubbish!

So after quite a search, I found a copy of *West with the Night*. Ah, what a grand and astounding book it is! I read it one day and again the next day. I blessed Hemingway and gave the book to Evan Connell, a friend who in my opinion is one of the two or three finest prose writers in America. (His *Mrs Bridge* is a classic.) Evan's enthusiasm and regard for your book matched mine and so we decided to send it to Jack Schumaker [sic] and William Turnbull, publishers and editors of North Point Press in Berkeley, two men with flawless literary taste and the courage of lions. They, too, fell under the spell of your wondrous book and set about securing US and British rights. I am sure you are pleased that North Point Press will re-issue *West with the Night* in late spring of 1983. Marvellous! Could not happen to a finer book. I am glad I am a careful, involved reader or I might have skipped right over Hemingway's tribute.

In appreciation of a beautiful book, I send my best regards to the woman who lived and wrote it.
George P. Gutekunst

George Gutekunst proved to be a larger-than-life character, whose love for literature and motion pictures ('the only twentieth-century art-form') knew no bounds. No doubt it was out of concern for Beryl's finer feelings that he edited Hemingway's letter about her, for he left out the following: '... and sometimes making them an OK pigpen. But this girl, who is to my knowledge very unpleasant and we might even say a high-grade bitch, can write rings around all of us who consider ourselves writers.' And later: 'She omits some very fantastic stuff which would destroy much of the character of the heroine; but what is that anyhow in writing?'[13]

Whatever George's motives, he was the moving force in this important chapter of Beryl's later years. A question screams to be answered. Why did Hemingway refer to her as 'very unpleasant' and what is the fantastic stuff that would destroy the character of the heroine? Bearing in mind the fact that Hemingway knew Beryl for only a matter of weeks, whilst he was convalescing in Nairobi from his unfortunate illness, and Beryl was engaged for most of that time in scouting for Blix on the Alfred Vanderbilt safari, he must have gained his impressions mainly from gossip. Hemingway, not renowned for his own saintliness, could surely not have been referring merely to Beryl's reputation for sexual promiscuity? One of the many rumours which abound says that Beryl spurned Hemingway's sexual advances – is this perhaps the reason for his personal condemnation? If so it makes his literary approval even more commendable.

In this way, though other people had begun to take an interest in Beryl's book, it was George Gutekunst who – without any personal reward – was the prime mover in its republication. After reading Hemingway's letter he went to his local library to see if they could locate a copy of the book – now, he realized, long out of print.

The librarian searched with the help of a computer and found that one copy of the book did exist within the Marin County library system, but it was lodged in an out-of-town location. Gutekunst immediately jumped into his car and drove to the library in question. He found that the book had been issued only seven times since 1942.

Taking a day off from running his sea-front restaurant, Ondines, at Sausalito, which is a short drive across the Golden Gate Bridge from San Francisco, Gutekunst settled down to read the book. He sat down at noon with a drink by his side and didn't rise from his chair until he finished it. The next day he read it again just to make sure that his enthusiasm hadn't been misplaced. On the second reading he knew he had rediscovered a literary gem.[14]

Over the previous half-decade there had been occasional perfunctory interest shown in Beryl's book by friends and others who had contacts in the publishing world. Pamela Scott had included it in a list of books recommended for republishing that she sent to a young relative embarking on a publishing career. Petal Allen, daughter of Sir Derek Erskine, had also taken an interest. And during these years Beryl found herself an object of interest from several writers. In particular two women writers, working independently on the biographies of Karen Blixen and

Denys Finch Hatton, interviewed Beryl and asked for her recollections about the two lovers. One of them who visited Beryl on a number of occasions read Beryl's book as part of her research programme and was particularly intrigued by it. She suggested to Beryl that something should be done with the property, and Beryl agreed to allow her to investigate film rights. Beryl signed a document agreeing to this course of action, which she later repudiated, claiming that she 'had been pressurized into signing it when she was ill'.[15]

When Jack took over Beryl's affairs, interest was being displayed in the film rights by another journalist, James Fox.[16] Several people were by then talking about obtaining the film rights, but Fox purchased a renewable option for a small sum, and renewed the option regularly. In a letter dated 17 September 1982 he advised Beryl that together with Mark Peploe, he had written a 'movie treatment' and was hoping to get the project off the ground. This was the situation prevailing when George Gutekunst came on the scene in 1982 and when Beryl's book was republished.

Jack Couldrey, who already knew about the proposed resurrection of the book, saw no great income resulting from the matter, but such was Beryl's parlous financial state that 'every little would help'. Beryl was still surviving on her annuity and on charitable donations from friends, backed up by cheques sent regularly from the Bathurst Norman family now living in England. The upkeep of her horses and her car was a constant drain on her income, but Jack realized that without these Beryl's life would be miserable indeed.[17]

Somewhat to the surprise of both Beryl and Jack, the republication of *West with the Night* was received by critics in the USA with rapture. The risks that North Point Press took in publishing a book so long out of print were many, and their courage was amply repaid by the critics' reaction and subsequent sales. Beryl, interviewed in 1983 by Associated Press journalist Barry Schlachter, who was then based in Kenya, said, 'I thought it couldn't possibly be as good as all that ... but if people like it so much the better.'

The article written about Beryl by Barry Schlachter was syndicated around the world and was taken up by a surprising

number of newspapers, some of whom used it as useful
background to the story of the republication of *West with the
Night*.

At the same time stories began to appear which cast doubt on
Beryl's ability to have been the sole author of *West with the Night*.
These seem to have been fuelled by telephone calls to North Point
Press and *Vanity Fair* by a friend of Raoul Schumacher's, in which
the caller stated that Raoul was the author, not Beryl. Following these calls the acknowledgement which Beryl had made
thanking Raoul for his 'constant help and encouragement' was
seen by some as more than a mere tribute to an editor.

Precisely how much 'help and encouragement' Beryl
received from Raoul in the writing of *West with the Night* has
perplexed many people, but the charge that Beryl may not have
been its author is weak. It is based on three tenets:

1. In America, some friends who knew the couple say that
   Raoul was the writer in the family, not Beryl. 'Beryl did not
   appear erudite enough to have written the book,' said one.[18]
   'Raoul told me he had written the book,' said another, 'and
   after Beryl and Raoul separated she never wrote another
   thing.'[19] In March 1987 another friend of Raoul's, Scott
   O'Dell, made a similar claim.
2. Among Beryl's acquaintances in Kenya there was disdain
   for small inaccuracies such as the printing of the word 'Arab'
   (as in Arab Ruta) when it should correctly be written *arap*,
   and there are spelling mistakes too in some of the Swahili
   words used in the text. With Beryl's intimate knowledge of
   the language and of tribal etiquette, they say, she would not
   have made such elementary errors.[20]
3. The general belief in Kenya (all part of the great
   'Beryl legend') that because of her upbringing Beryl was
   virtually illiterate. This appears to be supported by
   Mansfield Markham's statement to his nephew that 'Beryl
   was almost illiterate, and that the only thing she could
   understand was signing her name on a cheque'.[21]

The few surviving manuscript pages for *West with the Night*
consist of typewritten foolscap sheets with handwritten editing
amendments which have been identified as Raoul's (compared
with a known sample on the flyleaf of a book in which he wrote a

message).[22] In addition there is clear evidence that he advised on the book's content, for there is one page of manuscript among Beryl's papers, on which Raoul's handwritten comments appear scrawled across the page: 'School at Nairobi. Balmy story. Cut school at Nairobi.' Balmy was the name of one of Clutterbuck's thoroughbreds and there is an anecdote about her in *West with the Night*.

But this proof of editing by Raoul, which some see as evidence that Beryl might not have been the sole author of the book, surely proved *only* that he acted as editor. Indeed his editing may have been responsible for the minor errors such as the title *arap* appearing as Arab. Together with the Americanization of Beryl's anglicized spelling, such changes could well have been standard editorial corrections (by either Raoul or Lee Barker – Houghton Mifflin's commissioning editor) for a work aimed primarily at an American readership.

The incorrect spelling of Swahili words has an obvious explanation. In all cases they are written as Beryl pronounced them. She had learned the language as a child from her African friends but had probably never given much thought to the spelling. Neither Raoul nor anyone at Houghton Mifflin would have known either way.

In his letter to *Vanity Fair*, and in two subsequent telephone conversations with me, Scott O'Dell claimed that after he introduced Beryl and Raoul 'they disappeared and surfaced four months later', when Raoul told him that Beryl had written a memoir and asked what they should do with it. This is at odds with the surviving correspondence and other archived material which proves that the book was in production from early 1941 to January 1942, and that almost from the start Beryl was in contact with Lee Barker of Houghton Mifflin.

When Raoul told his friend that it was he who had written the book, could the explanation not be that he was embittered by his own inability to write without Beryl's inspiration? That he exaggerated his editorial assistance into authorship to cover his own lack of words as a writer?

From the series of letters between Beryl and Houghton Mifflin, it is clear that Beryl had sent regular batches of work to the publishers from Nassau before Raoul came into the picture. As explained earlier, Dr Warren Austin lived in the Bahamas from 1942 to 1944, was physician to HRH the Duke of Windsor and became friends with Major Gray Phillips. Subsequently Dr Austin lived for a while with Beryl and Raoul whilst he was looking for a house in Santa Barbara. The two often discussed their mutual connections in Raoul's presence. Dr Austin is certain that Raoul had never visited the Bahamas, reasoning that it would certainly have been mentioned during these conversations if he had.[23] This speaks for itself. If Raoul was not even present when such a significant quantity of work was produced, then that part – at the very least – must have been written by Beryl.

My opinion is that Beryl's acknowledgement of Raoul's help was probably no more than a generous gesture to the man who without any question was responsible for editing the manuscript, and for valued advice regarding content and format. More important, by the time the book was completed he had become her supporter and lover, and it is not beyond credibility that her tribute served a dual purpose, embodying also a public acknowledgement of her love for him.

The argument that Beryl was virtually illiterate because of her upbringing is the weakest of all. She was clearly not illiterate. Her letters reveal a simple elegance in phrasing, her spelling (English) is faultless and she could also type well.[24] From the time of her relationship with Finch Hatton she had consciously directed her mind to educating herself, and her permanent collection of books (which I saw when I visited Beryl in 1986) reveals a wide-ranging literary taste.[25] She was able to acquire a commercial pilot's licence by passing an examination which required considerable mathematical knowledge, and her ability to plot complex navigational courses is beyond question. But is it necessary to labour the point? Has not this controversy already been given more exposure than is warranted by the flimsy evidence?

If Beryl had a problem it was not one of literacy, but a lack of confidence in her own ability. Saint-Exupéry encouraged Beryl to start the book, and Raoul gave her the confidence to complete it.

Conversely, there is no evidence whatsoever that Raoul had the literary ability to produce *West with the Night*. Indeed it is highly unlikely that the man who wrote 'The Whip Hand' was ever capable of writing in such a stylish manner. That he acted as the book's primary editor is not questioned, and in this respect he was masterful. But a good editor is not necessarily a good writer and the only works ever published under his name were three short stories, the style of which is totally different, and arguably inferior to *West with the Night* and to Beryl's other autobiographical works. It is however very similar to the style of all but one of the fictional works published in Beryl's name and this is almost certainly the truth behind his statement to friends that he was a ghost writer, for there is no evidence of such activity except for the work he did with Beryl. He is not listed in any of the usual sources as having a known pseudonym. His own description of his literary career consists of a sentence in a weekly magazine interview, where he told a journalist that between 1940 and 1945 he 'wrote short stories and doctored other people's books'.[26] Though several of his friends told me they thought Raoul wrote under a pen-name none knew what it might have been. Scott O'Dell said he thought it might have been a woman's name but even Schumacher's New York literary agents (MacIntosh and Otis) had no knowledge of this.

The American writer Kay Boyle is on record as stating that *West with the Night* is too detailed and too impassioned to have been written at second hand.[27] I agree with this opinion, and find no difficulty in believing that Beryl Markham wrote her book with no more help than any other author receives from an editor.

Nor was her memoir her only work. Later she was to write other autobiographical works in the same style, such as 'The Captain and his Horse':

> Nor is our challenger alone. I see not one but a dozen buffalo heads emerging from the bush, across our path like links in an indestructible chain – and behind us the walls of the donga are remote and steep and friendless.
>
> Instinctively I raise my revolver, but as I raise it I realize that it won't help. I know that even a rifle wouldn't help. I feel my meagre store of courage dwindle, my youthful bravado become a whisper less audible than my pounding heart. I do not move, I cannot. Still grasping the reins, but unaware of them, the fingers in my left hand grope for The Baron's mane and cling there. I do not utter them, but the words are in my

heart: 'I am afraid. I can do nothing. I depend on you'.

Now, as I remember that moment and write it down, I am three times older than I was that day in the donga and I can humour my ego, upon occasion, by saying to myself that I am three times wiser. But even then I knew what African buffaloes were. I knew that it was less dangerous to come upon a family of lions in the open plain than to come upon a herd of buffaloes, or to come upon a single buffalo; everyone knew it – everyone except amateur hunters who liked to roll the word 'lion' on their lips. Few lions will attack a man unless they are goaded into it; most buffaloes will. A lion's charge is swift and often fatal, but if it is not, he bears no grudge. He will not stalk you but a buffalo will. A buffalo is capable of mean cunning that will match the mean cunning of the men who hunt him, and every time he kills a man he atones for the death at men's hands of many of his species. He will gore you, and when you are down he will kneel upon you and grind you into the earth...

You can find many easy explanations for the things that animals do. You can say that they act out of fear, out of panic, that they cannot think or reason. But I know that this is wrong. I know now that The Baron reasoned, though what he did at the moment of our greatest danger seemed born more of terror than of sense.

He whirled, striking a flame of dust from his heels, he reared high into the air until all his weight lay upon his great haunches, until his muscles tightened like springs, then he sprang...[28]

There are three stories in this vein. The other two are 'Something I Remember', a story about her first pony, the Arab stallion Wee Macgregor, and 'The Splendid Outcast', which is the story of a woman trainer trying to buy a beautiful but unmanageable stallion at the horse sales. In the story the horse is brought into the ring in chains and held down by two grooms for he has recently killed a man. Again the main facts, and the setting, are true, but in reality Beryl was able to buy the horse whose name was Messenger Boy, whilst in her story she loses him to a scruffy little warned-off jockey who loves the horse and offers his last penny to buy him.

The other stories published under her name are pure fiction, though one, 'Brothers are the Same', may quite possibly be based on an incident she experienced or was told about. It concerns a young African tribesman who is facing the biggest moment of his life; in order to prove his manhood he has to stalk and kill a lion single-handed with his spear. Far worse than the trial to come is his knowledge that all the warriors of his tribe are watching from a distance and that the slightest hint of fear in his demeanour will be noted by them.

All but two of Beryl's stories ('The Quitter' and 'The Splendid Outcast') have an African setting and all have an aviation and/or equine background. The four stories which are wholly romantic fiction, 'The Transformation', 'Appointment in Khartoum', 'Your Heart will Tell You' and 'The Quitter', are written in a style different from her autobiographical stories. Here the writing lacks the sensitivity of her earlier work and of these, the last story was known to have been edited by Stuart Cloete. The other three appear to have been influenced to a great degree by Raoul and there are distinct similarities between them and the stories written under Raoul's own name, but there is enough of Beryl's unique manner of enhancing a statement using staccato supportive sentences and in the background information to betray the fact that she had some involvement and that they were not merely written by Raoul in her name.

Despite extensive research it has not been possible to find any works by Raoul Schumacher other than the handful of short Western stories which were published under his own name, 'The Whip Hand', published June 1944; 'Peaceable and Easy', published June 1945; and 'Sucker for a Trade', published in November 1945. In addition it is known that he wrote two radio playlets shortly after he and Beryl were separated. Although he is known to have received further commissions he was not able, for reasons which cannot be explained, to produce published work.

Asked the outright question: 'Did Raoul Schumacher write your book?' Beryl grimaced and raised her eyes heavenwards. 'Oh that again? No of course he didn't.' Asked how she answered the people who said she couldn't have written the book, she said simply: 'I don't bother.'[29]

Whilst researching this book I discussed this question of authorship with Miss Pamela Scott who lives near Njoro and who knew Beryl when she was Mrs Jock Purves. Miss Scott asked me: 'Does it really matter whether she actually wrote the book or not? It is quite obviously her own story; no one else could have imagined those experiences and whether or nor she put the words down on paper is surely irrelevant...' But I feel it *is* important that Beryl be given credit for her writing, for it reveals yet another facet of the talented, intricate character of a remarkable woman. My own opinion, having met Beryl, is one of astonishment that anyone could doubt her authorship. It is an opinion shared by those who knew her best.

June 22 1983

Dear Beryl Markham,

Today's post brought an interesting letter from Barry Schlachter along with enclosures of stories on Beryl Markham and *West with the Night* from the *Kansas City Star*, an Atlantic paper and one from Kenya... I loved the photo of you and that beautiful thoroughbred in the Nairobi paper! But can the beast run? Is it another Camsiscan? No, I suppose not, for it would somehow be improper if the racing world was blessed with another Camsiscan...! Barry Schlachter's excellent story based on his interview with you has been picked up by many newspapers – big metropolitan papers as well as local and regional papers. Astonishing really, since your book has only been out a little over a month.

All the best
George P. Gutekunst

Shortly after this letter was posted, George Gutekunst received a telephone call from Barry Schlachter. Whilst interviewing Beryl, he had learned of George's role, and now he was interested to see if George would be prepared to take his interest any further. 'How?' George asked. Barry's idea was that they should collaborate on a television documentary about Beryl's life. Could George arrange any financing? George was very interested and promised to do some research.

Barry Schlachter meanwhile had some strings he could pull. His brother-in-law, Andrew Maxwell-Hyslop, was a British film director who was holidaying in India. Coincidentally Andrew had just finished reading *West with the Night* when Barry telephoned to ask if he would be interested in working on the

TV documentary. Having secured Andrew's interest, Barry went on to work on a treatment – an outline which the documentary might follow. He then rounded up Garry Streiker, a respected news cameraman based in Kenya, and two sound recordists. As a long shot they filmed interviews with Sir Michael Blundell, a Kenya notable from the old days, and James Fox, who had already given them an assurance that the TV documentary would not conflict with his interest in any feature film. With this footage Barry travelled to the USA and there with George Gutekunst showed his film treatment along with the two interviews to a few would-be investors whom Gutekunst had lined up.[30]

In the early spring Andrew Maxwell-Hyslop received a telephone call from Gutekunst. 'When will you be free to go to Kenya and start work on the documentary?' he asked. Within weeks the crew were assembled and work started on the documentary.

April 12 1984

Dear Beryl,
I arrived in Nairobi early in the moring of June 24 for a 14 day stay. Needless to say, I am profoundly excited! As you may know through either J.A. Couldrey or Barry Schlachter, there is a strong possibility of doing a documentary (one hour) for Public Television here and for BBC in England tentatively entitled *Beryl Markham's Africa*. After my rediscovery of your splendid book and its republication here in the United States, a great deal of interest in you and your remarkable life has ensued – so much that I have had no trouble in raising a great deal of commitment money if we can put the documentary package together. I am sure you know that *West with the Night* has sold and continues to sell remarkably well here and I'm sure will do equally well in Britain when it is released in August . . . It is my hope that you are fit enough to participate in the documentary if we can make it. After all Beryl, you are the 'star of the show!'

George

Beryl had been suffering from back and stomach pains which resulted in an enforced stay in hospital and had caused her friends great concern; for when discharged, Beryl, always slim,

was skeletally thin. Many thought this dramatic weight loss
sinister, but Beryl recovered and was soon back at the racetrack.
She was well aware of the physical penalties of age, and disliked
them intensely.

There began, at about this time, a series of visits by reporters
and journalists, which was to continue for the rest of her life.
Beryl's role in the lives of Karen Blixen and Denys Finch Hatton
was now well known, and a major feature film, based on the
couple's love affair, called *Out of Africa* after Karen Blixen's
book, was in production. Beryl was represented in the film as a
minor character named Felicity. Among the first of these was
the British journalist Lesley Ann Jones who interviewed Beryl in
January 1983 and wrote an article for a women's magazine.[31]
She had been warned prior to her visit that Beryl might be
difficult and 'bloody vague'. Beryl was neither. She was pleased
to see her, and came to the door all smiles, wearing flared jeans,
a loose shirt and a pink scarf. She was barefoot of course. With
her blonde hair she appeared twenty years younger than her
eighty years. Beryl ended the interview by saying that though
Kenya had been her home for most of her life she was lonely
there and thought she'd like to go back to America.

Another visitor, James Fox, produced a colourful article
published in the UK by the *Observer* and in the USA by *Vanity
Fair*. Beryl was unhappy about the article and some of the
implications. She told me, 'I can't think where he picked them
up. He was a charming man, though. He was here writing
about Joss Erroll's murder. I helped him with it – I think I'm
mentioned in the book.'[32]

George Gutekunst had meanwhile formed a small corporation[33] to finance what he called a 'guerrilla shoot', a technical
term meaning, apparently, filming without a detailed script,
though Schlachter's treatment was used throughout as a guide.
With promised financial backing of $115,000 and the guarded
verbal backing of KQED – a San Francisco television station –
George threw in $20,000 of his own money and flew to Africa.
Schlachter had also done the ground work and located many
people from Beryl's past, including Sonny Bumpus, who rode
Wise Child to the Kenya St Leger victory in 1926 and Bunny
Allen, one of the white hunters on the 1928 and 1930 royal
safaris.

Beryl was a poor performer on camera. Many hours of filmed interviews had to be discarded because she simply would not cooperate when the camera was running. Part of the problem was that the interviewer required Beryl to talk about her experiences in a situation which Beryl later described to me as 'a crowd'. Beryl has never boasted of her achievements, nor has she ever talked of her various liaisons and friendships, except to close friends on the few occasions when intimacy has been appropriate. When the interviewer overstepped these bounds her annoyance showed. 'Oh I'm fed up with this . . . I'm going!' Her answers to the questions often appeared rambling, but this might have been a deliberately evasive tactic. She was quite willing to participate in the film, enjoying all the attention and hairdressing sessions. But she wasn't giving anything away.

Two or three scenes only were able to be used in the documentary. Beryl at the racetrack during an early morning workout. Here she must have felt securely at home. Her greetings to the grooms, softly spoken 'Jambo, jambo, jambo . . .' The tall, fair-haired figure moves slowly, and now there is a shadow of a stoop to the once upright posture. Dressed in pale blue shirt and denims with a colourful shawl about her shoulders providing a touch of chic, she watches a horse gallop around the track. Cameras forgotten, her face is a study in professional concentration.

Another shot shows her seated on the veranda outside her cottage, pointing out old navigational plots marked on her aviation charts. 'Nairobi, Kilimanjaro, Naivasha, Nairobi,' she intones, indicating the route of a single flight culled from the log book at her elbow. Finally she is shown about to embark in a modern aircraft for a flight to Njoro. Seated and strapped in, she smiles and waves from the rear window. It is a poignant moment captured on film, for the smile recaptures a ghost of the shy, boyish grin of the woman stepping into the Vega Gull nearly fifty years earlier.

George, busy with administrative details of the filming, managed to see Beryl privately only on one day. One evening after a hard day's shooting, he had been out to dinner and afterwards to a nightclub and had arrived back at his hotel in the early hours. It seemed a very short time later that he was awakened by the insistent shrilling of his bedside telephone.

'Georgie Porgie! Is that you?' Beryl's unmistakable cultured voice demanded. Shaking the sleep from his brain George grunted that it was. 'Where are you?' 'Well, I'm in bed,' he said, squinting at his watch to find that it was only shortly after seven a.m. 'Alone?' asked Beryl. 'Yes,' said George, grinning into the phone. 'Oh how perfectly dreadful for you, sweetie. Come over here right away and have a vodka!' Several hours later George appeared at Beryl's cottage and the two spent the day chatting and drinking.[34]

'I fell in love with her,' he told me, but explained that this is in addition to his love for his wife Berta to whom he has been married for over forty years. When he was first introduced to Beryl she responded quickly, 'George... ah yes, like Georgie Porgie.' George, uninitiated into English nursery rhymes, was perplexed by the sobriquet until it was explained to him, and then he was enchanted. The nickname stuck, as much at his insistence as for any other reason.

In all, during that three weeks or so of filming, the crew managed to amass some twenty-four hours of film, but the planned documentary was to run only an hour. A mammoth task lay ahead in the cutting room to edit and produce a documentary from the colourful material George bore home in triumph.

The mass of film, which included archive material from British newsreel sources such as EMI Pathé and Movietone, gathered by Maxwell-Hyslop during a period of frenzied activity covering four or five weeks, was delivered to KQED's Steve Talbot. 'A lot of it was useless but there was the germ of a very good documentary,' Talbot said.[35] Using Barry Schlachter's researches, Talbot wrote a script following the biographical line of Beryl's life. He then called in Joan Saffa as editor and producer and Judy Flannery as executive producer, and the huge footage, backed up by stills and US newsreel clips, was distilled into a manageable unit of one hour. With Diana Quick, the British actress,[36] reading Beryl's own words in voice-overs, the documentary entitled *World without Walls* was first shown in the Bay area of San Francisco in January 1986.

Beryl's book, though (as before) lauded by critics, had by no means been a big seller before the documentary. The first print of 5000 copies seemed adequate for a book which was considered a specialized subject. After the first year and another reprint it had sold 9100 copies. By the end of 1985 it had sold 15,000. But after the documentary was televised, bookshops in the area served by KQED sold out of copies overnight. North Point Press immediately set about reprinting and within months had sold 100,000.[37] But earlier, in 1984 it was the publicity surrounding the filming and the interest from journalists, rather than the first small royalty cheques from her book, that gave Beryl a new interest in a life which she told many had recently become 'rather boring'.

Her ancient Mercedes, although repaired after its assault by bullets during the attempted coup, had finally given up. Part of the problem was Beryl's driving. She used to drive two or three times a week to the local shopping centre at Ngong. 'More often than not she'd get in, put the car into first gear and drive all the way without ever changing up,' Jack Couldrey told me. Eventually the repair bills were so huge that Couldrey told Beryl the car could no longer be considered repairable – it was just too costly.[38] Beryl tried a smaller replacement and loathed it. 'Nasty little thing,' she said, 'I could never get on with it.' There was an upsetting incident in 1984 when one of Beryl's dogs was kidnapped, but her friends were able to ransom it back for her after some weeks.

Despite all the interest, money was still slow in filtering through to Beryl's account. Publishers have what are called 'accounting days', on which royalties due on books sold during the previous six months are calculated. It may be weeks or even months after the accounting date that the author receives a cheque. So despite all the growing interest in the United States, Beryl was still only moderately better off, and at times Jack Couldrey was driven to asking friends such as the Bathurst Normans for more financial help to make ends meet.

Moves were also afoot to make a film version of *West with the Night*, though at the time of Beryl's death these had still not crystallized. Age was making her forgetful and eventually Couldrey had to recommend that her remaining horses should go. There were only three: one of them – Supercharger – was the horse with bowed tendons belonging to David Sugden, and there were two belonging to Charles Ferrar, the professional golfer. For a while Beryl was left with only Supercharger. David

Sugden had returned to England leaving the horse there. 'Really for her to keep, to give her an interest,' he said. 'Beryl used to say to me, "I'll get that horse right one day, you know." She was convinced that the horse had tremendous potential if she could only keep him sound.'[39] But eventually even Supercharger had to go as Beryl's health deteriorated. 'She stopped training only when some of us, by sleight of hand, disposed of her last horses which were costing her a fortune to maintain,' Jack Couldrey recalled.[40]

She must have read the following letters with mingled amusement and pleasure:

> 2nd August 1985
> Mrs B. Markham
> Nairobi.
>
> Dear Mrs Markham,
> At a meeting of the Jockey Club of Kenya held in the Members' Room, Nairobi Racecourse, on 28th July 1985 it was agreed to invite you to become an Honorary Member of the Jockey Club of Kenya.
>   Please let me know if you are willing to accept this invitation.
> Yours sincerely,
> D.C. Bowden – Managing Director

> July 22 1985
>
> My Very Dearest Beryl,
> I know you feel that I have not been a good boy about writing you. Well, my darling, *you never write me* ...! Had I been his same age don't you think for a moment I would not have tried to replace Tom Campbell Black in your life ... or any of your lovers. I ADORE YOU! Beryl darling I really want you to 'hang in there' and take care of yourself and behave and go to the doctor when you are supposed to. Damn it, don't you know how much I love you? And how much I worry about you? You are a very special person to me. My dear darling Beryl, please be a good girl and take care of yourself until I can ... see and kiss you again. *Promise me!* With all my love.
> Georgie Porgie

Beryl was still driving herself about, 'dangerously',[41] when in October 1985 she suffered a thrombosis. On that afternoon, which was Kenyatta Day – a public holiday – Paddy Migdoll received a telephone call from Beryl's manservant, Odero. 'Please come quickly,' he said. 'The memsahib is very ill.' Paddy knew at once that it was serious, for Odero only called her in emergency. She rushed over to the race course, a journey of sixteen miles or so, to find Beryl unconscious on the floor. 'She had had a massive thrombosis and was dying,' said Paddy.[42]

Beryl didn't die, though she was very ill for a long time. She pulled through only because of a fierce determination to live. She could not talk much at first, but Paddy could read the will to live in her eyes. Her legs were terribly swollen and as she recovered she was unable to walk. She was particularly distressed that her long slim legs and pretty feet were often red and puffy following her illness. 'Hideous!' Beryl recalled with revulsion. Through the winter and spring she made a slow recovery, confined to her armchair and waited on, literally hand and foot, by her two servants.

Occasionally friends came to call, and as her book sold all over the world, visitors to Kenya stopped off at the cottage just to meet her or ask for an autograph. She loved to meet new people, but now, sometimes, her mind wandered and those unfortunate enough to time their visits badly reported to the world that she was senile. It was not so, but clearly it was the prelude to such a condition.

Mercifully Beryl did not know of these small lapses, though she was understandably annoyed and 'a look of despair came into her eyes'[43] when she tried to recall an incident in her past but could not summon it to mind. She had great support from Paddy Migdoll and Daphne Bowden, but even the visits that they were able to make seemed to Beryl to occupy a small time in her long, interminably long days. 'I'm so bored, I hardly ever see anyone,' she complained.

With her two servants she enjoyed an almost farcical relationship, calm and insouciant in her manner one minute – the graceful English lady ordering tea – lashing them with her tongue in rapid Swahili the next. Usually they took this in good part but on one occasion when both were badly hungover after a night spent drinking a bottle of brandy purloined from Beryl's drinks cabinet, she reduced Adiambo to tears and Odero to an anxious hovering shadow who could do nothing to please. A nurse called several times a week, visits which Beryl did not relish. 'Why does everyone treat me like a two-year-old?' she asked fiercely.

When I visited her in March and April of 1986 Beryl welcomed the daily visits with a flattering eagerness. 'Are you sure I'm not tiring you?' I asked constantly. 'No-o. I love to have company, sweetie. What shall we talk about?' she would invariably reply.

In early April, showing indomitable determination, she was able to walk a little. Upright she seemed to shed years and the tall, slim woman standing so triumphantly on her veranda was ageless. On 6 April it was Derby Day in Nairobi and Beryl decided quite suddenly, a few hours before the race, that she would like to attend. It was her first social engagement since the previous October. She dressed for the outing with care in an outfit as modern as the day – crisply pressed pale blue denim trousers, a pale blue silk shirt, a scarf in bright shades of pink and cerise tied stylishly at her neck. A blue leather blouson jacket completed the ensemble. Her hair, silvery ash blonde, was carefully styled, and her fingernails and toenails were painted a matching glossy clear red. Her skin still glowed with pink and white colour, showing no traces of the effects of hot climates.

I drove her to the races with George Gutekunst. Though with determination she could walk a little, the seat organized with admirable promptitude by the Jockey Club was on a high vantage point overlooking the finishing post and she had to be carried up the narrow stone stairway to the terrace of the Owners', Breeders' and Trainers' Club. She enjoyed watching the races and flirting with her male friends. 'How lovely to see you, darling.' She reminisced with Lady Elizabeth Erskine about old times, and chatted to Lady Erskine's daughter Petal. It was the start of the rainy season, and though the rain held off during the afternoon, a chill wind sprang up and she borrowed a headscarf to save her hairstyle from being blown awry.

But the day of triumph and happiness, enhanced by the numerous friends who came over to greet her, turned sour. When Beryl asked to leave, a volunteer came forward to carry her downstairs. He was young and strong and used to the task, for he regularly carried an invalid friend in similar circumstances. Beryl grinned as he swept her up into his arms. But descending the steep, narrow stairway, and failing to notice a wet patch on the stairs, he slipped and fell and the pair tumbled to the bottom.

It was a horrifying moment, and though it was quickly established that no bones were broken, Beryl was clearly in pain from the bruising her legs and ribs suffered in the fall. Her carrier had gallantly taken most of the impact and actually landed with Beryl on top of him, but it was an anxious little party who rushed Beryl back to her cottage and awaited the doctor's arrival. Beryl was sedated and slept well, probably – according to friends – the best night's sleep she'd had for a long time.

Although no damage was sustained her doctor thought it best to use the opportunity to get Beryl into hospital for X-rays and general care. Despite her dislike of hospitals, she did not appear to find this stay unpleasant. News of her accident brought her visits from many friends. Each day her two dogs were brought in by her servants and Beryl was allowed to have her customary glass of vodka and orange each afternoon. She was clearly seriously undernourished and the hospital used the opportunity to make sure she ate well and properly; she gained weight rapidly on a good diet and seemed happy and talkative. She even walked a little. On her discharge from hospital, bolstered by renewed vigour which came from a combination of good diet and lots of mental stimulation, she spent the summer happily enough. Paddy Migdoll wrote regularly to me saying that Beryl was in better health than she had been for a long time.

As the date of the fiftieth anniversary of her flight drew closer, plans were made by various bodies to celebrate the day. Beryl was almost the last of the great aviation figures in a line which had included Charles Lindbergh, Amelia Earhart, Wiley Post, Amy Johnson and Jim Mollison. At Abingdon, the Royal Air Force particularly wanted to mark the anniversary, and with the help of the original sponsors of Beryl's flight, Smith's Industries and Castrol, and surprisingly, the Province of Nova Scotia, they commissioned a bronze model of the Vega Gull. This they hoped could be presented to Beryl in person at Abingdon on the anniversary of the flight. Though there was never really any hope of Beryl being fit enough to make the journey, she talked happily about her supposed trip, but also about an invitation through George Gutekunst to visit California. 'I think I'd like to go back and see my lovely house,' she said.

One day towards the end of July she was pottering around in her cottage – she managed to walk a little now and then – when she tripped over her dog Tookie, whom she had just stopped to pat. She broke her hip in the fall and was again rushed to hospital. Paddy Migdoll saw her there on 29 July, propped up with pillows and disagreeing violently with the theory that her leg was broken. Beryl was still experiencing the numbness that occurs after fracture and may also have been given pain-killing drugs. She and Paddy spent the time discussing the proposed trip to England in September. Beryl was still determined to attend if she could, and if Paddy had any doubts this was not the time to voice them.

The X-rays revealed a bleak picture. Beryl's hip joint was badly shattered. It was not a clean break but a complex shattering of the joint. 'The surgeon told me that if they did not operate she would certainly die. If they did operate, there was a fifty-fifty chance she'd make it,' Jack Couldrey stated. 'I had no option really.'[44] Following the long operation Beryl showed signs of fighting back and the hospital were pleased with her progress. Paddy visited her in post-operative recovery and found her friend remarkably happy and mentally strong, and so she was surprised when two days after the operation she learned that Beryl had been moved into intensive care. It was pneumonia.

Even Beryl could not fight this killer of the aged, and in the early hours of 3 August she slipped quietly from life. She had been unconscious for most of the previous day and did not speak to anyone.

On 4 September 1986, the fiftieth anniversary of the famous flight across the Atlantic, a Thanksgiving Service for Beryl's life was held at St Clement Dane's Church in London. Unlike the day – fifty years earlier – when Beryl had lifted her little Vega Gull into glowering clouds and fitful stormy rain, this was a golden September day full of blue sky and autumn colours. The sunlight streamed through the stained-glass windows of the lovely Wren church, catching the massed white chrysanthemums which held knots of ribbons in Beryl's racing colours.

A packed congregation of friends from every sphere of life in which Beryl had been involved – racing, aviation and literature, from Kenya, America and all corners of the British Isles – heard Beryl's friend George Bathurst Norman read an eloquent tribute to the woman he had recognized as unique even as a small boy, being taught by her to play cards in her house at Naro Moru.

'Around Beryl,' he said, 'life was never dull. Like a comet passing through the firmament she lit up all around her. None who came into contact with her could fail to recognize the genius of a truly remarkable person. I like to think that the place where she now is, is a happier and more interesting place because of her presence ... Kwaheri, Beryl; God bless you and God speed.'

APPENDIX I

Published works by Beryl Markham
West with the Night   1942 Houghton Mifflin (USA)
                      1943 Harrap & Co Ltd (UK)
West with the Night   1983 North Point Press (USA)
                      1984 Virago Press Ltd (UK)

Short stories published in the USA:
'The Captain and his Horse'
(first published August 1943, *Ladies' Home Journal*)
'Something I Remember'
(first published 29 January 1944, *Collier's Magazine*)
'Your Heart will Tell You'
(first published January 1944, *Ladies' Home Journal*)
'Appointment in Khartoum'
(first published 22 April 1944, *Collier's Magazine*)
'The Splendid Outcast'
(first published 2 September 1944, *Saturday Evening Post*)
'Brothers are the Same'
(first published 24 February 1945, *Collier's Magazine*)
'The Transformation'
(first published January 1946, *Ladies' Home Journal*)
'The Quitter'
(first published June 1946, *Cosmopolitan*)

Note: Beryl Markham's short stories have now been compiled into an anthology for publication in 1987 under the title *The Splendid Outcast*, by Century Hutchinson (UK) and North Point Press (USA).

APPENDIX II

CLASSIC WINNERS TRAINED BY BERYL MARKHAM

Date	Horse	Race
1926/27	Wise Child	Kenya St Leger
1958/59	Little Dancer	Kenya St Leger
	Niagara	Champagne Stakes
1959/60	Niagara	East African Derby
	Niagara	Kenya Guineas
	Niagara	Kenya St Leger
1960/61	Speed Trial	Champagne Stakes
1961/62	Rio Grande	Kenya Guineas
	Speed Trial	East African Derby
1962/63	Cutlass	East African Derby
	Mountie	Champagne Stakes
1963/64	Blue Streak	Kenya Oaks
	Fair Realm	Kenya Guineas
	Lone Eagle	East African Derby
	Spike	Champagne Stakes
1964/65	Athi	East African Derby
	Athi	St Leger
1971/72	Heron	Kenya Guineas
	Heron	East African Derby
	Heron	Kenya St Leger
	The Sultan	Breeding Futurity
	The Sultan	Champagne Stakes
1978/79	Sailor Beware	Kenya St Leger

Note: Beryl's best season was 1963/64 when she achieved a total of forty-six winners (including the above classics). This represented a major number of winners at every meeting held during that year in Kenya.

NOTES

Unless otherwise stated interviews were conducted by the author.

CHAPTER 1

1. Correspondence with Secretary of Old Reptonian Society.
2. Archive Records, Royal Military Academy, Sandhurst.
3. Private correspondence between the author and Colonel Ward, Regimental Secretary, King's Own Scottish Borderers.
4. Details extracted from the 'Last Will and Testament of Richard Henry Clutterbuck who died on 29th June 1891 at Durran Hill, Carlisle'.
5. ibid., and information supplied by Mr Nigel Clutterbuck, Salisbury, September 1986.
6. Private correspondence between the author and Colonel Ward, Regimental Secretary, King's Own Scottish Borderers.
7. *English Fox Hunting*, Raymond Carr, Weidenfeld & Nicolson, 1976.
8. Mrs Frankie Iceley, in private correspondence with the author, recalled that even in old age Clara's voice retained its sweetness.
9. Clara's father was Josiah William Alexander, late of the Indian Civil Service in Indore.
10. Each pack of foxhounds has its own territory in which it may hunt. This territory is defined by the Masters of Foxhounds, and is referred to as 'the country'. At Melton Mowbray in Leicester the borders of The Quorn, The Belvoir and The Cottesmore come together – hence its place in foxhunting lore.
11. Entry in Parish Register, St Mary's Church, Ashwell, Rutland. Technically, the county of Rutland no longer exists; the village of Ashwell, three miles from Oakham and Whissendine, is now part of the county of Leicestershire, whilst the Cottesmore country with its copse-crowned hills and open rolling vales, is still considered to provide the cream of English foxhunting.

12. Interview with Mrs Doreen Bathurst Norman, Jersey, 1986.
13. Private (unpublished) hunting diary of Miss S. Chaplin, 1880–1900. Property of the author.
14. Kelly's *Directory for the Counties of Leicestershire and Rutland*, 1904.
15. 'Nearly ten thousand pounds a mile were expended upon its construction.' See *My African Journey*, Winston S. Churchill, Hodder & Stoughton, 1908.
16. *The Lunatic Express*, Charles Miller, Macdonald, 1971; and J.J. Toogood mss, Rhodes House Library, Oxford. ref: AFR s.782.
17. Unpublished memoir, Miss Margaret Elkington, Rhodes House Library, Oxford, ref: AFR s.1558.
18. *My African Journey*, Winston S. Churchill, Hodder & Stoughton, 1908.
19. *East African Standard*, 30 July 1904.
20. *My African Journey*, Winston S. Churchill, Hodder & Stoughton, 1908.
21. *African Rainbow*, H.K. Binks, Sidgwick & Jackson, 1959.
22. *White Man's Country*, Elspeth Huxley, Chatto & Windus, 1935.
23. *East African Standard*, 4 August 1904.
24. *White Man's Country* by Elspeth Huxley (Chatto & Windus 1935) is the authorized biography of Lord Delamere and the standard work on white settlement in Kenya.
25. Beryl Markham, during interview March 1986, Nairobi.
26. *White Man's Country*, Elspeth Huxley, Chatto & Windus, 1935.
27. Rhodes House library; Elspeth Huxley interview with C.B. Clutterbuck, Elburgon, Kenya, 1932: ref AFR s.782 (the rupee equates to 20 new pence).
28. *White Man's Country*, Elspeth Huxley, Chatto & Windus, 1935.
29. *The Lunatic Express*, Charles Miller, Macdonald, 1971.
30. For further reading see *No Easy Way* by Elspeth Huxley. This book was a commissioned history of the Kenya Farmers' Association, and Unga Ltd, published in Nairobi by the *East African Standard* in 1957.
31. *The Lunatic Express*, Charles Miller, Macdonald, 1971.
32. *East African Standard*, 30 July 1927.
33. Interview with Mr Langley Morris, Herefordshire, 1986.
34. ibid.
35. ibid.
36. *East African Standard*, 21 January 1905. The term 'hh' refers to the height of a horse or pony, which is measured in 'hands'.
37. 'At the race meeting of February 4th C.B. Clutterbuck rode the following horses: "Dawn" and "The Toy" belonging to Lord Delamere; "Silver King" owned by R.J. Church; "Vivander"

owned by W.H. Griers; "Wee Woman" owned by H. Cravens and "Gladys" owned jointly by R.B. Cole and C.B. Clutterbuck.' *East African Standard*, February 1905.

38. Rhodes House Library, Elspeth Huxley interview with C.B. Clutterbuck, Elburgon, Kenya, 1932: ref. AFR s.782.

39. Unpublished memoir by Miss Margaret Elkington, Rhodes House Library, Oxford, ref. AFR s.1558.

40. *Kenya Chronicles*, Lord Cranworth, Macmillan, 1939.

41. Reports in both *East African Standard* and *The Times of East Africa*, 28 April 1906.

42. *Kenya Diary 1902–1906*, Richard Meinertzhagen, Oliver & Boyd, 1957; and republished by Eland Books, 1983. Charles Clutterbuck had gone up to Molo to buy some land for Lord Delamere when this incident took place.

43. ibid.

44. Unpublished memoir by Miss Margaret Elkington, Rhodes House Library, Oxford, ref. AFR s.1558.

45. *East African Standard*, 4 August 1906.

46. *The Times of East Africa*, 4 August 1906.

47. *White Man's Country*, Elspeth Huxley, Chatto & Windus, 1935.

48. Rhodes House Library, ref. AFR s782.

49. *White Man's Country*, Elspeth Huxley, Chatto & Windus, 1935.

50. Interview with Mr Langley Morris, Herefordshire, 1986.

51. *The Lunatic Express*, Charles Miller, Macdonald, 1971.

52. *The East African Protectorate*, Sir Charles Eliot, Edward Arnold, 1905.

53. *My African Journey*, Winston S. Churchill, Hodder & Stoughton, 1908.

54. 'Master Richard Clutterbuck (aged six years) sailed on s.s. *Natal* 28 August 1906 northbound for Brindisi and Trieste, thence overland to England via Paris and Calais.' See *East African Standard*, 1 September 1906. Richard travelled in the company of 'Mr and Mrs Cholmley and Miss Cholmley'.

55. *Kenya Chronicles*, Lord Cranworth, Macmillan, 1939.

56. 'Mrs Clara Clutterbuck sailed on 28 November 1906, aboard s.s. *Djemnah* to Marseille and overland to England.' *East African Standard*, 1 December 1906.

57. Reports in *East African Standard*: 22 July 1905: 'Major H.F. Kirkpatrick came down [to Nairobi] from Kismayu by the s.s. *Juba*; subsequently went to England "on leave".' Returned to Kenya on 17 February 1906.

CHAPTER 2

1.   Evanson Muwangi, who worked at Green Hills farm when Beryl was a child, interviewed by the production team of *World without Walls*, Njoro, 1984. Mr Muwangi lost a leg in Clutterbuck's saw mill and has worked on the site ever since for a succession of owners. He is now employed as a wool-spinner.
2.   Private correspondence between Doreen Bathurst Norman and the author.
3.   'Something I Remember' by Beryl Markham (c. 1944).
4.   Private correspondence between Doreen Bathurst Norman and the author.
5.   Interview with Beryl Markham, Nairobi, April 1986.
6.   Mrs Tobina Cole (wife of Lady Delamere's nephew) told the author that the two farms were about eight miles apart and as the only method of transport was riding, she doubted if the two families had daily contact as claimed by Beryl in her memoir. 'Clutterbuck,' Mrs Cole recalled, 'could talk of nothing except horses and perhaps one would not wish to see that sort of neighbour every day,' but she felt that Lady Delamere would have been very kind to the motherless little girl.
7.   *Kenya Diary 1902-1906*, Richard Meinertzhagen, Eland Books, 1983.
8.   Rhodes House Library, Oxford, notes on E. Huxley's interview with C.B. Clutterbuck, Elburgon, 1932, ref. AFR s.782.
9.   *White Man's Country*, Elspeth Huxley, Chatto & Windus, 1935.
10.   Interview with Mr Langley Morris, Herefordshire, April 1986.
11.   Rhodes House Library, Oxford, ref. AFR s.782.
12.   *My African Journey,* Winston S. Churchill, Hodder & Stoughton, 1908.
13.   *Isak Dinesen the life of Karen Blixen*, Judith Thurman, (p 153).
14.   Interview with Beryl Markham, Nairobi, March 1986.
15.   *Something I Remember*, by Beryl Markham (c. 1944).
16.   *My African Journey,* Winston S. Churchill, Hodder & Stoughton, 1908.
17.   Interview with Doreen Bathurst Norman, Jersey, 1986.
18.   Unpublished memoir by Miss Margaret Elkington, Rhodes House Library, Oxford, ref. AFR s.1558.
19.   Extract from a short story by Beryl Markham entitled 'Something I Remember', written in 1943.
20.   Extract from unpublished page of manuscript in Beryl Markham's papers, by kind permission of the late Beryl Markham.

21. There were two sons of Richard Henry Clutterbuck's first marriage: Henry Baldwin Clutterbuck, and Charles Baldwin Clutterbuck – Beryl's father.
22. Interview with Mr Nigel N. Clutterbuck, Salisbury, 1986.
23. Beryl made this statement to Associated Press journalist Barry Schlachter during an interview in 1983.
24. Interview with Langley Morris, Herefordshire, April 1986.
25. Interview with Beryl Markham, Nairobi, March 1986.
26. Interview with Langley Morris, Herefordshire, April 1986. Mr Morris explained that it became customary to dose any farm animal which was dying of natural causes with strychnine. Prior to this practice the Africans would often deliberately injure or poison an animal in order to be given the meat. 'They were not above breaking an animal's leg, or feeding it with some herb which made it appear sick in order to provide meat for some feast. I even heard that they poured boiling water down one cow's throat.'
27. Interview with Langley Morris, Herefordshire, April 1986.
28. Mr Ian Quiller Orchardson, son of William Quiller Orchardson, RA, eventually produced a huge manuscript entitled 'The Kipsigis'. It is well written, highly readable and covers all social customs from birth to death, as well as a section on language. He says in the introduction: 'Why write a book on the Kipsigis? Simply because it has not been done previously... the well known book on the Nandi by Sir A.C. Hollis treats of an adjacent tribe – differing no more from the Kipsigis than Yorkshiremen do from the men of Kent.' The manuscript is lodged at the Rhodes House Library, Oxford.
29. Interview with Miss Pamela Scott, Deloraine, Kenya, March 1986.
30. Interview with Mrs Doreen Bathurst-Norman, Jersey, May 1986.
31. ibid.
32. ibid.
33. *Out in the Midday Sun*, Elspeth Huxley, Chatto & Windus, 1985; unpublished memoir by Miss Margaret Elkington, Rhodes House Library, Oxford, ref. AFR s.1558.
34. Even in those days, when the accounts of killing 'big game' read like unmitigated carnage, it was considered wrong or 'unsporting' to kill any animal 'in milk'.
35. Unpublished memoir by Miss Margaret Elkington, Rhodes House Library, Oxford, ref. AFR s.1558.

36. *West with the Night*, Beryl Markham, Harrap, 1943 and Virago Press, 1986 (UK).
37. Unpublished memoir by Miss Margaret Elkington, Rhodes House Library, Oxford, ref. AFR s.1558.
38. ibid.
39. Interview with Mr Nigel N. Clutterbuck, Salisbury, 1986.
40. Short story by Beryl Markham, entitled 'Brothers are the Same' written in 1944.
41. *Black Laughter,* Llewelyn Powys, Macdonald, 1953.
42. Interview with Beryl Markham, Nairobi, March 1986.
43. ibid.
44. Interview with Beryl Markham, Nairobi, March 1986 and letter from Doreen Bathurst Norman to author, April 1986.
45. Interview with Mr Buster Parnell, Copenhagen, June 1986.
46. Interview with Beryl Markham, Nairobi, March 1986. 'I loved running about barefoot. The worst part about it was the jiggers, but the boys were very good about digging them out.' Jiggers are tiny burrowing fleas which tunnel under the toenail where they lay their eggs. This creates a very painful and irritating sore. The Africans were adept at removing the infestation with a needle.
47. *White Man's Country*, Elspeth Huxley, Chatto & Windus, 1935.
48. *Kenya Chronicles*, Lord Cranworth, Macmillan, 1939.
49. Interview with Mr Ryan 'Buster' Parnell, Copenhagen, June 1986. Beryl had talked to him of her hunting adventures saying that she 'always kept her lower body covered with a lungi'.
50. Interview with Countess of Enniskillen, London, 1986.
51. *West with the Night*, Beryl Markham, Harrap, 1943 and Virago Press, 1986 (UK).
52. Interview with Mr Ryan 'Buster' Parnell, Copenhagen, June 1986.
53. *Ernest Hemingway - Selected Letters*, ed. Carlos Baker, Granada Publishing, 1981.
54. Interview with Mrs Doreen Bathurst Norman, Jersey, May 1986 and Mrs Sybil Llewelyn, Salisbury, July 1986. Mrs Llewelyn's syce is arap Ruta's son.
55. Interview with Mrs Doreen Bathurst Norman, Jersey, May 1986.
56. Interview with Mr Ryan 'Buster' Parnell, Copenhagen, June 1986.
57. *White Man's Country*, Elspeth Huxley, Chatto & Windus, 1935.
58. Letter to the author from Mrs Hilda Furse, May 1986.
59. *East African Standard*, 25 February 1919.

60. Interview with Beryl Markham, Nairobi, April 1986.
61. ibid; and story recounted by Mrs Doreen Bathurst Norman in private correspondence with the author, spring 1986.
62. Interview with Beryl Markham, Nairobi, April 1986.
63. Letter to the author from Mrs Hilda Furse, May 1986.
64. Interview with Mr Ryan 'Buster' Parnell, Copenhagen, June 1986.
65. Letter to the author from Mrs Hilda Furse, May 1986.
66. From transcript of filmed interview with the late Mr Sonny Bumpus by the film crew of *World without Walls*, Kenya, 1984.
67. Interview with Mrs Doreen Bathurst Norman, Jersey, May 1986.
68. ibid.; and interview with Beryl Markham who said she had merely encouraged 'everyone to run away back to their homes'. The plan failed when a less daring pupil told a teacher.
69. Decree Absolute dated 24 November 1914, London. In 1916 Clara gave birth to a son, Ivone. In 1918 she was to bear another son, James, who was born some months after Harry died of wounds received in action in France.
70. Interview with Mrs Doreen Bathurst Norman, Jersey, May 1986.
71. Interview with Beryl Markham, Nairobi, March 1986.
72. ibid.
73. The protectorate became a colony in 1920.
74. Letter from Mrs Hilda Furse, May 1986.
75. Interview with Mrs Doreen Bathurst Norman, Jersey, May 1986.
76. F.O.B. Wilson was one of several gentlemen who formed 'cavalry units' or 'scout corps' when war was announced in 1914. These units were given colourful names such as Monica's Own (after the governor's daughter), Bowker's Horse, Wilson's Scouts, etc.
77. Interview with Beryl Markham, Nairobi, April 1986, and excerpt from a page of discarded, unpublished manuscript written in 1943, part of which were later used in 'The Captain and his Horse' published in 1944.
78. 'The Captain and his Horse', a short story by Beryl Markham, published in 1944.
79. ibid.
80. Interview with Mrs Doreen Bathurst Norman, Jersey, May 1986.

CHAPTER 3

1.   Letter to the author from Mrs Hilda Furse, June 1986.
2.   Interview with Mrs Doreen Bathurst Norman, Jersey, May 1986.
3.   Interview with Evanson Muwangi by the film crew of the television documentary *World without Walls*, 1984.
4.   The late Sonny Bumpus, interviewed by the film crew of *World without Walls*, Kenya, 1984.
5.   It is only comparatively recently that the spelling Maasai has been accepted as the accurate one. Throughout this book, when quoting from other works, the spelling used in the original work has been used.
6.   The original Nairobi race course was sited in the present-day Racecourse Road; the Ngong Forest Course was not established until 1954 – see *Then and Now – Nairobi's Norfolk Hotel* by Jan Hemsing.
7.   Interview with Miss Pamela Scott, Deloraine, Kenya, March 1986.
8.   Mr R.A. Cole-Hamilton, Keeper of the Register at Fettes College, 1986.
9.   ibid.
10. Obituary: *The Times*, 1945.
11. Told to the author by Mrs Elspeth Huxley and others.
12. Racehorses do not add a year to their age on the anniversary of their birth, but on a specific date each year. Thus, in England, the unfortunate horse born on 1 December of one year would become a yearling four weeks later on 1 January, that is on the same day as a horse born in the previous spring. In an industry where huge sums of money are staked on the performance of two-year-olds, the more mature horse has an obvious advantage. In Kenya the ageing date was 1 August.
13. Story told to Miss Pamela Scott by her father.
14. Letter from Mr Barry Schlachter (Associated Press), May 1986.
15. Mrs Doreen Bathurst Norman thought that it was tuberculosis that was responsible for Richard's tragically early death. However there was a severe outbreak of cerebral malaria in the highlands in 1922 and Beryl told Buster Parnell that this was what killed her brother. Richard was already ill when the disease attacked.
16. *White Man's Country*, Elspeth Huxley, Chatto & Windus, 1935.
17. Remark by HRH Princess Alice, Duchess of Gloucester, in letter to the author.

18. *East African Standard,* 8 January 1921.
19. ibid., 6 January 1921.
20. ibid., 21 January 1922.
21. ibid., 8 October 1921.
22. ibid., 10 December 1921.
23. ibid., 7 January 1922.
24. ibid., 14 January 1922.
25. ibid.
26. Interview with Mrs Rose Cartwright, Nairobi, March 1986.
27. Interview with Mr Ryan 'Buster' Parnell, Copenhagen, June 1986.
28. Interview with Mrs Rose Cartwright, Nairobi, March 1986.
29. The author of *Out of Africa, Seven Gothic Tales,* etc.; also known by the pen-name Isak Dinesen.
30. Interview with Beryl Markham, Nairobi, April 1986.
31. Beryl always referred to Karen Blixen as Tania. To avoid confusion therefore I have also referred to her as Tania in the text, except when quoting from other works or when using her full name as an author.
32. Extract from letter: Karen Blixen to her mother, 29 April 1923. All translations of Blixen letters from Danish to English were made by Ms Anne Born.
33. Lord Carbery had renounced his title and called himself John Carberry (additional 'r' added by deed poll) before this date.
34. Extract from letter: Karen Blixen to her mother, 6 May 1923.
35. ibid., 21 May 1923.
36. ibid., 15 July 1923.
37. Interview with Sir Charles Markham, Nairobi, March 1986.
38. Extract from letter: Karen Blixen to her mother, 29 December 1923.
39. Papers of E.A. Dutton, Rhodes House Library, Oxford, ref. Mss AFR s.782.
40. Interview with Mrs Rose Cartwright, Nairobi, April 1986.
41. Beryl repeated this accusation several times to me, saying that Jock became very 'kali' (a Swahili word which can mean tough, fierce, hard or angry) when he drank too much.
42. Interviews with Mr Hugh Barclay, Mrs Rose Cartwright and Mrs Molly Hodge, Nairobi, March and April 1986.
43. Report of the court proceedings, *East African Standard.*
44. I was not able to locate any papers for this divorce despite research in archives in Nairobi. Eventually I ran out of time. Formal research is more difficult in Kenya because of the change in administration after 1963.

45. Obituary, *The Times*, April 1945.

46. Extract from letter: Karen Blixen to her mother, 27 January 1924.

47. Born Jaqueline Alexander. First married Ben Birkbeck, second by Baron Bror von Blixen, and finally Jan Hoogterp.

48. Interview with Mrs Cockie Hoogterp, Newbury, May 1986.

49. Extract from letter: Karen Blixen to her mother, 29 July 1924.

50. Mr Carsdale-Luck had a firm conviction that the Maasai belong to one of the lost tribes of Israel and wrote a lengthy book in support of his theory.

51. Letter to the author from Mrs Hilda Furse, June 1986.

52. Interview with the late Mr Sonny Bumpus by the production team of *World without Walls*, Kenya, 1984.

53. She was Lady Alice Montagu Douglas Scott, later HRH Duchess of Gloucester. See her autobiography, *Duchess of Gloucester*.

54. Interview with Mrs Doreen Bathurst Norman, Jersey, May 1986.

55. Letter to the author from Gwyneth, Duchess of Portland, 1986.

56. *East African Standard*, 27 June 1925.

57. Interviews with Mrs Doreen Bathurst Norman, Jersey, May 1986, and Miss Florence Desmond and Miss Greta Nissen, Surrey, February 1986.

58. *Sju Ar I Talt – Bland vita och Svarta*, Hjalmar Frisell, Lars Hokerbergs, Stockholm, 1937. Translated for the author by Anneleise Bang.

59. Letter to the author from Doreen Bathurst Norman, September 1986.

60. Extract from letter: Karen Blixen to her mother, 27 April 1926.

61. Interview with the late Mr Sonny Bumpus by the production team of *World without Walls*, Kenya, 1984.

62. ibid.

63. Reports in the *East African Standard* and information provided by Mr Muraguri, the Jockey Club, Nairobi, April 1986.

64. *East African Standard*, 25 December 1936.

65. *East African Standard*, 6 February 1926, 'Bending race won by Beryl Purves on Pegasus'.

66. In fact Wrack did eventually live up to his early promise and won many races as a six-year-old in the hands of a different trainer.

67. Interview with Miss Pamela Scott, Deloraine, Kenya, April 1986.

68. *Happy Valley*, Nicholas Best, Secker & Warburg, 1979.

69. Interviews with Doreen Bathurst Norman and Ryan 'Buster' Parnell, 1986.

70. *White Mischief*, James Fox, Jonathan Cape, 1982.

71. Interview with the late Mr Sonny Bumpus by the production team of *World without Walls*, Kenya, 1984.

72. Oserian was a vast and beautiful white castle on the shores of Lake Naivasha, a resort about fifty miles north of Nairobi. Built in Moroccan style with minarets, christened the Djinn Palace, and predictably mispronounced Gin Palace, it was the home of Lord Erroll and his second wife Molly, and reputed to be the site of the wilder Happy Valley parties. Story related to the author during interviews with Mr Ryan 'Buster' Parnell, Copenhagen, June 1986.

73. In an interview with Beryl, I referred to 'your brother'. 'Which brother?' Beryl asked. 'I had three, you know.' Further questions revealed that she was talking of Ivone and James Kirkpatrick, her half-brothers by Clara's second marriage.

74. Interview with Miss Pamela Scott, Deloraine, Kenya, March 1986. Beryl subsequently lightened her dark blonde hair by several shades.

75. Karen Blixen to her mother, 29 May 1927: '... The engagement is still on despite all the spiteful rumours.'

76. Extract from letter: Karen Blixen to her mother, 10 July 1927.

77. Interview with Mrs Rose Cartwright, Nairobi, April 1986.

78. Extract from letter: Karen Blixen to her mother, 21 August 1927.

79. *East African Standard*, 3 September 1927.

80. Extract from letter: Karen Blixen to her mother, 28 August 1927.

81. Extract from letter: Karen Blixen to her mother, 9 September 1927.

CHAPTER 4

1. From the – as yet – unpublished memoirs 'Yesterday, Today and Tomorrow' by Sir Charles Markham, kindly loaned to the author during research.

2. Interview with Sir Charles Markham Bt, Nairobi, April 1986.

3. The former US president Theodore Roosevelt. His safari in autumn 1909 set up a record for its size and organization. There were 500 porters each carrying a 60-pound load.

4. Private correspondence with Mr Bunny Allen, June 1986.

5. Interview with Mrs Cockie Hoogterp, Berkshire, August 1986.

6. Interviews with Mrs Rose Cartwright, Nairobi, March 1986, and Mrs Doreen Bathurst Norman, Jersey, May 1986.

7. Extract from letter: Karen Blixen to her mother, 1 November 1927.

8. ibid., 9 September 1927.

9. Interview with Mrs Cockie Hoogterp, May 1986.

10. Interview with Sir Charles Markham Bt, Nairobi, April 1986.

11. Interview with Mrs Doreen Bathurst Norman, Jersey, May 1986.

12. Interview with Sir Charles Markham Bt, Nairobi, April 1986.

13. ibid.

14. ibid.

15. ibid.

16. Extract from letter: Karen Blixen to her mother, 18 March 1928.

17. The English trainer Fred Darling regarded Hurry On as the best racehorse he ever trained: the horse was never beaten on the English turf, won the St Leger in 1916 and sired three Derby winners. Fifinella, the dam of Messenger Boy (he was originally named For'ard) was equally impressive. She was the last filly to win the English Derby and she won the Oaks in the same year (1916). Messenger Boy foaled in 1924 and was shipped to Kenya in 1928 where he became a significant sire. Ref: *The Stud Book*.

18. Short story entitled 'The Splendid Outcast', written by Beryl Markham in 1944.

19. Interview with Sir Charles Markham, Nairobi, March 1986.

20. Interview with Mrs Doreen Bathurst Norman, Jersey, May 1986.

21. Extract from letter: Karen Blixen to her mother, 25 March 1928.

22. ibid., 1 April 1928.

23. Beryl had previously secured an abortion (with the help of Cockie Hoogterp) in London during her visit there in the spring of 1924. Information given to Elspeth Huxley by Cockie Hoogterp, June 1986.

24. Interview with Mme Viviane Markham, widow of Gervase Markham and Beryl's daughter-in-law, London, June 1986.

25. Gervase told his wife that Mansfield had never behaved to him 'as a father'. There was never any outward show of love until the last few weeks of Mansfield's life. See Chapter 16.

26. Extract from letter: Karen Blixen to her mother, 22 July 1928.

27. ibid., 16 September 1928.

28. Private correspondence with Mr Bunny Allen, June 1986.
29. Interview with Mrs Doris Smart, Sussex, May 1986.
30. Private correspondence with Mr Bunny Allen, July 1986.
31. *Sport and Travel in East Africa*, compiled from the Prince of Wales's diaries by Patrick R. Chalmers, Philip Allan, 1934.
32. Private correspondence with Mr Bunny Allen, June 1986.
33. ibid.
34. Interview with Sir Charles Markham Bt, Nairobi, April 1986.
35. Extract of filmed interview with Mr Bunny Allen by the film crew of *World without Walls*, Kenya, 1984.
36. Private correspondence with Mr Bunny Allen, July 1986.
37. ibid.
38. This was written some years after the events referred to. Beryl had not learned to fly at the time of the royal safari.
39. *Prince Henry: Duke of Gloucester*, Noble Frankland, Weidenfeld & Nicolson, 1980.
40. *Out of Africa*, Karen Blixen, Penguin, 1984.
41. *Isak Dinesen: The Life of Karen Blixen*, Judith Thurman, Weidenfeld & Nicolson, 1982.
42. Lord Dawson of Penn, the king's surgeon.
43. *Out in the Midday Sun*, Elspeth Huxley, Chatto & Windus, 1985.
44. *Sport and Travel in East Africa*, compiled from the Prince of Wales's diaries by Patrick R. Chalmers, Philip Allan, 1934.
45. ibid.
46. *Prince Henry: Duke of Gloucester*, Noble Frankland, Weidenfeld & Nicolson, 1980.
47. Private correspondence with the General Register Office, 1986.
48. When this writer asked Beryl Markham why she had not denied the rumours surrounding Gervase's birth, though she knew they were widely believed, she said, 'I didn't think it was any of their business.' This attitude was also conveyed by Mrs Doreen Bathurst Norman: 'Beryl never stopped to think how her behaviour must look to other people, and if she had she wouldn't have cared.'
49. A comedy by Ludwig Holberg. Information kindly supplied by Ms Anne Born during translation of Karen Blixen letters.
50. Extract from letter: Karen Blixen to her mother, 17 March 1929.
51. *The Compleat Jockey and the most exact Rules and Methods to be Observ'd in Training up of Racehorses*, Gervase Markham, 1568, reprinted by London Woodstock Press, 1933.
52. *Prince Henry: Duke of Gloucester*, Noble Frankland, Weidenfeld & Nicolson, 1980.

53. Obituary for Prince Henry, *The Times,* 11 June 1974.

54. 'Who is Beryl Markham?', James Fox, *Observer Magazine,* 30 September 1984.

55. This silver cigarette box was returned to Beryl by Prince Henry. She kept it with her until her death and it is now in the possession of Mr George Bathurst Norman.

56. Interviews with Mme Viviane Markham, London, June 1986, and Sir Charles Markham Bt, Nairobi, March 1986. Many people stated that Beryl saw almost nothing of Gervase during his infancy but of these informants both Sir Charles Markham and Mme Viviane Markham are in a position to know this for fact.

57. Interview with Mrs Doreen Bathurst Norman, Jersey, May 1986.

58. *Prince Henry: Duke of Gloucester,* Noble Frankland, Weidenfeld & Nicolson, 1980.

59. 'Who is Beryl Markham?', James Fox, *Observer Magazine,* 30 September 1984. In this article James Fox refers to the RAF Club in Piccadilly as the place where Beryl was living. Since Beryl was a member of the Royal Aero Club (RAC), also in Piccadilly, this is more likely to have been her address after her separation from Mansfield.

60. Beryl had been a frequent visitor to this club since 1928 – interview with Mrs Doris Smart, Sussex, May 1986.

61. *Prince Henry: Duke of Gloucester,* Noble Frankland, Weidenfeld & Nicolson, 1980.

62. Sir James Ulick Alexander GCB, GCVO, CMG, OBE, was educated at Eton and served in the Coldstream Guards. He was Comptroller to HRH the Duke of Kent 1928–36, Keeper of HM's Privy Purse and Treasurer to His Majesty the King 1936–52, and to Her Majesty Queen Elizabeth II 1952.

63. Mr C.D.S. Clogg died on 5 June 1986.

64. Interviews with Sir Charles Markham and Mrs Cockie Hoogterp. Sir Charles was kind enough to question his aunt, Mrs Mary Markham, widow of Mansfield Markham, about this matter and transmit the result to the author.

65. ibid.

66. This documentation from informal sources mainly consisted of bank statements which various interviewees had kept as 'souvenirs'.

67. Interview with Mrs Cockie Hoogterp, May 1986.

68. Some interviewees insisted on anonymity. Where this occurred their information has been used only when the author was

convinced of its accuracy and value to the biography.
69. Interview with Mrs F. Migdoll, March 1986.
70. The Civil List is a fixed sum (agreed by Parliament) paid anually to meet the salaries and expenses of the royal household, including the pensions of former employees.
71. Mrs Cockie Hoogterp to Elspeth Huxley, relayed to the author in private correspondence, August 1986.
72. Interview with Mrs Cockie Hoogterp, May 1986. Research reveals that HRH Prince Henry did not shine in court social circles. His real pleasures in life were country pursuits, riding and hunting etc., and this is where his personality really sparkled. He would have been a far happier man had he been born a country squire rather than a prince.
73. *Bad 'Uns to Beat*, Guy Paget, Collins, 1936.
74. Extract from letter: Karen Blixen to her mother, 2 March 1930.
75. Interview with Mrs Doreen Bathurst Norman, Jersey, May 1986; and the writer's own experience.

CHAPTER 5

1. The Honourable Denys George Finch Hatton was born in 1887, the second son of the 13th Earl of Winchelsea and 8th Earl of Nottingham.
2. Doreen Bathurst Norman, telephone conversation, October 1986.
3. *Isak Dinesen: The Life of Karen Blixen*, Judith Thurman, Weidenfeld & Nicolson, 1982.
4. Interview with Beryl Markham, Nairobi, April 1986. Beryl also hinted at a characteristic which other informants (among them Sir Charles Markham) had mentioned. 'He was something you wouldn't like,' she told me. 'Do you mean he liked men and women equally?' I asked. 'Oh you knew, did you?' To me it seemed perfectly in line with Denys' extraordinary sensitivity but I felt that Beryl was disappointed that I was not shocked.
5. *Isak Dinesen: The Life of Karen Blixen*, Judith Thurman, Weidenfeld & Nicolson, 1982.
6. Letter from Bunny Allen, July 1986.
7. *Isak Dinesen: The Life of Karen Blixen*, Judith Thurman, Weidenfeld & Nicolson 1982.
8. *African Hunter*, Bror von Blixen-Finecke, Cassell, 1937.
9. *Isak Dinesen: The Life of Karen Blixen*, Judith Thurman, Weidenfeld & Nicolson, 1982.

10. Interview with Beryl Markham in Nairobi, April 1986. Asked for her opinion of the theory that Bror had infected Tania with syphilis, in view of Cockie Hoogterp's claims that it was not possible, Beryl responded, 'He had lots of other women you know, has anyone else ever complained of getting it from him?' This writer was unable to discover any other complaints. However this is not conclusive, for few women would have aired such a problem had it occurred. Nevertheless it is a point to consider.

11. *Isak Dinesen: The Life of Karen Blixen*, Judith Thurman, Weidenfeld & Nicolson, 1982.

12. ibid.

13. Transcript of interview made with Mr Bunny Allen for the telvision documentary *World without Walls*, Kenya, 1984.

14. *Inside Safari Hunting*, Dennis Holman, W.H. Allen, 1969.

15. *Black Laughter*, Llewelyn Powys, Macdonald, 1953.

16. *East African Standard*, 17 May 1931.

17. *Out of Africa*, Karen Blixen, Penguin, 1984.

18. James Fox, 'Who is Beryl Markham?', *Observer Magazine*, 30 September 1984.

19. *Isak Dinesen: The Life of Karen Blixen*, Judith Thurman, Weidenfeld & Nicolson, 1982.

20. ibid.

21. ibid.

22. *Silence Will Speak,* Errol Trzebinski, Heinemann, 1977.

23. The Gipsy Moth was a two-seater bi-plane built by De Havilland. It was the first light aircraft to gain 'popular' acceptance and did much to promote civil aviation.

24. *Silence Will Speak,* Errol Trzebinski, Heinemann, 1977. After Denys's death his family accepted Tania, possibly because she formed some sort of link with Denys. She made many visits to their home and became a favourite surrogate aunt to the Finch Hatton children.

25. In *Silence Will Speak* Errol Trzebinski says this 'gave a vital fillip to their relationship... In the way that a new child, whose birth is neither planned nor hoped for will sometimes postpone a rift in a foundering marriage, flying brought interest and a feeling of temporary peace.'

26. *Out of Africa*, Karen Blixen, Penguin, 1984.

27. Percy Bysshe Shelley, 'Invocation':

> Rarely, rarely comest thou,
> Spirit of Delight!

Wherefore hast thou left me now
Many a day and night?
Many a weary night and day
'Tis since thou art fled away.

How shall ever one like me
Win thee back again?
With the joyous and the free
Thou wilt scoff at pain.
Spirit false! thou hast forgot
All but those who need thee not.

As a lizard with the shade
Of a trembling leaf,
Thou with sorrow art dismayed;
Even the sighs of grief
Reproach thee, that thou art not near,
And reproach thou wilt not hear.

Let me set my mournful ditty.
To a merry measure;
Thou wilt never come for pity,
Thou wilt come for pleasure;
Pity then will cut away
Those cruel wings, and thou wilt stay...

I love Love – though he has wings,
And like light can flee,
But above all other things,
Spirit, I love thee –
Thou art love and life! Oh, come!
Make once more my heart thy home.

28. *Isak Dinesen: The Life of Karen Blixen*, Judith Thurman, Weidenfeld & Nicolson, 1982.
29. ibid.
30. Interview with Mrs Doreen Bathurst Norman, Jersey, May 1986.
31. *Out of Africa*, Karen Blixen, Penguin, 1984.
32. Mrs Doreen Bathurst Norman in telephone conversation, October 1986.
33. Interview with Mrs Doreen Bathurst Norman, Jersey, May 1986.

34. *Isak Dinesen: The Life of Karen Blixen*, Judith Thurman, Weidenfeld & Nicolson, 1982.
35. ibid.
36. *The Times*, 21 September 1936.
37. *Out of Africa*, Karen Blixen, Penguin, 1984.
38. ibid.
39. ibid.
40. Interview with Beryl Markham, Nairobi, April 1986; and transcript of interviews with Beryl by film crew of the documentary *World without Walls*, Kenya, 1984.
41. ibid.
42. *The Times*, 21 September 1936.
43. *Hunters' Tracks: Great Men – Great Hunters*, J.A. Hunter, Hamish Hamilton, 1959.
44. ibid.
45. *The Times*, 17 May 1931.
46. *Hunters' Tracks: Great Men – Great Hunters*, J.A. Hunter, Hamish Hamilton, 1959.
47. *Silence Will Speak*, Errol Trzebinski, Heinemann, 1977.
48. Interviews with Mrs Doreen Bathurst Norman, Mrs Sybil Llewelyn, Mr Buster Parnell, and others who wish to remain anonymous.
49. *Silence Will Speak*, Errol Trzebinski, Heinemann, 1977; and *Isak Dinesen: The Life of Karen Blixen*, Judith Thurman, Weidenfeld & Nicolson, 1982.
50. *East African Standard*, 16 May 1931.
51. *Out of Africa*, Karen Blixen, Penguin, 1984.
52. *Isak Dinesen: The Life of Karen Blixen*, Judith Thurman, Weidenfeld & Nicolson, 1982.
53. There is a story that Beryl was pregnant by Denys when he died and that she chose to terminate the pregnancy. This information was repeated by two separate sources, neither of whom would agree to their names being given here; and neither knew of the other's disclosure. I did consider omitting the incident. However it has been included here because of its obvious importance and because I was able to substantiate other things told me by the same people.

   On numerous occasions I came across a barrier whenever the subject of Beryl's relationship with Denys came up. Interviewees who had seemed willing to talk freely suddenly appeared vague, or said they weren't prepared to talk about it. This seems odd in view of the fact that over fifty years have now passed and attitudes towards sexual mores have changed. I was left with the distinct impression that there is still something about the affair which has not been told.

54.   Telephone conversation with Doreen Bathurst Norman, October 1986.

CHAPTER 6

1.   General; also George Bathurst Norman's tribute, 4 September 1986; interview with Jack Trench by team of television documentary, *World without Walls*, Kenya, 1984; article by G.D. Fleming, 'Popular Flying', July 1936: 'Once I shot an 8 ft 4 in lioness beside our hangar and despite the six-foot ditch and barbed wire fence we often got game inside, and several times lions made their kills inside the aerodrome.'
2.   *The Times*, 21 September 1936.
3.   *Florence Desmond*, Florence Desmond, Harrap, 1953.
4.   *Pioneers' Scrapbook*, ed. Elspeth Huxley and Arnold Curtis, Evans Brothers, 1980.
5.   *Then and Now: Nairobi's Norfolk Hotel*, Jan Hemsing, Sealpoint, 1975.
6.   *Pioneers' Scrapbook*, ed. Elspeth Huxley and Arnold Curtis, Evans Brothers, 1980.
7.   ibid.
8.   *Sport and Travel in East Africa*, compiled from the Prince of Wales's diaries by Patrick R. Chalmers, Philip Allan, 1934.
9.   Interviews with Miss Florence Desmond, Surrey, March and June 1986; and *Florence Desmond*, by Herself, Harrap, 1953.
10.   ibid.
11.   Interview with Beryl Markham, Nairobi, 1986.
12.   ibid. Reconstruction based on what Beryl could remember and the writer's own experiences.
13.   Beryl Markham's first log book; entries date from 11 June 1931 to 10 October 1934.
14.   *East African Standard*, various issues, 1930 and 1931.
15.   Interviews with Beryl Markham, Nairobi, March and April 1986; and transcript of a filmed interview with Beryl Markham for the television documentary *World without Walls*, Kenya, 1984.
16.   Information extracted from Beryl Markham's first log book.
17.   Interview with Beryl Markham, Nairobi, April 1986.
18.   *Daily Express*, September 1936.
19.   Civil aircraft are recognized by a 'registration number',

consisting of a prefix and suffix. Each country has its own prefix – i.e. British civil aircraft carried the prefix GE initially, followed by three letters of the alphabet. Later the British prefix was changed to GA. The Kenya prefix was VP.

20. Mr John Dawson of Melton Mowbray in personal correspondence with the author. The purchase price of the Avian in 1928 was £600 'ex-aerodrome'; but the price was later lowered to compete with the ubiquitous De Havilland Gipsy Moth which sold for £395.

21. Mike Cottar, 20 November 1931.

22. Interview with Mrs Cockie Hoogterp, Berkshire, 1986. Downdraughts generally occur near mountains in hot weather. They are invisible of course and can vary from annoying to extremely unpleasant. A light aircraft will fight to gain altitude but any gains the pilot is able to make are invariably lost in a series of alarming bumps.

23. Interview with Florence Desmond, Surrey, 1986: 'Tom had more silver trophies for his horseriding activities than for his flying.'

24. Campbell Black made the round trip between England and Kenya thirteen times between 1929 and 1934.

25. Paddy Migdoll, Buster Parnell and Sir Charles Markham were among many of Beryl's friends who were given the impression by Beryl that Tom had been 'the love of her life'. This view is not shared by Doreen Bathurst Norman who thought that Denys Finch Hatton had meant more to her. Beryl made the following statements: 'When my beloved flew to England I followed him...' Question: 'Do you mean Tom when you say beloved?' 'Him, yes – who else would I mean?' and (when talking of her transatlantic flight) 'Then my beloved was killed and I went home quickly.'

26. *Famous Flights*, John Frayn Turner, Arthur Barker, 1978.

27. *East African Standard,* May and October 1936.

28. *Little Gloria, Happy at Last*, Barbara Goldsmith, Macmillan, 1980.

29. *The Heart Has its Reasons*, Duchess of Windsor, Michael Joseph, 1969.

30. *Little Gloria, Happy at Last*, Barbara Goldsmith, Macmillan, 1980.

31. Letter from Tom Campbell Black to Beryl Markham, July 1934.

32. *East African Standard,* October 1936. The Waco belonged to East

African Airways, a company jointly owned by John Carberry.

33. *Daily Sketch*, May 1932.
34. *East African Standard*, May 1932.
35. Standard instrumentation in the Avro Avian Sports model.
36. Log Book entries July 1932.
37. Interview with Sir Charles Markham, Nairobi, March 1986.
38. *Daily Express*, 13 August 1932.
39. *The Flying Duchess*, John Duke of Bedford, Macdonald, 1982.
40. *East African Standard*, 'Mrs Markham's return'; and extract from private diary of Lady Moore provided by Mrs Elspeth Huxley.
41. Extracts from Beryl Markham's log books, December 1932.
42. *Out in the Midday Sun*, Elspeth Huxley, Chatto & Windus, 1985.
43. *White Mischief*, James Fox, Jonathan Cape, 1982.
44. *Out in the Midday Sun*, Elspeth Huxley, Chatto & Windus, 1985.
45. *The Spotted Lion*, Kenneth Gandar Dower, Heinemann, 1937.
46. *Out in the Midday Sun*, Elspeth Huxley, Chatto & Windus, 1985.
47. Letter from Mr Bunny Allen to the author, 1986.
48. Private correspondence between the author and Miss Juanita Carberry, July 1986.
49. Log book entries and interview with Beryl Markham, April 1986.
50. Interview with Beryl Markham, April 1986.
51. *Alone in the Sky*, Jean Batten, Airlife Books, 1979.
52. Article by Beryl Markham, *Daily Express*, September 1936.
53. Mr John Dawson of Melton Mowbray in private correspondence with the author, 1986.
54. Interview with Beryl Markham, Nairobi, March 1986.
55. Article by Beryl Markham, *Daily Express*, September 1936.
56. *Out in the Midday Sun*, Elspeth Huxley, Chatto & Windus, 1985.
57. 'Flying Luck', G.D. Fleming (RAFO), *Popular Flying*, July 1936.
58. Interview with Mr Jack Trench by production team of *World without Walls*, Kenya, 1984.
59. *Pioneers' Scrapbook*, ed. Elspeth Huxley and Arnold Curtis, Evans Bros, 1980. There are twenty Kenya shillings to the Kenya pound.
60. *Blue is the Sky*, G.D. Fleming, William Earl & Co, 1945.

CHAPTER 7

1. Mr Muraguri, Jockey Club, Nairobi, April 1986.
2. Interview with Beryl Markham, Nairobi, March 1986.

3.   *London Evening Standard,* 9 December 1933.
4.   Transcript of filmed interview with Bunny Allen, *World without Walls*, Kenya, 1984. Beryl still had one of these message bags in her trunk in 1986.
5.   ibid.
6.   *The Short and Happy Life of Francis Macomber*, Ernest Hemingway, Jonathan Cape, 1944.
7.   *Ernest Hemingway*, Carlos Baker, Collins, 1969.
8.   *Ernest Hemingway – Selected Letters,* ed. Carlos Baker, Granada Publishing, 1981.
9.   *East African Standard,* 28 August 1934.
10. Florence Demsond stated that Tom changed his mind about Hitler in 1935 when stories of the dictator's excesses started to filter through. However prior to this Tom, in common with many others, thought that Hitler was a good strong leader for the German people.
11. Beryl had retyped this letter heading it 'extracts from a letter from Tom', probably because she intended to use part of it in *West with the Night*. It is therefore not possible to say whether she deliberately chose to omit any original endearments.
12. Letter to the author from Gustaf 'Romulus' Kleen, September 1986.
13. ibid.
14. 'Your Heart will Tell You', Beryl Markham, *Ladies' Home Journal,* January 1944. Despite the unreliablity of the Pobjoy engine, two heroic flights were made using these tiny radial engines; one to Australia and the other across the Andes.
15. Log book entries, 1934.
16. After-dinner conversation with David Allen, Nairobi, April 1986.
17. *Florence Desmond:* by Herself, Harrap, 1953; and personal interviews with Miss Desmond, Surrey March and June 1986.
18. C.W.A. Scott. Aviation editor of the *News Chronicle* and a pilot with great experience dating from World War One. Broke the England–Australia record three times and was a renowned long-distance pilot.
19. *Florence Desmond:*, by Herself, Harrap, 1953.
20. ibid.; and personal interviews with Miss Desmond, Surrey, March and June 1986.
21. ibid.
22. ibid.
23. *East African Standard,* 27 October 1934.
24. ibid.

25. Interviews with Miss Florence Desmond, Surrey, March and June 1986.
26. Interview with Beryl Markham, Nairobi, April 1986.
27. Interview with Buster Parnell, Copenhagen, June 1986.
28. Interview with Mrs P. Barclay, Nairobi, April 1986.
29. *Florence Desmond:*, by Herself, Harrap, 1953; and personal interviews with Miss Desmond, Surrey, March and June 1986.
30. ibid.
31. Log book entries, 1934.
32. Interviews with Beryl Markham, Nairobi, April 1986.
33. Interview with Cockie Hoogterp, June 1986.
34. *Out in the Midday Sun*, Elspeth Huxley, Chatto & Windus, 1985.
35. ibid.
36. ibid.
37. A wealthy American sportsman whose winning temperament and prowess in sporting and sexual achievements won the friendship and admiration of Ernest Hemingway and Bror Blixen. A well-known polo player, Guest kept a string of ponies in Kenya to ride down buffalo. Blixen worked for Guest in the late 1930s as a hunstman. According to Judith Thurman (see *Isak Dinesen: The Life of Karen Blixen*): 'Guest found it difficult to believe that Blicky suffered from tertiary syphilis and described him at fifty as a man of undiminished appetite, stamina and extravagance.'
38. *Brev Fran Afrika*, Bror Blixen, trans. Gustaf Kleen (Bror's nephew).
39. ibid.
40. 'Beryl Markham', Mervyn F. Hill, 1964 (Kenya).
41. Interview with Mr Ryan 'Buster' Parnell, Copenhagen, June 1986.
42. *East African Standard*, 27 November and 4 December 1936.

CHAPTER 8

1. English translation of *Letters from Africa* (published in Sweden 1942 as *Brev fran Afrika*) by Baron Bror von Blixen-Finecke, trans. Gustaf Kleen, Sweden, 1986.
2. ibid.; and interview with Beryl Markham, Nairobi, April 1986.
3. ibid.
4. ibid.
5. Interviews with Miss Florence Desmond, Surrey, 1986.
6. *Florence Desmond*, by Herself, Harrap, 1953; and personal

interviews with Miss Desmond, Surrey, March and June 1986.

7. ibid.
8. Interview with Mme Viviane Markham, June 1986.
9. Beryl with Sir Charles Markham Bt, Nairobi, March 1986.
10. Interview with Beryl Markham, Nairobi, April 1986. I asked Beryl whether she had met the king and Wallis Simpson. 'Yes, I saw them both, at dinners and dances and things like that, you know.'
11. *Daily Express*, 8 July 1937.
12. *Daily Telegraph*, 4 December 1936.
13. *Daily Express*, 24 September 1936.
14. *Whitaker's Peerage, Baronetage, Knightage and Companionage 1929.*
15. *White Mischief*, James Fox, Jonathan Cape, 1982.
16. *Whitaker's Peerage, Baronetage, Knightage and Companionage 1929.*
17. *East African Standard*, 17 March 1928.
18. Interview with Beryl Markham, Nairobi, March 1986.
19. *Playboy of the Air*, Jim Mollison, Michael Joseph, 1937.
20. *Flight Magazine*, July, August and September 1934.
21. *New York Times*, 6 September 1936.
22. *Daily Mail*, 7 September 1936.
23. *Flight Magazine*, 10 September 1936.
24. *Playboy of the Air*, Jim Mollison, Michael Joseph, 1937.
25. *News of the World*, 9 August 1936.
26. *Reuter* syndicated article, 19 September 1936 (see *Daily Express*; *East African Standard*; others).
27. *Daily Express*, 19 August 1936.
28. *East African Standard*, 18 September 1936.
29. Interview with Mrs Rose Cartwright, Nairobi, March 1986.
30. *East African Standard*, 18 September 1936.
31. *Daily Express*, 2 September 1936.
32. ibid., 5 September 1936.
33. *Daily Express*; *Daily Mirror*; other English national dailies, 5 September 1936.
34. Interview with Ryan 'Buster' Parnell, Copenhagen, June 1986.
35. *Daily Express*; *Daily Mirror*; other English national dailies, 5 September 1936.
36. ibid.
37. *Sunday Dispatch*, 6 September 1936.
38. *Daily Express*, 5 September 1936.
39. Interviews with Miss Florence Desmond, Surrey, March and June 1986.

CHAPTER 9

1. *Sunday Dispatch,* 6 September 1936.
2. *New York Times,* 6 September 1936.
3. *Reuter* syndicated to many newspapers, 5 September 1936.
4. *New York Times,* 6 September 1936.
5. *Daily Express,* 7 September 1936.
6. *Alone in the Sky,* Jean Batten, Airlife, 1979.
7. *Daily Express;* many other daily newspapers, 7 September 1936. *East African Standard,* 16 October 1936. Note minor variations in each version.
8. Interview with Beryl Markham, Nairobi, April 1986.
9. *New York Times,* 7 September 1936.
10. *Sunday Dispatch,* 6 September 1936.
11. *Daily Express,* 7 September 1936.
12. ibid.
13. *Sunday Dispatch,* 6 September 1936.
14. ibid.
15. ibid.
16. *East African Standard,* 11 September 1936.
17. *New York Times,* 6 September 1936.
18. ibid.
19. *East African Standard,* 18 September 1936.
20. *New York Times,* 6 September 1936.
21. *Daily Mail,* 8 September 1936 and *New York Times,* 9 September 1936.
22. *Daily Telegraph,* 8 September 1936.
23. *New York Times,* 10 September 1936.
24. *Daily Mail,* 10 September 1936.
25. *New York Times,* 23 September 1936.
26. ibid., 7 October 1936.
27. ibid., 5 November 1936.
28. *The Times;* report on accident also other British national newspapers; *Liverpool Echo,* 19 September 1936.
29. Interview with Miss Florence Desmond, Surrey, March 1986.
30. *Florence Desmond,* by Herself, Harrap, 1953; and personal interviews with Miss Desmond, Surrey, March and June 1986.
31. Interview with Beryl Markham, Nairobi, March 1986.
32. *New York Times,* 23 September 1936.
33. *Cape Times,* 17 November 1936.
34. Interview with Miss Florence Desmond, Surrey, March 1936.
35. *New York Times,* 4 October 1936.
36. ibid.

CHAPTER 10

1. 'Your Heart will Tell You', Beryl Markham, *Ladies' Home Journal*, 1944.
2. *Daily Express*, 28 September 1936.
3. *Florence Desmond*, by Herself, Harrap, 1953; and personal interviews with Miss Desmond, Surrey, March and June 1986.
4. *Florence Desmond*, by Herself, Harrap, 1953.
5. *East African Standard*, 9 October 1936.
6. ibid., 16 October 1936.
7. ibid., Tommy Rose, 9 October 1936.
8. Contemporary newspaper reports; *The Dangerous Skies*, A.E. Clouston, Cassell, 1954; and *The Story of the British Light Aeroplane*, Terence Boughton, John Murray, 1963.
9. Interviews with Miss Florence Desmond, Surrey, March and June 1986.
10. *East African Standard*, 16 October 1936; *Theatre World*, September 1936.
11. *Daily Telegraph*, 16 October 1936.
12. *East African Standard*, 16 October 1936.
13. *New York Times*, 4 October 1936.
14. ibid., 9 October 1936.
15. Transcript of interview with Mr Jack Trench by film crew of television documentary *World without Walls*, Kenya, 1984.
16. *Daily Express*, 11 November 1936.
17. Interview with Beryl Markham, Nairobi, April 1986.
18. Interviews with Miss Florence Desmond, Surrey, March and June 1986.
19. ibid.; and *Florence Desmond*, by Herself, Harrap, 1953.
20. Interviews with Miss Florence Desmond, Surrey, March and June 1986.
21. ibid.
22. *Daily Express*, 21 February 1937.
23. *The Dangerous Skies*, A.E. Clouston, Cassell, 1954.
24. I.W. Schlesinger – a wealthy South African with a flair for publicity and money making. In 1936 he bought a property in the centre of Maritzburg for £25,000. When the city council refused permission for development as a department store he turned the building into a rest home for down and outs, saying, 'I am sure that the City Council will be glad to cooperate in my scheme for social uplift and as the property is to be used for charitable purposes no doubt they will be willing to remit part of the rates.'

25. *Los Angeles Times,* 6 July 1937.
26. *Women of the Air,* Judy Lomax, John Murray, 1986.
27. *The Sky's the Limit,* Wendy Boase, Osprey, 1979.
28. *Women of the Air,* Judy Lomax, John Murray, 1986; and *Biography of Jackie Cochrane,* Katherine Moore, unfinished manuscript (1986).
29. *The Stars at Noon,* Jacqueline Cochran, Robert Hale 1955.
30. ibid.
31. *Los Angeles Times,* 6 July 1937.
32. *Kiss Hollywood Goodbye,* Anita Loos, W.H. Allen, 1974.
33. ibid.
34. *Truth* (Australia), 2 January 1938.
35. ibid.
36. Telephone interview with Scott O'Dell, February 1987.

CHAPTER 11

The collection of letters between Houghton Mifflin and their authors, referred to in Chapters 11 and 12 and indicated by the symbol 'HL', is lodged at the Houghton Library, Harvard University, by whose generous permission they are included in this book.

1.   *Truth* (Australia), 2 January 1938.
2.   *New York Times,* 23 June 1939.
3.   *East African Standard,* 20 May 1938.
4.   *Letters from Africa,* Bror Blixen, trans. Gustaf Kleen.
5.   ibid.
6.   Letter to the author from Sir Charles Markham, 1986.
7.   English newspaper cutting, (source unknown) 26 February 1938.
8.   *East African Standard,* March 1939.
9.   Interview with Mme Viviane Markham, London, June 1986.
10. Josslyn Hay Erroll, Earl of, whose murder at Nairobi in 1941 caused a sensation.
11. Lady Idina, formerly Countes of Erroll. A woman of great beauty and charm, whose hobby was collecting husbands.
12. Captain Roger A.F. Hurt (later Lieutenant Colonel Hurt DS0, CO of the 5th KAR), known variously by the nicknames Raf and Roddy.
13. *New York Times,* 23 June 1939.
14. From photographs among Beryl's papers apparently taken on different days (according to clothes, weather conditions, locations etc.).

15. There is no record of an American licence issued to Beryl Markham or Beryl Schumacher. Lady Nancy Enniskillen states that Beryl told her she gave up flying 'because of her heart'. This could mean that she failed the medical examination, although there is no evidence that Beryl was ever anything other than superbly fit.

16. Programme distributed by studio for the premiere of *Safari*; and various reviews by film critics.

17. ibid.

18. ibid.

19. Paramount Studios PR material.

20. ibid.; and interview with Beryl Markham, Nairobi, March 1986.

21. Statement by Mr Douglas Fairbanks Jr in a letter to the author.

22. *Daily Mirror*, 16 January 1940.

23. *The Moon's a Balloon*, David Niven, Hamish Hamilton.

24. Signed picture among Beryl's papers: 'To Beryl, from your loving... Harry Richman (with my flaps down, Toots).'

25. *Antoine de Saint-Exupéry – His Life and Times*, Curtis Cate, Heinemann.

26. ibid.

27. ibid.

28. Letter from Mrs Tiny Cloete, South Africa, to the author, September 1986.

29. *Wind, Sand and Stars*, Antoine de Saint-Exupéry, Heinemann (London), p. 260.

30. *West with the Night*, Beryl Markham, North Point Press (USA); Virago (London), p.267.

31. Interviews with Beryl Markham, Nairobi, April 1986.

32. ibid., confirmed in interviews with Dr Warren Austin.

33. *The Duke of Windsor's War*, Michael Bloch, Weidenfeld & Nicolson, 1982.

34. ibid.

35. *Appointment with Destiny*, Rosita Forbes, Cassell, 1946.

36. Interview with Dr Warren Austin, October 1986.

37. *Appointment with Destiny*, Rosita Forbes, Cassell, 1946.

38. HL. Paul Brooks to LeBaron Barker, 26 June 1941.

39. HL. LeBaron Barker to Paul Brooks, 2 July 1941.

40. HL. Beryl Markham to LeBaron Barker, 29 June 1941.

41. HL. Beryl Markham to LeBaron Barker, 23 July 1941.

42. The name of this man is not known, but Mr Jørgen Thrane remembers Beryl telling him about the matter and showing him

a photograph of the man. Letter from Mr Jørgen Thrane, Kenya, to the author, September 1986.

43. United States emigration department stamp in Beryl's passport.

CHAPTER 12

1. Telephone interview with Scott O'Dell, February 1987.
2. Letter to the author from E.D. Baring-Gould, September 1986.
3. Although Beryl's first flying licence bears the correct date, subsequent renewals and two passports give Beryl's date of birth as 26 October 1904. In several interviews she gave incorrect dates of birth, inconsistently dropping two or four years.
4. In his letter to *Vanity Fair* in March 1987, Scott O'Dell stated that Beryl and Raoul met in the summer of 1940. But subsequently in two lengthy telephone interviews Mr O'Dell (and his wife) explained that the date was open to question. 'I am two months short of my eighty-ninth birthday,' he told me. 'You get to forget that sort of detail at my age.'
5. *Santa Barbara News Press*, 21 September 1962.
6. *Collier's Weekly Magazine*, 30 June 1945.
7. Telephone interview with Scott O'Dell, February 1987.
8. Letter to the author from Mrs Doreen Bathurst Norman, June 1986.
9. HL. Paul Brooks to Beryl Markham, 19 September 1941.
10. HL. Beryl Markham to Paul Brooks, 23 September 1941.
11. This house no longer exists but in July 1986 I visited the site and spoke to Mr Charles Fox – a former neighbour of Beryl's – who kindly described the former building and its tenants.
12. HL. R.N. Linscott to Mr Greenslet, 20 October 1941.
13. HL. Paul Brooks to Beryl Markham, 23 October 1941.
14. Osa and Martin Johnson were the husband and wife team who pioneered filming in the 'jungles' of Africa for early movies. Beryl was notably scathing about their work and in particular thought their zebra-striped seaplane vulgar.
15. HL. Beryl Markham to Paul Brooks, 25 October 1941.
16. HL. Paul Brooks to Beryl Markham, 27 October 1941.
17. HL. Beryl Markham to Paul Brooks, 31 October 1941.
18. HL. R.N. Linscott to Beryl Markham, 4 November 1941.
19. HL. Beryl Markham to R.N. Linscott, 12 November 1941.
20. HL. Paul Brooks to Beryl Markham, 18 November 1941.
21. HL. Beryl Markham to Paul Brooks, 22 November 1941.

22. HL. Beryl Markham to Paul Brooks, 29 November 1941.
23. HL. Paul Brooks to Beryl Markham, 5 December 1941.
24. HL. Beryl Markham to Paul Brooks, 5 December 1941.
25. HL. Paul Brooks to Beryl Markham, 22 December 1941.
26. HL. Beryl Markham to Paul Brooks, 23 December 1941.
27. Letter in Beryl's private papers.
28. Telephone interview with Mr Bertrand Rhine, Los Angeles, July 1986.
29. Letter to the author from Doreen Bathurst Norman, July 1986.
30. Letter (HL), 2 June 1942.
31. Letter (HL), 14 July 1942.
32. Scott O'Dell told me that the original version of *With with the Night* sold 30,000 copies, although Houghton Mifflin were unable to confirm this figure from their existing files. The book sold at three dollars so assuming that Mr O'Dell's statement is accurate and allowing for agency commission Beryl probably earned about $10,000 in royalties.
33. *New York Times*, 6 and 10 October 1942.
34. HL. Stuart Cloete to Dale Warren, undated but marked 'filed on 28 November 1942'.
35. HL. Stuart Cloete to Dale Warren, undated but marked 'filed on 12 November 1942'.
36. Letter and interviews with Sir Charles Markham, 1986.
37. HL. Stuart Cloete to Dale Warren, January 1943.
38. HL. Stuart Cloete to Dale Warren, 25 February 1943.
39. HL. Stuart Cloete to Dale Warren, undated but marked 'filed on 16 February 1943'.
40. Letter to the author from Mrs Doreen Bathurst Norman, June 1986.
41. Interview with Doreen Bathurst Norman, June 1986.
42. Interview with Beryl Markham, Nairobi, 1986, and transcript on television documentary *World without Walls*, filmed in Kenya, 1984, in which Beryl makes the same statement.
43. Telephone interview with Scott O'Dell, February 1987.
44. *Crusader* by Stuart Cloete, a short story about a temperamental horse tamed by a young girl.
45. HL. Stuart Cloete to Dale Warren, 7 September 1943.
46. See a collection of short stories by Beryl Markham, *The Splendid Outcast*, compiled by Mary S. Lovell, Hutchinson, 1987.
47. Telephone interview with Mr John F. Potter (France), December 1986.
48. Many people who knew Raoul Schumacher well thought that he wrote under a pen-name. No one, including two very close

friends and his stepson, knew what the pen-name might be, but Scott O'Dell thought it was a woman's name. Most people were surprised to learn that he had ever written under his own name.

49. *Colliers Magazine,* 29 January 1941, p. 54.
50. *Vanity Fair,* March 1987.
51. Telephone interview with Scott O'Dell, February 1987.
52. Antoine de Saint-Exupéry was killed whilst on active service in France, 31 July 1944.
53. Houghton Mifflin contracts files show that Beryl and Raoul received a $2,500 advance to write 'An African Novel'. The contract is dated 9th January 1944 and was palced through Raoul's literary agents, MacIntosh & Otis. This falls far short of Raoul's claim to Scott O'Dell that Beryl received an advance for $15,000 and Houghton Mifflin confirmed that this would have been considered an enormous sum at that date. It is highly unlikely that an author of Beryl's (or Raoul's) stature could have looked for such an advance based on an outline for a novel.

CHAPTER 13

1. Information provided by C.M. Schrader, US Military Personnel Records Center, Missouri.
2. *New York Herald Tribune,* 18 March 1938.
3. *Little Gloria, Happy at Last,* Barbara Goldsmith, Macmillan, 1980.
4. *The Heart Has its Reasons,* Duchess of Windsor, Michael Joseph, 1969.
5. *Little Gloria, Happy at Last,* Barbara Goldsmith, Macmillan, 1980.
6. ibid.
7. Interviews with Mr Lee Van Atta, Montecito, July and August 1986.
8. Interview with Dr Douglas Hall (current owner of the ranch), August 1986, and his subsequent letters to the author.
9. Index files and extract from 'Noticias', archives of Santa Barbara Historical Society.
10. Interviews with Mr Van Atta, Montecito, July and August 1986.
11. Dr Warren R. Austin, telephone interview (Washington–California), July 1986.
12. After-dinner conversation with Dr Austin, Hampshire, October 1986.
13. ibid.
14. Telephone interview with Mr John F. Potter, France, December 1986.

15. Transcript of filmed interview with Mrs Maddie de Mott by film crew of television documentary *World without Walls*, Kenya, 1984.
16. *Santa Barbara News Press,* 8 June 1958.
17. Dr Warren R. Austin, telephone interview (Washington–California), July 1986.
18. ibid.
19. Interview with Mme Viviane Markham, London, June 1986.
20. Conversations with Fleur and Valery Markham, Beryl's granddaughters.
21. After-dinner conversation with Dr Austin, Hampshire, October 1986.
22. Telephone interview with Mr John F. Potter, France, December 1986.
23. Telephone interview with Scott O'Dell, 9 February 1987.
24. ibid., 10 February 1987.
25. Conversation with Warren Austin, Hampshire, 23 October 1986. During research for Beryl's stories this one eluded me until a chance remark to Juanita Carberry caused her to volunteer the information, 'I've got that story tucked into my copy of *West with the Night!*'
26. 'The Quitter' by Beryl Markham, written 1946, first published by *Cosmopolitan,* June 1946.
27. *Cosmopolitan,* June 1946, p. 48.
28. Interview with Barry Schlachter, Boston, July 1986.
29. *Mombasa Times,* January 1946.
30. Conversation with Mrs Warren 'Bunny' Austin, Wiltshire, November 1986.
31. Interview with Mr Buster Parnell, Copenhagen, June 1986.
32. These letters, together with some bank statements, are currently in the possession of a good friend of Beryl's, who does not wish to be named.
33. Telephone interview with Mr John F. Potter, France, December 1986.
34. ibid.
35. *Santa Barbara News Press,* 28 April 1953.
36. Ref 1750/212, Hall of Records, Santa Barbara, California.
37. Telephone interview with Scott O'Dell, 10 February 1987.
38. Interview with Mr John B. Greene Jr, Santa Barbara, July 1986.
39. Interview with Mrs J. Whiting, Santa Barbara, July 1986.
40. Interviews with Mr John Yabsley, Santa Barbara, July and August 1986.
41. *Santa Barbara News Press,* 21 September 1962.

42. Interviews with Mr John Yabsley, Santa Barbara, July and August 1986, and Mr John B. Greene Jr. After Mrs Gertrude Schumacher died her family apparently burned all the couple's papers, as part of a general clear-out of their home prior to its sale.

CHAPTER 14

Much of the information in this chapter is the result of interviews, telephone calls and letters exchanged with Mrs Doreen Bathurst Norman, who was a mine of information. I have therefore not made individual attributions since these will be obvious from the text.

1. Interview with Sir Charles Markham, Nairobi, March 1986.
2. Letter to the author from Mrs Tiny Cloete, 1986.
3. Probably *The Curve and the Tusk* by Stuart Cloete. Mrs Cloete does not recall Beryl doing any secretarial work, but Beryl told Doreen Bathurst Norman that she had done this typing for him.
4. Letter to the author from Mrs Tiny Cloete, 1986.
5. Various racing reports in the *Cape Argus*, 1948; and article entitled 'Beryl Markham', Mervyn F. Hill *Kenya Weekly News*, 1964, Kenya.
6. Interview with Sir Charles Markham, Nairobi, 1986.
7. I have purposely steered clear of African politics and do not see it as a function of this book to document or comment on the political situation at any stage in Kenya's development. There are many books on the subject by authors more qualified than I and this short paragraph is merely to illustrate the apprehension of the European settlers during the time of Mau Mau, because of its effect on Beryl's life.
8. Extract from 'The Tribute to Beryl Markham', given at a Thanksgiving Service for her life on 4 September 1986, by George Bathurst Norman.
9. In Kenya there exists what is called 'Fusion' in legal practice. This allows barristers to act as solicitors and appear in courts.
10. See *Inside Safari Hunting* by Dennis Holman for Rundgren's interesting history.
11. There are twenty shillings to the pound which was then worth about $2.50 (US).
12. Interview with Mme Viviane Markham in London, May 1986, and her subsequent series of letters to the author. Also, interviews with Beryl's granddaughters, Fleur and Valery Markham.

13.   Interview with Mr Ryan 'Buster' Parnell, Copenhagen, June 1986.
14.   Extract from 'The Tribute to Beryl Markham', given at a Thanksgiving Service for her life on 4 September 1986, by George Bathurst Norman.
15.   Letter to the author from Mr E.R. 'Tubby' Block; and telephone conversation with Mr Robin Higgin.
16.   'Beryl Markham', Mervyn F. Hill, *Kenya Weekly News*, 1964.
17.   ibid.
18.   Letter to the author from Mr G. 'Romulus' Kleen, Sweden.
19.   Interview with Mr Ryan 'Buster' Parnell, Copenhagen, June 1986.

CHAPTER 15

Because most of the information in this chapter was provided in a series of interviews with Mr Ryan 'Buster' Parnell, individual items attributed to him are not sourced, to avoid inevitable repitition. It should be noted, however, that a great deal of background information was also provided by other informants and where appropriate these are detailed.

1.   Letter to the author from Mr E.R. 'Tubby' Block.
2.   *East African Standard*, July 1960; and Mr Ryan 'Buster' Parnell, June 1986.
3.   General, but specifically see *Flame Trees of Thika*, Elspeth Huxley, Penguin, 1984.
4.   Racing report in *The Nation*, Nairobi, 3 August 1960 by 'Blenheim'. The horses were: Sea Lord, Muffindi, Rio Grande, Dancing Flame, Title Deed, Speed Trial, Frigate and Bridgeway.
5.   Information provided by Mr Muraguri of the Jockey Club, Nairobi, April 1986.
6.   Several informants who knew Beryl in 1936 made a similar statement that it was important to Beryl to 'prove something' to Tom at any cost.
7.   Lucerne is a green clover-like fodder plant, capable of rapid growth and having great water-retaining properties.
8.   Copenhagen and Malmo race courses, June 1986.
9.   The late Mervyn F. Hill had known Beryl since her first success as a trainer in 1925, when he acted as timekeeper for the Jockey Club at the old Nairobi Race Course. Mr Hill was a well-known writer in Kenya and his book *Permanent Way* is regarded as the

standard work on the Uganda Railway and its effect on the history of Kenya during the colony's development. He was also owner of and writer for the *Kenya Weekly News*, in which his article 'Beryl Markham' originally appeared.

Robin Higgin was well known in Kenya racing circles. He died suddenly in the summer of 1986 whilst on a visit to England. Some months before his death he wrote an article about Beryl's racing career for the American racing magazine *Bloodhorse* (see: 'In Africa', 29 March 1986) and was interviewed by the author when he repeated his views on Beryl's feeding methods.

10. Independence (Uhuru) was achieved on 12 December 1963 and a republic was proclaimed in the following year when Kenyatta was declared president.
11. Letter to the author from Mr E.R. 'Tubby' Block.
12. *Then and Now: Nairobi's Norfolk Hotel*, Jan Hemsing, Sealpoint, 1975.
13. Letter to the author from Mr E.R. 'Tubby' Block.
14. 'Beryl Markham', Mervyn F. Hill, Kenya, 1964.
15. A well-known open-air café built around a thorn tree. Traditionally, messages for out-of-town friends were left spiked on this tree in the early settlement days.
16. Telephone interviews with Mrs Anna Parnell during 1986.
17. Letter to the author from Mr G. 'Romulus' Kleen, Sweden, September 1986.
18. Interview with Mrs Doreen Bathurst Norman, Jersey, April 1986.
19. *East African Standard*, 3 February 1964.
20. 'Beryl Markham', Mervyn F. Hill, Kenya, 1964.
21. Letter from Mrs Doreen Bathurst Norman, Jersey, September 1986.

CHAPTER 16

1. Telephone conversation with Mrs Patricia O'Neill.
2. Often called 'Duke' – a diminutive of his christian name – Lord Furness was also known to some as 'Jockey' Furness in later years.
3. Telephone conversation with Mrs Patricia O'Neill.
4. Interview with Mrs Doris Smart, Sussex, May 1986.
5. The Bathurst Norman family returned to England in 1960 because Charles was suffering from pyrethrum poisoning. He returned to Kenya in 1963 having taken a job as resident

magistrate. Doreen followed him that autumn.

6.   Interview with Mrs Doreen Bathurst Norman, Jersey, June 1986.
7.   ibid.
8.   Interview with Mrs Patricia O'Neill.
9.   ibid.
10.   ibid.
11.   *Cape Times,* 3 August 1965.
12.   ibid.
13.   Interview with Mrs Patricia O'Neill.
14.   ibid.
15.   Interview with Mrs Anna Parnell, September 1986.
16.   Interview with Mr Ryan 'Buster' Parnell, Malmo, Sweden, June 1986.
17.   ibid.
18.   Interview with Mrs Anna Parnell, September 1986.
19.   Interview with Beryl Markham, Nairobi, April 1986.
20.   Interview with Mrs Patricial O'Neill, September 1986.
21.   Interview with Mrs Doris Smart, Sussex, May 1986.
22.   Interview with Mrs Anna Parnell, September 1986.
23.   Now Zimbabwe.
24.   *Sunday Mail* (Rhodesia), 23 June 1968.
25.   Letters from Mr Peter Leth, Cornwall, 1986.
26.   *East African Standard*, Michael Clower, 1972.
27.   Interview with Mme Viviane Markham, London, June 1986.
28.   Interview with Sir Charles Markham Bt, Nairobi, March 1986.
29.   Interview with Mr Ulf Aschan, Nairobi, March 1986.
30.   Telephone conversation with Mr Robin Higgin 30 May 1986.
31.   Letter from Mrs Doreen Bathurst-Norman, June 1986.
32.   Introduction to *West with the Night*, Virago, 1984.
33.   ibid.
34.   Interview with Dennis Leatherby by production team of television documentary *World without Walls*, 1984.
35.   'Turf Chatter' by 'The Squirrel' (Paddy Migdoll), *East African Standard*, 7 January 1976.
36.   'In Africa', Robbin Higgin, *Bloodhorse*, 29 March 1968.
37.   Interview with Mrs Flora 'Paddy' Migdoll, Nairobi, March 1986.
38.   Interview with Mr F.D. Erskine, Nairobi, April 1986.
39.   Interview with Ryan 'Buster' Parnell, Copenhagen, June 1986.
40.   Interview with Mr F.D. Erskine, Nairobi, April 1986.
41.   'In Africa', Robin Higgin, *Bloodhorse,* 29 March 1968.
42.   Now Duchess of Portland.

43. Interview with Mr F.D. Erskine, Nairobi, April 1986.
44. Letter provided by Beryl Markham during interview in Nairobi, April 1986. When I read it aloud she said, 'Do you see what they tried to do to me? That's what I had to put up with then...'
45. Interview with Sir Charles Markham Bt, Nairobi, March 1986.
46. Interview with Mr Buster Parnell, Copenhagen, June 1986.
47. Interview and letters from Nancy, Countess of Enniskillen, 1986.
48. Letter from Gwyneth, Duchess of Portland, 1986.

CHAPTER 17

1. Interviews with Jack Couldrey, Nairobi, March and April 1986.
2. Ulf Aschan is the godson of, and author of a biography of, Bror Blixen, published Sweden 1986.
3. Odero, who is a member of the Luo tribe, was the senior house-servant of the Bathurst Normans until they returned to England.
4. Conversations with V.J. Varma, Nairobi, April 1986; and transcript of interviews by the crew of *World without Walls*, 1984.
5. Interviews with Paddy Migdoll, Nairobi, March and April 1986; and transcript of interviews by the crew of *World without Walls*, 1984.
6. Interview with Beryl Markham, Nairobi, April 1986.
7. Interview with Sir Charles Markham, Nairobi, March 1986.
8. Telephone conversation with David Sugden, September 1986; and transcript of interviews by the crew of *World without Walls*, 1984.
9. ibid.
10. Letter from Bill Purdy, August 1986; and transcript of interviews by the crew of *World without Walls*, 1984.
11. *East African Standard*, August 1982.
12. Extract from Eulogy given by Jack Couldrey at Beryl's funeral, Nairobi, August 1986.
13. *Ernest Hemingway – Selected Letters,* ed. Carlos Baker, Granada Publishing, 1981. The phrase 'and we might even say a high-grade bitch' appears in the original letter but was omitted from the above work to avoid possible legal problems. This information generously provided by Carlos Baker in correspondence with the author.
14. Series of interviews and letters between George Gutekunst and the author.
15. Letter, Jack Couldrey to James Fox, 5 December 1980.

16. The author of *White Mischief*; and of 'Who is Beryl Markham?' *Observer Magazine*, 30 September 1984.
17. Interviews with Jack Couldrey, Nairobi, March and April 1986.
18. Letter to the author from Mr E. Baring-Gould, California, September 1986.
19. Telephone conversations with Mr John F. Potter, France, December 1986.
20. Comments made by Sir Charles Markham Bt, Elspeth Huxley and others to the author.
21. Interview and letters from Sir Charles Markham.
22. Santa Barbara Historical Society library.
23. Telephone conversation with Dr Warren R. Austin, October 1986.
24. Letter to the author from Doreen Bathurst Norman, August 1986; interview with Paddy Midgoll, Nairobi, April 1986; and others.
25. Besides a large number of inevitable books on horseracing (such as Gordon Richards' biography, *Veterinary Notes for Horse Owners* and *Sods I Have Cut on the Turf* etc.), and on Africa (such as *The Lunatic Express* and *Last Chance in Africa*), there were many classic books such as Ransen's *Maasai Lands*; *A book of African Legends*; *The Life of Christ*; *A Biography of Doc Holliday*; *Air Navigation – British Empire Edition*; *Rubaiyat of Omar Khayyam*. There were also books which no writer would be without: *Roget's Thesaurus*, and the complete edition of *Webster's New English Dictionary*; and there were novels by: Somerset Maugham; John Steinbeck; Ernest Hemingway; Nancy Mitford; Stuart Cloete; Dick Francis and others.
26. *Colliers Weekly Magazine*, 30 June 1945.
27. Transcript of filmed interview with Kay Boyle by film crew of television documentary *World without Walls*.
28. *The Splendid Outcast*, Beryl Markham, compiled by Mary S. Lovell, Hutchinson, 1987, and North Point Press (USA) 1987.
29. Interview with Beryl Markham, Nairobi, 1986.
30. Telephone interview with Andrew Maxwell-Hyslop, September 1986.
31. Article, Lesley Ann Jones, *Ladies' Home Journal*, London, December 1982.
32. Interview with Beryl Markham, Nairobi, April 1986.
33. SHG Productions Inc.
34. Interviews with George Gutekunst, Nairobi, London, San Francisco, 1986.

35. 'West with the Rights', *The Monthly*, San Francisco, October 1986.
36. Diana Quick starred in the television series *Brideshead Revisited*.
37. Telephone conversation with George Gutekunst, October 1986. (Note that by October 1986 the actual sales had reached 202,000 and *West with the Night* had reached Number 2 in the *New York Times* paperback-sales charts. In December 1986 it reached Number 1 where it remained for some weeks, and sales had risen to over 300,000.)
38. Interview with Jack Couldrey, Nairobi, April 1986.
39. Telephone conversation with David Sugden, September 1986.
40. Interview with Jack Couldrey, Nairobi, April 1986.
41. ibid.
42. Interview with Paddy Migdoll, Nairobi, March 1986.
43. Extract from Eulogy given by Jack Couldrey at Beryl's funeral, Nairobi, August 1986.
44. Telephone conversation with Jack Couldrey, August 1986.

BIBLIOGRAPHY

ALICE, PRINCESS, *Duchess of Gloucester* (Collins, 1983).

ALTRINCHAM, LORD, *Kenya's Opportunity* (Faber & Faber, 1955).

ARCHER, SIR GEOFFREY, *Personal and Historical Memoirs of an East African Administration* (Oliver & Boyd, 1963).

BAINBRIDGE, J., *Garbo* (Doubleday, 1955).

BAKER, CARLOS, *Ernest Hemingway* (Scribner, 1969).

———, *Ernest Hemingway: Selected Letters* (Scribner, 1981).

BATTEN, JEAN, *Alone in the Sky* (Harrap, 1938).

BEATY, D., *The Water Jump* (Harper & Row, 1977).

BEDFORD, JOHN, DUKE OF, *The Flying Duchess* (Macdonald, 1982).

BEST, NICHOLAS, *Happy Valley* (Secker & Warburg, 1979.)

BILLQUIST, F., *Garbo* (Putnam, 1961).

BINKS, H.K., *African Rainbow* (Sidgwick & Jackson, 1959).

BLIXEN, BARON BROR VON, *African Hunter* (Knopf, 1938).

———, *Brev Fran Afrika* (Sweden, 1942).

BLIXEN, KAREN, *Letters from Africa: Isak Dinesen*, ed. Frank Lasson (Phoenix, 1984).

———, *Out of Africa* (Modern Library, 1952).

BLOCH, MICHAEL, *The Duke of Windsor's War* (Weidenfeld & Nicolson, 1982).

BLUNDELL, SIR MICHAEL, *So Rough a Wind* (Weidenfeld & Nicolson, 1964).

BOASE, W., *The Sky's the Limit* (Macmillan, 1979).

BOUGHTON, TERENCE, *The Story of the British Light Aeroplane* (John Murray, 1963).

BUXTON, M. ALINE, *Kenya Days* (Longmans, 1927).

CARR, RAYMOND, *English Fox-hunting* (Weidenfeld & Nicolson, 1976).

CATE, CURTIS, *Antoine de Saint-Exupéry: His Life and Times* (Heinemann).

CHALMERS, PATRICK R., *Sport and Travel in East Africa*; compiled from the Private Diaries of HRH The Prince of Wales (Dutton, 1935).

CHASINS, ABRAM, *Leopold Stokowski: A Profile* (Hawthorn, 1979).

CHURCHILL, WINSTON SPENCER, *My African Journey* (Doran, 1909).

CLAUSON-KASS, E.A., *Fra Lindberg Til Dan Viking* (Catir Andersens Forlag, Copenhagen, 1947).

COCHRAN, JACQUELINE, *The Stars at Noon* (Little, 1954).

CLOUSTON, A.E., *The Dangerous Skies* (Cassell, 1954).

COVENTRY, ARTHUR, and ALFRED WATSON, *Racing and Steeplechasing* (Longman Green & Co., 1886).

CRANWORTH, LORD, *Kenya Chronicles* (Macmillan, 1939).

CURTIS, ARNOLD, *Memories of Kenya* (Evans Bros., 1986).

DANIEL, OLIVER, *Stokowski: A Counterpoint of View* (Dodd, Mead & Co., 1982).

DESMOND, FLORENCE, *Florence Desmond: by Herself* (Clarke, Irwin, 1953).

E.A.W.L., *Sixty Years: 1917–1977* (Nairobi, 1977).

———, *They Made it Their Home* (Nairobi).

ELIOT, SIR CHARLES, *The East African Protectorate* (Edwd Arnold, 1905).

ELLIS, FRANK, & E.M., *Atlantic Air Conquest* (William Kimber, Ltd.).

FARRANT, LEDA, *The Legendary Grogan* (Hamish Hamilton, 1981).

FLEMING, G.D., *Blue is the Sky* (William Earl, Ltd., 1945).

FORAN, W. ROBERT, *A Cuckoo in Kenya* (Hutchinson, 1936).

FORBES, ROSITA, *Appointment with Destiny* (Dutton, 1946).

FOX, JAMES, *White Mischief* (Random, 1983).

FRANKLAND, NOBLE, *Prince Henry: Duke of Gloucester* (Weidenfeld & Nicolson, 1980).

FRISELL, HJALMAR, *Sju Aritalt* (Lars Hokerbergs Bokforlag, Stockholm, 1937).

GANDAR DOWER, KENNETH, *Amateur Adventurer* (Ryerson, 1934).

———, *The Spotted Lion* (Ryerson, 1934).

GOLDSMITH, BARBARA, *Little Gloria, Happy at Last* (Knopf, 1980).

HAMILTON, GENESTA, *A Stone's Throw* (Hutchinson, 1986).

HEMSING, JAN, *Then and Now: Nairobi's Norfolk Hotel* (Sealpoint Publicity, Nairobi, 1975).

HERNDON, BOOTON, *Mary Pickford and Douglas Fairbanks* (Norton, 1977).

HILL, MERVYN FREDERICK, *Permanent Way* (Crown Agents for Colonies, 1950).

HOBLEY, C.W., *Kenya, from Chartered Company to Crown Colony* (Frank Cass, 1970).

HOLMAN, DENNIS, *Inside Safari Hunting* (Putnam, 1969).

HUNTER, J.A., *Hunters' Tracks* (Hamish Hamilton, 1959).

HUXLEY, ELSPETH, *Flame Trees of Thika* (Penguin, 1984).

———, *Nellie* (Weidenfeld & Nicolson, 1984).

———, *No Easy Way* (East African Standard, 1957).

———, *Out in the Midday Sun* (Chatto & Windus, 1985).

———, *White Man's Country* (Macmillan, 1935).

———, *With Forks and Hope* (Morrow, 1964).

————, and ARNOLD CURTIS, *Pioneers' Scrapbook* (Evans Bros., 1980).

JABLONSKI, EDWARD, *Atlantic Fever* (Macmillan, 1972).

JACKSON, SIR FREDK, *Early Days in East Africa* (Humanities, 1970).

LOMAX, JUDY, *Women of the Air* (John Murray, 1986).

LOOS, ANITA, *Kiss Hollywood Goodbye* (Viking Pr., 1974).

MARKHAM, BERYL, *Kwaheri, Kwaheri* (Hutchinson, 1987).

————, *West with the Night* (North Point Press, 1983).

MARSH, ZOE, and KINGSNORTH, G.W., *A History of East Africa* (Cambridge University Press, 1961).

MAY, CHARLES PAUL, *Women in Aeronautics* (Thos. Nelson).

McDONOUGH, K., *Atlantic Wings* (Model Aero-Press, 1966).

MEINERTZHAGEN, RICHARD, *Kenya Diary 1902–06* (Eland Books, 1983).

MIGEO, MARCEL, *Saint-Exupéry* (McGraw, 1960).

MILLER, CHARLES, *The Lunatic Express* (Macmillan, 1971).

MOLLISON, J.A., *Death Cometh Soon or Late* (Hutchinson, 1932).

————, *Playboy of the Air* (Saunders, S.J.R., 1937).

NICOLSON, HAROLD, *Diaries and Letters 1930–1939* (Collins, 1966).

————, *King George the Fifth* (Constable, 1952).

OAKES, CLAUDIA M., *United States Women in Aviation* (Smithsonian Studies Number 6).

PAGET, GUY, *Bad 'Uns to Beat* (Collins, 1936).

PARSONS, BILL, *The Challenge of the Atlantic* (extract only, publisher and date unknown).

PENROSE, M., *British Aviation—Ominous Skies* (HMSO, 1980).

POWYS, LLEWELYN, *Black Laughter* (Macdonald, 1953).

ROSEBERRY, C.R., *The Challenging Skies* (Doubleday, 1966).

SAINT-EXUPÉRY, ANTOINE DE, *Flight to Arras; Wind, Sand and Stars* (Harcourt, 1969).

————, *Southern Mail and Night Flight* (Heinemann, 1971).

SEATON, HENRY, *Lion in the Morning* (Transatlantic, 1964).

SHARP, C. MARTIN, *The History of De Havilland* (Airlife, Ltd., 1982).

SORRENDSEN, M.P.K., *Origins of European Settlement in Kenya* (Oxford University Press, 1968).

THURMAN, JUDITH, *Isak Dinesen—The Life of Karen Blixen* (St. Martin's, 1982).

TRZEBINSKI, ERROL, *Kenya Pioneers* (Heinemann, 1985).

————, *Silence Will Speak* (U. of Chicago Press, 1985).

TURNER, JOHN FRAYN, *Famous Flights* (Arthur Barker, Ltd., 1978).

VAN HOOREBEECK, A., *L'Epopèe de L'Atlantique Nord* (Bruxelles Aéro Astronautique, Belgium, 1961).

WINDSOR, DUCHESS OF, *The Heart Has its Reasons* (McKay, 1969).

ACKNOWLEDGEMENTS

This book could never have been written without the help and support of many people. Whether such assistance amounted to the answering of letters and telephone calls, or submitting to the trauma of a lengthy interview or – as in some cases – the offer of generous hospitality, I am deeply grateful and wish to thank everyone involved. Some informants wished for anonymity and are therefore not named here, nevertheless my thanks to those persons is included. I am particularly indebted to the Markham family, the Bathurst Norman family and Mr Nigel Clutterbuck.

Kenya:
Bunny Allen; David Allen; R Anjeo (Standard Newspapers); Ulf Aschan; Cptn Hugh Barclay OBE, MC; E.R. Block; David Bowden; Juanita Carberry; Rose Cartwright; Jack Couldrey OBE; David Dykes; Lady Elizabeth Erskine; F.D. Erskine; the late Robin N. Higgin; Molly Hodge; Mrs F. Iceley; E. Maina Kimani (McMillan Library); Nicholas M. Kioko (Standard Newspapers); Sir Charles Markham Bt; Flora 'Paddy' Migdoll; Mickey Migdoll; Hugh Morton; Mr Muraguri (Jockey Club, Nairobi); K. Musangi; E. Muwangi; Odero and Adiambo (Beryl's servants); Charles and Eve Satchwell; Pamela Scott; Jørgen Thrane; Bill Purdy; V.J. Varma.

Great Britain:
Hon. Doreen Bathurst Norman; His Hon. Judge George Bathurst Norman; Patricia Barclay; Katy Belcher; Allen Bell (Rhodes House Library, Oxford); Doris Briggs; Nigel Clutterbuck; Tobina Cole; Sharon Cornwell; John Dawson; Florence Desmond; the Countess of Enniskillen; Victoria Eyre; Jacqueline 'Cockie' Hoogterp; John Grigg; Elspeth Huxley; James Fox; Hilda Furse; Lady Claud Hamilton; Jane Leggett; Mary Lewis; Peter Leth; Sybil Llewelyn; Graeme Lovell; Fleur Markham; Katherine Moore; Pam Moore; Langley Morris; Greta Nissen; Anna Parnell; Gwyneth, Duchess of Portland; Lady Connie Sorsbie; Doris Smart; Mr and Mrs Stuart Taylor; Lt Col Ward (KOSB); Reginald Wooley; Mary Wright.

USA:
Dr Warren and Mrs Bunny Austin; Edward Baring-Gould; Oliver Daniel; Douglas Fairbanks Jr; Florence Feiler; Judy Flannery; John B. Greene Jr; Dr Sadja Stokowski Greenwood; George Gutekunst; Dr Douglas Hall; Col. Hopper (CAP); Gloria Loomis; Scott O'Dell; Donald Ott; Bertrand Rhine; Harold Troxel; Fay Troxel; Barry Schlachter; Lee Van Atta; John T. De Blois Wack; Wendy Withington; Judy Whiting; John Yabsley.

Elsewhere:
Viviane Markham (France); Valery Carol Markham (France); John F. Potter (France); Anneleise Bang (Denmark); Else Brundbjerg (Denmark); Ryan 'Buster' Parnell (Denmark); Clara Selborn (Denmark); Robert Leader (Spain); Gustaf Kleen (Sweden); The Hon. Mrs Patricia O'Neill (South Africa); Mrs Tiny Cloete (South Africa).

I wish to record an immense debt to my agent and friend, John Belcher, who provided incalculable help and support during the entire project. John died with devastating suddenness a few weeks before this book was published and so never saw the results of his hard work on my behalf. My thanks to a large number of friends who loaned books and magazine articles, and to Andrea Ranson and Patricia Taylor Chalmers at Century Hutchinson. Finally – but certainly not least – my editors: Tony Whittome at Century Hutchinson, and Susan Rabiner at St Martin's Press; both of whom have made many constructive suggestions and with whom it has been my great privilege to work.

In addition to assistance from individuals, I have received enormous help from the staff of organizations and libraries. In particular I should like to thank the staff of the Salisbury (Wiltshire) Public Library, who have diligently acquired out-of-date and rare books on Kenya on my behalf; and to the staff in the archive room of Standard Newspapers in Nairobi.

Special Collections and Reference Libraries:
Houghton Library, Harvard, Cambridge, Mass., USA; Butler Library, Columbia University, NY, USA; UCLA Ref. Library, and Theatre Arts Library at the University of California in Los Angeles, California, USA; UCSB Ref. Library, Santa Barbara, California, USA; Santa Barbara City Library; California, USA; Santa Barbara News-Press, California, USA; Reference Library: University of Southern California (USC) Los Angeles, California, USA; Academy of Motion Picture Arts and Sciences, Los Angeles, California, USA;

National Personnel Records Centre, Mo. USA: Rhodes House Library, Oxford University, Oxford, England; Wiltshire County Library, Salisbury, Wiltshire, England; British Library, Colindale, London, England; *Daily Express* Library, London, England; McMillan Library, Nairobi, Kenya; Kenya National Archives, Nairobi, Kenya; Jockey Club, Nairobi, Kenya; Jockey Club, Newmarket, England; *East African Standard* Archives Library, Nairobi, Kenya; Newarke House Museum, Leicester; Army Records Office, Chelsea.

Newspapers:
U.K.:
The Times; *Daily Telegraph*; *Daily Express*; *Daily Mirror*; *Southern Evening Echo*; *Liverpool Echo*.

Elsewhere:
New York Times (USA); *Los Angeles Times* (USA); *East African Standard* (Kenya); *Leader* (Kenya); *Globetrotter* (Kenya); *Mombasa Times* (Kenya); *Cape Times* (South Africa); *Cape Argus* (South Africa); *Santa Barbara News-Press* (USA); *Truth* (Australia).

Extract Rights:
My particular thanks go to the Runstedlund Foundation for their permission to quote from Karen Blixen's works including previously unpublished letters, and to Anne Born who provided translations for these from the original Danish. Grateful thanks are also extended to the Houghton Library, Harvard University for permission to quote from the collection of letters between Beryl Markham and her publishers Houghton Mifflin. In addition the following publishers, authors and literary executors generously gave permission to quote from copyrighted materials:

The Lunatic Express by Charles Miller: permission granted by Macdonald & Co Ltd and by the author's representative Gunter Stuhlmann.
Ernest Hemingway – Selected Letters compiled by Carlos Baker; permission granted by Grafton Books, a division of Collins Ltd, and the Ernest Hemingway Foundation.
Black Laughter by Llewelyn Powys; permission granted by the Society of Authors.
Out of Africa and *Letters from Africa* by Karen Blixen (Isak Dinesen); permission granted by Florence Feiler on behalf of the Runstedlund Foundation.

Out in the Midday Sun and *White Man's Country* by Elspeth Huxley, permission granted by Chatto & Windus Ltd and The Hogarth Press.
Kenya Diary by Richard Meinertzhagen; permission granted by Eland Books.
Kenya Chronicles by Lord Cranworth; permission granted by Macmillan and Co. Ltd.
Florence Desmond by Florence Desmond; permission granted by Harrap Limited.
Hunter's Tracks by J.A. Hunter; permission granted by Hamish Hamilton Limited.
Silence will Speak by Errol Trzebinski; permission granted by William Heinemann Limited and the Chicago Press.
Inside Safari Hunting by Dennis Holman; permission granted by W.H. Allen & Co PLC
Isak Dinesen: The Life of Karen Blixen by Judith Thurman; permission granted by Weidenfeld & Nicolson Ltd and St Martin's Press.
Prince Henry: Duke of Gloucester by Noble Frankland; permission granted by Weidenfeld & Nicolson Ltd.

INDEX